Neolithic Tombs
of Wales

Watercolour of Pentre Ifan by Catherine Jones

Neolithic Tombs
of Wales

George Nash

LOGASTON PRESS

COVER IMAGE: Carreg Sampson, Pembrokeshire, and its dramatic backdrop (© George Nash).
FRONT FLAP, FROM TOP: Nineteenth-century engravings published in *Archaeologica Cambrensis*: Bachwen, Gwern Einion and Ystum Cegid Isaf.

First published (as *The Architecture of Death*) in 2006 by Logaston Press.
This edition published in 2024 by Logaston Press
The Holme, Church Road, Eardisley HR3 6NJ
www.logastonpress.co.uk
An imprint of Fircone Books Ltd.

ISBN 978-1-910839-72-0

Text copyright © George Nash, 2024.
All photographs and illustrations copyright © George Nash
unless otherwise stated beneath each image.

All rights reserved.
The moral rights of the author have been asserted.

Without limiting the rights under copyright reserved above, no part of this publication may be reproduced, stored in or introduced into a retrieval system, or transmitted, in any form or by any means (electronic, mechanical, photocopying, recording or otherwise), without prior written permission of the copyright owner and the above publisher of this book.

Designed and typeset by Richard Wheeler in 10.5 on 14 Minion.
Cover design by Richard Wheeler.

Printed and bound in Poland www.lfbookservices.co.uk

Logaston Press is committed to a sustainable future for our business, our readers and our planet. The book in your hands is made of FSC® certified and other controlled material.

British Library Catalogue in Publishing Data.
A CIP catalogue record for this book is available from the British Library.

CONTENTS

	PREFACE/ RHAGAIR	vii
	ACKNOWLEDGEMENTS	xiii
ONE	Being Neolithic	1
TWO	The Black Mountains Group	35
THREE	The Gower Peninsula Group	75
FOUR	The South-East Wales Group	85
FIVE	The Ynys Môn Group	97
SIX	The North Wales Group	131
SEVEN	The Harlech Group	147
EIGHT	The Llŷn Peninsula Group	161
NINE	The South-West Wales Group	175
TEN	Isolated Monuments	233
	CONCLUDING REMARKS	239
	APPENDIX 1: SUMMARY OF SITE DATA	243
	APPENDIX 2: RADIOCARBON DATES	247
	NOTES	249
	BIBLIOGRAPHY	255
	SITE INDEX	265
	GENERAL INDEX	269

For my best ever friends
James, John & Hannah

PREFACE/ RHAGAIR

It has been estimated that there are over 40,000 megalithic structures in Europe. The later prehistoric landscapes of the north-western European Atlantic zone, from the Iberian Peninsula to southern Norway, are notable for an outstanding monument assemblage belonging to the oldest architectural tradition in Europe, if not the world (Daniel 1958). The form and distribution of these monuments – some now merely piles of stone – have occupied the imagination of generations of scholars. As a result, numerous ideas have been proposed relating to their origin, construction methods, use and abandonment. It is now thought that these enigmatic structures – ostensibly a Neolithic phenomenon (New Stone Age *c.*4,000–2,000 BCE) – appeared in the landscape, not as a result of random or arbitrary decision-making on the part of Neolithic communities, but in response to a complex set of long-term processes that had influenced the organisation of social and ritual space since the preceding Mesolithic (Middle Stone Age *c.*10,000–4,000 BCE), or earlier. Indeed, several monuments occupy sites that appear to have been utilised during the Upper Palaeolithic (Old Stone Age *c.*35,000–10,000 BCE). As a result of the working out of these processes, spaces became places; chaotic nature became structured, tamed, manipulated, controlled.

One of the most important works produced by a British scholar in this field is Glyn Daniel's seminal volume *The Prehistoric Chambered Tombs of England and Wales* (1950). Many have attempted to repeat or update Daniel's achievement but, arguably, the enthusiasm and integrity of subsequent works have often appeared lacking. Regarding Wales, a number of researchers have, over the past 45 years, discussed the Neolithic in a number of regional studies that embrace ideas initially discussed by Daniel. But many of these studies have been limited by the tendency of researchers to concentrate exclusively on 'their patch' without considering external influences. One must acknowledge that these ideas transcend modern political boundaries. In some ways this approach is understandable: confining one's research to an area defined by political boundaries is convenient, facilitating the production of an orderly piece of work – as is the case with this volume. That said, one *can* consider the megalithic architecture of Wales to be unique and different from other Neolithic areas of Britain and Europe.

Research for this volume led me to a number of key texts that would establish an overview. Most of these address the problems of regionality, architectural form and influence. One of these key texts is *Megalithic Enquiries in the West of Britain* (Powell et al.), which was published in 1969 by Liverpool University Press. In many respects, this volume remains unsurpassed. Not only does it deal with monument regionality, but it also establishes an important framework for books such as this. This volume has spawned a number of more specific and detailed regional studies, including Frances Lynch's *Prehistoric Anglesey* (1970, 1991), Christopher Barker's excellent monograph *The Chambered Tombs of South-West Wales* (1992) and volumes by Children & Nash – *The Prehistoric Sites of Monmouthshire* (1996), *The Neolithic Sites of Cardiganshire, Carmarthenshire and Pembrokeshire* (1997) and *The Prehistoric Sites of Breconshire* (2001). Specific research has been undertaken by Britnell & Savory (1984), Britnell & Whittle (2022), Gibson (1999) and Lynch & Smith (1987), who investigated, respectively, the Gwernvale (BRE 7) and Penywyrlod (BRE 14) monuments in Breconshire, the Neolithic enclosure at Hindwell and the Ynys Môn tombs of Trefignath (ANG 1) and Din Dryfol (ANG 5).

In addition to the above, the Royal Commission for Historical and Ancient Monuments in Wales (RCAHMW) has brought much of the monument evidence together. Its county studies, although sometimes appearing somewhat dated in approach, have provided sound and essential empiricist data. The Royal Commission's more recent inventory on Breconshire (1997) has enlightened the study of this, the only inland Neolithic monument group in Wales. All of these volumes, ancient or modern, have proven an important resource.

Finally, there are a handful of research papers and volumes that have attempted to set these monuments into a theoretical framework, looking at such concepts as the importance of location within the landscape or the way architecture interplays with burial and ritual aspects of monumentality. Foremost among these is Christopher Tilley's *A Phenomenology of Landscape* (1994) which includes chapters on the Black Mountains and South-west Wales. Other volumes include Richard Bradley's trilogy: *The Significance of Monuments* (1998), *The Archaeology of Natural Places* (2000) and *The Past in Prehistoric Societies* (2002); Mark Edmond's *Ancestral Geographies of the Neolithic* (1999); Julian Thomas's *Rethinking the Neolithic* (1991) and *Understanding the Neolithic* (1999), Ray and Thomas's *Neolithic Britain: The Transformation of Social Worlds* (2018) and Alasdair Whittle's *Problems in Neolithic Archaeology* (1988), *Neolithic Europe: A Survey* (1985); *The archaeology of people: dimensions of neolithic life* (2003), and the later edited collaboration with Bill Britnell on the site of Gwernvale (Britnell & Whittle 2022). Although some of these books only touch on Wales, they are, nonetheless, essential reading, as they discuss why people locate monuments in particular places within the landscape. Also well worth considering is Gabriel Cooney's *Landscapes of Neolithic Ireland* (2000). Although this volume does not deal specifically with Wales, it is a fine example of how regional landscape studies should be written.

Over the past 40 years, and where possible, radiocarbon dating has been used in order to assess fixed dating in time for a small number of monuments. Radiocarbon dates, though, are too limited in number to make any valid attempt on the datable chronology, with the exception of sites such as Trefignath (ANG 1) and Gwernvale (BRE 7) (APPENDIX 2). However, since the publication of the first edition of this book, a new and more accurate database has been formulated and updated.

In this book, I have used calibrated dates, and these will be termed BC[E] (see Stuiver 1998 et al.). Where this is not possible, uncalibrated BC dates are used. In addition, I have also occasionally used BP dates (before present) that have usually been applied to environmental research data. These dates are derived from direct sources and are, in most cases, referenced as such.

Within this book, I have followed an established system of classification (also used by Daniel 1950, Powell et al. 1969, Lynch 1970, and Barker 1992). This classification system, based on a three- or four-letter county prefix coding, was used in order to prevent possible site duplication. It appears that over the recent past, new sites (of which there are very few) have not followed on this classification system. I have therefore decided to rectify this and where possible continue the system in numerical order.

A NOTE ON PLACE-NAMES

The author has taken the utmost care to ensure that the correct Welsh spellings are used for sites that appear in this book. However, there may be discrepancies with the spelling of certain names. This appears to be an inherent problem, not just with the SMR county lists, but also with the CADW and RCAHMW inventories and the Ordnance Survey. Where possible, I have listed all published names for each site.

RHAGAIR

Fe amcangyfrifir bod dros 40,000 o strwythurau megalithig yn Ewrop. Mae tirweddau cynhanesyddol hwyr rhanbarth ogledd-orllewinol y Môr Iwerydd, o Benrhyn Iberia i dde Norwy yn nodweddiadol am gasgliad hynod o henebion a berthyn i draddodiad pensaernïol hynaf Ewrop, os nad y byd (Daniel 1958). Mae ffurf a dosbarthiad yr henebion hyn – sydd ddim mwy na phentyrrau o gerrig erbyn hyn – wedi mynd â bryd ysgolheigion am genedlaethau. Fel canlyniad, awgrymwyd syniadau di-rif ynghylch eu gwreiddiau, dulliau adeiladu, y defnydd a wneid ohonynt a'r rhesymau dros eu dirywiad. Erbyn hyn, meddylir bod y strwythurau enigmatig hyn – sydd i bob golwg yn ffenomen Neolithig (Yr Oes Garreg Newydd 4,000–2,000 CC) – wedi ymddangos yn y dirwedd nid fel canlyniad penderfyniadau mympwyol a damweiniol ar ran cymunedau Neolithig, ond fel adwaith i set gymhleth o brosesau hirdymor a oedd wedi dylanwadu ar drefniant gofod cymdeithasol a defodol ers y cyfnod Mesolithig (Yr Oes Garreg Ganol 10,000–4,000 CC) neu'n gynharach. Yn wir, mae nifer o henebion yn sefyll ar safleoedd a ymddengys fod wedi cael eu defnyddio yn ystod y cyfnod Uwchbalaeolithig (Yr Oes Garreg Hen 35,000–10,000 CC). Fel canlyniad i'r prosesau hyn, trodd gofodau yn lleoedd; cafodd anrhefn natur ei strwythuro, ei dofi, ei manipiwleiddio, ei rheoli.

Un o'r gweithiau pwysicaf a gynhyrchwyd gan ysgolhaig Prydeinig yn y maes hwn yw cyfrol flaengar Glyn Daniel *The Prehistoric Chambered Tombs of England and Wales*. Mae sawl un wedi ceisio efelychu neu ddiweddaru campwaith Daniel ond, gellir dadlau, heb na'i frwdfrydedd na'i ddidwylledd. Parthed Cymru, mae nifer o ymchwilwyr dros y 45 mlynedd ddiwethaf wedi trafod y Neolithig mewn nifer o astudiaethau rhanbarthol sy'n coleddu'r syniadau a drafodwyd gyntaf gan Daniel. Ond, cyfyngwyd ar lawer o'r astudiaethau hyn gan duedd ar ran yr ymchwilwyr i ganolbwyntio ormod ar eu "milltir sgwâr" eu hunain heb ystyried dylanwadau o'r tu allan. Dylid ystyried nad oes a wnelo'r syniadau hyn mewn gwirionedd â ffiniau gwleidyddol modern. Ar lawer cyfrif, mae hyn yn ddealladwy ddigon; mae cyfyngu maes ymchwil i ardal a ddiffinnir gan ffiniau gwleidyddol yn gyfleus gan hwyluso cynhyrchu darn trefnus o waith – fel yn achos y gyfrol hon. Ond, gellir dadlau bod pensaernïaeth fegalithig Cymru yn unigryw ac yn wahanol i eiddo ardaloedd eraill o Brydain ac Ewrop y cyfnod Neolithig.

Wrth ymchwilio'r gyfrol hon, fe'm harweiniwyd at nifer o destunau allweddol a fyddai'n sefydlu arolwg eang. Un o'r testunau allweddol hyn yw *Megalithic Enquiries in the West of Britain* (Powell et al.) a gyhoeddwyd ym 1969 gan Wasg Prifysgol Lerpwl. Ar lawer ystyr, erys y gyfrol hon heb ei hail. Nid yn unig yr ymdrinia â natur ranbarthol yr henebion, ond mae hefyd yn sefydlu fframwaith pwysig ar gyfer llyfrau fel hyn. Mae'r gyfrol wedi esgor ar nifer o astudiaethau rhanbarthol manwl a phenodol, gan gynnwys *Prehistoric Anglesey* (1970, 1991) Frances Lynch, monograff ardderchog Christopher Barker *The Chambered Tombs of South-West Wales* (1992) a chyfrolau gan Children a Nash – *The Prehistoric Sites of Monmouthshire* (1996), *The Prehistoric Sites of Cardiganshire, Carmarthenshire and Pembrokeshire* (1997) and *the Prehistoric Sites of Breconshire* (2001). Gwnaed rhagor o ymchwil ar safleoedd unigol gan Britnell a Savory (1984), Gibson (1999) and Lynch a Smith (1987) a archwiliodd, yn ôl eu trefn, henebion Gwernvale (BRE 7) a Phenywyrlod (BRE 14) ym Mrycheiniog, y caeadle Neolithig yn Hindwell a beddrodau Trefignedd (ANG 1) a Din Dryfol (ANG 5) ar Fôn.

Yn ogystal â'r rhain, mae'r Gomisiwn Frenhinol ar Henebion yng Nghymru wedi casglu at ei gilydd lawer o'r dystiolaeth am yr henebion hyn. Mae eu hastudiaethau sirol, er o bosibl braidd yn hen ffasiwn eu hymdriniaeth, wedi darparu gwybodaeth empirig ddibynadwy ac anhepgor. Mae astudiaeth ddiweddarach y Gomisiwn ar Frycheiniog (1997) wedi goleuo'r ymdriniaeth â'r unig glwstwr mewndirol o henebion Neolithig yng Nghymru. Mae'r cyfrolau hyn i gyd, yn hynafol neu'n fodern, wedi bod yn ffynonellau pwysig.

Yn olaf, mae dyrnaid o bapurau ymchwil a chyfrolau sydd wedi ceisio gosod yr henebion hyn mewn fframwaith damcaniaethol, gan ymdrin â chysyniadau fel pwysigrwydd eu lleoliad o fewn y dirwedd neu'r modd y mae'r bensaernïaeth yn cyd-chwarae â chladdedigaethau a defodau. Y ceffyl blaen yn eu plith yw *A Phenomenology of Landscape* (1994) gan Christopher Tilley sy'n cynnwys penodau ar y Mynyddoedd Duon ac ar dde-orllewin Cymru. Mae cyfrolau eraill yn cynnwys trioleg Richard Bradley: *The Significance of Monuments* (1998), *The Archaeology of Natural Places* (2000) and *The Past in Prehistoric Societies* (2002); *Ancestral Geographies of the Neolithic* (1999) gan Mark Edmonds; *Rethinking the Neolithic* (1991) ac *Understanding the Neolithic* (1999) gan Julian Thomas a chyfrolau Alasdair Whittle *Problems in Neolithic Archaeology* (1988), *Neolithic Europe: a Survey* (1985) ac yn fwy diweddar *The Archaeology of People: Dimensions of Neolithic Life* (2003). Er mai dim ond braidd-gyffwrdd â Chymru mae rhai o'r llyfrau hyn, maent serch hynny yn anhepgor gan y trafodir ynddynt yn benodol paham y bu i bobl godi henebion mewn lleoedd arbennig o fewn y dirwedd. Gwerth ei ystyried hefyd yw *Landscapes of Neolithic Ireland* (2000) gan Gabriel Cooney. Ar nad yw'r gyfrol hon chwaith yn ymdrin yn uniongyrchol â Chymru, mae'n enghraifft ardderchog o sut y dylid ymgymryd ag ysgrifennu astudiaethau tirwedd rhanbarthol.

Dros y 40 mlynedd diwethaf a lle bu'n bosibl, defnyddiwyd dyddiadau radio carbon er mwyn asesu dyddiadau gosodedig nifer fechan o henebion. Serch hynny, mae dyddiadau radio carbon yn rhy brin o lawer i wneud unrhyw ymgais dilys at gronoleg gyflawn (ac eithrio mewn achos safleoedd fel Trefignedd (ANG 1) a Gwernvale (BRE 7) (ATODIAD II).

Yn y llyfr hwn, yr wyf wedi defnyddio dyddiadau calibredig a ddynodir gan CC (gweler Stuiver et al. 1998). Lle nad yw hyn yn bosibl, defnyddir dyddiadau cc heb eu calibreiddio. Yn ogystal, yr wyf hefyd wedi defnyddio dyddiadau CP (cyn y presennol) sydd fel arfer wedi'u cymhwyso i ddata ymchwil amgylcheddol. Cafwyd y dyddiadau hyn mewn ffynonellau unigol a chyfeirir atynt felly.

O fewn y llyfr hwn, yr wyf wedi dilyn system ddosbarthu gydnabyddedig (a ddefnyddiwyd hefyd gan Daniel 1950; Powell et al. 1969, Lynch 1970 a Barker 1992). Defnyddiwyd y system ddosbarthu hon, wedi'i seilio ar fyrfoddau sirol gyda thair neu bedair llythyren, er mwyn osgoi'r posibilrwydd o ddyblu henebion. Dros y blynyddoedd diwethaf hyn, mae'n ymddangos na ddilynwyd y system hon ar gyfer henebion newydd a ddarganfuwyd yn ddiweddar. Penderfynais felly gywiro hyn o wall gan barhau, lle mae'n bosibl, gyda'r system mewn trefn rifiadol.

NODYN AR ENWAU LLEOEDD

Cymerodd yr awdur gryn ofal i sicrhau cywirdeb yr enwau Cymraeg a ymddengys yn y llyfr hwn. Serch hynny, fe all fod anghysonderau a gwahaniaethau gyda sillafiadau enwau arbennig. Mae hyn y broblem gynhenid, mae'n debyg, nid yn unig gyda rhestrau sirol yr SMRau ond hefyd gyda rhestrau Cadw a'r Gomisiwn Frenhinol a chydag Arolwg yr Ordnans.

ACKNOWLEDGEMENTS

This volume has, like its author, gone through a number of metamorphoses. I had the idea of publishing something large-scale in 1993. However, with one thing or another, the text was not started properly until nearly ten years later. Before this, I had the pleasure of dragging my children around all 100 Neolithic cromlech sites (and more), and I am sure they are scarred for life. The photography used in this book is a testament to the lengths I have gone to get the imagery right second time around. I am sure that each photograph will speak a thousand words, and I hope that they will be used to visit these most enigmatic prehistoric monuments, come rain or shine.

This volume could not have been written without the support from my fellow colleagues and friends. I would like to thank the following people who helped with the production of the original version of this book – Andy Johnson and George Children. Sincere thanks also to the four Welsh Trusts: Dyfed Archaeological Trust, Clwyd-Powys Archaeological Trust, Glamorgan-Gwent Archaeological Trust and Gwynedd Archaeological Trust – now collectively known as *Heneb*, and colleagues at the Royal Commission on the Ancient and Historical Monuments of Wales (RCAHMW).

I would also like to thank the members, either deceased or living, of the Cambrian Archaeological Association. It is their inquisitive and tenacious minds that provided much inspiration for writing this book.

From the original version of this book, I would also like to thank Christopher Barker, Peter Dorling, Ian Kinnes, Tim Malim, Sian Rees and Terry Williams who took the time to read through and comment on the various chapters. Special thanks also to Frank Olding and Ian Jones, who translated the preface into Welsh, and to my oldest friend of nearly 46 years, George Children. It was George with whom I worked on four books on Welsh and Marches prehistory, copious notes from which were used for this book. I am also most grateful for a grant from the Brook-Bryant Foundation.

In terms of much needed assistance with the publication of this book, I must express my sincere thanks to Ian Jones (Oriel Môn Museum), Arwyn Owen and Dr Mike Woods, Kim Allen, Dewi Bowen, Ian Tog Jenkins, Dr Edith Evans, Carol James, Kim Iannucci and James Athelstan Nash. Also, thank you to the various landowners of Wales who allowed me to traipse over their land in order to study these sometimes-large stone piles. Finally, a special big thank you to my dear friends who undertook many geophysical surveys around this remarkable country, Les Dodd and Phil Dell.

Thanks also to my dear friends Abby George and Thomas Wellicome who read through the various sections of the original text and made invaluable comments. Thanks to Richard and Su Wheeler at Logaston Press who made this long-awaited project possible and turned it into such a handsome book.

Finally, I would like to thank all my loyal friends, who gave support through difficult times, especially my family. All mistakes are of course my own responsibility.

Construction in progress of the Lligwy monument in Anglesey (Illustration © Cadw)

XV

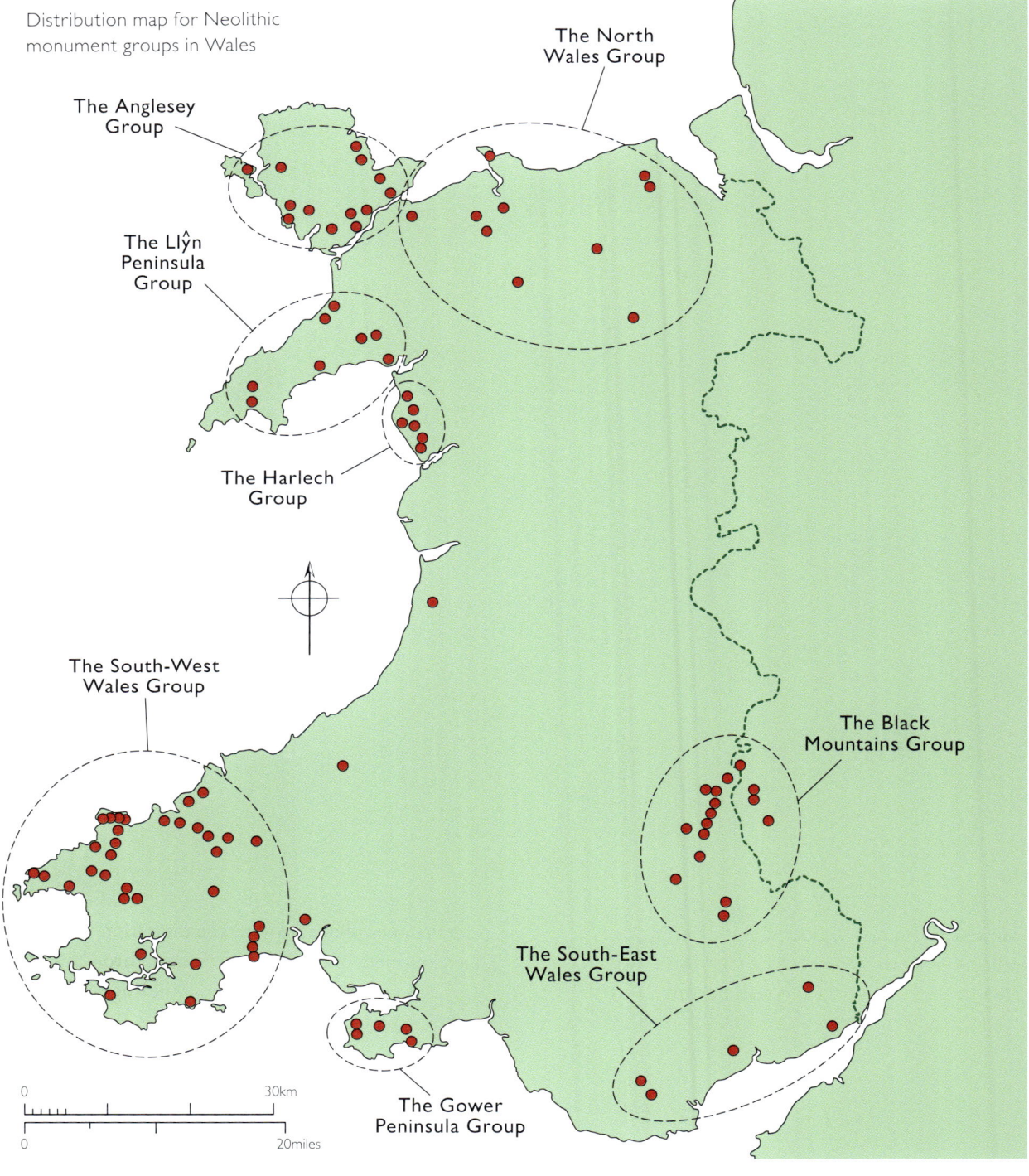

ONE

Being Neolithic

What is Neolithic?

A DEAR FRIEND of mine, Christopher Chippindale, once remarked that we (today) are all a product of the Neolithic. All our actions in terms of food production, storage and consumption, landscape organisation, settlement dispersal, material culture, craft specialisation and ritual habits (in other words, the way we dispose of and venerate the dead) all stem from that 2,000-year period – what we call the *Neolithic*, between 4,000 and 2,000 BCE.

The term *Neolithic*, first conceived by John Lubbock (later Lord Avebury) in 1872, envisaged economy and technology as the primary mechanisms that controlled and manipulated society (Lubbock 1872). Secondary to this was the ritual and symbolic *act of burial* of the dead, and the evidence that accompanied it. Prehistorians have tended to suggest that the Neolithic is a period that reflects death, whilst the preceding Mesolithic (10,000–4,000 BCE) is a period that reflects economy. The evidence in Wales and in other Neolithic core areas of Western Britain for this *act of burial* can be seen through a series of monuments that are generically referred to as 'stone burial chambered tombs'. These monuments, usually remaining as no more than a confused pile of stones, conjure an evocative picture of how people in this distant time prepared and buried their dead (Chapman, Kinnes, Randsborg 1981). However, in complete contrast, the archaeological evidence for economy and society is limited to a handful of settlement sites, some of which are little more than lithic scatters. The burial evidence and limited settlement, plus the associated material culture, form what is termed the *Neolithic Package*. Also associated with this package are farming and the making and use of pottery.

It was originally thought, prior to the application of radiocarbon dating, that the duration of the Neolithic spanned around 400 years (Piggott 1954, 379–81). At this time the period was divided into two phases: Primary and Secondary Neolithic. The Primary phase represented the colonisation of settlers from the Continent, whilst a secondary phase included the possible integration with the indigenous Mesolithic hunter/gatherer/fisher communities (Stanford 1980). The Primary phase also saw the migration from the Continent of tomb-builders; and, through a diffusionary process, the idea of building mausoleums for the dead spread to many areas of Britain.

Subsequently, Savory (and others) divided the Neolithic into three stages: Early Neolithic (4,500–3,750 BCE), Middle Neolithic (3,750–3,250 BCE) and Late Neolithic (3,250–2,000 BCE) (Savory

1980, 207). Both the earlier and later dates of the Neolithic would have merged into the Mesolithic and Early Bronze Age (EBA)[1] periods respectively. The date of the Early Neolithic is represented not by the introduction of burial monuments but the introduction of domestication, and in particular woodland clearance, as witnessed through palynology and sedimentological analysis. Monument building appears to have gained momentum during the Middle Neolithic, arguably following a period of social-political crisis (Ashbee 1978, Burgess 1980). This movement of architectural ideas and trends is not only confined to the western British Isles but also to Neolithic Europe (Hodder 1990). The various design concepts are, in my view, evidence on the design, dimensions and shape of monuments. A good example is the concept of the long mound, from its *Linienbandkeramik* (LBK) beginnings in the northern plains of Europe to southern Britain (see Kinnes 1992), and eventually occupying the landscapes of Wales and Scotland. What we see is a 2–3,000-year journey of idiosyncratic change through hybridisation.

FARMING THE PROMISED LAND

In terms of farming, this can be seen as merely an economic system, whereby the knowledge of when and which crops to harvest, and the management of domesticated animals, comes into practice. Indeed, this is the primary mechanism that supposedly divides the hunter-gatherers of the Mesolithic from the agriculturists of the Neolithic. The reliance on one, two or maybe three harvests per year could be considered risky. However, it is probable that a more complex economic system was in place. I have previously suggested that the Mesolithic-Neolithic transition was no overnight affair and regionally, was not synchronous (Smith 1992; Nash 1998). A transition from an economy based on hunting, fishing and gathering to limited agriculture, in the form of allotment-style cultivation along with animal husbandry, probably took over 1,000 years (between 4,500 and 3,500 BCE). Anthropologist Barbara Bender suggests 'food production was a question of technique; agriculture a question of commitment, in this case, a long-term commitment' (1987, 204). I would further add that hunting, fishing and gathering remained the primary economy throughout the Neolithic. The mechanisms of change evident through the material culture, although dominating the archaeological record, do not fully reflect Neolithic society, and what I would term a mixed economy in which hunting and gathering are as important to society as farming. In the coastal areas, there would have been a greater emphasis on estuarine and marine resources. Large marine mammals such as seal, porpoise and whale would have been important food resources. Freshwater fish and estuarine shellfish, according to Jarman et al. (1982) would also have provided an important source of protein. For example, limpet shells have been found within the floor debris in hut platforms at the Clegyr Boia settlement (Williams 1953, 24–9), whilst salmon bone was found at Coygan Camp (Wainwright 1967, 190). Within a burial context, limpet, mussel shells, and fish bones have also been found at Barclodiad y Gawres (ANG 4) and Lligwy (ANG 14) in Ynys Môn (Anglesey) (Powell & Daniel 1956, 16–7 and Lynch 1970, 53), suggesting that people using these monuments had an affinity with the sea. The food residues found within a burial-ritual context may reflect the symbolic power of certain food stuffs. It is important to stress that 75% of monuments in Wales lie within 2km of the sea, suggesting a ritual affinity with the sea.

It was considered initially that the first farmers came to southern Britain during the early fourth millennium BCE in boats laden with cattle, sheep and

The possible henge at Bryn Celli Ddu showing the first phase of the monument (Illustration © Cadw)

grain (Case 1969). When in Britain, it is suggested that these colonists began to clear small areas of woodland and create allotment-style gardens. However, according to pollen evidence, some of these areas were abandoned and forest regeneration was pursued. Subsequently, the same areas were again cleared. This process, sometimes referred to as *landnam*, would have incorporated slash-and-burn clearing. The burning of shrubs and undergrowth would have provided the necessary nutrients to the soils. It would also have encouraged woodland fauna to graze cleared areas, thus providing an ideal opportunity for hunting and foraging. This process of woodland clearance can also suggest Late Mesolithic communities, rather than early farmers, were utilising the woodlands.

On the deeper, more fertile soils, permanent clearances provided long-term settlement stability, thus establishing sedentism. According to Evans (1975), mixed agricultural regimes were in practice whereby wheat (*emmer* variety) and barley were grown. Archaeological evidence shows that the fields prior to cultivation were prepared using ploughs. When harvested, crops would have been harvested using hoes, spades and reaping knives. Once harvested, grain would have been stored in clay-lined storage pits like those found at the Late Neolithic/Early Bronze Age site of Four Crosses, near Llandysilio, Powys (Warrilow 1986, 60).

The system of one, two or even three crops-per-year-cultivation would have been supported by hunting, fishing and gathering, and this form of mixed economy probably continued throughout the Neolithic and beyond. Storage pits also contained wild foods such as hazelnuts, as found within a crop-marked enclosure at Bryn Derwen, Llandysul (Gibson 1990, 13). This discovery suggests that there was still a need to 'farm' the landscape. According to Smith (1974) there appears to be a change in emphasis from a mixed agriculture to a more pastoral society, and less evidence within the archaeological record of cereals, but an increase in cattle and, in particular, pig. At the same time, forest and woodland regeneration occurred, and the domestication and husbandry of pigs became an important practice.

As well as farming, comprising this Neolithic package and associated with monumentality, are artefacts. Artefacts are usually classified as either mundane (utilitarian tools) or symbolic. Interestingly, mundane items such as flint tools are also occasionally considered symbolic – usually when found in burial deposition. A number of monuments have contained a series of diagnostic tools including blades, scrapers and leaf shaped arrowheads. This desire to include flint tools, and also pottery, suggests that Neolithic people believed in an afterlife in which the deceased would have a use for these items. Also recovered, but in small numbers, are polished flint and stone axes. However, the extent of what else was placed within each burial chamber has not survived the archaeological record.

Moreover, finds from recently excavated monuments suggest that grave good assemblages were small.

One of the earliest material culture assemblages recognised within this early chronology, and one that survives the archaeological record, is pottery. Recognised wares found within the Welsh Neolithic include Abingdon, Ebbsfleet and Peterborough wares (Abingdon wares being the earliest). Each of these wares is noted for its distinct shape and design, in particular the impressed cord and stamped comb coarse pottery belonging to the Peterborough ware assemblage (Peterson 2003). Although Neolithic pottery assemblages are found across much of Wales, very few burial-ritual sites have yielded significant quantities. This is largely due to the acidic nature of the soil or unrecorded historic interventions/disturbances caused by antiquarian plundering. Over the past 20 years or so, I have had the honour to excavate four Neolithic burial monuments in Wales and the Marches. Of these four, only two have yielded Neolithic pottery. One of these sites is Trellyffaint, which was investigated between 2014 and 2019 (Nash 2020). Retrieved from a shallow pit, close to the chamber area of the monument, were 35 sherds of Grooved Ware pottery (forming a near-complete vessel), along with a small assemblage of flint.

Architecture and death

The Neolithic in Britain, and in particular western Britain, is generally agreed to span some 2,000 years, between 4,000 and 2,000 BCE. However, it is unlikely that monuments were continually in use throughout this period, but represent a substantial period of time occurring sometime within that 2,000-year span. To add more confusion, the very idea that the Neolithic neatly occupies a distinct chunk of time is, at best, naive, relying – implicitly or explicitly – on the idea of invasion, conquest and colonisation. It is clearly unrealistic to assume that brand new forms of social organisation, economic exploitation and symbolic behaviour appeared in Britain overnight, as it were, sometime around 4,000 BCE, and that this lifestyle disappeared just as abruptly in 2,000 BCE, to be replaced immediately by another. Researchers have tended to compartmentalise prehistory: one period and its distinct and dominant material culture ends and another begins. To come closer to the truth, we must regard the onset of the Neolithic as a gradual process – what one might refer to as *Neolithicisation* – rather than as a specific, revolutionary event. Over time, gradual social, political, economic and symbolic change influenced the behaviour of mobile hunting and gathering societies and their relationship with the landscape. Many textbooks proposed two distinct worlds – the Mesolithic and the Neolithic – and ne'er the twain shall meet. Mesolithic and Neolithic cultures are seen as mutually exclusive: where one existed, the other could not flourish (see discussion in Thomas 1993). It was said that they represented radically different economies: one extensive in its harvesting of natural resources; the other exploiting land intensively in order to increase its productivity. The adoption of a Neolithic cultural package, therefore, meant the sudden and irreversible extinction of the Mesolithic way of life. Such rigidity has been a convenient fiction. As we shall see, these worlds did not collide; they merged, coalescing gradually, perhaps imperceptibly, over time.

A theme of this book is the interplay between the economy and ritual of the Old World and that of the New. Arguably, there was a degree of co-existence. The same process of assimilation and integration of material culture is true of the Neolithic–Bronze Age transition (between 2,500 and 2,000 BCE). It is suggested, therefore, that any invasion is likely to have been one of ideas rather than conquering tribal groups. Although one cannot ignore the possibility of migration and the introduction and utilisation of Continental food stuffs and livestock (Case 1969).

In Wales, as in southern Britain, the Neolithic is most visibly (and in some cases spectacularly) represented by stone and earthen burial monuments. It is more than probable that chambered monuments were used by and for social elites (Atkinson 1968). There has been much debate about when and what type of monument was constructed first. Indeed, in the limestone areas in north-east Wales, Mesolithic and Early Neolithic burials occur in a number of natural caves. Could this transition between natural and artificial caves (i.e. stone chambered tombs) be part of a local transition in terms of changing place and architecture? It is more than probable that the earliest monuments were constructed during the mid-fourth millennium BCE. Powell (1969, 264–71), Lynch (1976, 65) and more recently, Whittle (2003, 118) suggest that the Portal Dolmens form part of the earliest Neolithic sequences in Wales and Ireland,

Carreg Coetan Arthur (PEM 3), a fine example of an Irish Sea Province Portal Dolmen

within what is referred to as the Irish Sea Province (Davis 1945; Cummings 2009). It appears that these monuments may have originated from (theoretical) wooden structures in southern Britain (see Kinnes 1992; Whittle 1985); themselves a product of design from the *Linienbandkeramik* (LBK) long mounds in central and Eastern Europe. However, whilst I accept the idea of a 'blueprint' for monument design moving across Europe, I would suggest that there is a more complex movement of architectural ideas within the Welsh Neolithic. Portal Dolmens have a greater design affinity with other Dolmens found in western France and southern Ireland. The lack of radiocarbon data for Neolithic structures with a *terminus anti-quem* date has hampered the problem of monument development; moreover, Powell and Lynch have based their assumptions on the excavation of only one monument, Dyffryn Ardudwy (MER 3), which was excavated in 1961. Early dates taken from the Cotswold-Severn monument of Penywyrlod (BRE 14), located within the Black Mountains Group, suggest that Portal Dolmens and Cotswold-Severn monuments, although sited in different areas, were in use at roughly the same time. There is a case that both monument types are similar enough to be considered, of course, to be one and the same (Kinnes 1981).

Chambered monuments occur throughout Wales, although each cluster contains a degree of regional architectural diversity.[2] Savory (1980, 219) has divided monuments into eastern and western groups. This, in my opinion, is too simplistic, essentially as Savory suggests that architectural influences come from either the Atlantic/Irish Sea area or southern Britain. I would suggest that Wales is more of a 'melting pot', whereby a number of influences from Ireland, southern Britain and western France affect the way monuments are designed and constructed. Further, architectural influences were being transmitted from one core area to another, especially during the Middle Neolithic (*c*.3,500 BCE). Although a construction date can be fixed with some precision, scientific excavation has cast doubt on the idea that these sites were first and last used by communities that had adopted a Neolithic way of life and death (Chapman, Kinnes, Randsborg 1981). Some at least have been shown to possess a pre-Neolithic past, and many remained in use during later periods in prehistory. For example, Mesolithic and Upper Palaeolithic flint has been found beneath the chambered tomb at Gwernvale (BRE 7), Breconshire (Britnell 1984, 2022). Others have revealed evidence of re-use, perhaps following a lengthy period of abandonment: for example, Ty Isaf (BRE 5) and Bryn Celli Ddu (ANG 7). In each case, a place appears to have been chosen and then shaped by ritual, social or economic activity over many thousands of years. Monumentality is not just a purely Neolithic phenomenon; the *Neolithicisation* of a place is part of an ongoing history.

Capel Garmon (DEN 3), the most northerly Cotswold-Severn monument in Wales

Regionalism and architectural form

The idea of transition and integration involves a complex set of variables. Architecture, landscape, material culture and time, together establish the regionalism evident throughout the core areas of Wales – those areas that have extensive burial evidence, usually in the form of chambered monuments, and occasionally evidence of settlement. There are two areas of Wales, however, which do not have stone burial monuments: the Walton Basin and Welshpool have, unusually, a probable late Neolithic circular palisade enclosure and several cursus monuments (Gibson 1999). These monuments, along with other henge-types found within the Central Marches area, represent a different type of Neolithic whereby the living and the monument interact, as opposed to the dead interacting with burial monuments. In the case of henges within the Walton Basin (which incidentally include the largest of its kind in Europe) their function may also have included the ritual corralling and slaughter of livestock, feasting, and social and political mediation.

Megalithic Enquiries, published in 1969, has done much to explore the problem of establishing how and where regionality through architecture emerges. The proposed classification system of the Cotswold-Severn tradition initiated by Corcoran is now more complex than once thought. This classification of monument, Middle Neolithic in date, is identified by the following architectural traits:[3] (i) cairns which have a simple terminal chamber (e.g. Lletty'r Filiast, CRN 1, and Tinkinswood, GLA 9); (ii) cairns which have transepted terminal chambers (e.g. Parc-le-Breos-Cwm, GLA 4, and Penmaen Burrows, GLA 5); and (iii) cairns which have lateral chambers (e.g. Capel Garmon, DEN 3, Gwernvale, BRE 7, and Penywyrlod, BRE 14). Many of these architectural traits can be considered to form part of a regional tradition. For example, the majority of monuments

Bryn Celli Ddu (ANG 7), one of three large passages graves in Wales

within the Black Mountains Group of central-eastern Wales are constructed using a lateral chamber along with the erection of a false portal within a horned forecourt area.[4] In the same area, Neolithic builders have also seen fit to construct inner and outer cairn – one for stability; the other for cosmetic purposes. However, using raw materials in a particular way cannot be collectively placed into a tradition. Regional variations usually incorporate a number of design traits. I would argue that within the core areas of Neolithic Wales and elsewhere, there are several architectural traditions that, to their builders and users, were considered the correct way of doing things. Furthermore, builders were establishing their 'mark' on the monument, creating a unique architectural identity, but at the same time allying themselves to a regional and identifiable tradition.

For example, during the Late Neolithic in Ynys Môn, a ritually induced necessity dictated that the place of burial must be round and contain a passage and a large chamber (Lynch 2000b). At the same time, in South-west Wales, there was a need to create a small, confined burial place using a capstone propped up by a single upright (or orthostat), usually with no covering mound. This is merely a generalisation; however, as many researchers will know, Ynys Môn and South-west Wales contain a number of monuments which are architecturally diverse and located in different landscapes. I would also suggest that within these core areas there are sub-groups that possess their own unique architecture and material culture, and have adopted their own attitude to landscape position. The term *Neolithicisation* must therefore embrace a number of traditions that are regionally influenced over time and space.

The group of monuments that I have chosen to discuss here lies within Wales and along its borders, and forms a diverse set of monuments occupying nine core areas. The Black Mountains Group, for example, includes a number of sites that lie within the fertile hinterland that includes west Herefordshire. The so-called Cotswold-Severn monument tradition has its roots in South-west England, but quite clearly some of the architectural traits associated with this tradition are found throughout Wales. Megalithic art provides a further example illustrating the poor fit between modern boundaries and the distribution of Neolithic cultural traits. Two sites in Ynys Môn – Barclodiad y Gawres (ANG 4) and Bryn Celli Ddu (ANG 7) – possess some of Britain's finest megalithic art, yet similar traditions are found at Loughcrew and Newgrange in the Boyne Valley of Co. Meath, Ireland, and at Clear Island, County Cork and the Calderstones (LANCS 1), near Liverpool (Forde-Johnson 1956). This megalithic art tradition, Middle to Late Neolithic in date, consists of a series of

The gallery grave of Bedd yr Afanc (PEM 27), located in Mynydd Preseli, Pembrokeshire

carved images, including spirals, concentric circles, footprints, shoe prints and cupmarks, and clearly transcends modern boundaries, extending across the Irish Sea as far east as Liverpool (Stewart, Nash & Cowell 2021).

Based upon architectural diversity and distribution, six core groups have been identified in Wales: Ynys Môn, the Black Mountains, the Gower Peninsula, the Llŷn Peninsula, North Wales and South-west Wales (Daniel 1950; Powell et al. 1969). Within each of these core areas a number of smaller sub-groups are evident, based upon architectural similarity, geographical proximity to various landforms and the coast, and similarities in landscape setting and monument orientation. For example, five such local monument-building

The Devil's Quoit (PEM 25), an example of a possible earth-fast monument

The King's Quoit (PEM 26), another example of an earth-fast monument. Engraving by E.L. Barnwell (*Archaeologia Cambrensis*, 1872)

traditions have been identified within the Black Mountains Group. Here, it is geography and topography, rather than architecture, which are emphasised. Within the Black Mountains area, and also in others, architectural style varies considerably from monument to monument, and even within sub-groups variation is significant. Why such diversity? One answer could be that, within each sub-group, different architectural techniques are being employed at different times – a suggestion that could be reinforced by radiocarbon dating were it not for several potential problems. Firstly, very few Neolithic burial places have been excavated in Wales over the last 50 years, and earlier excavations were usually undertaken without the necessary scientific rigour. Consequently, there is little datable material available. The other problem is that radiocarbon dating only fixes a monument's use at one particular point in time; and (as stated earlier) one must consider the burial place prior to it becoming *Neolithicised*. Within the South-west Wales Group, up to six sub-groups have been identified, and within these groups a diverse monumentality is evident that is clearly based on chronological variables (Barker 1992; Children & Nash 1996). This can be stated with some conviction because the antiquarian accounts available indicate a clear distinction between monuments in terms of material culture and – more importantly – burial practice. For example, a number of simple 'earth-fast' monuments (Daniel 1950) have been identified. These consist of a capstone propped up at one end by a single upright stone (or orthostat), while the other end rests on the ground. A small chamber excavated beneath the capstone was usually found to accommodate cremated human remains. It is clear that the burial practice evident in these monuments is very different from the method found, for example, at Parc-le-Breos-Cwm (GLA 4) on the Gower coast, or at Ty Isaf (BRE 5) in the Black Mountains – of interring disarticulated skeletal remains. This variation in burial practice can either be explained in terms of regional preference or as a product of changes over time. Britnell (1984, 5) suggests that skeletal remains from monuments within the Black Mountains Group were deposited in an incomplete state, suggesting either excarnation or disarticulation practices were in operation (or both). One can suggest that identical practices are occurring within similar monuments elsewhere in western Britain. If one looks at modern material culture and the changes, say, in rites within English communal burial since the fifteenth century, one is able to see that change is both subtle but at the same time, significant.[5] If we are able to witness ongoing change within the space of 600 years, then we can perhaps accept that similar changes in Neolithic burial practice would be likely to occur over a period of 2,000 years or more.

Multi-phased building activity

Monument building in Wales and elsewhere cannot be regarded as a single event. The archaeological record suggests that nearly all the burial monuments in Wales possess more than one building phase. Even hybrid monuments, recognised by Corcoran (1969), have some form of secondary phasing. Their long use, maybe over many hundreds of years, could not have escaped the numerous architectural influences and trends that moved around the Neolithic landscape. For example, the Black Mountains monument of Ty Isaf (BRE 5) has at least two phases of building activity. Grimes (1939a) suggests that Phase 1 consisted of a circular mound with a single passage and chamber, which was followed by Phase 2, a trapezoidal-shaped mound added to the northern section of the circular mound. It appears that during the middle Neolithic, c.3,000 BCE, trapezoidal mounds became popular, and this is shown in the hybrid trapezoidal monuments that are found throughout Wales. At Heston Brake (MON 3), there is, according to Daniel (1950, 212), a passage that was added to an existing chamber. At the passage grave of Bryn Celli Ddu in Ynys Môn, excavations by Hemp between 1925 and 1929 showed that beneath this already impressive monument, were the remains of a circular alignment consisting of 14 stones (1930). In the centre of the circle was a pit that was covered by a recumbent stone slab. Lying next to this was a stone that had an incised, abstract, meandering design. Archaeological evidence suggests that this monument has an earlier henge monument that underlies the mound and certainly predates the burial activity of the site. Probably the most spectacular addition to any monument is the cairn and eastern chamber to Dyffryn Ardudwy (MER 3). According to Powell (1963) the first chamber, which was enclosed by a semicircular cairn, was later incorporated into a trapezoidal mound built of cairn.

Antiquarian engraving of the complex, multi-phased Dyffryn Ardudwy monument (MER 3), north-west Wales

At the eastern end of the monument a rectangular chamber was constructed within a forecourt area; and, as with monuments of this date and form, two horns were added either side of the new chamber.

It is not just additions to the architecture that are present; one can also see changes in society through the limited material culture that is present in these monuments. In some cases, one can witness different types of burial activity occurring within the same chamber. However, due to adverse soil conditions and medieval and post-medieval disturbance, evidence is somewhat limited. There are a number of monuments, in particular in Ynys Môn, which clearly indicate multi-period activity. At Lligwy (ANG 14) near Penrhos-Lligwy, excavations in 1908 revealed the remains of 15–30 individuals of all ages (Baynes 1908). Also present were an array of animal bone, mussel shell and pottery fragments. Interestingly, the pottery dated from the Neolithic and Bronze Age. Similarly, at the Ty Isaf monument (BRE 5) there is evidence of different types of burial activity, including crushed, disarticulated bone from the western chamber, articulated skeletons from the eastern chamber and passage, along with associated Neolithic and Bronze Age grave goods. It is clear from the burial evidence that this monument was in use for at least 1,500 years. The difference in time between the construction of the circular mound and its incorporation into a larger trapezoidal mound may only be a few years. Dating of the burials is based partly on what was going on elsewhere in Britain and western Europe at that time.[6]

A large number of Welsh monuments have an earlier, non-megalithic origin, and culminate in the alteration or destruction of the megalithic structure. One of the most celebrated excavations of the modern era was that carried out at Gwernvale (BRE 7), near Talgarth, in 1977–78 (Britnell 1984), which revealed a period of use spanning some 10,000 years. Beneath the actual fabric of the monument were a number of lithics dating as far back as the late Upper Palaeolithic period, *c*.12,000 BCE. Overlying this material was diagnostic flint of the Mesolithic period (Healey & Green 1984). Incorporated into what can now be described as a multi-phase monument was recent evidence of the chambers being used as a sheep shelter. The nearby monument of Ty Illtyd (BRE 6) has evidence of a hermit known as St Illtyd using the chamber as a hermitage during the medieval period. A series of Christian symbols are faintly scratched on several of the uprights inside the chamber. Within the Nevern group of monuments in South-west Wales, six monuments that surround the Nevern Valley are embedded within a number of landscapes, both prehistoric and historic. On the capstone of Trellyffaint (PEM 2) are up to 75 cupmarks which probably date from the Late Neolithic or Early Bronze Age and are probably additions to the monument during use (Nash, Brook & Wellicome 2020). At Pentre Ifan (PEM 5) and running along the edge of the mound on the eastern side, are a series of ritual pits which, according to Grimes (1948, 3–23), appear to pre-date the mound. On two uprights within the forecourt area, Lynch (1972) has argued that rock art exists which may date from the Bronze Age; however, these potential engravings are difficult to define. Similarly, at Carreg Coetan (PEM 3) diagnostic Mesolithic flint lies close to the robbed-out mound. Similar acts of multi-phased activity are present on monuments in North Wales and in Ynys Môn.

Within modern times and especially in Wales, one sees additions to ritual buildings. More importantly, some of these buildings, although recognised as ritual buildings, change their meaning over time. For example, one will see in Wales, changes of meaning and status to Nonconformist chapels. These buildings, which were part of popular religious movements during the seventeenth, eighteenth and nineteenth centuries, have invariably been changed both in form and meaning; many now being domestic buildings, or even restaurants and garages. There is of course a period of transition when the initial meaning of the building ceases. At this point, the building may fall into decay. The graveyard becomes unattended. The meaning of the building becomes forgotten. However, visually, the building is vaguely recognised as a place of worship. This is seen through the style, the distinct architecture of the building and where the building stands within the settlement. After a period of transition, the modern planning procedure will invariably allow the building to be transformed. However, due to its ritual importance, its age and architectural style, the main fabric of the building will be protected. After planning permission is granted, the building, which is now a shell (its internal form and freestanding furniture removed) is transformed into a space with different meaning. Despite this transformation the original meaning – that of a chapel – stays the same. This simplistic approach to style and change in architecture and its meaning can be applied to the multi-phased activity of chambered monuments. Nowadays, we are in a fortunate position, through the access to detailed historical records and the Listed Buildings Register, to know when, why and how buildings such as chapels changed their identity (but not their form). In the case of chambered monuments, the when, the why and the how are near impossible to assess. However, we do know that change did take place at some point in time of use.

The Mesolithic–Neolithic transition

When dealing with prehistoric chronology, one is often misled into thinking that transition occurs within an instant; that one day Mesolithic people were hunting, fishing and gathering, and leaving very little trace of a material culture, whilst the next day Neolithic people were corporately burying their dead in artificial caves, being sedentary, making flint tools and pottery. Based on the archaeological evidence, this is obviously not the case. Transition entails a very long process of ideological change. Only hints of this change are seen through a fragmented material culture. Indeed, concerning the Neolithic, archaeologists may only be witnessing up to five per cent of this material culture.

Traditionally, the Mesolithic of Wales (and indeed western Britain) spans roughly 6,000 years from 10,000 BCE to 4,000 BCE (Wymer 1977). These transition dates vary according to the author, and conveniently mark either environmental or material culture change (see Evans 1975; Smith & Cloutman 1988). At around 10,000 BCE there was a progressive warming of the climate in Western Europe. Prior to this, between 40,000 and 15,000 BCE, the Devensian Ice Sheet had scoured the Eurasian landscape. Over the next 5,000 years there had been several cold snaps, but generally the climate was gradually warming. At about the time of the Late Upper Palaeolithic–Mesolithic transition, hunter/fisher/gatherer tool kits became more specialised, mainly due to the varied and prolific fauna that was being hunted and the wide range of resources present (Lillie 2015). However, this change did not occur at once. There was a lengthy transition from the Late Upper Palaeolithic (LUP) to the early Mesolithic, that probably spans at least 2,000 years.

The changes in lithic industries, from broad blades to shaped blades and microliths, occurred with the change from coniferous to broad-leaved woodland (Lillie 2015). Obviously, with this gradual change in vegetation there was a need to rethink new resource strategies. The wildwood (or 'climax woodland' as it is referred to), began to colonise the valleys and intermediate slopes of Wales from around 8,500 BCE. This change can be seen as a sweep from south to north, and includes tree species such as oak, elm, hazel and alder. With the emergence of climax woodland, a new set of forest dwellers began to emerge, including roe and red deer, wild cattle and pig.

There is sporadic settlement evidence in Wales during this period. Caseldine (1990) has identified up to 19 sites that indicate anthropogenic activity. In the southern part of Breconshire, for example, at Nant Helen and Coed Taf, quantities of datable charcoal and tree pollen have been found which suggest the encroachment of early Holocene (post-glacial) forests, along with possible pre-Neolithic communities following a slash-and-burn woodland clearance strategy. It has been suggested by Huntley (1990) and Lille (2015) that by around 10,000 BCE, birch, willow, juniper and, in some areas, pine had started to migrate northwards to northern Britain. These species were later replaced with alder, elm and lime. They later integrated with the hazel and oak that marks the so-called 'Climatic Optimum' that commenced around 8,000 BCE when average summer temperatures were around 18–20 degrees centigrade. Jacobi (1980, 105) charts this part of the Holocene into three broad stages. The first stage was a warming phase that lasted for up to 3,500 years until 6,500 BCE when ash and lime began to colonise the wooded valleys and encroach up to altitudes of 450m. At around the same time, the land bridge across the Bristol Channel began to close. This was followed by an optimum phase, which lasted for a similar duration until 3,000 BCE. The final stage was a cooling phase that continued into the historic period. This climatic process was ongoing throughout north-west Europe.

Settling the Promised Land

Today, the places of the dead are extremely visible, yet the living have left few traces. The archaeological record in Wales contains around 150 freestanding monuments of Neolithic date; 100 of these are discussed within this volume (Appendix 1). Perhaps another 3–400 monuments have been either lost or destroyed, some of which have been documented. Associated with these monuments are numerous find spots and lithic scatters. Other monuments that date to the Neolithic and have been found in Wales include henges, pit alignments and a possible causewayed enclosure. Henges appear to be found sporadically throughout Wales; sometimes incorporated into later monuments such as Bryn Celli Ddu (ANG 4). However, large-scale formal settlement is less evident. Only a handful of sites have been discovered and fully investigated. Whether one wishes to include large flint scatters as settlement is open to debate. Two multi-phased sites in South-west Wales, Clegyr Boia and Coygan Camp, have revealed evidence of Neolithic, as well as Bronze Age and Iron Age activity. A further site is located in west Herefordshire on Dorstone Hill, close to Arthur's Stone, in an area referred to as the Golden Valley. The importance of this lithic site is down to two factors: its size and the quantity of the diagnostic lithic assemblage.

The site was discovered by field-walkers on Dorstone Hill and is equidistant between Arthur's Stone (HRF 1) and Cross Lodge Long Barrow (HRF 4). Excavated by Christopher Houlder and Roger Pye between 1965 and 1970, this extensive settlement (SO 326 423) covers approximately 18 acres (Children & Nash 1994).

The settlement was enclosed on the west side by a crude stone wall, on top of which was a wooden 'stockade' fence. Also present were storage pits (possibly used for grain), occupation floors and undisturbed 'buried soils', ideal for dating. Within this, ancient soils were discovered that contained over 4,000 pieces of flint (including many arrowheads), pottery, and more than 50 polished stone axe fragments. The stone and flint used to

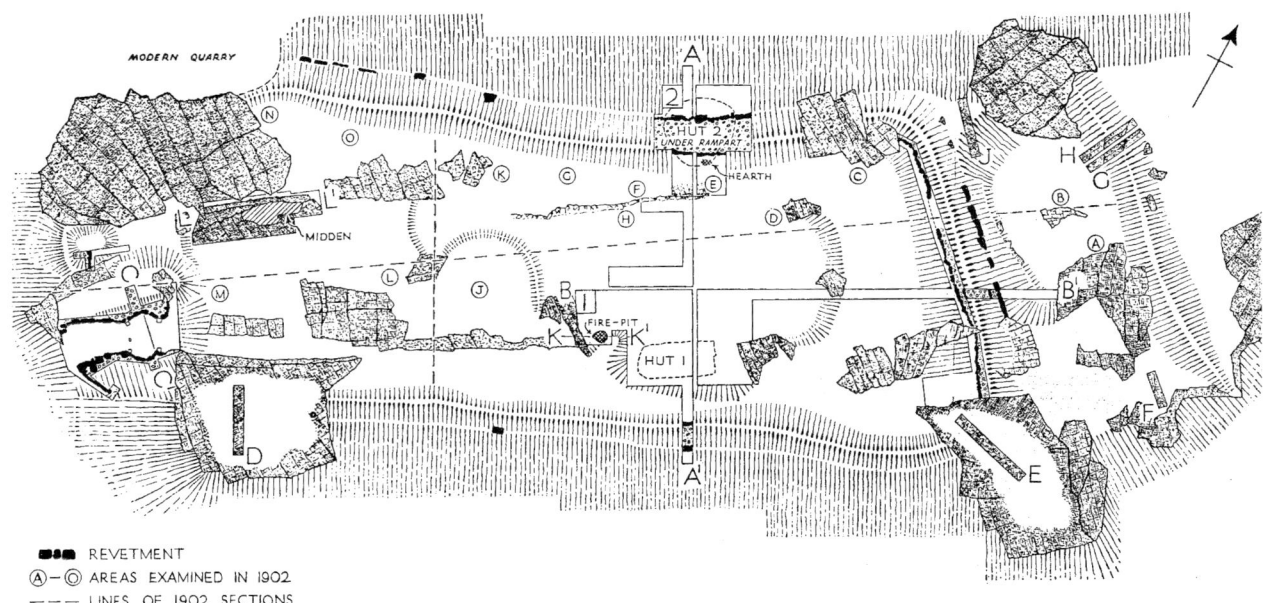

Early twentieth-century plan of the Clegyr Boia, St David's Head, south-west Wales

create these prestige items were, in part, imported from as far away as South Wales and the Cotswolds. The contact/exchange of axes between all three areas highlights the importance and prestige of farming groups within the Golden Valley.

The size of the Dorstone settlement suggests that a large population (probably in excess of 250 people) occupied the upland areas of the Golden Valley during the Neolithic. This settlement utilised the slopes, ridges and tops of the eastern uplands – from Merbach Hill in the north-east to Canns Hill in the south. By settling on the eastern slopes, the community would have lived within full view of the Golden Valley – and, more importantly, of the symbolically significant Black Mountains. Below, the fertile woodland of the valley floor would have been slowly cleared for allotment-style farming. More land would have been brought into production as the population grew. Remaining pockets of woodland scattered throughout the valley would have contained red deer and wild boar, additional resources that could have been exploited by Neolithic people in the same way as their Mesolithic ancestors.

The two settlements in South-west Wales, in particular Clegyr Boia, are difficult to research as the soils are very acidic and shallow. Much of the stratigraphy of Clegyr Boia was extremely ephemeral because of subsequent disturbance. The settlement is set within later rectangular ramparts, measuring 100m x 25m, which is possibly of Iron Age date.

Clegyr Boia settlement consists of three possible Neolithic house structures, a fire pit and a midden. Outside the settlement area, a large number of Mesolithic flint scatters suggest continuous occupation of the peninsula for well over 4,000 years.

One of the houses was oval; the other rectangular. The excavation revealed a possible third hut, located centrally within the rampart area (Baring-Gould, 1902). This rectangular structure measuring 7m x 3m in plan, and probably representing a dwelling, comprised two rows of posts, which may have supported a timber roof (Williams, 1953: 24–9). An *unused pit* investigated inside this structure by Audrey Williams in 1943, was compared by the excavator to similar pits discovered under the Pentre Ifan monument (PEM 5).

The oval hut yielded evidence of extensive burning. Barker (1992) has suggested that, in addition, the deposition of pottery indicates possible ritual abandonment. I would argue that the settlement and the two nearby monuments are contemporary, and that the former may have died out naturally towards the end of the Neolithic. Pottery from the oval hut appears to be identical to examples found in the rectangular structure and in the midden to the west. Three different Neolithic pottery styles have been identified in all, and have been compared to wares found in Cornwall, southern Ireland and the Wessex region, suggesting that a possible exchange network linked these areas. Barker (1992) proposes a Middle Neolithic date (3,200–2,700 BCE) for the pottery from this site.

A series of hearths to the west of the oval hut yielded a flint arrowhead and a partly polished stone axe of gritty volcanic tuff (Houlder, 1988). Limpet shells, pottery and oak and birch charcoal was recovered from the midden. Cattle bone was found in both huts. The bone, together with the shells, suggests that the people of Clegyr Boia thrived on a mixed economy of hunting/gathering/fishing with an element of domesticated herding. The settlement may have supported only two or three small family units at any one time.

The second settlement identified in South-west Wales is located on Coygan Hill and dates from the Early Neolithic, around 3,750 BCE (3,050 ± 95 cal years BCE). An earlier phase of Mesolithic occupation has also been suggested (Castleden, 1992). Located close to the sea and the mouths of the

Decorated and painted, later prehistoric vessel, drawn in 1869

Afon Tywi (Towy) and Taf, Coygan Camp revealed a number of datable organic remains, including charred hazelnut shells and animal bone recovered from a small fire pit (Taylor 1980). The shells and the bone, which date to 5,000 ± 95 BP, suggest hunting and gathering remained an important component of daily Neolithic life.

Approximately 3km to the north of the Clegyr Boia settlement are two stone chambered monuments that belong to a cluster of tombs that occupy St David's Head. These are regarded as earth-fast in form and small enough to be constructed and managed by small a group. To the east of both monuments is a series of prehistoric field systems that are arguably of a later date. Nevertheless, apart from the rearing of cattle and the fishing of seasonal marine fauna, including mammals such as porpoise and seal, communities on this peninsula may have relied upon the produce from small garden allotments, although no pollen record suggests this.

Another Neolithic settlement worthy of mention is sited within the central part of Ynys Môn, near the monuments of Presaddfed (ANG 2) to the

Flint and chert blades and points from Tenby Museum

south-east and the damaged Cromlech monument (ANG 15) to the north. Dispersed within the same landscape are a number of standing stones that were probably in use at the same time. The site at Llanfaethlu yielded over 2,000 artefacts (including 600 flints) and uncovered the fragmentary remains of four buildings (Rees & Jones 2015). The settlement appears to have been in use for at least a millennium, spanning the middle part of the Neolithic. Based on post-hole arrangements, the buildings were considered longhouses (similar to the LBK buildings of the Early Neolithic, found in northern and eastern Europe). Internally, each building was subdivided into a series of rooms, probably engender or craft encoded. Within the settlement area were numerous storage pits containing significant quantities of food residues. Also found was evidence of axe production, where rough-outs from the Penmaenmawr axe factory were being shaped and polished.

The choice of different economic resources would have established a safety net against the slowly deteriorating climate that commenced from the mid to late Neolithic onwards. Peter Fowler has suggested that the coastal areas of South-west Wales and North Wales (including Ynys Môn) were ideal for agriculture. He postulates further that there were up to 365 potential crop-growing days per year in these areas, as opposed to 240 days within central Wales, where the Black Mountains Group is located (Fowler 1983, 24).

In order to utilise time constructively, tomb-building may have been undertaken during the winter months when there was less time given to cultivation. Alternatively, it may have been the first task undertaken by the first farmers in order to establish ritual control and social-political identity within the locality.

Megalithic art: the physical act of applying ritual

Within Britain, megalithic art dating from the Neolithic is rare and is mainly associated with the passage grave tradition. Savory (1980, 222) suggests megalithic art has its origins in Iberia. According to Joussaume (1985, 73) megalithic art was either engraved or painted; however, the latter in the British Isles has probably long since disappeared. Within western England and Wales there are three passage grave sites which possess complex carved designs. Two of them are in Ynys Môn: Barclodiad y Gawres (ANG 4) and Bryn Celli Ddu (ANG 7). Also, if one is to ignore political boundaries, one could include within this group the Calderstones in Liverpool (LANCS 1 – SJ 405 875). All three sites have similar carved designs. Apart from these three, there are a number of other sites that contain cupmarks, both single and multiple (for example, Bachwen, CRN 7, and Trellyfaint, PEM 2). This phenomenon, however, is regarded as a later tradition probably dating to the Early Bronze Age. It is from this period in prehistory that many stones, isolated and in groups, possess singular or multiple motifs, usually cupmarks and cup-in-rings (see Nash 2023; Nash & Pope 2023).

A rare occurrence of a cup-and-ring motif, located on the Garn Turne monument (PEM 11) in South-west Wales

These monuments are usually associated with burial cairns and barrows and are generically referred to as *landscape monuments*.

When Barclodiad y Gawres was excavated in 1952–3, five uprights with complex carved decoration were recorded. In the excavation report, they are referred to as stones 5, 6, 8, 19 and 22 (Powell and Daniel 1956).[7] These stones are located within the inner passage and chamber areas. Stone number 5, located at the interface of the passage and chamber, contains a series of pecked lozenges and chevrons. Stone 6, lying immediately south of Stone 5, has, within its design coding, two interlocking anticlockwise spirals, a series of lozenges and a series of zigzag lines that link the lozenges. According to Shee-Twohig (1981, 299) this stone is extremely weathered. One could, therefore, suggest that other designs once adorned this stone. Stone 8, located within the eastern part of the chamber, is decorated with six spirals, one of which is integrated with a lozenge design. Four of the spirals extend in a line across the face of the upright and are both clockwise and anticlockwise. The pecking for all spirals is rather faint. In the western section of the chamber and incorporated into an antechamber is Stone 19, which has a single clockwise spiral in its centre. Finally, Stone 22, probably the most complex example of megalithic art within this monument, lies at the junction of the passage and chamber. This stone, measuring 1.47m in height, contains three sets of designs. At the top of the stone is an anticlockwise spiral, part of which is missing. Immediately below this are five complete horizontal zigzag lines and three incomplete zigzag lines. Forming part of the lower zigzag are two chevrons, one below the other. Either side of the face of this upright and continuing the lower set of incomplete zigzag lines is a multi-lined curvilinear pattern that continues to the base of the upright. This particular design has certain similarities with the nearby Pattern Stone at Bryn Celli Ddu.

Bryn Celli Ddu was excavated by F.D. Lucas in 1865 and later by W.J. Hemp in 1930. It was the latter excavation that revealed an ornately-carved stone referred to as the Pattern Stone. Uniquely, this stone was carved on both faces, and on the top the designs on both faces appearing to be interlinked. The Pattern Stone, measuring 1.5m in height by 1.64m in width, was found during the Hemp excavation, and was overlying a central pit. It is not known if this stone, along with an undecorated one, belonged to the passage grave or an earlier henge monument. Interestingly the pit is centrally located within both monuments; however, the rear section of the chamber belonging to the passage grave is not physically connected, suggesting the Pattern Stone and its associated pit belonged to an earlier

Concentric circles engraved on the uprights that once formed the passage or chamber of the Calderstones, Liverpool

monument phase. Shee-Twohig (1981, 230) suggests that the Pattern Stone may have once stood at the centre of the henge monument, or it may have been a dedication stone for some form of ritual during construction of the passage grave. The decoration only covers two-thirds of the stone, with the lower third of the stone buried into the ground. On one of the faces, is a double *serpentiform* (snake-like design) pattern that has the end terminating into an anticlockwise spiral. One section of this pattern is similar to the lower section of patterns on Stone 22 in Barclodiad y Gawres. There appears to be very little symmetry to the patterning on this face. However, the pattern does appear to be emerging from the top of the stone and spreading outwards. Likewise, on the reverse the lines appear to be running down the stone. On this face the patterns are similar in form yet more confused. Centrally located within this plethora of design is a single cupmark.

Engraved feet on the uprights that once formed the passage or chamber of the Calderstones, Liverpool

The Calderstones (LANCS 1) in Calderstone Park, Liverpool are believed to be part of a large passage grave, and possess similar designs which are arranged in a more complex way than those designs found in Ynys Môn (Forde-Johnson 1956, 73). All six stones are decorated and include clockwise, anticlockwise spirals, merging spirals, concentric circles and lozenges. There are also eight carved footprint designs on three of the stones and a Maltese Cross (Shee-Twohig 1981, fig. 265). These designs, however, may be later additions to megalithic art (Stewart, Nash & Cowell 2021).

The fundamental question to be asked is: why do only three monuments in this part of Britain possess this form of complex megalithic art? I have stated earlier that the idea of constructing chambered tombs is based on a transmission of ideas: *we came, we saw, we copied*. Both Daniel (1950) and Powell et al. (1969) have discussed extensively the architectural links between certain monuments: for example, the replication of the Cotswold-Severn type of monument within Wales. It is clear that certain architectural traits, such as the introduction of horns and false portals, must have originated from somewhere, and these fashionable traits were transmitted to other monuments, such as those found within the Black Mountains Group in central eastern Wales. Likewise, there must have been a point in time during the Middle Neolithic that megalithic art became important.

The distribution of such an art form is concentrated in nine areas of western Europe: Portugal, northern Spain, central west France, the Paris Basin, Brittany, the Channel Islands, Orkney, Ireland and North Wales (Shee-Twohig 1981, 12). Each of these areas has a unique set of artistic designs, all of which are carved onto megalithic monuments. The megalithic art recorded throughout southern Ireland, although more complex than the North Wales examples, does have similar traits. The Four Knocks site in Co. Meath has identical spirals on several stones, which are also found at Barclodiad y Gawres. Similarly, spirals are found at Loughcrew and at Newgrange, in Co. Meath. The distribution of megalithic art in Ireland is confined to the east, within the central valleys such as the Boyne Valley, and within Northern Ireland. An even larger concentration of sites with megalithic art is also found in Brittany, the most ornate of these being the passage grave of Gavrinis, located in the Gulf of Morbihan. This passage grave, now located on an island, has all its passage and chamber uprights carved with complex abstract imagery. It was probably at Gavrinis, along with other Breton megalithic sites, that the megalithic art tradition was born in north-western Europe, based on the concentration of sites, and the complexity of the art. According to Burl (1985, 14) megalithic art in Brittany commenced around 4,600 BCE. Lynch (1969a) claims that Bryn Celli Ddu is one of the latest megalithic burial monuments in Ynys Môn, despite replicating the architecture of some of the Breton passage graves. If this is the case, the Irish megalithic art probably commences after contact with the Breton groups, almost certainly through contact/exchange. The concept of decorating a burial monument in this way finally reached Ynys Môn, possibly sometime after 2,800 BCE.

The power and prestige of the axe

The detailed study of Neolithic polished stone axes has revealed a variety of distribution patterns that involve probable contact and exchange mechanisms between individuals and communities. The axe appears to have been a desired commodity, that was in circulation for many hundreds of years. Sourcing the geological origins of stone and flint axes has resulted in the discovery of at least 30 axe factories, the majority of which are located in the western British Isles. These include igneous stone from Cornwall, Cumbria, Isle of Man, Northern Ireland, North Wales, South Wales and Western Scotland. Communities desiring such items appear to have been attracted by the colour, lustre and mineral, shape, size and texture of the stone, before and after it was extracted, hewn, shaped and eventually manufactured (see Clough & Cummins 1988; Walker 2018).

Generally speaking, grave good assemblages from Welsh chambered tombs are poor (Savory 1980, 220). There are a handful of sites, however,

The axe factory of Langdale, Cumbria

An assemblage of polished stone axes from South-west Wales (housed in Tenby Museum)

One of the Tenby Museum axes, originating from one of the axe factories of the Western British Isles

where there has been a wealth of finds including an array of ceramics, polished stone and flint axes and occasional adornment. It has been regarded that these items have ritual and symbolic associations, and that they would have accompanied the deceased to the next world. Axes, although limited in number, have been found within the chambers at the destroyed Ffynnondruidion monument (PEM 28) in Pembrokeshire. Accounts state that five flint axes (celts) were found here in the early nineteenth century (Fenton 1811, 24). Axes have also been found at Bryn yr Hen Bobl, Angelsey (ANG 8), Din Dryfol (ANG 5), Ty Isaf (BRE 5) and Ty Newydd (ANG 3).

Despite the limited funerary deposition, the majority of axes that have been found are usually classified as un-provenanced stray finds. However, one cannot assume that these finds are the result of accidental loss. Their functionality has been widely discussed and it would appear that they are more than just utilitarian items. Axes found within non-funerary provenance in each of the Neolithic core areas of Wales, originate from a variety of unique geological source areas, sometimes outside Wales. The time and effort, of either trading with other Neolithic groups or embarking on long-haul expeditions to axe-sourced areas, collecting the rough-outs and then shaping and polishing, suggests that these are special items. It would appear these items possessed a number of uses for the living as well as the dead.

Stray finds may form part of a votive offering, again suggesting a ritual-symbolic use. Axes in a burial context were probably gender-encoded, representing maleness. They are usually associated with other prestige items such as leaf-shaped arrowheads, diagnostic flint tools, flint debitage and pottery. There were probably many other items associated with burial that have not survived the archaeological record.

Apart from burial and possible votive deposition, polished flint and stone axes offer a unique insight into axe production, trade and exchange mechanisms. Axes found within Wales originate from a number of areas of Britain whereby exchange formed part of the mechanism which ensured contact with other Neolithic groups. It also provided the impetus for Neolithic people to travel many hundreds of kilometres in order to successfully trade other goods. Contact and exchange would also have provided the impetus and knowledge to replicate new forms of monument design as well as new ideas of ritual – especially in the treatment and disposal of the dead.

According to a number of researchers, in particular Grimes (1951, 23), axe shapes conform to four basic types: a) axes with pointed butts; b) axes with broad, thin butts; c) elongated forms; and d) double-edged axes with square ends. These axe types do not correspond to certain dates within the Neolithic. It would appear that several types were in use at the same time and may represent two different regional trends. Prior to experiments undertaken by Danish archaeologist Ivenson in 1946, it was thought that polished jadeite flint and stone axes were considered functional tools; in particular, used for cutting down trees. However, after several blows, these axes had splintered or shattered on impact. Given the fracturing qualities of the geology of axe type, similar results could be expected for axes made in Britain.

In Wales, it is not just the distribution of axes, but also the production; these form part of the national petrological group numbering 1–24 (I–XXIV). Research in particular by Houlder (1988, 133–6) has outlined the frequency of axe factories in Wales, of which six have been identified. Three of these are located in South-west Wales (Groups VIII, XIII and XXIII); one on the Llŷn Peninsula (Group XXI), one west of the Great Orme at Penmaenmawr (Group VII), and one in central Wales close to the source of the River Severn (Group XII). According to Darvill (1982), these groups are divided into Early Neolithic and Late Neolithic stone sources. It would appear that axes from these areas are widely distributed throughout Wales and England, and were collectively in circulation for at least 2,000 years. This may be the result of social exchange and interaction between neighbouring and more distant groups. One should also note that axes that have been quarried and polished outside Wales are also found in Wales, in particular axes from the factories of Cumbria (Groups VI, XI, and XV) and Cornwall (Groups I and III) (Clough & Cummins 1988, 253).

Although axes geologically sourced from outside are occasionally found in Wales, the frequency of distribution of Group VII axes, for example, appears to be localised, with 70% of all axe finds from this group being found within a 70km radius of the axe factory. The same axe group accounts for 20–30% of all axe finds within central and North Wales. Five per cent of all finds from this group is found outside central and North Wales, suggesting periodic or limited contact/exchange between local and regional Neolithic groups. Likewise, a similar graduated distribution is witnessed with Group VIII, located in Pembrokeshire. Here, 40–50% of axes from this group are found within a 30km radius of the Preseli Mountains, and 20–30% of axes are found within South-west Wales; again, suggesting periodic or tentative links with other Neolithic groups outside South-west Wales. A small percentage of this group is found within the Cotswold-Severn group in Gloucestershire.

It is only since the emergence of experimental archaeology that polished stone axes have been regarded as prestige items. Tilley (1993) argues that axes were an extremely important mechanism for the ritual and the burying of the dead. Within southern Scandinavia, polished stone and flint axes form an integral part of the burial package.

There appear to be a number of complex issues surrounding the deposition of axes within burial monuments. I would suggest that axes had an aesthetic value and were regarded as objects of desire, which more than likely denoted status, especially within a burial context. However, as stated earlier, twice as many axes have been found in non-burial contexts. In South-west Wales, there is the likely evidence of both exchange and trade (as well as evidence for axe deposition in funerary monuments). Many axes appear to have come in from other areas in Wales and England, suggesting that power and prestige were to be gained by acquiring axes from production centres outside the locality. Within the central uplands of the Preseli Mountains, is one of the major sources for the production of axes in South Wales (Group VIII). The distribution of axes from this area, and axes coming from other areas of Wales and England, gives some idea of the extent and influence of communities trading in axes. Clough & Cummins (1988, 246–55) list a total of 89 polished stone and flint axes found within Pembrokeshire, and a further 41 and 45 in Cardiganshire and Carmarthenshire respectively.

Approximately 40% of these are from specific axe manufacturing areas, the majority of which lie within the Preseli Mountains. Within the same area, a few axes have been found which originate from factories in North Wales. It is clear that, since the Early Neolithic, both indigenous and expeditionary groups have used stone from the Preseli Mountains as a prestige raw material.

Three individual quarries from the Preseli Mountains have been discovered. Cummins (1988) and others have recognised one of these Preseli axe factories – Group VIII – as an Early Neolithic stone source. This source, located on the southern flank of the Preseli Mountains, is igneous tuff and the quarry dates between 3,000–2,500 BCE. The stone from the other two groups, XIII and XXIII, is spotted dolerite and was used to manufacture axes after 2,500 BCE. Pitts (1980, 8) has suggested that igneous tuff has a predominant flaking characteristic, while dolerites have a pecking quality. Both stones would have served different uses: the tuffs for axes and the dolerites for later (Neolithic and Early Bronze Age) perforated implements. Within the area, both types are well represented. Outside – in particular within the Cotswold-Severn region – axes from the Preselis frequently occur. This distribution possibly suggests expedition and trading alliances between different communities. Communication would have provided the impetus to establish valuable trading partners, which would involve the exporting of commodities in and out of each area, as well as ideas, innovation and knowledge.

It could also be that axes from the three local quarries were so valuable/rare that an exchange imbalance between local axes and other goods was in operation. An axe from the Ffynnondruidion monument (PEM 28), made from either gabbro or quartz diorite (both coarse-grained igneous rocks), probably originated from the Isle of Man or Cornwall. However, these isolated finds are rare. It should also be noted that the famous bluestones (blue-grey dolerite) which form the inner circle at Stonehenge, derive from three outcrops at Carn Meini, within the heart of the Preselis, close to several axe factories (Groups VIII, XIII and XXIII). These alone would have attracted interest from social elites outside South-west Wales.

The axe factories in North Wales are located between 180m and 350m AOD on the outcrops and scree slopes of Penmaenmawr Mountain, and are referred to as the Graig Lwyd axe factory group.[8] The site covers an extensive area, the limits of which have yet to be determined. Excavations undertaken in 1920 revealed the method of extracting stone and, more importantly, how the process of manufacture was undertaken. According to Savory (1980, 223) axes from Penmaenmawr date from the mid to late Neolithic and dominated the local 'market' in North Wales. Apart from North Wales, axes from this factory have been found in Paviland Cave on the Gower, Merthyr Mawr and Kenfig. Outside Wales, axes have been found at Avebury, Cairn Papple, Woodhenge and Upware (Castleden 1992, 391; Grimes 1951, 23). A fragment of a Graig Lwyd mace head was also found within the causewayed enclosure at Windmill Hill. Dates taken from the archaeological excavations suggest that the axe factory was in use between the mid to late Neolithic.

Rough-outs, probably taken away from their geological source and shaped into the finished axe, would invariably be ovate or oblong, and, according to Grimes, 'flat and tabular or spindle-like' (1951, 23). According to Houlder (1988, 134) there are only 27 rough-out finds sourced from Wales. It was more than probable that some axes were either being polished at their geological source or the success rate for polishing was high, with little accidental fracturing or wastage.

Other finds identified by Houlder include battle axes, axe hammers and mace-heads. However, these account for a small percentage of the total number of stone tools found and sourced within Wales, and can be associated with high status so their numbers would be small. It is also probable that these particular items extend into the Early Bronze Age, and therefore represent a different form of burial. Also found within the 1920 excavation was a stone plaque, which had been decorated with hatched chevron symbols. This measured 13cm across and may have been a talisman. Similar finds have been found at other mine and quarry sites, such as Grimes Graves in Norfolk and Harrow Hill in Sussex.

Over the recent past, many of the potential stone extraction sites on Penmaenmawr Mountain in North Wales, have been largely destroyed by modern quarrying; or, according to Castleden, some are buried beneath quarry waste (1992, 391). From the scree slopes, the stone used for Neolithic axe manufacture is augite granophyre, also known as Penmaenmawr granite. According to Grimes (1951, 21) this rock is extremely tough and difficult to utilise, which is certainly reflected in the large number of broken axes that have appeared on the site. Some of these axe fragments, according to Grimes, could be joined together and in a number of cases each of the fragments showed different patterns of weathering. Unlike most Neolithic axe factory sites in Britain, Graig Lwyd does not continue beyond the Neolithic.

Populating the Promised Land
During the preceding Mesolithic, there were a large number of coastal sites that lie close to or beneath Neolithic sites, in particular burial monuments. These sites vary in size, from small lithic scatters, for example, around Freshwater East, to large, exposed settlement on Nab Head (both in Pembrokeshire). The Nab Head site comprises early (Nab Head I)

and late Mesolithic (Nab Head II) assemblages, and includes evidence of a number of (dwelling) structures and datable features, including a shallow pit that was filled with burnt soil and charcoal which was radiocarbon dated to 7,360 ± 90 BP (OxA-860). On the same site, a possible hearth has also been found, dated to 6,210 ± 90 BP (OxA-861) (David 1990, 210–12). Despite this site, evidence for Mesolithic settlement overall is rather fragmentary. It is probable that small bands of semi-sedentary hunter/gatherers exploited small, well-defined territories and that settlement was all but temporary, consisting of makeshift encampments.

In order to gain a clearer picture of settlement, one must look outside Wales – for example, to southern Scandinavia, due mainly to excellent waterlogged conditions. The large habitation sites at Sveardborg (excavated by Friss Johansen 1919), Klampenborg (excavated by Westerby 1927), Åamosen (excavated by Mathiassen 1943) and Vedbaek (excavated by Mathiassen in 1946) have revealed a mixed economy whereby marine and terrestrial resources were being utilised. During the early part of the Late Mesolithic (known as the Kongemose phase, 5,500–4,300 BCE) the area around Åamosen (bog) would have been densely populated, and possibly marks a zenith for inland habitation. The main food resources would have been red deer, fish, shells and woodland fruits and berries. The density of occupation of such areas has prompted researchers such as Peter Rowley-Conwy (1981) to suggest that the population of such settlements would support between 45 and 250 individuals. However, I am not saying that such numbers were present on sites in Wales; though certainly, the complexity of society and land division may have been comparable. Because of the absence of major settlement, the evidence we have for the Neolithic is more difficult to assess. It has been suggested that early Neolithic settlement within the core areas of Wales is similar to that of the late Mesolithic settlement distribution. More or less, the same resources for both the Mesolithic and Neolithic were available.

Population density may also be roughly assessed with the distribution of flint. Contained within each of the core areas are a large number of flint sites. Sites vary in size and diagnostic tool type. Some sites have evidence of multi-phased activity suggesting long periods of use. In the case of Gwernvale (BRE 7), it is not only Mesolithic flint that is present but also Upper Palaeolithic stone tools and accompanying debitage.

In addition to flint distribution, pollen evidence suggests that many of the fertile valleys within these core areas were densely wooded (Caseldine 1990, 43–7). For example, at Mynydd Troed (BRE 10) within the Black Mountains, there is pollen evidence within a buried soil deposit (referred to as a *palaeosol*), suggesting the area was a mixture of heathland and open woodland (Crampton & Webley 1966). Similarly, at Dyffryn Ardudwy (MER 3), the pollen evidence portrays a landscape covered in broad-leaf woodland (Dimbleby 1973). These essential open and wooded habitats would have provided the necessary resources for the establishment and function of settlement.

It is probable that as populations became more sedentary and increased in number, due to the wide availability of seasonal resources during the Climatic Optimum (10,000–6,000 BP), over time, settlement moved inland to occupy the fertile valleys of the main tributaries around coastal Wales. It is clear that the distribution of chambered tombs in, for example, the hinterlands of the Black Mountains or those monuments occupying the Llŷn Peninsula, shows not only ritual use of the landscape but also indicates a landscape whereby settlement, social and economic space was equally important.

Frances Lynch (2000a, 46–7) has identified up to 96 megalithic tombs in Wales, along with numerous polished stone axe and pottery finds. The axe finds are usually confined to the Neolithic core areas. This distribution of both tombs and axes suggests that the population was indeed concentrated. I would suggest that, based on the four regional Historic Environment Records (HERs) and also using Archwilio[9] and Coflein[10] for Wales, this density was far more complex, in that axes are usually found in clusters. However, this phenomenon may in part be due to concentrated field-walking surveys. It is likely that Wales had 300 active megalithic tombs or more, as well as numerous lithic scatters, some of which may represent habitation sites.

The limited number of henge monuments and Late Neolithic/Early Bronze Age stone circles should also be taken into consideration, adding to this complexity. Even so, assuming a minimum of 300 chambered monuments, one must consider there would have been at least 300 settlement sites. If one envisages that several settlements accompanied a single monument, then the number of settlements would be higher still.

During the late Mesolithic and throughout north-western Europe, there is evidence for hunter/gatherer/fisher societies becoming more permanent within proscribed landscapes where resources were abundant. This idea of sedentism may be based on winter and summer encampments within a defined territory, such as the seasonal habitation sites at Star Carr in the Vale of Pickering, Yorkshire. One of the components of the Neolithic package is the construction of monuments, and where evidence prevails, the concept of permanent settlement. In the case of the Neolithic core areas of Wales, it is likely that the main component of the Neolithic package – farming – was not necessarily adopted; more that Neolithic communities were opting to take advantage of natural, seasonal resources. Metaphorically speaking, these communities were 'farming' the sea, the rivers and woodlands of Neolithic Wales. Over a 2,000-year period, sedentism would have allowed communities to become established and prosperous, and this is sometimes seen with the construction of some of Wales' larger monuments, such as Bryn Celli Ddu (ANG 7), Gop Cairn (FLT 1) and Tinkinswood (GLA 9). The monuments themselves are a testament to the success of the settlements.

Peter Fowler (1983, 24) has suggested that the ideal conditions for year-round agriculture prevailed in three main areas of Wales, with 365 growing days present in Ynys Môn, St David's Head and the Gower coast. These three areas benefit from the warm currents of the Gulf Stream and a mild Atlantic climate. Areas offering 300 growing days include the Llŷn Peninsula, the Menai Straits, South-west Wales and the Gwent Levels. The Black Mountains in south-east Wales, and land stretching as far as Snowdonia, offered only 240 potential growing days. Interestingly, the monumentality for each of these areas is extremely diverse and, in many ways, cannot relate to the number of growing days available. However, Startin and Bradley (1989, 289–96) have estimated that a tomb such as Ty Isaf (BRE 5) – what they term a medium-sized monument – could take between 7,000 and 16,000 hours of labour to construct. This would depend on the hardness of the stone or bedrock quarried, and the distance the materials had to be moved to the site. It was also dependent on the availability of a workforce. Startin and Bradley suggest an average of ten people working an eight-hour day, seven days a week for three to seven months. This simplistic formula does not take into account additions to the monument or the idea that a monument was treated as an organic structure, in that it was constructed over a long period of time. Either way, it is important to stress that the monument belonged to a community. It is probable that communities were stratified, and only certain people were allowed to use such monuments. Their construction and use would have involved a large amount of time utilising many people. I would argue further that inter-group co-operation may have been the only way of constructing monuments such as Arthur's Stone (HRF 1), Tinkinswood (GLA 9) and Garn Turne (PEM 11), all of which have massive capstones – one that weighs an estimated 60 tons in the case of Garn Turne (Children & Nash 1997, 91). I would also suggest that smaller monuments would have received the same inter-group co-operation, especially if one considers Colin Renfrew's hypothesis of core-periphery distribution. This suggests that monuments are located along the boundaries between neighbouring groups and act as political markers within the landscape, as well as repositories for the dead. One could also add that such monuments would have provided a sense of collective security and identity between neighbouring groups.

On St David's Head in South-west Wales, the Clegyr Boia settlement boasts up to two houses, a fire pit and a midden of Neolithic date (Williams 1953, 24–9). Each house was probably home to between 10 and 15 individuals who would have constructed small earth-fast monuments such as Coetan Arthur (PEM 23) and Carn Llidi (PEM 21 & 22), both located on St David's Head. The size and construction methods used for these two monuments would have been ample for an extended family unit of this size. However, one must question how many individuals would have been needed to construct, and more importantly place the capstones on, Pentre Ifan (PEM 5) and nearby Carreg Samson (PEM 18)? Monuments of this size throughout Wales would have required complex planning prior to and during their construction. Assuming that there were 300 monuments in existence and that perhaps 150 were being constructed and in use at any one time during a 2,000-year period; and assuming that an average community of the style of Clegyr Boia, consisting of 20–30 individuals, would have constructed one tomb, it can be deduced that the adult population of Neolithic Wales was around 4–5,000 people. This very rough estimate also assumes that collective co-operation between neighbouring groups was present for larger tomb-building as well as the more mundane activities in Neolithic society.

Another determining factor that could give some indication of population is the number of individuals that have been found within a limited number of monuments (albeit the usually acidic soil means that relatively few bones have survived). Dependent on burial practice, a number of archaeologists have been able to determine the gender and age group that have been interred in monuments such as Ty Isaf (BRE 5) and Parc-le-Breos-Cwm (GLA 4). According to the nineteenth-century excavator, John Lubbock, the Parc-le-Breos-Cwm monument contained up to 24 skeletons 'much broken and in no regular arrangement,' which were found within the chambers. One then has to consider whether these remains are just those of the elites over a long period of time, or do they represent a communal grave for an extended family group. If an elite section of the community is using this monument as a repository over a long period, would carbon dating have detected a chronological sequence? Assuming that the average life expectancy was up to 40 years of age, with a high infant mortality rate[11] (Hedges 1987, 174–84), then probably the answer is *no*. Likewise, at Ty Isaf, up to 33 individuals were found within the western chamber, a further two in the eastern chamber and further remains in the passage. Again, are we looking at corporate monumentality or communal burial? Unfortunately, the problem in Wales is made more difficult by the inconsistency of burial material from each of the monuments. For example, in South-west Wales, within the earth-fast group of monuments, the preferred burial practice appears to be cremation; and, in some cases, in particular Morfa Bychan A, there is a stratified sequence that includes a few fragments of charred bone (Ward 1918, 69–70) and little else.

As for people themselves, Lynch has suggested that they were 'of small stature', ranging from 1.5m to 1.64m in height; that they lived an active life, thus developing 'well marked muscle channels and flattened shin bones' (2000). Furthermore, from the limited number of skulls recovered from a burial context, they are described as dolichocephalic (having an elongated skull). These pronounced features are derived from only a limited number of burials, and in essence I would suggest that these people are no different from ourselves. I would further suggest that damp climatic conditions contributed to short life expectancy, and that ailments such as rheumatoid arthritis and osteoarthritis were prevalent, as evidenced by the burial record from this period. Concerning diet, Neolithic communities would have utilised both domestic and wild resources. Also, although not present in a Welsh context, there is evidence for Paget's Disease and Rickets elsewhere in Neolithic Europe, which may be the result of poor diet. Further, one cannot rule out that within a 2,000-year period, some form of natural catastrophic epidemic event may have affected the population (Manchester & Roberts 1995, 175–85). For example, bovine tuberculosis, a disease in cattle, can spread secondarily to humans. According to Sherratt (1981) the milking of domestic cattle occurred in southern Europe from the fifth millennium. Roberts & Manchester (1995, 134) suggest that the spread of diseases such as bovine tuberculosis, contracted through the drinking of infected milk or the eating of cattle meat, attacks the most vulnerable in society, such as children, the infirm and older members of the community. This and other diseases recorded in the Neolithic, such as infantile paralysis (poliomyelitis), could have tipped the balance in small Neolithic communities. This type of event may have occurred during the Neolithic–Bronze Age transition, when there is a change in monument-building, from corporate monumentality to single status burial.

Monuments and their recent past

In 1993, I can remember walking around Falköping, a provincial town in central Sweden. The town boasts of having over 35 megalithic chambered monuments within its bounds. Many of these monuments, referred to as *gongriffen* (or passage graves), had been incorporated into garden bedding, whilst several have been used as ornamental features within public spaces (see overleaf). In certain places, sites that are constructed of local sandstone and are in various states of preservation, dominate the locality. In the recent past, there appears to have been a desire to include these monuments within the townscape. Despite their heritage value, it is clear that the original meaning of these monuments is not fully understood. To many, they are merely stones that have been symmetrically constructed by ancient people; they are divorced, alien from the modern world. Likewise, there are a number of monuments in Wales that have been placed into modern landscapes such as gardens and parklands: for example, Plas Newydd (ANG 9) and the Hanging Stone (PEM 24). There are others which have provided shelter to cattle, sheep, even families and hermits. Monuments of the dead have therefore become dwellings for the living as well, taking on a more practical role in their long history. Monuments such as Plas Newydd (ANG 9) have been incorporated into a recent historical setting, whereby their formal arrangement of either stones

The monument in the park: Kyrkerör, Falköping, Vastergötland, Central Sweden

or a mound has been set into a recently constructed artificial landscape. Arguably this artificiality exhibits and complements the artificiality of the monument; itself an ancient social construct.

Many Neolithic and Early Bronze Age monuments continue to exist as striking features within the landscape. Others are more unobtrusive, either because they were deliberately hidden, accessible only to those possessing the necessary ritual knowledge, or because the physical traces of their existence have been eroded over the millennia and are now barely discernible (for example, incorporated into stones and turf boundaries). A few monuments survive only in the pages of antiquarian journals or as folklore: for example, a couple of sentences and a picturesque engraving by Theophilus Jones, made in 1809, are all that remain of the Black Mountains monument of Croesllechau (BRE 11).[12] A plan published in Lhwyd's *Parochalia* (1699) informs us that there was once a burial chamber, probably a passage grave, at Llanymynech Hill, Montgomeryshire. Likewise, an antiquarian sketch of unknown date, probably nineteenth-century, depicts the original chambered monument at Llanfechell, Ynys Môn (ANG 15) – today just 'a heap of fallen stone' (Lynch 1970, 43). Following their abandonment or partial destruction many monuments remained largely intact until the seventeenth century. It is only during the last 300 years that destruction has occurred on a significant scale. There are a number of reasons for this. One is the increasingly common practice of plundering monuments for building stone. The antiquarian accounts of Arthur's Stone in Herefordshire (HRF 1) suggest cairn-robbing accounted for the partial destruction of the monument during the eighteenth century (*cf.* Crawford 1925). Superstition no doubt also played a role, but the evidence for this is rather sparse.

Concurrent with these instances of destruction, however, was the rise of scholarly and artistic interest in the Neolithic tombs of Wales, coinciding with William Stukely's studies of the Wessex megaliths. Stukely (1687–1765) produced a large number of panoramic illustrations during the early to mid eighteenth century, that reveal the condition of the monument and, in the case of Stonehenge, the agricultural regime that surrounded it. In some cases, a methodology for the surveying of monuments was also provided. For Stukely and other artists, of course, romance and mysticism must also have played a role. The spread of antiquarianism can be accounted for in part by the fact that Neolithic chambered tombs and the monuments of the Bronze Age, particularly those of stone, offered the artist an ideal focus for any landscape composition, in some cases embellished by the liberal use of artistic license.

The eighteenth- and nineteenth-century artistic movement in Wales focused on a number of sites that were usually set within a dramatic backdrop. The Bachwen monument (CRN 7), painted in watercolour by Moses Griffith, shows the Portal Dolmen with a series of outliers and recumbent stones, centrally placed with a backdrop of a field boundary and mountains beyond. The once-recumbent stone and outliers are no longer present. To the right of the monument is an ancient bard paying homage to the monument, probably inferring druidical links. Richard Tongue, a painter from Bath, painted the most famous of all megalithic scenes, that of Pentre Ifan (PEM 5), in 1830. Like all painters of this period, Tongue was concerned with what was going on around the megalith. The subsequent researcher is shown the remains of a chamber outline within the centre of the monument. The backdrop appears to show a very rugged Mynydd Carningli. To the right of the picture is a peasant-like figure sitting on one of the outliers. This figure gives some idea of scale as well as a romantic feel to the painting.

Staying with the theme of nineteenth-century landscape painting and the dramatic changes to monuments since then, there is Pryce Carter Edwards' sepia drawing of the Gwernvale monument (BRE 7) painted in 1832. Here, the monument is not centrally located, but is nonetheless visible. To the left of the monument is a track that is now the A40 trunk road between Talgarth and Crickhowell. The monument overlooks what can be regarded as a figment of the artist's imagination – the backdrop shows a dramatic mountainscape with what appears to be a lake between the monument and the intermediate slopes of the mountains. The actual view from this position is very much less dramatic. The drawing shows the monument consisting of a series of uprights with a supporting capstone. Nowadays, the chamber uprights still exist, but the capstone has long since gone. It could be the case that the capstone was considered to be part of the romantic image of the past and it is probable that Gwernvale no longer possessed any of its chamber or passage capstones when Edwards made his drawing.

Within the Neolithic core areas of Wales, several seventeenth-, eighteenth- and nineteenth-century antiquarians have published a number of important volumes that give some insight of how these monuments appeared. Some antiquarians have merely described what they have seen; others have gone somewhat further and excavated the monument. Most of the descriptive accounts occur during the mid to late eighteenth century, when Thomas Pennant undertook his *Tours in Wales*, published in 1783. His monument accounts are regarded as descriptively useful but are limited to monuments in north Wales. David Thomas's list of monuments in the *Cambrian Register*, published in 1796, provides a list of sites and shows the number that have been destroyed, many used as quarries.

I now want to turn to the Reverend John Skinner's *Ten day's Tour through the Isle of Anglesea*, published in 1802. This important account describes a number of monuments, some of which have been completely destroyed. It is probable that Skinner was in part influenced by earlier antiquarians, such as

Antiquarian engraving of Bachwen, Llŷn Peninsula, North Wales. Note the cupmarks. Engraving by E.L. Barnwell (*Archaeologia Cambrensis*, 1868)

Antiquarian engraving of Arthur's Stone (HRF 1), also known as the Bredwardine Cromlech (by E.L. Barnwell, 1873)

David Thomas (1796) and Thomas Pennant (1783). Accompanying Skinner's descriptions are a series of sketches and references to folklore. The sketches show each monument as a curiosity rather than a site of historical and archaeological interest. A number of monuments sketched by Skinner are now either collapsed or destroyed. Skinner provides the best account of Bryn Celli Ddu (ANG 7) following the near destruction in 1780 of a cairn that once lay few metres west, and the discovery of the chamber and passage of the eastern cairn during the mid eighteenth century.

With the birth of archaeology as a scientific discipline during the mid nineteenth century, journals such as *Archaeologia Cambrensis* started to reproduce engravings that concentrated purely on the monument. These engravings have proven to be invaluable when assessing the condition of the monument and, of course, the potential for excavation. For example, the mid nineteenth-century engraving of Bryn Celli Ddu shows the site to be in a ruinous state. Present is the central chamber with a supporting capstone and a confused arrangement of stone, probably representing the remains of a passage. On top of the capstone, there is what appears to be a mixed earthen cairn deposit that is probably the remains of the covering mound. The engraver has skilfully placed a shepherd figure close to the passage entrance in order to give some idea of scale. A similar noteworthy engraving is Henry Longueville's depiction of Ty Illtyd (BRE 6) in 1887. Again, the archaeologist is given some idea of the state of preservation of the site, a state that seems not to have changed since the late nineteenth century. Over a period of 50 years, *Archaeologia Cambrensis* published up to 40 illustrations showing the condition of Neolithic monuments throughout Wales. Accompanying these illustrations were,

The Bachwen Portal Dolmen dipping towards the sea

Antiquarian photograph of Pentre Ifan, c.1920

Reconstruction of a ritual event at Pentre Ifan
(Illustration by Elle McQueen)

in some cases, quite detailed descriptions of both the monument architecture and, in cases where excavation was taking place, detailed accounts of the stratigraphy in particular, within the chamber areas. Some of these illustrations appear later in this book.

I intimated earlier that Neolithic sites possess a history both before and after that of the monument itself. It has been stated, for example, that the chambers at Gwernvale (BRE 5) were used as sheep pens during the eighteenth and nineteenth centuries. Arthur's Stone (HRF 1) and Penywyrlod (BRE 14) were used as quarries. In some cases, the monument has been incorporated into later field boundaries. One can therefore suggest that although the site has a physical presence, its meaning, status and use have changed. There is, however, a resurgence in Wales concerning the symbolic status of Neolithic burial monuments. Many will be aware that over the past 100 years, there have been erected stone circles that symbolise the resurgence of Welsh culture and identity through the annual gathering of the Eisteddfod. The revival of the Eisteddfod occurred in the late eighteenth century through the efforts of Edward Williams. Williams, also called *Iolo Morgannwg*, was obsessed with creating a mythical past for the Welsh. One aspect of this was the Gorsedd of the Bards that was first performed on Primrose Hill in 1792. Part of the ceremony included the throwing down of a circle of pebbles that symbolised a miniature stone circle in which Williams and his brethren could act out their rites. In 1819 Williams went to the Eisteddfod in Carmarthen with the same pebbles and created another stone circle within the grounds of the Ivy Bush Hotel. At this time the symbolism had little to do with chambered monuments and Druids. During the mid to late nineteenth century, the Gorsedd of Bards became firmly associated with the Eisteddfod, and every year a stone circle is constructed to

Antiquarian engraving of Coetan Arthur in *Archaeologia Cambrensis* by E.L. Barnwell (1872)

commemorate each festival. Associated with the idea of ancient ancestry – in particular, the lunar and solar cycles – many of the rites associated with the Eisteddfod are now performed around the Neolithic monuments. Interestingly, this interest in Welsh identity and religion has added to the history of such monuments, in particular the link between stone monuments and druidism.

Although one can appreciate the value of the illustrations of both antiquarians and nineteenth-century archaeologists, more transformative were the systematic approaches of excavation and recording which first made their entrance during the late nineteenth and early twentieth centuries, through the recording methods of people such as E.N. Baynes, O.G.S. Crawford, W.J. Hemp and General Pitt-Rivers (to name but a few). One should also mention Sir Mortimer Wheeler who was Director of the National Museum of Wales and did much to professionalise archaeology during the early part of the twentieth century.

Although systematic recording techniques were in place, many Neolithic sites were still excavated in an unsympathetic manner. For example, the Morfa Bychan monuments in Carmarthenshire (CAR 2–5) were each excavated (in 1910) within a couple of days. Similarly, the chambers of the Ffostyll North and South (BRE 3 & 4) monuments were 'dug' in 1921 in the space of two days, in order to retrieve artefacts. The excavator was not interested in the stratigraphic sequence of the chamber deposits. As a result, the position of the entrances to the chambers is not fully understood.

Despite this, there were a number of sites that were excavated throughout the twentieth century that did receive a sympathetic approach. According to the inventories listed by Daniel (1950), Grimes (1951) and Powell et al. (1969), the majority of excavations and non-intrusive investigations in Wales took place between 1910 and 1975. In 1921, for example, W.E.T. Morgan and George Marshall, members of the Woolhope Naturalists' Field Club, excavated Pen-y-wyrlod (BRE 1)[13] to reveal a circular/oval mound some 11m in diameter. Within the centre of the mound was a simple rectangular terminal chamber that contained the remains of a number of individuals. Close by, at Ty Isaf, W.F. Grimes excavated a 30m-long trapezoidal cairn. The systematic excavation revealed a false portal, three chambers and associated passages along with two phases of monumentality. Within the chambers, up to 33 individuals, along with cremated bone and an array of artefacts, were discovered. One of the most notable excavations was that of Pipton Long Cairn (BRE 8). Pipton was excavated by Herbert Savory in 1949. Accompanying the report were a series of plans that gave an insight to the chamber architecture and the stratigraphy, in particular the location of artefacts and human remains within the chamber area. This approach is all-important to understanding how burial practice may have been performed during the Neolithic.

Accompanying the systematic approaches to excavation during the twentieth century was the use of photography. Like its predecessors the engraving and the painting, photography gave an insight into the methodologies used in excavation. More importantly, photography was largely able to curb fanciful speculation and the use of artistic license.

Following the publication of the first edition of this book in 2006, Dr Jennifer Woodcock (University of Liverpool) kindly gave me a rare copy of *The Transactions of the Honourable Society of Cymmrodorion* (1912). Within this journal was an article by E.N. Baynes, which was concerned with the megalithic remains of Ynys Môn. Baynes not only reproduced antiquarian and contemporary plans of most of the extant monuments but also included a rare photographic essay. The publication provided a unique insight into the state of preservation and conservation of many Ynys Môn monuments.

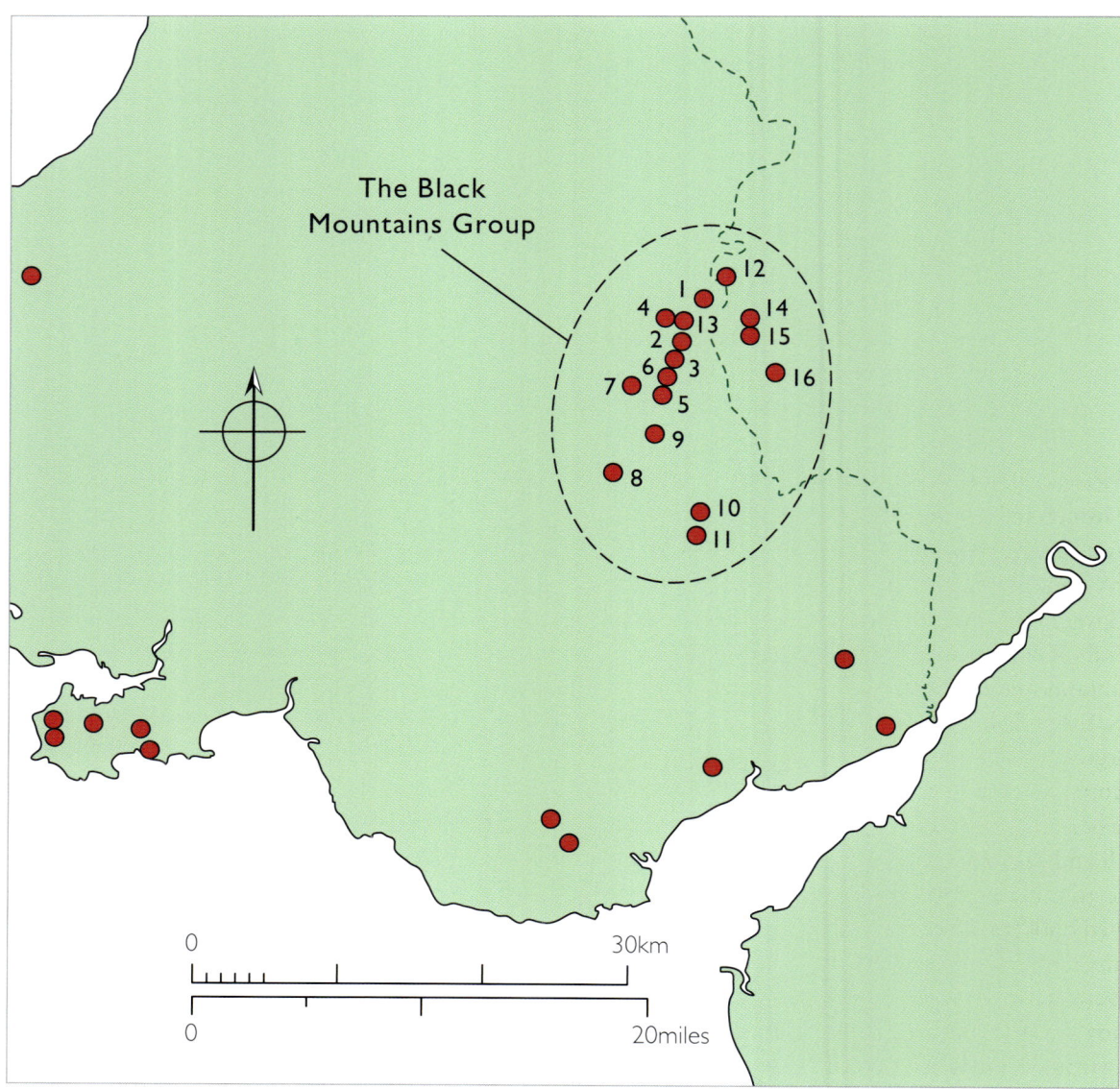

1 Pen yr Wyrlod	5 Ty Isaf	9 Mynydd Troed	13 Little Lodge Barrow
2 Ffostyll North	6 Croesllechau	10 Gwernvale	14 Arthur's Stone
3 Ffostyll South	7 Penywyrlod	11 Garn Goch	15 Cross Lodge Barrow
4 Pipton Long Cairn	8 Ty Illtyd	12 Clyro Court Farm	16 Dunseal

TWO

The Black Mountains Group

This group of monuments lies within the fertile hinterlands of the Black Mountains: a large, basal sandstone massif of some 35sq km, which forms a boundary between the undulating valleys and lowland pastures of the Welsh Marches and the uplands of central Wales. The geology of the Black Mountains and its hinterland has done much to shape the archaeology of the area (Pringle & Neville George 1970). The Black Mountains and the Brecon Beacons (Bannau Brycheiniog) form the mountain zone of Breconshire and are located mainly in the south and east of the county. Geological uplifting, some 40 million years ago during the Cenozoic era, formed both the Black Mountains, rising to over 600m, and, to the west, the Brecon Beacons, rising to 700m above sea level. The Black Mountains gently dip towards the south-east, while the Brecon Beacons are oriented along a NE–SW alignment.

The basal geology consists mainly of Old Red Sandstone (fine marls, mudstones, siltstones and occasional sandstone conglomerates) formed 370 million years ago during the Devonian period when much of the area was covered by a warm, brackish sea; however, the rocks have produced very little fossil evidence. The sandstone beds are up to 950m thick. To the south of the county, along the border with Monmouthshire, is an extensive outcrop of limestone and millstone grit dating from the Carboniferous period (280–345 million years ago).

The shaping of the landscape during the last ice age (referred to as the Late Devensian Glaciation) completes the geomorphological story. The rapid retreat of the Welsh Ice Cap left large accumulations of till (boulder clay deposits) and reshaped the valley profiles, creating numerous fluvioglacial landforms (such as eskers, kames, meltwater channels, moraines and ice-dammed lakes). Llangorse Lake and the classic U-shaped Cwm Sorgwm Valley, near Talgarth, are products of the glacial retreat around 14,500 BP.

It is around these rich, fertile valleys that one starts to witness the utilisation of the landscape by people of the Mesolithic and Neolithic periods. Webley (1959) suggests that the freely drained base-rich soils are a major factor for settlement. According to the dating of lithics found at Gwernvale, this utilisation of the landscape dates to the Upper Palaeolithic. This continuous use of landscape is important since the Neolithic cannot be considered in isolation. What we are probably witnessing is a gradual social, political and economic use of the valleys, from hunting, fishing and gathering in the wild wooded areas to the woodland clearance and the formation of enclosed allotment-style field systems. This change in landscape utilisation would have taken several millennia.

During the proceeding Late Mesolithic and prior to monuments being constructed, the landscape would have been inhabited by small, mobile hunter-gatherer groups that arguably would have seasonally farmed the land (Children & Nash 2001, 14). The knowledge of when to harvest wild berries, fruits, and nuts, as well as hunting particular animals such as wild cattle and pigs at certain times of the year, would have been essential. Monument-building, which forms an integral part of the Neolithic package, would have derived from one of two ideologies: either there was a migration of people (supported by Case 1969; Stanford 1990; Savory 1980) or a migration of ideas. The migration of ideas would have initially involved contact and exchange networks between hunter/fisher/gatherer groups, who would have imported ideas from the Continent and Ireland. If the former is true, Britnell (1984, 3) has suggested that competition between Late Mesolithic hunter-gatherers and incoming migrating agriculturists may have created severe demand for land. I would suggest, however, that an invasion of ideas is the more likely course in that the Eastern and Central European agricultural revolution was very much ideologically fuelled by already well-established communities who would still rely on some form of hunting/foraging strategy.

Marking a special landscape

This group is the only inland group of chambered tombs in Wales, and comprises 18 extant structures, five of which stand in neighbouring Herefordshire. The group extends in an arc around the northern, western and south-western hinterlands of the Black Mountains. It is possible that further monuments to the south and south-east may exist and thus completely encircle the Black Mountains. Monuments appear to be locally oriented, either with the valley or towards prominent features of the immediate landscape (Tilley 1994), and usually occupy the intermediate slopes facing the mountains. Beyond, there appears to be little or no Neolithic activity (Children & Nash 1994, 17).

Monuments within this group are in various states of preservation. An important review of this group has been produced by Britnell (1984, 3–9) and, recently, by Britnell & Whittle 2022. These reviews focus on the excavated monuments of Gwernvale (BRE 7) excavated by Britnell (Britnell 1984), Penywyrlod (BRE 14) excavated by Savory (Savory 1984), but also include essential discussions on other monuments within the group, including Pipton (BRE 8) excavated by Savory (Savory 1956) and Ty Isaf (BRE 5) excavated by Grimes (Grimes 1939). These four monuments arguably provide the most detailed evidence of burial deposition within this group. From the four monuments, human bone was found within the chamber and passage areas, and appeared to be disarticulated: a trait not uncommon with other monuments of this architectural style. Both sexes and all age groups are represented. Several heaps of human bone were found in one of the chambers at Pipton Long Cairn and were interpreted as a (ritualised) foundation deposit, possibly representing a symbolic offering following the construction of the monument (Savory 1956). These bone heaps may have originally been placed within a wooden box (Atkinson 1965, 130–1). I would suggest that they represent secondary deposits, which may have originated from other nearby tombs. Within each of the four monuments, overlying the bone heaps, was evidence of deliberate infilling of the chambers with soil. Similar deposition has been found in the chambers at West Kennet Long Barrow

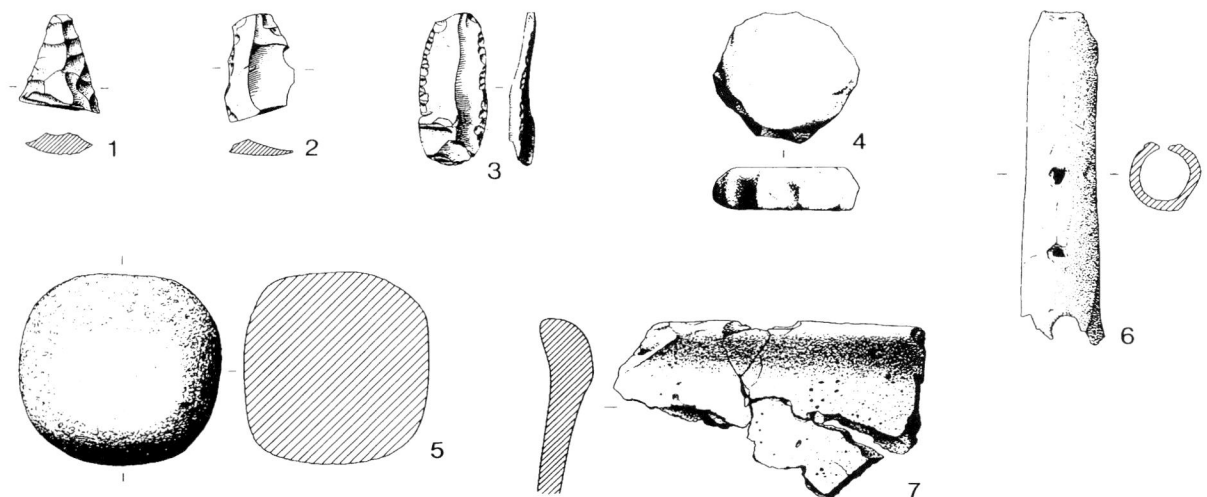

Artefacts from the Penywyrlod excavation: 1–3 lithics, 4–5 stone items, 6 bone flute, 7 pottery (after Britnell & Savory 1984)

(WILTS 4; Piggott 1962, 68). Did this act of 'burial' mark the end of chamber use?

The first coherent account of this group was made by Crawford in 1925 and was later refined by Grimes in 1936. Early sources suggest there were once as many as 21 monuments around the rivers Dore, Rhiangoll, Usk and Wye (Crawford 1925, Daniel 1950, Nash 2000, Olding 2000, Powell et al. 1969). The majority of these belong to the Cotswold-Severn tomb tradition; a label first coined by Daniel in 1937 (Daniel 1937), and were either influenced by or influenced other tomb builders in regions to the east and south, probably through contact/exchange links. Although their architectural style clearly originates from the Cotswold-Severn region (i.e., side chambers incorporated into a long trapezoidal mound), there exist a number of idiosyncratic localised traits that makes the Black Mountains Group altogether unique. Architectural traits include Cotswold-Severn façades and associated horns and extensions being added to existing monuments (e.g. Ty Isaf; BRE 5) and side chambers with distinct kinks within their passage alignments.

It has been argued that many of these architectural traits, that appear to have their origins in western France, date to the fifth millennium BCE (Savory 1980, 222); however, their development appears to be far too complex to be traceable to a single area of origin. Architectural features for the Cotswold-Severn group within this part of Wales include terminal and side chambers, passages leading to these chambers, a forecourt area and a false entrance (also referred to as a false portal); they are also built within an elongated or trapezoidal mound frequently enclosed by drystone walling. The Black Mountains monuments exhibit a number of unique characteristics that are found outside the area to the south and east, and beyond the shores of the British Isles (Children & Nash 2001, Nash 2000, Olding 2000). Britnell has argued that there is still little or no consensus as to how the architecture was used (1984, 7). Dating of the monuments in this region of Wales is problematic in that only two have been successfully radiocarbon-dated. Human bone for Penywyrlod (BRE 14) has been dated to around 3,020 BCE, whilst radiocarbon dates from Gwernvale suggest that the monument was in use for up to 600 years; construction dating to 3,100 BCE and formally closing at around 2,500 BCE. Recent investigations at Arthur's Stone in west Herefordshire may yield further dates.

A number of the tombs are found on high upland ridges and plateaus, close to and in full view of the mountains, such as Ffostyll North and South (BRE 3 & 4) and Ty Isaf (BRE 5). To the north and east, the Wye and Dore provide a focus for eight monuments, including Arthur's Stone, Dunseal and Cross Lodge Barrow,[14] and the lost barrow of Parkwood (HRF 2).[15]

Despite the significance and ritual draw of the Black Mountains to most monuments in the group, farther west are two that appear to ignore their influence. Instead, both have commanding views over the Brecon Beacons and lowland pastures of Llyn Llangors and Afon Honddu. Mynydd Troed (BRE 10) is one of the least impressive mounds, yet it is set in one of the most dramatic of all Black Mountain landscapes. Lying between the mountains of Mynydd Troed and Mynydd Llangors, the monument faces south-east towards Cwm Sorgwm and Pen Allt-mawr. It also has views to the west, towards Llyn Llangors. Both Mynydd Troed and another monument, Ty Illtyd (BRE 6), are sited around 3.5km from Llyn Llangors and may be linked territorially. The area around the mound may have marked the transition from open scrub to woodland (Grimes 1932; 1936a); and, if so, the mound would have been concealed from view, in spite of standing well over 254m AOD. However, clearing a swathe of vegetation from around the monument may have enhanced visibility (e.g. Cloutman 1983). The oval mound is oriented NE–SW and encloses a simple terminal chamber and at least one other. Recent historical disturbance makes reconstruction near-impossible. However, Mynydd Troed does resemble other monuments within the group, notably Ty Illtyd, Ffostyll North and Penywyrlod.

Outside the main group, but possibly associated with Mynydd Troed, is the isolated Ty Illtyd monument. Positioned on a west-facing ridge approximately 6.6km due west of Mynydd Troed, Ty Illtyd incorporates a visual setting that includes the eastern portion of the Brecon Beacons. Both chamber and capstone are aligned towards Pen y Fan, the highest point in the Beacons. The monument comprises a single capstone overlying a rectangular chamber delineated by eight uprights, and is set into a raised oval earth mound. The mound and chamber are oriented N–S with a small rectangular forecourt or antechamber at the northern end that has been interpreted as a second chamber (Corcoran 1969).

The southern and western monuments are less concentrated and follow a different pattern of construction, suggesting different communities and their tomb builders were probably being influenced by different groups externally. Here, we may be witnessing a temporary development in monument design, indicating the importance of particular areas at different times. Several monuments appear to have been in use for long periods. Ty Isaf, near Talgarth, reveals evidence of multi-phased building; whilst Gwernvale, Crickhowell shows that the site was periodically in use for up 6,500 years before the construction of the monument.

Only two tombs, Gwernvale and Carn Goch (BRE 12), near Crickhowell, stand close to the flood plain of the lower Usk Valley. Both are set on low terraces: Carn Goch takes in the views of Table Mountain (3km to the north-east) as its focus, while Gwernvale is aligned to the River Usk (Afon Wysg) and the Black Mountains to the east. Of the four passages at Gwernvale, three are oriented towards the Usk and to local spurs and escarpments. The south-eastern passage is slightly angled. A large doorway stone suggests visual access to the chamber was restricted, while the angled doorway hints at secret ritual-symbolic activity (see below). Similar passage plans are found at Arthur's Stone (HRF 1) and Pipton Long Cairn (BRE 8).

Garnishing the dead

Finds from these monuments can be considered limited, which may be due to antiquarian plundering, environmental conditions and the slow but inevitable decay of items made from, say, leather or wood. The majority of finds originate from the four monuments that have received sympathetic excavation: Gwernvale, Penywyrlod, Pipton and Ty Isaf. A small but significant assemblage of finds, including human remains, has also come from Little Lodge Barrow (BRE 2). Only one flint was found in Chamber I at Pipton, whilst in Chamber I at Ty Isaf, two polished flint axes, a bone pin and pottery fragments were uncovered. Found in chamber II at Ty Isaf, were the remains of at least six pottery vessels (referred to as Western pottery style). Small artefact assemblages were also found in the chambers at Penywyrlod, including part of a leaf-shaped arrowhead, a flint knife and a few sherds of pottery. The pottery from each of the monuments is classified according to Smith (1974, 108) as Abingdon ware, dating to the Early Neolithic. Interestingly, and in chronological sequence, later Neolithic Ebbsfleet and Peterborough wares appear to be associated with the blocking (abandonment) deposits at Gwernvale (Savory 1984, 6). These small but significant grave good assemblages would have been important items for the dead and their journey into the next life.

Life, death and resurrection in the east

Neolithic activity in Herefordshire is divided into two small but definitive areas: the Golden Valley, which has the extant monuments and settlement, and the Goodrich-Doward area, which has no burial monuments but a significant lithic presence. Both areas have yielded the majority of Neolithic finds in Herefordshire, including at least 30 polished stone and flint axes. The largest pocket lies in the Golden Valley, which forms part of the Black Mountains monument group. Apart from monuments and associated artefacts, there is clear evidence of Mesolithic activity, indicating the importance of an ancestral presence over many generations, usually within the curtilage of a site (e.g. Gwernvale). This near-continuous presence over, say, a 2–4,000-year period is evidenced by the retrieval of diagnostic tools and associated debitage from settlement activity (e.g. Gavin Robinson 1934; Ray & Thomas 2020; Rees and Jones 2015). Such familiarity with the landscape would have involved social, economic, and ritual knowledge, creating a sense of belonging.

Of the four known monuments within west Herefordshire, only Arthur's Stone has been archaeologically investigated: the first time (as far as the author is aware) in 2005/6, then in 2011, and recently in the summers of 2022 and 2023. The 2005/6 excavation concentrated on a small parcel of land immediately north of Arthur's Stone Lane. It was considered by the author that the present extant monument, south of the lane, was incorporated into a trapezoidal mound (Nash 2008). A series of seven test pits of varying size were excavated, five of which yielded *in situ* cairn. The presence of cairn material allowed the author to reconstruct a trajectory of the rear section of the trapezoidal mound. Based on this excavation, the author ascertained that Arthur's Stone possessed a similar architecture to the other 18 Cotswold-Severn monuments that encircled the Black Mountains.

Apart from the more obvious remains, such as Arthur's Stone and Cross Lodge Long Barrow (HRF 4), other smaller, damaged and lost monuments exist along the northern and eastern portions of the valley, and include Parkwood Chambered Cairn (HRF 2), Bach Long Barrow (HRF 5) and Dunseal Long Barrow (HRF 6). A number of standing stones within close vicinity of these monuments may be contemporary, their function as yet unknown.

As with many other areas of high Neolithic activity, Herefordshire has revealed very little evidence of settlement. However, one notable example was discovered by field-walkers on Dorstone Hill, equidistant between Arthur's Stone and Cross Lodge Long Barrow. Excavated by Christopher Houlder and Roger Pye between 1965 and 1970, and later by teams from Herefordshire Archaeology and Manchester University between 2015 and 2019 (Ray and Thomas 2020), this extensive settlement covers approximately 18 acres (SO 326 423). It was enclosed on the west side by a crude stone wall, on top of which was a wooden stockade fence. Also present were storage pits (possibly used for grain), occupation floors and undisturbed palaeosols (similar in morphology to Clegyr Boia in South-west Wales). Many finds were unearthed from within the soil stratigraphy, including a large quantity of diagnostic flint, pottery and polished stone axe fragments. The stone and flint used to create these prestige items were, in part, imported from as far away as north and south Wales, and the Cotswolds. The contact/exchange of axes and other commodities between these areas highlights the importance and prestige of farming groups within the Golden Valley.

The size of the Dorstone settlement suggests that a large population, probably in excess of 250 people, occupied the upland areas of the Golden Valley during the Neolithic, utilising the slopes, ridges and summits of the eastern uplands – from Merbach Hill in the north-east to Canns Hill in the south. By settling on the eastern hills, the community would have lived within full view of the Golden Valley, and, more importantly, of the symbolically significant Black Mountains. Below, the fertile woodland of the valley floor would have been slowly cleared for allotment-style farming. More land would have been brought into production as the population grew. Remaining pockets of woodland scattered throughout the valley would have harboured red deer and wild boar and cattle, additional resources that could have been exploited by Neolithic communities in the same way as their Mesolithic hunter ancestors. This pattern of settlement was probably repeated by small farming communities that occupied the hinterland valleys elsewhere around the Black Mountains massif.

1. Pen yr Wyrlod, Llanigon
SO 2248 3986, SM NO. BR012
County Reference Number: BRE 1

The Pen yr Wyrlod monument is located on a north-west facing slope, some 250m AOD. According to the RCAHMW (1997, 60) the monument is sited on the edge of farmland which was probably enclosed during the late eighteenth century; a field bank cuts across the north-western side of the mound and until 1991 was covered with trees. It is highly likely that the material from this field bank was once derived from the mound. The site has been further damaged by a road that runs from the village of Llanigon, and by local quarrying. Further reshaping of the monument has been caused by excavation – in particular through investigations by the Woolhope Club in 1921–2 under the direction of the Reverend W.E.T. Morgan and George Marshall (1922).

The remains of this denuded monument comprise four sandstone uprights, measuring approximately 2m by 1m[16] (the chamber uprights standing 1m above the existing ground level), and traces of an elongated, pear-shaped mound, approximately 18.5m long and

The chamber of Pen yr Wyrlod, looking east

9.6m wide. Presently, the uprights splay outwards, suggesting that they would have supported a heavy capstone, although settlement from resetting of these stones during the excavation is more probable. In 1898 a reference was made to the site being a 'Druidical Altar', hinting that a capstone was present (Morgan 1898, 40). It has been suggested that many, if not all, the *in situ* uprights were reset during the excavation (RCAHMW 1997, 60).

During the 1921–2 excavation the mound was found to consist of large flat stones that were irregularly placed on top of one another. Smaller stones were used as infill. This arrangement suggests that sections of drystone walling were in place; a style of architecture present at other Black Mountain sites, and one of the main architectural traits of the Cotswold-Severn Group of monuments.

The 1921–2 excavation methodology has been heavily criticised. The excavation of the terminal chamber revealed a black earth deposit that contained several human bones. More human bone was found at the base of the chamber, along with two black coarse potsherds.[17] The chamber base was constructed of irregular paving slabs. The bones can be considered the remains of a primary inhumation. Very few artefacts were found, but among them were fragments of 'rough pottery and a few flint flakes'. Vulliamy and, later, Gwynne investigated spoil heaps left by the excavators and found flint, traces of Beaker pottery, a Roman brass coin with the head of Crispus (dated AD 317–326),[18] and many blue glass beads and tubes believed to be from an early (possibly sixth-century) Anglo-Saxon or Romano-British burial. Sir Arthur Keith, responsible for the osteology of the 1921–2 excavation, claimed that the bone and teeth represented up to 20 individuals, including children of various ages, men and women.[19] However, the provenance of the bone material was difficult to determine due to poor excavation conditions.

According to excavation records, a charcoal deposit was found to the south-east of the eastern chamber, measuring up to 5cm in thickness. It is not clear from the excavation report if this deposit was analysed.

A plan published by Vulliamy in 1922 suggests that the eastern chamber was an enclosed structure and access to it was via the top of the mound (1922). However, the plan in Grimes (1936b, 275) argues that the remains of a passage may have existed several metres to the north. Grimes's plan also shows the mound to be oval rather than pear-shaped.

At the north-western end of the mound are traces of a small-chambered structure, consisting of three uprights. A small roofing slab would have also covered this small chamber. Both Vulliamy and

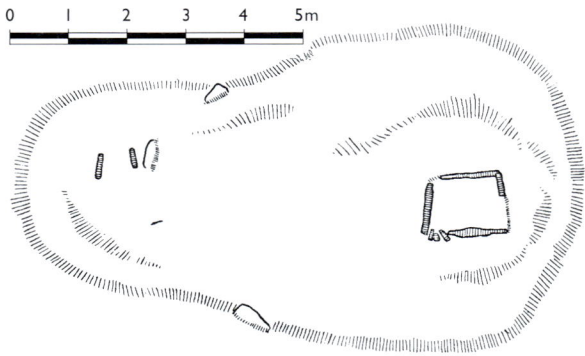

Plan of Pen yr Wyrlod (after Grimes, 1936b)

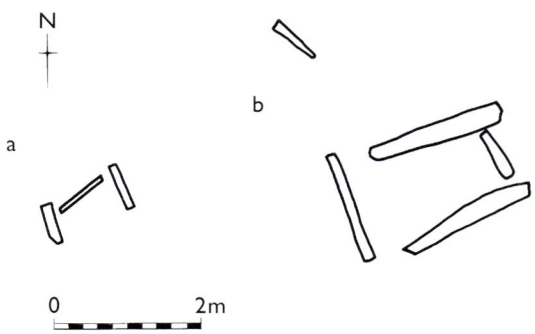

Pen yr Wyrlod: detailed plan of the chamber arrangement (after RCAHMW, 1997)

Grimes place a fourth stone in different locations, to the north or east of this small chamber respectively.

It has been suggested that the shape of the mound may be the result of multi-phased building activity, with the eastern section of the mound along with the chamber once forming a circular mound (Corcorcan 1969). If this were the case, Pen yr Wyrlod would have been in use over a long period of time, serving over many generations. However, the poor drawing record plus the disturbance made by the field bank, road and excavation makes any idea of such multi-phasing difficult to promote. I would suggest that Pen yr Wyrlod was constructed as a single-phased monument, mainly based on the idea that so many architectural traits found within this monument are present within other single-phased monuments found elsewhere.

Its position within the landscape suggests a symbolic strategic importance, in that the orientation of the mound (SW–NE) follows the orientation of the upper Wye Valley. The tomb also stands on a high, truncated spur with views across the valleys of the Wye and Llynfi; but it is not intervisible with the Neolithic monument at Clyro Court Farm (3.5km), nor Little Lodge Barrow (4–7km) and Pipton Long Cairn (7km). It would appear that Pen yr Wyrlod was sited in order to visually control the hinterlands to the west. Ironically, one only has to walk a few paces north in order to achieve intervisibility with Clyro Court Farm, its closest neighbour.

2–3. Ffostyll South & North, Llanelieu
SO 1789 3489 (South); SO 1791 3495 (North)
SM NO. BR175
County Reference Number: BRE 3 & 4

Ffostyll North and South stand about 70m apart in a field some 200m north of Ffostyll Farm. The two barrows stand around 312m AOD and are the highest within the Black Mountains Group. The mounds have been widely reported since the mid nineteenth century when, in 1842, Reverend T. Price observed that:

> … the most notable grave mounds I saw in Wales are in the parish of Llanelieu, Brecknockshire, on the land of the farm called Ffos-t-yll. The biggest of these mounds is 45 yards [41m] long, 20 yards [18m] yards wide and about two yards [1.8m] high; and they showed that they were full of cistvaens [cists or small chambers] of the same

size – one of which was lately broken for the sake of the stones. There are still enough left to show its size and its workmanship. It was 10 feet long, five feet wide and eight feet deep, formed of great stones one at each end and two at each side and covered with corresponding stones.

Both monuments, along with others within the group, were subjected to poor excavation, especially during the early part of the twentieth century. Indeed, O.G.S. Crawford unsuccessfully attempted to impose Statutory Protection for both monuments in order to prevent any further damage to the mounds following Vulliamy's excavation of 1921–3. However, evidence of earlier destruction of these monuments dates to the late nineteenth century when it was reported by the owner of Ffostyll Farm that the southern mound had been quarried for road ballast around 1875. As a result of the quarrying, human bone had allegedly been found and the height of the mound greatly reduced.

The monuments are directionally opposed. Ffostyll North (BRE 3) is oriented roughly E–W, while Ffostyll South has a N–S orientation. The latter (the smallest and best preserved of the pair) has a single 3m gallery-type chamber at the north-eastern end. Here, ten uprights support two dislodged capstones. According to Vulliamy, who investigated the mounds in three very brief seasons between 1921–3, both had been disturbed. He remarks:

> At first glance, the southern one appeared to have suffered a more searching devastation. Here, we have found that a vast amount of stone had been moved from the southern end, and there was considerable disturbance which I expected to contain the principal cist. Furthermore, a large covering stone lay tilted on the face of the mound. On examination, I concluded that neither of these disturbances had touched the burial chamber, which, though its form was not clear, was traceable in the centre of the highest part of the barrow. From information supplied by Mr Gwillym the tenant of the farm, I learned that the stone had been removed from the lower southern end of the barrow about forty-five years ago (c.1875), to supply material for roadmaking; and at that time quantities of human bone had come to light. (Vulliamy 1923)

2. Ffostyll South

According to the RCAHMW (1997, 41) the Ffostyll South monument measures 36m in length by 23m in width and is oriented NNE–SSW. However, it should be noted that at the southern terminal end there is an extensive rubble spread that distorts the actual shape of the mound. The rubble may be the result of spoil generated by the Vulliamy excavation.[20]

This monument was excavated on 20 September 1921, with the excavation lasting just four days! An entire stone cist, measuring 3.35m long by 1.2m wide with a displaced roofing slab (measuring 2.4m x 2.1m) was uncovered. According to excavation records, the eastern section of the chamber had collapsed inwards, revealing a series of individual slabs with a maximum height of 2m. Evident within the chamber were at least two deposits. Located at the base of the chamber was a layer of burnt human bone, a limited assemblage of domestic animal bone including those of a cat, and some bones which could not be properly identified. Overlying this was a further burnt charcoal deposit that contained mainly the remains of domesticated animals such as goat, ox and pig. According to Vulliamy:

> The bones were in the utmost confusion; only in a few instances were they in anatomical relation to each other, and by far the greater number were

split and broken. Some of the bones were wedged between the surrounding stones. The remains included 70 cranium fragments and a lower jaw (mandible), 36 metacarpals, metatarsals and phalanges, six vertebrae, 30 detached teeth, 135 fragments of long bone and 240 unidentified fragments, including non-human remains. Subsequent osteological analysis revealed some interesting characteristics: There was a man of about forty years old, whose head was very narrow, relatively high, and rather small. There was an old woman who must have had a face cast in a small, almost delicate mould. There was another man with a prominent ridge over his eyes; and there were children. In no instance was there a complete skeleton. All the individuals were short, the adult males being about 5 feet 4 inches in height. (1929, 162)

It was concluded that the bone material represented at least nine individuals.[21] Sir Arthur Keith, of the Royal College of Surgeons, commented on the pathology of the bones, suggesting that the material was typical 'of an ancient date' (it must be remembered that radiocarbon dating was not available during the 1920s). No traces of pottery were discovered, but three pieces of flint were found in the cist.

Vulliamy also excavated the chamber at the northern end, revealing more cremated remains, including those of an adult and a very young child, as well as pig or goat bone. Fragments of crude, black pottery (later interpreted as the remains of a round-bottomed bowl of Neolithic A type), and 17 pieces of flint and chert were also recovered, all of which had been burnt (1923, 320–4). Vulliamy noted a surprisingly low number of vertebrae within the skeletal assemblage. Indeed, a large percentage of bone material was absent, suggesting Ffostyll South

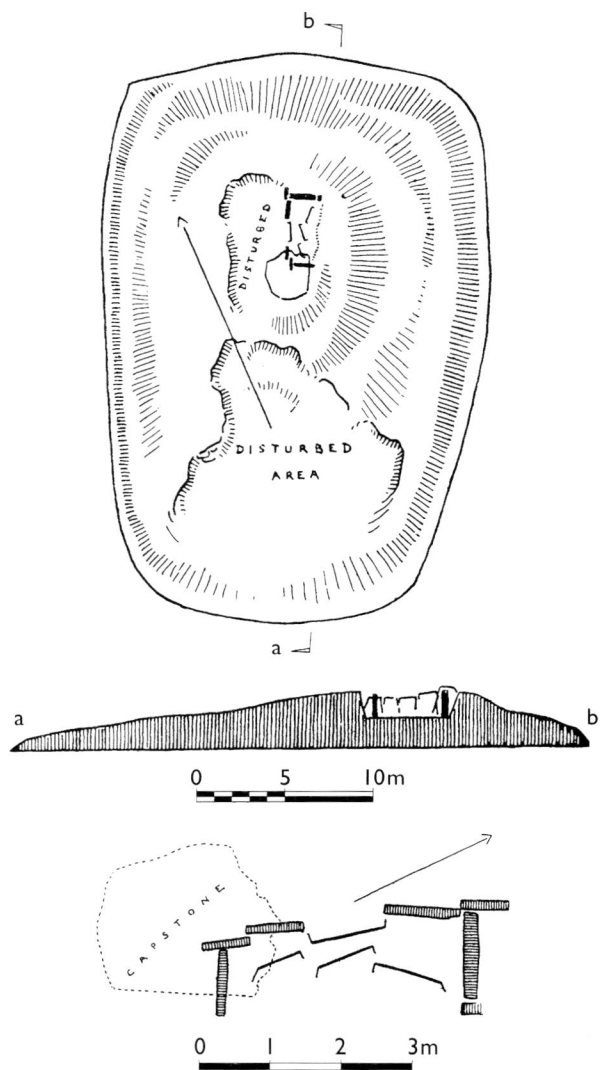

Plan and cross-section Ffostyll South (Vulliamy, 1929)

(and North) may have been a final ancestral resting place (i.e. the two sites acting as an ossuary). This monument may have had a similar purpose as that of the Neolithic monument at Quanterness, on Orkney, where ancestral bones were moved around the landscape from tomb to tomb, before eventually coming to rest in the largest monument within a specified group (Renfrew 1979). Interestingly, the Ffostyll monuments are indeed the largest, most visible and, arguably, the most central to monument activity within the Black Mountains group.

The chamber belonging to the Ffostyll South monument

Detail of the chamber architecture, with the Black Mountains visible beyond

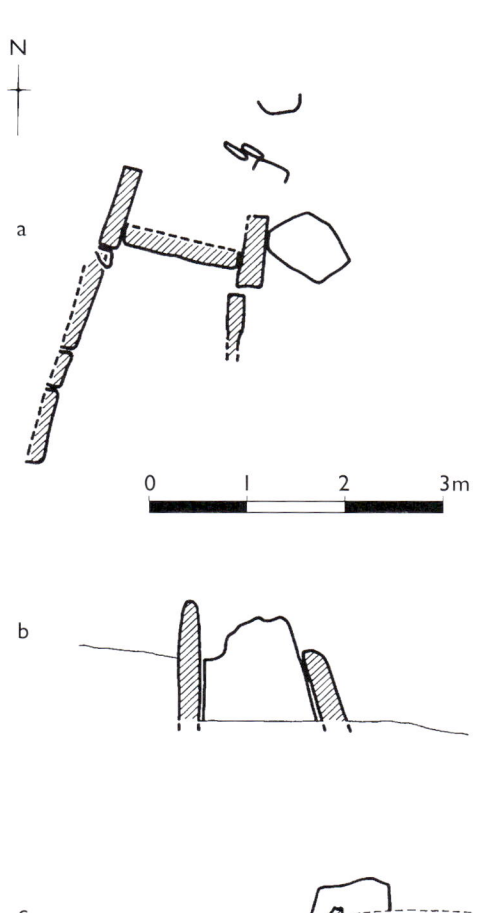

Plan and section of the Ffostyll North chamber arrangement (after RCAHMW, 1997)

3. Ffostyll North

The larger northern mound is considered multi-phased and possibly trapezoidal in plan (Corcoran 1969). The mound, which has been damaged by excavation and livestock, incorporates three chambers. A destroyed eastern chamber consists

THE BLACK MOUNTAINS GROUP 45

The mound of the Ffostyll North monument

of five upright stones of local sandstone, with no surviving capstone. Two further chambers are located centrally and at the south-western end. Unfortunately, none of the chambers has evidence of a passage. The main chamber contained human remains and those of horse, dog, ox and pig. These were found over the chamber floor in undisturbed deposits, some of them retaining their correct anatomical relationship. Flint flakes and pottery fragments were also recovered. Vulliamy describes the human remains thus:

> One of the men had been the possessor of massive thigh bones, and a remarkably heavy but well-modelled jaw. The neck-bones of a woman showed that she had suffered from rheumatism. Two of the burials were those of children, six and eleven years of age … (1925, 163)

The northern mound is positioned slightly higher up-slope than Ffostyll South, so may be considered the dominant monument and perhaps the earlier. Although directionally opposed, this pair of monuments may be considered to comprise a single, harmonious whole, in that, together, they encompass the localised landscape and have outstanding compass views towards Mynydd Troed to the south and the Wye Valley to the north.

The intact eastern chamber belonging to Ffostyll North

4. Pipton Long Cairn, Glasbury

SO 1604 3727, SM NO. BR029
County Reference Number: BRE 8

The remains of Pipton Long Cairn consist of a single *in situ* upright, several recumbent stones and disturbed cairn material. They stand at around 145m AOD, in the corner of an east-facing field, overlooking the north-western extent of the Black Mountains. The monument, one of four known hybrid Cotswold-Severn monuments within this group, stands between the River Wye and its tributary the Afon Llynfi. The site was excavated by Hubert Savory in 1956 (Savory 1956a).

The topography of the area is similar to the surroundings of other nearby tombs. Ffostyll North and South, Little Lodge Barrow and Pipton all appear to acknowledge corresponding features within the landscape – the spurs of Y Das and Hay Bluff. This small group of monuments also shares intervisibility. The monuments of Penywyrlod, Ffostyll North (BRE 3) and South (BRE 4), and Little Lodge Barrow (BRE 2) can be clearly seen from Pipton. The cluster may, therefore, constitute a ritualised territory.

The mound, once covered with trees and thought to be originally oval in shape (Grimes 1936b, 269), measures 37m in length and 22m in width.[22] The mound was delineated by a drystone revetment wall (first published in 1925 and later excavated by Hubert Savory). Although trapezoidal in shape, the mound has two horns and a 'dummy' or false portal at the northern end. These features are also present at Penywyrlod (BRE 14), Ty Isaf (BRE 5), Gwernvale (BRE 7) and now Arthur's Stone (HRF 1). There is evidence to suggest that the monument may have been constructed in a number of phases; a circular structure at the end of the monument may predate the main mound. This feature is recognised as an internal revetment wall that may have been of structural use in supporting the inner cairn, whilst the outer revetment wall was merely cosmetic. Both revetment walls, also found at Gwernvale, Penywyrlod and Ty Isaf, would have been constructed as a single phase. The mound is oriented roughly N–S and overlooks the River Wye.

There are a number of similarities with other monuments within the Black Mountains Group. For example, Arthur's Stone (HRF 1), has an identical T-shaped northern chamber and passage arrangement. The west-facing passage, centrally placed within the cairn fabric, is angled in two places, with two door-stones, thereby inhibiting visual access. The passage entrance, which is on the north side, has a small sill formed by a series of upright slabs and is narrower than the central, deeper sections. Headroom within the main chamber (also referred to as 'the gallery') was, like

Pipton Long Cairn: one of the uprights that formed a chamber

Arthur's Stone, around 1.3m. The chamber is divided into two. A north transept, measuring 3.5m x 1m, is further subdivided by a door-stone halfway along its length. The smaller south transept, measuring 1m x 0.8m, was blocked by a single (door-stone) slab. A second chamber (Chamber II), measures internally 1.9m x 1m, faces south-west and has no passage. However, an earlier phase of construction has been recognised (Savory 1956). The second chamber may be a closed cist, entered from above, suggesting that a passage would not be necessary. The outer cairn may originally have attained a height of nearly 2m (RCAHMW 1998, 49).

The plan suggests a similarity with the multi-phased construction at Ty Isaf. At the terminal end of the mound on the south-western side, are two canted slabs which may be an earlier architectural feature. Prior to construction, the ground was carefully prepared. On the southern side, an earthen deposit was scooped away to create a level surface. Charcoal, sandstone chips and a piece of unidentifiable Neolithic pottery were found within this context. Whilst the sandstone fragments may be associated with the building process, the charcoal could be the remains of ritual activity associated with the preparation of the ground. Savory also

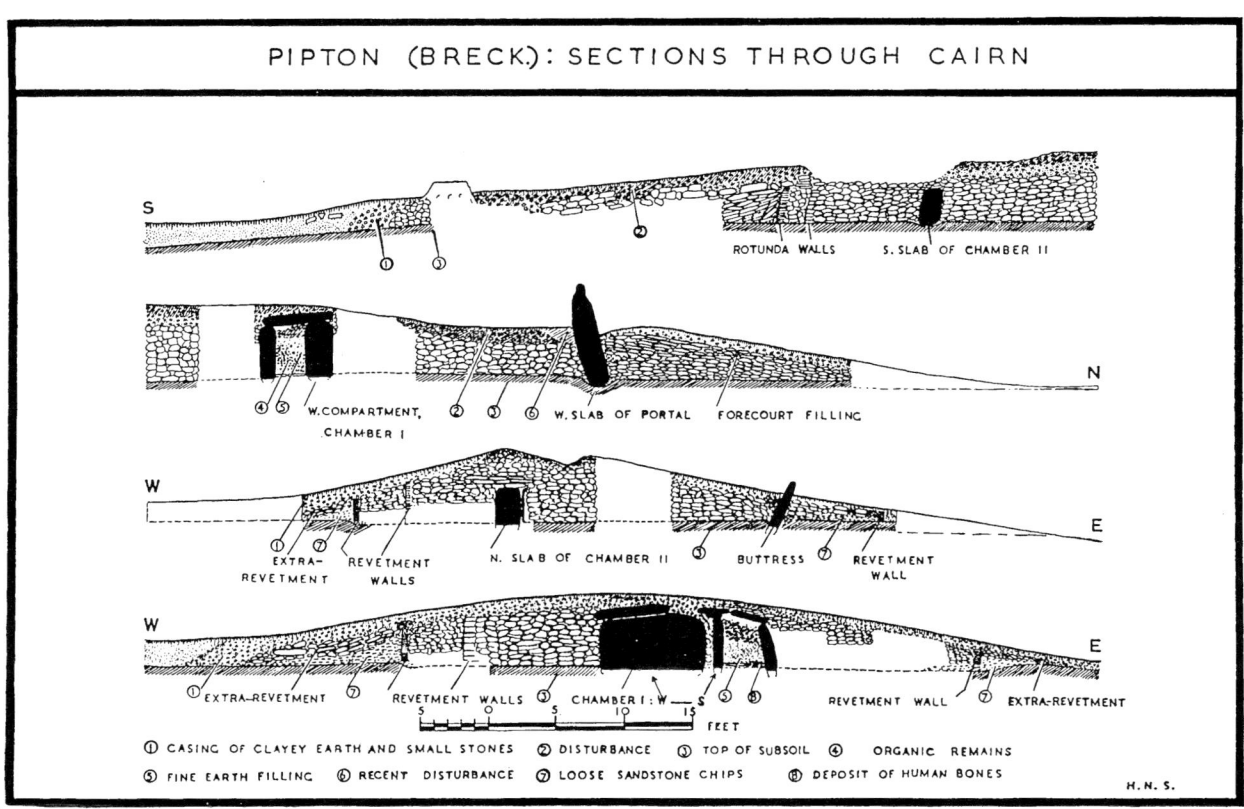

Pipton Long Cairn: sections (after Savory 1956)

noted a number of low, upright stones that appear to have had no structural significance and which may be interpreted as marker stones delineating this section of the monument (Savory 1956). Like other monuments within the group, the chambers were surrounded by a cairn of angular sandstone blocks and flags. Water-rolled blocks and pebbles would have been brought up from the nearby Afon Llynfi. The mound is supported by a series of revetment walls that may represent different construction phases. The inner revetment appears to be more crudely constructed than the outer wall, which, in places, rises to 24 courses, to a height of 0.75m. A need to amplify monumentality in order to create something more visually impressive (see also the plan of Ty Isaf) could be in evidence here, as elsewhere within the Cotswold-Severn region. Alternatively, the reason could be structural rather than aesthetic (Children & Nash 2001).

In Chamber I and the passage, an incomplete assemblage of disarticulated human bone was found beneath the floor slabs of the south transept, representing possibly four individuals. Human as well as animal bone and a flint flake were found in the passage area. Human bone was also discovered beneath the floor of Chamber II, and seven bone heaps representing possibly seven individuals were placed against the side wall of the chamber. Covering the bone was a layer of earth, which may have been introduced as part of an interment ritual. The bone may have come from elsewhere (Savory 1956a), and if so Pipton was either the final abode of the dead or an interim resting place.

The seven bone heaps do have similarities with the way the dead were interred into the chambers at the Neolithic passage grave of Le Déhus, in north-west Guernsey, Channel Islands (Jelly & Nash 2016). Here, finds from this complex monument included a large assemblage of limpet shells, found mainly within the main chamber. Below this deposit were two adult burials and a child, along with later cremated remains. The later burials were accompanied by a copper-tanged dagger and the fragmentary remains of a Bell Beaker vessel. In Chamber A, located north of the passage, further human remains were uncovered along with Neolithic and Early Bronze Age pottery and a polished stone axe made from imported serpentine. Further burials were also found inside Chambers B, C and D, including two individual sitting skeletons that were discovered side by side and facing in opposite directions in Chamber B. When excavated, these and other interments were recorded as bone heaps. It would appear that interred individuals were propped up and placed into sitting positions, thus replicating the living!

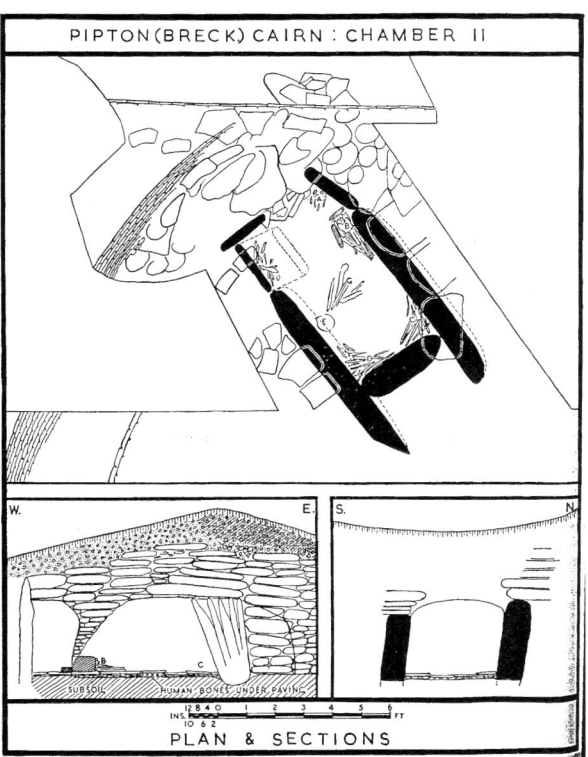

Cairn chamber II: plan & sections (after Savory 1956)

5. Ty Isaf, Talgarth
SO 1819 2906, SM NO. BR006
County Reference Number: BRE 5

One of the more carefully excavated tombs in Wales, Ty Isaf stands on a small east-facing ridge in a field above a farm at around 211m AOD. The monument was excavated in 1938 by W.F. Grimes and is regarded as a Cotswold-Severn-type monument (1939a). Typically, it has a complex series of chambers and passages set within a trapezoidal mound (oriented N–S), a false portal or doorway, extended horns, and a deeply recessed forecourt area. Although the excavation plan is complex, today the remains comprise a few protruding uprights and traces of an elongated mound (measuring 30m x 18m). However, the monument's landscape setting may be regarded as an important element of its overall meaning.

The monument, sited on a small knoll and close to two small streams is set in one of the most dramatic landscapes within the Black Mountains Group. The land rises steeply to the east and west. Mynydd Troed to the west reaches 609m AOD and Waun Fach to the east rises to 811m AOD. To the north and within view is a circular knoll on which an Iron Age hill enclosure stands. According to Grimes (1936b, 263), located between the hill enclosure and Ty Isaf is the remains of primeval woodland.[23] It is within this woodland that the badly damaged Cwmfforest monument stands (BRE 9). Grimes postulates, correctly in my view, that (damp oak) woodland would have extended over the site of Ty Iasf and that extensive clearance would have been necessary in order to construct this monument (ibid. 264).

The plan reveals that Ty Isaf is a multi-phased monument, with at least three phases of construction and use. The earliest phase consists of a small oval cairn, about 12m in diameter, and located at the southern end of an extended mound. Within the cairn, a passage runs S–E, and the chamber is oriented SW–NE. The cairn has been seen as an addition to the larger mound (Corcoran 1969), but it is probably the earliest structure (Castleden 1992). The principal mound, which contains two chambers (with passages), and a curious false portal (or doorway), probably represents the second phase of construction. The mound itself has a

The outline of the mound belonging to Ty Isaf

The stone outline of one of the four chambers of Ty Isaf

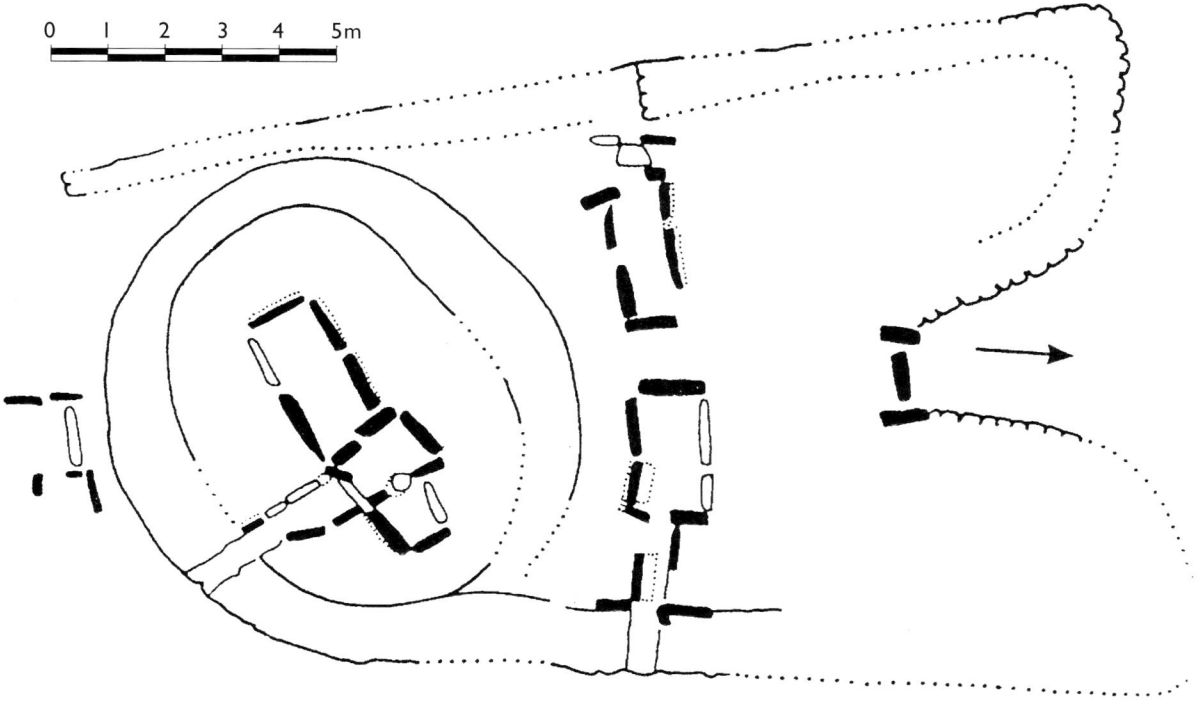

Plan of Ty Isaf (after Grimes 1939a)

double drystone revetment wall. The false portal is located at the northern end, between two horns. The monument is very similar in terms of plan and orientation to Arthur's Stone (HRF 1) and Pipton Long Cairn (BRE 8) – hybrid tombs in this group. The lateral passages open out towards Mynydd Troed to the west, and Waun Fach to the east, while 100m or so to the west the Afon Rhiangoll flows southwards. These landscape features may be symbolic components of the strategic position of the monument.

Ty Isaf has revealed much information about the treatment of the dead during the Neolithic. The crushed bones of 17 of the 33 individuals recovered from the tomb were found in the western chamber,[24] accompanied by leaf-shaped arrowheads, a flint axe and undecorated Neolithic pottery; while the eastern chamber contained a possible complete skeleton and at least six Western (Neolithic) bowls. A light grey, asymmetrical, lozenge-shaped, partially polished and ground axe was also found (Grimes 1939b, 130–2). Savory (1980, 219) suggests that bones from this and other Cotswold-Severn monuments may represent a reburial phase, either originating from other chambers within the monument or from other monuments. The crushed bones appeared to have been deliberately placed in small piles against the sides of the chamber. They were also placed in niches between the chamber walls and the uprights. In contrast, the remains of two articulated skeletons were recovered from the passage area of lateral chamber II on the eastern side of the mound.

THE BLACK MOUNTAINS GROUP

A sandstone pendant with an hour-glass-type perforation (25mm in diameter) and more pottery were found near the entrance of this chamber. Pottery was also recovered from the old land surface against a section of the eastern wall. The chamber and passage of the southern circular cairn (chamber III) contained the remains of five individuals with the articulated remains of a further four individuals inside the passage. The burials from the passage may have been the last to be interred.

A small, isolated and heavily disturbed chamber (chamber IV) at the southern end of the monument, probably representing the final construction phase, contained a middle Bronze Age cremation urn and a series of burnt wooden boxes. The successive phases of building and the varied manner in which the dead were interred suggest Ty Isaf remained in use for hundreds of years, certainly throughout the latter part of the Neolithic and the Early Bronze Age.

6. Croesllechau, Bronllys
SO 1672 3626, SM NO. BR007
County Reference Number: BRE 11

This monument, now lost and probably destroyed, possesses a unique antiquarian history. This includes several plans (the earliest dating to the seventeenth century and sketched by Edward Lhuyd), and a later one by Theophilus Jones in 1809. The site, named from the field in which is stood, is also known as Byrn-y-Groes (after the name of the farmstead). Textual information describing the site relies heavily on the sketch and notes made by Lhuyd in *c*.1700. Although the precise location of the site is open to debate, Croesllechau stands close to the Ffostyll North and South monuments, on a small hillock at 120m AOD.

Lhuyd describes the site as a cromlech (Dolmen), using five individual sketches. The first of these

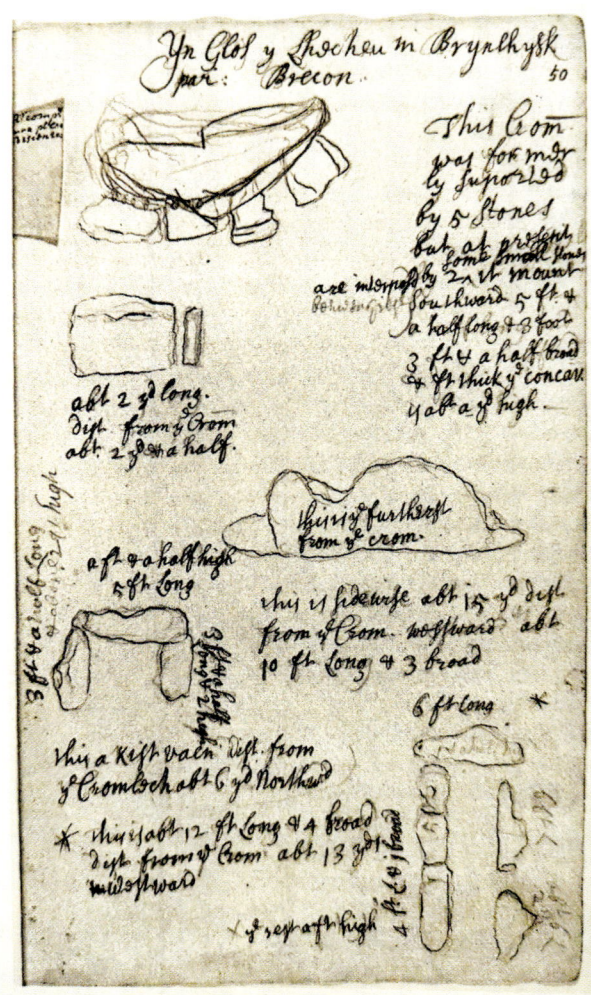

Detailed plan of the now-lost site of Croesllechau, sketched by Edward Lhuyd, c.1700

shows a classic dolmen chamber, comprising a large flat capstone that is supported by at least five short uprights. Lhuyd also sketches several outliers, along with a plan of a long chamber, formed from 6/7 uprights (see transcription in the RCAHM 1997, 47, Fig. 32). This structure, measuring 6ft (1.8m), stood around 13yds (11.8m) westward of the dolmen. The spatial distribution of the various structures recorded

CROESLLECHAU

Antiquarian engraving of the destroyed Croesllechau, by Theophilus Jones, 1809

by Lhuyd indicates that this monument probably formed the remains of a Cotswold-Severn monument, similar to others within the Black Mountains Group.

According to the RCAHM (1997, 48), the site appears to have survived up until the first decade of the nineteenth century. Prior to destruction, the site was noted by Richard Colt Hoare and Richard Fenton who place the monument in a field known as Clos y llechau. The Ordnance Survey 1 inch map of 1832 locates this site with a cromlech symbol.

Theophilus Jones in 1809 provides several clues to the whereabouts of the monument by stating:

> In a field called Croeslechau about two miles eastward of this town or village [Talgarth] but in the parish of Bronllys and on a farm called Bryn-y-groes, is a cromlech, not merely interesting on account of its antiquity, but from the circumstance of a white thorn growing close, and indeed under part of it, which has gradually

raised the horizontal or covering-stone several inches out of its original position; it is therefore not only venerable as a relic of very ancient days but as a natural curiosity.

Later, in the early twentieth century, the eminent archaeologist O.G.S. Crawford commented:

Now the site is unknown and all memory of it has completely vanished in the neighbourhood. Mr. Evan Morgan has visited the site and reports that no traces of the "cromlech" were visible; nor were enquires of the farmer at Bradwys any more successful in identifying the site. It is not unlikely that the monument was destroyed when a new road was made at some date probably soon after 1832. (Crawford 1925, 54)

Despite the destruction and disappearance of all traces of the monument, its sketchy location and description provides an important missing element in the distribution of Cotswold-Severn monuments within the Black Mountains Group of central Wales.

7. Penywyrlod, Talgarth
SO 1505 3156, SM NO. BR175
County Reference Number: BRE 14

Standing 253m AOD on the crest of a ridge above the Afon Llynfi valley, the monument is clearly valley aligned, although the orientation is directly towards Mynydd Troed. Also worth noting is that the monument is intervisible with three other nearby tombs – Ffostyll North and South (BRE 3 & 4) and Pipton Long Cairn (BRE 8). All are similar architecturally and appear to share an affinity in terms of both landscape topography and valley alignment.

Not to be confused with Pen-y-wyrlod (BRE 1), Llanigon, this monument stands on a small rise overlooking Mynydd Troed. Partly hidden by tree cover, Penywyrlod was discovered during quarrying, when human remains were reported to the National Museum of Wales on 27 June 1972. It was excavated later that year by Hubert Savory (Savory 1973). The mound, one of the largest in the Black Mountains Group, is considered a laterally chambered hybrid-type of the later Cotswold-Severn design: in other words, constructed as a single-phase monument (Savory 1984). The mound is oriented roughly N–S, whilst three chambers (referred to as Chambers NE I, NE II and NE III) with associated passages, open out towards the Black Mountains. The western side of the monument that opens out towards the Brecon Beacons was not excavated. Previous comments by Children & Nash (2001, 66) have incorrectly stated that no chamber activity existed on this side of the mound. However, there is evidence of a large chamber located immediately west of Chamber NE I that would have opened out towards the Brecon Beacons.[25] Further chambers on the western side of the mound may exist, which symmetrically oppose chambers of the eastern side.

Quarrying had nearly destroyed one chamber (NE I), exposed another (NE II) and revealed a false portal and central chamber lying beyond the main axis. Quarrying had also revealed sections of the original outline of the mound, which incorporated substantial revetment walling at the north-eastern end and south-eastern forecourt area. Exposed within this excavation trench was a probable lintel stone that was found lying in the central area of the forecourt. This stone probably once lay on top of three portal stones that constitute a false portal, located between the horns. Also recovered were small fragments of human skull (some were burnt). These fragments may represent some form of

The quarried area of Penywyrlod and the landscape to the west

The landscaped, quarried area of Penywyrlod

excarnation activity. A temporary timber mortuary structure, similar to that suggested by post-hole evidence within the forecourt area at Gwernvale, may have been utilised (Britnell 1984, 6).

Excavation trenches at both ends of the axis suggest the mound measured 52m x 22.5m. A total of five trenches, mainly along the north-east side of the mound, were excavated. The excavation exposed three side-chambers, the inner remains of a western (main) chamber and the revetment wall of the north-eastern horn. The unexcavated western chamber, which probably opens out to the west, comprises two uprights (still visible) infilled with earth and sandstone. I would suggest that this is not a 'main' chamber but a side chamber similar to that of NE I or NE II. Savory's excavation report suggests these were tilted inwards in order to support a large capstone(s) (1984). This structure was covered by a sandstone rubble block and slab cairn that consisted of two building phases. Sections of the revetment wall that delineates the cairn survive up to 0.3m in height. Savory (1984) suggests that the revetment walls of the mound would have not exceed 0.5m. However, the revetment walls around the forecourt area are considerably higher, measuring up to 1.5m in height.

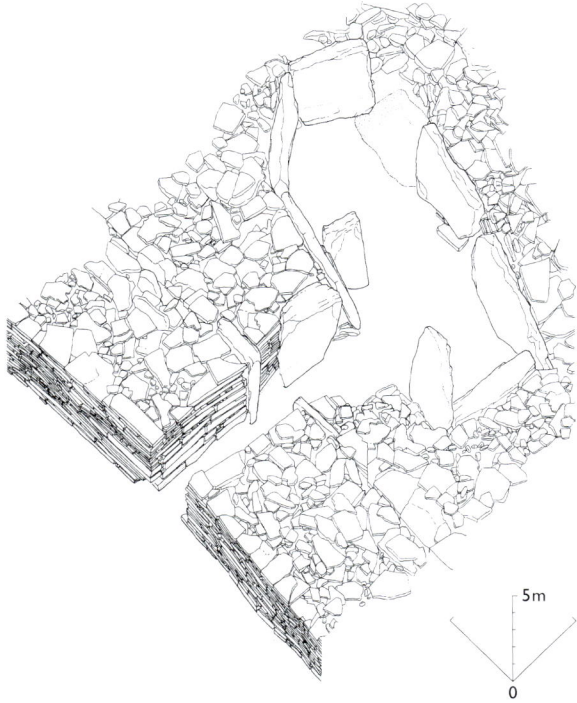

Isometric plan of one of the side chambers (after Savory 1984)

THE BLACK MOUNTAINS GROUP   55

The north-eastern chamber (NE I) had been almost destroyed; only the plan of the western section of the chamber appeared to show any form. The chamber formed two separate compartments measuring 2m x 1.2m and 1.6m x 1m. The latter was entered from a short passage between two revetment walls. Fallen uprights indicated that a second chamber (NE II), which measured 2.85m x 1m x 1.3m, was located 9m north-west of the Chamber NE I. A slab sealed the chamber, giving the impression of a false entrance, a feature commonly found within the Cotswold-Severn region. The two chamber compartments of NE II comprised 10 uprights and were entered by a short passage opening out to the west. The third excavated chamber (NE III) lay at the terminal end of the mound and revealed an entrance with supporting revetment walls, which supported a capstone.

The human remains from Chamber NE I are considered to represent a dedicatory deposit. Disarticulated human bone, possibly representing more than six individuals, was recovered from Chamber NE II where long bones were piled against the base of the side walls. This structure may be the remains of an ossuary deposit (RCAHMW 1997, 40). Recovered from Chamber NE III, where the fragmented remains of seven individuals were found, a further two partial skeletons were discovered in various deposits within the entrance blocking. In the entrance area of Chamber NE III, a further possible ossuary deposit was discovered. Also found was a flint knife, a bone flute and numerous animal bones. Several fragments of Abingdon ware were recovered from within the same chamber area, beneath the entrance.

The probable incomplete bone flute, found within the entrance of chamber NE III, is regarded as one of Britain's oldest musical instruments, radiocarbon dated to 3020±80 BCE. The bone, from an *ovicaprid*

The earliest musical instrument in the British Isles: a flute made from sheep bone

(sheep) metapodial, measures 74mm in length and has three holes punched into it (Megaw 1984, 27–8).

Savory concludes that Chambers NE I and NE II were utilised and sealed when the monument was first constructed. Further bone deposits found within a small cist located underneath the north-eastern horn, suggest these burials may represent foundation activity whereby human remains rather than building stone legitimises the place as a site for burial.

The Penywyrlod and nearby Gwernvale sites were re-evaluated in an important edited volume published in 2022 (Britnell & Whittle 2002). The book places both sites into a wider landscape and monument group context, and also includes up-to-date analysis on the architecture and finds that were recovered in the original excavations. The study also discusses the long-term conservation issues associated with site denudation and visitor footfall. These issues were mitigated when Penywyrlod was subjected to a comprehensive conservation programme in 2015. This programme of work involved further limited excavation and the sympathetic covering or loose cairn.

8. Ty Illtyd, Llanhamlach
SO 0984 2638, SM NO. BR011
County Reference Number: BRE 6

Ty Illtyd (also known as Ty Illtud and Maen Iltyd) stands opposite Manest Court Farm, approximately 215m AOD, on a west-facing ridge. Although classified within the Black Mountains Group, it stands apart and appears to take the Brecon Beacons as its focus, overlooking the flood plain of the Usk and the eastern extent of the Brecon Beacons. Both chamber and capstone are aligned towards Pen y Fan, the highest point of the Beacons. John Aubrey first investigated the site in the seventeenth century, and it was later examined by Edward Lhuyd, who described the monument as having three uprights and a capstone, with clear graffiti on both side stones (leading to the chamber). He also noticed that the chamber stood within a circular structure/mound.

The monument itself comprises a single capstone overlying a rectangular chamber, delineated by eight uprights which are set into a raised, oval, earthen mound measuring 23m (N–S) x 15.7m (E–W). The mound slopes away to the south and west, and the chamber, measuring 1m x 2m, is oriented N–S, with a small rectangular forecourt or antechamber at the northern end, which may be a second chamber (Corcoran 1969). Rather than repeat an apparently endless set of dimensions (RCAHMW 1997), it is perhaps sufficient to draw attention to an engraving by Henry Longueville Jones (1867), which clearly shows the uprights and capstone. The two outer uprights depicted may represent the inner sections of two horns.

Antiquarian engraving of the monument by Henry Longueville Jones (*Archaeologia Cambrensis*)

The chamber and entrance remains of Ty Illtyd

Medieval symbols engraved on the walls of the chamber at Ty Illtyd (after RCAHMW, 1997)

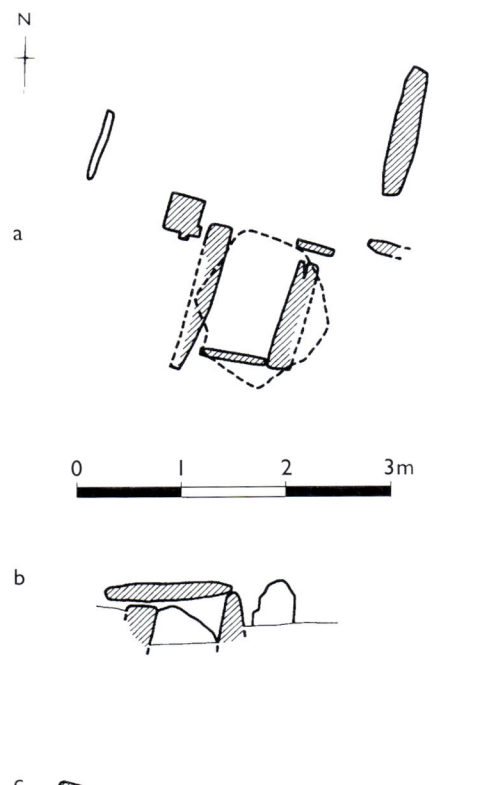

Plan and section of the chamber arrangement (after RCAHMW 1997)

Five uprights are inscribed with what appear to be medieval graffiti, including a harp (five-stringed lyre) and the dates 1312 (in Roman numerals) and 1510. A side-chamber upright bears at least eight crosses and what are presumed to be personal initials. Another has at least 60 carvings, mostly lozenges, diamonds and crosses. Longueville Jones (*Archaeologia Cambrensis* 1867, 347–55) considered them to be the work of shepherd boys. However, O.G.S. Crawford (1925, 156) and the Abbe Breuil (c.f. RCAHMW 1997, Fig. 16) have argued that some of the graffiti is prehistoric and possibly contemporary with the use of the tomb. On the other hand, the graffiti are similar to masons' marks and are contemporary with the robbing of the monument for building stone (RCAHMW). However, Grinsell (1981, 131–9) thought the tomb had been reused by St Illtyd as a hermit's cell and that the symbols are therefore medieval in date. The marks, as illustrated, do not appear to be prehistoric, for there are no direct parallels with prehistoric art elsewhere. I would suggest that this is no 'idle graffiti'. If the crosses are of Christian origin, they may signify a refuge against religious persecution (similar to incised art I have found in caves around the Cathar region of south-west France).

9. Mynydd Troed, Talgarth
SO 16145 28417, SM NO. BR013
County Reference Number: BRE 10

Mynydd Troed, one of the less impressive mounds within the Black Mountains Group, stands 350m AOD at the foot of Mynydd Troed (and is thus the highest monument within the group). The site was discovered by O.G.S. Crawford in 1921, and sketched by W.F. Grimes in 1926. The sketch shows three exposed stone uprights within the centre of the mound, which form a probable cist. There was also extensive disturbance within the southern section of the mound, suggesting possible unrecorded antiquarian activity. In 1966, Crampton & Webley excavated a series of sections that were cut into the western and eastern sides of the mound. The trenches were excavated in order to locate any walling and to take environmental samples (Caseldine 1990, 49–54). The excavation identified 22 courses of drystone perimeter wall approximately 0.43m high and 11m long (RCAHMW), which had collapsed on the western side but was protected by 'a canted pile of slabs' on the eastern side (ibid. 35). The

The plundered mound of Mynydd Troed, looking east towards the Black Mountains

The monument stands between Mynydd Troed and Mynydd Llangorse, facing south-east towards Cwm Sorgwm and Pen Allt-mawr. Views westwards take in Llangorse lake and the surrounding hinterlands. Ty Illtyd (BRE 6) and Mynydd Troed (BRE 10) are equidistant, suggesting the monuments may be linked territorially.

The area around the mound marks the boundary between open scrub and woodland (Grimes 1936b, 265). In spite of the monument standing at well over 350m AOD, such a location would have inhibited visual access. If Mynydd Troed was constructed in order to be seen, as it probably was, a large area of scrub and woodland must have been cleared by the users of the monument in order to expose the mound to the surrounding landscape.

wall was similar to that recorded at Gwernvale (BRE 7). The excavation also yielded an assemblage of cherty flint flakes and a range of Neolithic pottery similar to types found at Ty Isaf.

Three definite hollows within the mound structure may represent chambers. The tops of a number of upright stones are visible in two of the hollows. Past interpretations suggest the stone alignments within the mound core represent a terminal chamber, although they may be the remains of a western passage that led to a central chamber. Had it not been for extensive recent disturbance, (especially within the northern section), investigations may have revealed further passage and chamber alignments, and an overall plan to rival that of nearby Ty Isaf (BRE 5) in complexity. It is precisely because the monument is so poorly preserved that very little has been said about it, though it does have architectural similarities with nearby Pen yr Wyrlod, Ffostyll North (BRE 3) and Ty Illtyd (BRE 6). Looking beyond the confines of the monument, however, more can be said, as Mynydd Troed is set within an impressive landscape.

10. GWERNVALE, CRICKHOWELL
SO 2110 1920, SM NO. BR016
County Reference Number: BRE 7

Gwernvale, a hybrid Cotswold-Severn monument, has been excavated many times. The most recent of these was undertaken by William Britnell in 1978

One of the two southern chambers at Gwernvale

THE BLACK MOUNTAINS GROUP

Completed excavation plan of the Gwernvale monument, showing the four excavation areas and respective chambers (after Britnell 1984, Fig. 31)

(Britnell 1979, 132–34; Britnell 1984, 42–154; Britnell & Whittle 2022). The discovery of Upper Palaeolithic flint suggests the site has been occupied for many thousands of years, though not continuously. Prior to the 1978 excavation, it was thought that very little of the monument had survived. Since early post-medieval times a main arterial route between the Marches and central and south-east Wales had cut into the northern section of the mound, destroying cairn revetment walling and the northern horn.

Gwernvale aroused some early interest from Theophilus Jones, who, in 1804, remarked:

> This cromlech, one end of which adjoined the Brecon turnpike road on the south side, was immediately opposite Gwernvale, about half-a-mile from Crickhowell: it consisted as usual of a huge tablet of unhewn stone mounted upon five supporters pitched edgewise in the ground, the super incumbent stone or cover inclining to the south and open in the front to the north; it was placed on a high mound, long overrun with brushwood and brambles, and formerly there seem to have been stones placed edgewise also round what is now almost a semicircle; whether before the turnpike road was made they extended it so as to describe an irregular circle I know not; but I am inclined to think that the appearance of the spot was materially altered by the intersection of the highway; and that upon that occasion the workmen ... anticipated our attempt to make discoveries under the cromlech; in that case the object, though far different from ours, was probably equally unsuccessful ....
> The experiment in 1804 proved nothing either way (as to the sepulchral or other object of the cromlech).

A quite different account, from the unpublished diary of Sir Richard Colt Hoare, states:

Saturday May 26th 1803. This morning was devoted to opening a cromlech or kistvaen adjoining the turnpike road near Crickhowell and opposite the house of Mr Everett: with some difficulty the upper stone measuring ten feet in length, being removed, we dug to the base of the surrounding upright stones, which had supported the recumbent one, but found no signs of an interment or relics; but a few pieces of charcoal seemed to indicate cremation. The history of the cromlech has not as yet been sufficiently ascertained, and it remains a doubt whether it was designed for an altar or sepulchre. The kistvaen or stone chest was clearly designed for an interment.

O.G.S. Crawford (1925, 60) noticed the chamber was being used as 'a receptacle for old pails, bottles and jam jars'.

Gwernvale and nearby Carn Goch (BRE 12) are valley monuments that stand on river terrace gravels and sand respectively (Grimes 1936b, 265). The site, standing at around 69m AOD, was occupied, albeit periodically, for at least 6,500 years prior to the construction of the long cairn during the Neolithic. The discovery, underneath the southern section of the cairn and within the forecourt area, of Late Upper Palaeolithic flint suggests the site was utilised as a probable encampment. The encampment may have been sited along an ancestral migratory route used seasonally by megafauna such as elk, horse and reindeer. Small hunter-gatherer groups may have used the site and its immediate area to make tools and utilise the carcasses of hunted animals, similar to sites like the Meiendorf and Stellmoor stations in northern Germany where significant reindeer carcass utilisation is evident (Grønnow 1987). Diagnostic tools included backed blades. Early and Late Mesolithic flint was also found within the same areas of the site, suggesting a spatial continuity between periods. This specialised tool kit, used for different hunting needs, included finished and unfinished microliths, microburins, notched and truncated flakes and awls (Healey & Green 1984, 113–32).

Forty-five metres in length and standing on a low, west-facing terrace, the mound was once thought to be circular in form (Fenton 1804, Crawford 1925). At the eastern end are two horns and a false portal. Two lateral chambers at the southern end of the mound are both clearly visible; the largest chamber comprising six large uprights. A passage opens towards two dominant topographic features – the River Usk and Mynydd Llangatwg in the south-west. A third chamber has been badly damaged, and a small, single chamber on the northern side has also been noted.

Very few human remains were found during the 1978 excavation; it is believed many were removed during investigations in 1804 (Jones 1804). From the 1978 excavation, human bone was found in Chambers I, II, III and IV. Skull fragments were also found within timber bedding trenches that extended beneath the northern section of the monument. The monument itself is believed to have been built over an earlier Neolithic settlement. Pits, associated pottery and the remains of two rectangular buildings have also been found. Evidence of intensive early farming activity has been dated to 3,900 BCE (Burnham 1995, 15). Two rows of three post-holes, probably forming a six post-hole structure, were found within the forecourt area, beneath the northern horn. These post-holes were located within two clear timber bedding trenches, and may represent an Early Neolithic shrine or, more probably, a mortuary house or platform. It has also been suggested that this may represent domestic activity (Britnell 1984, 6). The platform may have been used to expose the dead (using excarnation) prior to interment. Similar structures have been found within and underneath the forecourt areas at Fussell's Lodge[26] and Wayland's Smithy (BERKS 1).

The elongated mound, which has a double-revetment wall, is oriented E–W. Traces of a possible ancient cement were noted between the uprights and walling during the 1977–8 excavation (Britnell 1979, 132–4). Following the excavation, the A40 was widened and has extensively damaged the southern section of Gwernvale, destroying the southern horn. Although the extant elements of the monument lie in a poor state of conservation, the valley location and orientation provide the onlooker with the concept of the impact such a monument would have had on the immediate landscape.

11. Garn Goch, Llangatwg
SO 2123 1771, SM NO. BR028
County Reference Number: BRE 12

Garn Goch (also referred to as Carn Goch) is possibly the remains of a hybrid Cotswold-Severn tomb. The monument stands on a small sandy rise, 84m AOD, overlooking the River Usk and surrounding mountains to the north and east. It measures 17.4m across and 1.6m high, is oval-shaped, with its northern end oriented towards Table Mountain, a prominent truncated spur at the southern extent of the Black Mountains. The mound has recently been disturbed by tree roots and further damaged by vandalism. Grimes (1936b, 265) suggests that this site, along with Gwernvale (BRE 7) was constructed within an open landscape, sited on riverine gravels and sands.

Garn Goch was discovered accidentally in 1847 by workmen clearing stones from Llangattock Park. According to an anonymous account (Anon 1864, 148) the mound contained a 'cist' or 'cromlech' supported by four 'rude uprights' under a covering stone. Inside were human remains, some of which had 'crumbled to dust' (extracts from *Gentleman's Magazine* 1847, Part 2, 526). A humerus, maxilla (with a row of teeth) and part of the skull were, however, found intact. It appears that the bones lay within a centrally-placed chamber measuring 2.6m x 1.22m x 0.7m. Accompanying the bones was a 'quantity of fresh-looking charcoal'. The bones and six coins that came from the cairn were sent to Lord

The denuded mound of Garn Goch

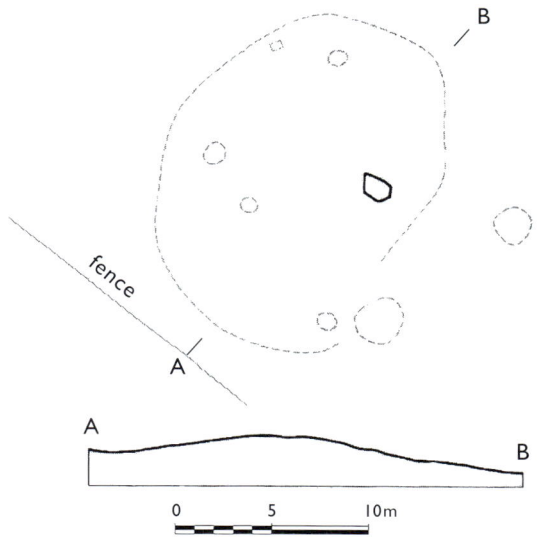

Garn Goch plan and cross-section

Northampton but have since been lost. It is believed that the coins dated to the reign of Constantine I (AD 307–37). On the north side, where the chamber was discovered, a large capstone measuring 1.6m x 1.5m is also present. Loose stones, probably originating from the cairn, lie on top of the mound.

The form of the monument is difficult to establish. Crawford, visiting in 1924 with Mortimer Wheeler, suggested it was a long cairn and typical of other Breconshire examples. Grimes (1936b) also suggested that Garn Goch was a long cairn, possibly similar in form to nearby Gwernvale. The mound is certainly oval and therefore typical of other megalithic structures in the region. Furthermore, large stones 'placed' on top of the mound delineate a simple rectangular chambered structure. Finally, many of the landscape traits attributed to Neolithic burial monuments in this region, such as topographic orientation, also apply to Garn Goch. Daniel (1950), however, argues that it is no more than a cist or round mound of Bronze Age date. I tend to concur with Crawford and Grimes, in that the denuded mound does form a long cairn and its orientation runs parallel with the River Usk.

12. Clyro Court Farm Long Barrow, Clyro
SO 2123 4313, SM NO. RD203
County Reference Number: RAD 2

Clyro Court Farm Long Barrow is located 20m south-west of the farm, on a ridge facing south-east, standing 90m AOD. The visible remains are restricted to a low mound and a few uprights, recognised as a barrow in 1973 by W.E. Griffiths; although the site has been referred to as *Carnaf* (or cairn) for at least 200 years. According to the RCAHMW (1997, 63) the area around the site has been disturbed and there is evidence at the northern end of the mound of stone dumping which has invariably and superficially changed the shape of the mound. At the north-western end of the mound are the remains of a low field bank, possibly medieval in date.

The locally quarried sandstone uprights, within the centre of the mound, delineate either a small

The chamber outline of Clyro Court Farm Long Barrow, looking west

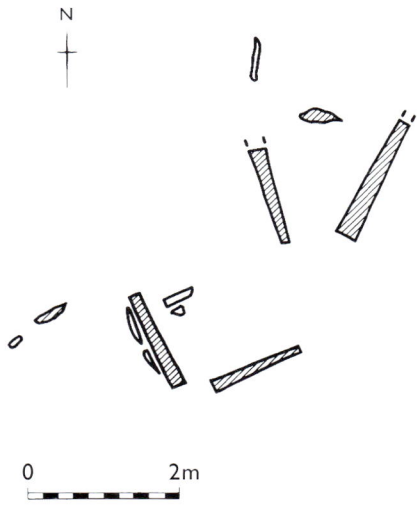

Plan of the chamber arrangement
(after RCAHMW 1997)

THE BLACK MOUNTAINS GROUP

chamber and passage or two chambers. This area measures roughly 4.4m by 2.5m and is marked by up to 12 uprights. These uprights are arranged into two chamber wall sections; the southern alignment forming a right-angled corner of a chamber, whilst the northern alignment is more difficult to discern. The two largest uprights appear to form the walls of either a chamber or, more likely, a passage that is oriented roughly north. The mound, measuring around 33m in length by 17m in width, has a maximum height of 1.1m (ibid. 63). The tomb has outstanding views across the Wye Valley, incorporating the north-western extent of the Black Mountains. In addition, Mynydd Troed, an isolated peak, can also be seen, approximately 15km SSW.

The mound is valley-oriented, being aligned SW–NE. Another long barrow several hundred metres to the south-east (SO 2159 5377), is now believed to be destroyed. In spite of their proximity, each tomb may have functioned in quite different ways from the other; similar to, say, Arthur's Stone (HRF 1) and Cross Lodge Long Barrow (HRF 4) at Dorstone. In neither case can any pattern of intervisibility be identified. The Clyro Court Farm monument is positioned in such a way that Pen yr Wyrlod (BRE 1, 3.5km) and Little Lodge Barrow (BRE 2, 4.6km) are completely hidden from the Clyro Court tomb's view. At the same time, however, the monument is positioned in full view of the south-western flanks of the Wye Valley and would have possessed intervisibility with the Bach chambered monument (HRF 5), located some 6.5km to the east.[27] Extensive lithic scatters, dating between the Mesolithic and Bronze Age, have been found within the vicinity of the monument. Also recently discovered by the landowner, were two Neolithic axes: one flint, the other polished stone (the latter probably deriving from the Penmaenmawr axe factory in North Wales).

13. Little Lodge Barrow, Aberllynfi
SO 1822 3806, SM NO. BR067
County Reference Number: BRE 2

Little Lodge Barrow stands some 340m west of Little Lodge Farm, within an old orchard. The monument, which possibly would have been intervisible with Pipton Long Cairn (BRE 8) some 2.3km due west, stands 137m AOD on a west-facing slope. The mound, which rises to a height of 1.8m, is constructed over a small platform, 56m x 22m (17m at the south end), above a tributary of the River Wye.[28] Over the recent past, the eastern side of the mound has suffered plough damage, and stone has been robbed for use elsewhere. According to Grimes, this monument had been heavily denuded by quarrying, the result of which has almost completely obliterated part of the cairn (Grimes 1936b, 270). In addition, parts of the mound and chambers have been severely disturbed by hawthorn roots.

Excavated in 1929 by C.E. Vulliamy, the monument contained unburnt human bone and charcoal flecks, and the remains of red deer,[29] sheep and cattle (1929).[30] The human bone was thought to represent five adult males, an elderly female and perhaps three children.

Little Lodge Barrow with its faint cairn mound

The stone outline of the main chamber

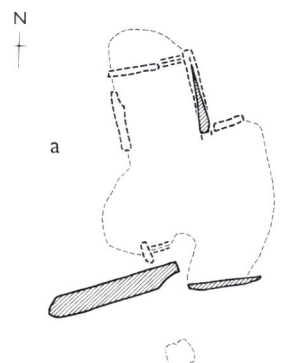

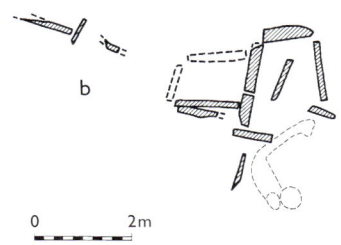

Plan of the chamber arrangement (after RCAHMW 1997)

However, a re-evaluation suggests four adults and one youth (all male).[31] A single red deer molar, apparently notched, was also re-examined. These remains were all found in a chamber complex just south of the centre of the mound.

The mound is oriented roughly N–S, with two or perhaps three chambers present: a simple chamber at the southern end; the remains of a lateral chamber opening out to the west, and a possible third chamber indicated by a single upright at the northern end. The southern chamber consists of 12 uprights. This confused area of the site was planned by Vulliamy but in not great detail. It would appear that a passage exists on the south-western side of the mound, suggesting that the chambers are side-transepted types. Interestingly, if this is the case, all the ritual activity of the monument orientates up-slope towards the prominent spur of Hay Bluff. Similar landscape affinities are recorded elsewhere within the group.

The mound appears to be typical of the Cotswold-Severn classification, with a possible horned forecourt to the northern section. The chambers may have been entered from passages on the western side of the mound, suggesting a false portal or entrance at the northern end, similar in architectural detail to Arthur's Stone (HRF 1) and Pipton Long Cairn (BRE 8). Both chamber and passage would have had extensive views across the Wye Valley. Vulliamy's hurried excavation failed to establish a clear architectural form, as he was probably interested only in the contents of the chambers; however, the external architectural detail may survive on the western side of the mound, which is protected by a hedge. In and around the site are a number of large stones, which may represent the remains of further chambers, especially within the northern section of the monument.

14. Arthur's Stone, Dorstone
SO 31885 43127, EHL NO. 1914
County Reference Number: HRF 1

This impressive barrow is one of the most notable of all prehistoric monuments along the Welsh border. However, it is also a monument that has received only superficial investigation and discussion, and was, up until 2005/6, unexcavated (Nash 2008). The site, however, has been extensively surveyed and discussed (Daniel 1950; Darvill 1982; Grimes 1936b; Hemp 1935a; HWCC 1981; Stanford 1990; Children & Nash 1994; Nash 1997, 2000; Olding 2000; Sant 2000; Watkins 1928). Fortunately, antiquarian interest has been limited to periodic site visits.

This monument, once referred to as *Artil's Stone*, is first described by Nathaniel Salmon in his *A New Survey of England* (1728–9). Comments by Salmon suggest the monument had changed little in appearance over the past 200 years. According to Crawford (1925, 147), the northern edge of Arthur's Stone Lane (which runs past the monument), forms part of the parish boundary between Dorstone and Bredwardine. The lane, which runs along the spine of Arthur's Stone ridge – from Merbach Hill to Dorstone Hill – is believed to be of ancient origin. During the recent past, the monument was probably used to delineate part of this recognised boundary.

Set within an oval mound (approximately 26m x 17m), the monument has nine upright stones forming a polygonal chamber, an unorthodox right-angled passage and an enormous capstone, estimated to weigh more than 25 tons (Corcoran 1969, 23). Hemp (1935b, 288) describes the chamber as kite-shaped, approximating the form of the capstone. The chamber is regarded by Daniel (1950, 74) as being laterally sited. Several metres south of the capstone and chamber is a large upright sandstone slab which, it is claimed, has as many as 12 large finger-dint cupmarks on the inner face; which, if so, probably date from the Bronze Age (Crawford 1925, 147; Daniel 1950, 118). Also present, and highly visible on the upper part of the stone, are a series of graffiti marks with clear dates, one of 1912. It is believed that this stone represents part of an antechamber (Daniel 1950); however, a recent hypothesis suggests that this architectural element is actually the inner section of a façade with a false portal stone and the remnant earthwork comprising two horns (Nash 2000, 2008).

The Old Red Sandstone capstone (measuring approximately 5.8m. x 3m.) is split into three pieces (as a result of weathering processes) and is oriented NE–SW, with the south-western end pointing towards the southern section of the Golden Valley. A large section of the capstone has also split horizontally, with an enormous fragment collapsing into the central chamber.

The western section of the chamber and the remains of a false portal area, looking east

The chamber has, at its western end, a false portal stone (partly blocking the doorway to the main chamber) and an inner passage that is oriented north. However, the passage changes direction to the north-west, pointing towards the impressive Hay Bluff and the northern extent of the Black Mountains (Children & Nash 1994, 26; Tilley 1994, 140).

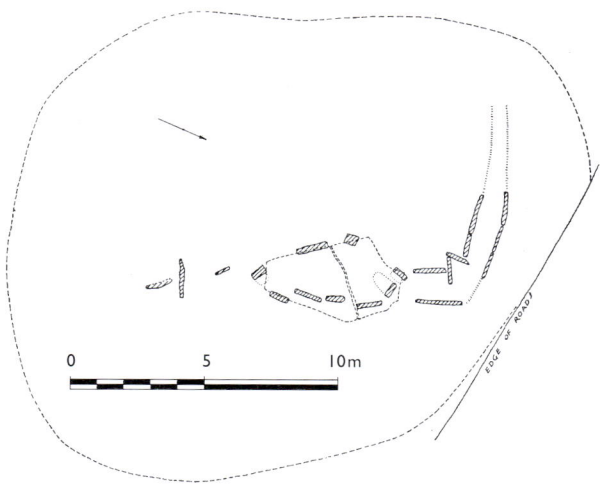

Plan showing the chamber and passage uprights, and the extent of the mound (after Watkins 1928)

Arthur's Stone, with its complex passage that leads to a large chamber, looking south-west

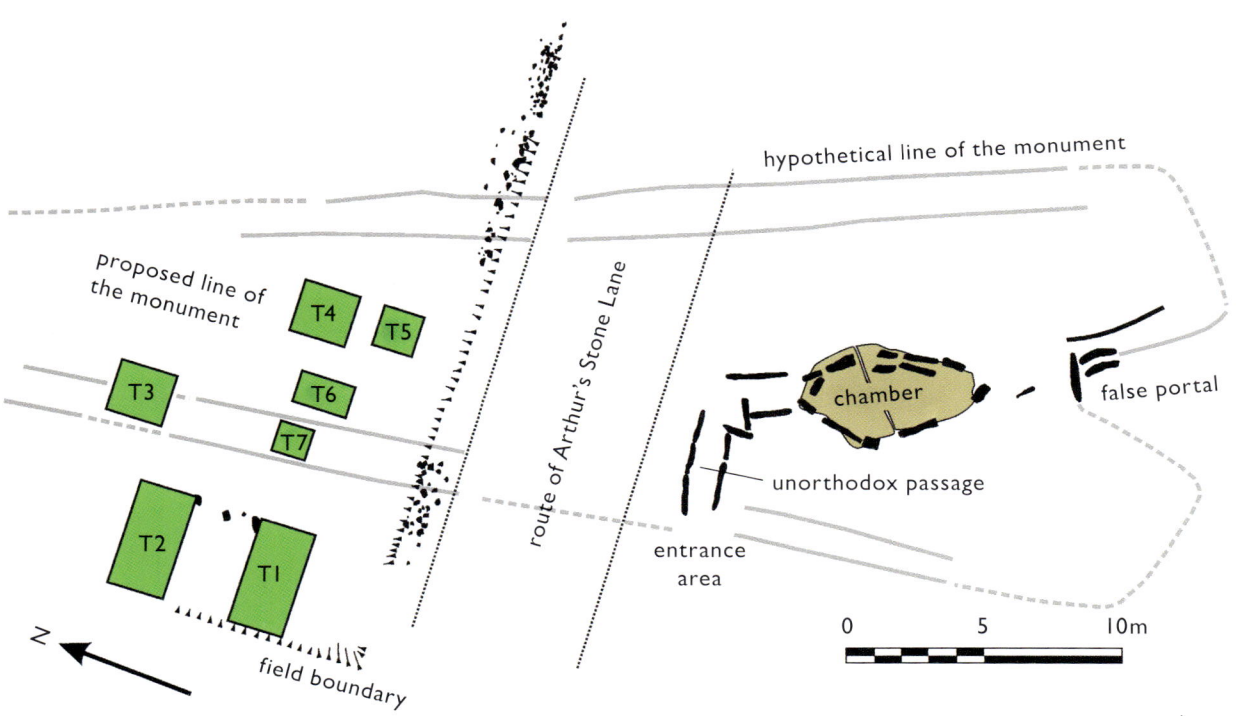

Plan of the extent areas of Arthur's Stone, overlaid with the outline of the Gwernvale Monument (Nash 2008)

THE BLACK MOUNTAINS GROUP   67

Crawford (1925, 147) has suggested that the chambers of Arthur's Stone and Gwernvale (near Crickhowell) are similar, although the former is much larger. The unorthodox redirection of the passage and the orientation of the capstone suggest that Arthur's Stone may have been positioned deliberately so as to completely encompass the visual aspect of the Black Mountains. The tomb also incorporates views from both the southern and northern extents of the Golden Valley (Nash 1997, 20). Many other tombs within the Wye, Lynfi and Usk valleys (in Powys) appear to be similarly positioned (Children & Nash 1994; Olding 2000). However, it is more than likely that what we are witnessing here is the presence of a western side chamber that is orientated in such a way as to be conveniently pointing to the northern extent of the mountains. Here, the tomb builders are merely replicating a Cotswold-Severn blueprint that includes side chambers, and not a deliberate requirement to orientate a side chamber to a particular focal point within the landscape.

Members of the Woolhope Naturalists' Field Club, visiting the site in July 1872, remarked that a series of stones laid out in a circular fashion surrounded the monument. These may represent the outer kerbing, or what eighteenth- and nineteenth-century antiquarians referred to as 'a peristalith alignment', enclosing the mound. However, there was no sign of any kerbing by 1928 (Watkins 1928, 150). An alternative view, and one that I support, suggests Arthur's Stone may have been trapezoidal in form, or at least elongated, and that the monument extended across the lane, with the present passage on the side of the monument, forming the remains of a Cotswold-Severn type monument.[32] The actual forecourt area (with false portal) would have been located in the south-east and is represented by the upright which is recognised as being an antechamber. Within fields north of the lane is a large selection of stones that cannot be considered as naturally occurring rock outcropping. Excavations by the author in 2005/6 revealed that these stones, along with a distinct stone spread, represent a cairn deposit that formed the rear section of the Arthur's Stone monument. The excavation of five of the seven test pits (T3 to T7) revealed clear evidence of a distinct, shallow cairn spread (Nash 2008, 8–12). Unfortunately, no organic material for dating was forthcoming.

The destruction of this part of the monument must have occurred prior to the early eighteenth century. Accounts by Nathaniel Salmon suggest Arthur's Stone was as it is today, although later witnesses remark that the site was being robbed of its stone for building (cf. Crawford 1925). Furthermore, discernible monuments such as Arthur's Stone, with its folklore and local superstition, would have suffered destruction, especially during the post-medieval period. In support of this, it would seem unlikely that Arthur's Stone was the only distinct oval mound within this group (except for the first architectural phase at Ty Isaf, near Talgarth). The other 18 monuments within the Black Mountains Group appear to use the long (or at least oval) mound as a blueprint. Those adopting the hybrid trapezoidal plan, including Gwernvale (BRE 7), Penywyrlod (BRE 14), Pipton Long Cairn (BRE 8) and Ty Isaf (BRE 5), are probably later monuments that have been specifically designed and built, but essentially developed from the long mound/oval principle.

In 2011, Headland Archaeology (report by Boucher & Rouse, commissioned by English Heritage) excavated seven test pits which would eventually house timber posts that currently form a protective timber fence that surrounds the earthwork of the mound. The test pit programme exposed disturbed and undisturbed sections of the cairn that formed the north and west sides of a former mound. Of particular interest was Post Hole No. 32 which revealed a clear wall section that extended to a depth of 0.50m below the existing ground level. Prior to excavation, the Headland Archaeology team undertook a detailed earthworks and geophysical survey of the monument area, south of Arthur's Stone Lane.

The 2022 and 2023 excavations undertaken by the Universities of Cardiff and Manchester and Herefordshire Archaeology were concentrated in the south and west sections of the monument. The interim reports suggest that an avenue was present at the southern end and would have terminated within or around the façade area where the false portal is present. At the time of the publication of this book, Keith Ray and Julian Thomas had turned their attention to excavating an area around the side entrance area that leads to the chamber and the rear section of the monument, where I conducted excavations in 2005/6 (the results of this work to be published in due course).

Drawing in the landscape

Arthur's Stone is one of the most northerly chambered tombs of the Cotswold-Severn Group, and is one of five tombs that dominate the Neolithic landscape of the northern reaches of the Golden Valley (Children & Nash 1994; Darvill 1982; Nash 1997). Other monuments within the group lie further south and west, and occupy the hinterlands of the western reaches of the Black Mountains.

Arthur's Stone shares a landscape affinity with many other Neolithic monuments, both within the Black Mountains Group and elsewhere. The monument stands on the western ridge of Merbach Hill and has clear, uninterrupted views across the northern, western and southern extents of the Golden Valley, across Cefn Hill and to the eastern slopes of the Black Mountains, from Hay-on-Wye to Pandy – a total distance of about 40km. To the east of the site, views are restricted to the nearby eastern ridge of Merbach Hill, some 300m away. Interestingly, there is no further substantial archaeological evidence for Neolithic activity, in the form of lithic scatters and monuments, further east (Children & Nash 1994). This would suggest that such activity is confined to the area within sight of the Black Mountains and the Golden Valley. A similar distribution of lithics and monuments is found along the lower Usk and Wye Valleys.

The relationship between Arthur's Stone and the immediate landscape, together with the spatial organisation of the tomb, suggests that its builders clearly understood how certain parts of the monument should be constructed and sited. Standing at around 274m AOD, views from outside the small forecourt area into the entrance and outer passage are uninterrupted. However, views into the inner passage and chamber are restricted due to the 90° bend halfway along the passage. Likewise, restricted visuality is in operation when viewing the outer passage and entrance from the chamber. It is as if a conscious attempt was being made to separate human space, the realm of order and control, from the outside world, from nature. The transition between the two is achieved precisely at that point, equidistant between chamber and entrance, where the passage abruptly changes direction. It is here that culture meets nature and social order. However, this is only part of the meaning behind the monument's construction. The redirection of the passage and the orientation of the capstone suggest Arthur's Stone may have played a key role in the socio-symbolic process of territory formation. The monument was probably constructed to visually encompass the entire length of the Black Mountains. In this way, the mountains were incorporated into the social and symbolic identity of the Neolithic settlers, helping to create a sense of belonging. Other tombs in the Wye and Usk valleys interact with the landscape in a similar way.

Like many other chambered burial monuments of this date, Arthur's Stone is not on the highest point within the immediate landscape but slightly away from Merbach Hill's summit (Nash 1997, 20). It could be argued that there is a clear attempt to control the surrounding landscape from the monument. However, the monument cannot be seen from any part of the Golden Valley. I would suggest that a form of restricted visual access was in operation, such that only certain members of the community would be allowed to see the monument, and then perhaps only periodically. If this was the case, then Neolithic communities could have been stratified on at least three levels. Those occupying the first, lower level would have had no visual access to the monument. The second tier may have been allowed visual access, but only to the outside (maybe around the façade and entrance area), while the third level were able to access the inside of the monument to bury the dead and perform ritual activities, probably associated with death, fertility and political and social consolidation. This could have been further complicated by the way in which the monument was planned and constructed.

Areas for the living

Located between nearby Cross Lodge Long Barrow (HRF 4) and Arthur's Stone is the Dorstone Hill settlement (SO 326 423) which was first excavated between 1965 and 1972 by Chistopher Houlder and Roger Pye, and later, teams from Herefordshire Archaeology and Manchester University between 2015 and 2019 (Ray and Thomas 2020). This rare example of a Neolithic settlement yielded from the Houlder and Pye excavation over 4,000 lithics, including more than 30 arrowheads and 60 polished stone axe fragments (HWCC 1981; Children & Nash 1994, 17). Based on high concentrations of flint, another possible settlement site may be present on nearby Cefn Hill at Abbey Farm, Craswall (Gavin-Robinson 1934).

Arthur's Stone and other chambered monuments in the area appear to represent, in part, a continuous human presence since at least the Late Mesolithic (6,000–3,500 BCE). Diagnostic lithics, in particular microliths, have been found beneath and around Arthur's Stone (Brown 1963, 76–91; Children & Nash 1994, 25; Gavin-Robinson 1934; Tilley 1994, 118). So, even during the Neolithic, Arthur's Stone would have possessed a history and, more importantly, an affinity with its ancestors. It should also be highlighted that diagnostic lithics dating to the Bronze Age have also been found along the west-facing slopes of Arthur's Stone ridge, including several barbed and tanged arrowheads (Brown 1963, 80). The continuous use of Neolithic sites is not uncommon, for example, Gwernvale, north of Crickhowell, where Upper Palaeolithic and Mesolithic flint assemblages have been found beneath the southern section of the forecourt area (Healey & Green 1984, 129–30). Similarly, along the western reaches of Merbach Hill to the south (along Arthur's Stone ridge to Vowchurch Common), a large number of lithic scatters have been found, which date to the Late Mesolithic (Brown 1963; Gavin-Robinson 1934). These sites may represent only a fraction of the total number of hunter/fisher/gatherer sites that once existed in this area.

Social complexity can be especially seen with the passage arrangement. Of the 12 Old Red Sandstone slabs recently recorded by the author (and previously by Grimes 1936a), eight large stones construct the walls of the passage. Stone 10 can be interpreted as a door-stone, similar to door-stones found at Parc-le-Breos-Cwm on the Gower Coast (GLA 4) and Ty

Isaf, near Talgarth (BRE 5). The upright stones would have supported a series of small capstones, thus enclosing the passage. What has been noticed within this arrangement is that the passage appears to be constructed in order to restrict visual access between the outside and the chamber. The door-stone blocks visual access from the entrance/forecourt to the chamber and vice versa. Further restricted visual access is also present in the way in which the passage stones are arranged. Between the entrance and the chamber, each of the stones appears to gain height. Between the door-stone and the chamber an individual can crouch through the upper section of the passage and then into the chamber. As well as witnessing a gradual rise within the passage roofing, the uprights appear to widen as one moves through the passage. A similar architectural trait occurs within the passage grave tradition in Wales, Ireland, central southern Sweden and Denmark (Children & Nash 1997; Tilley 1993). It could be the case that the passage acts as a boundary between life (outside the monument) and death (inside the chamber), creating a liminal space or a rite of passage – similar to the spatial divisions inside a Christian church.

I have suggested in previous research (1997) that Arthur's Stone, along with other monuments within the Black Mountains Group, utilises both organic and inorganic architecture in its construction; monuments that have chamber and passage stones (inorganic) which were also once covered by a mound (organic). Recently, the siting of monuments has been interpreted fundamentally as a form of statementing the landscape; turning a space into a place (Bradley 1993; 1998). Both ritual and socio-political knowledge make this place special. In part, this is fair comment. However, I would stress that Arthur's Stone, with its covering mound, was hidden away, organic and incognito with its surroundings.

15. Cross Lodge Long Barrow, Dorstone
SO 33247 41697, EHL NO: 106126
County Reference Number: HRF 4

This monument, also known as Great Llanafon Farm, is classified as a long mound (Powell et al. 1969) and stands at around 180m AOD. Cross Lodge Long Barrow is built on a west-facing slope, approximately 300m from Llanafon Farm. To the south-west of Cross Lodge Long Barrow is the River Dore which flows SSE. Three large ash trees mark the location of the monument. The northern section of the mound has been damaged by ploughing, with some of the stones littering the field. This material may once have formed part of the tomb structure, perhaps as cairn material or even kerbing. Possibly much larger during the Neolithic, the elongated oval mound currently measures approximately 18m x 10m x 3.5m in height, and is locally oriented (NW–SE) to the direction of the Golden Valley. Like Arthur's Stone (HRF 1), the monument also appears to visually encompass the Black Mountains. Currently, on top of the barrow are two large stones which may be the remnants of the architecture.

Cross Lodge Long Barrow, looking south

Northerly view of the Cross Lodge Long Barrow

The site was designated a Scheduled Monument in 1954, and was described by archaeologist R.S.G. Robinson following reports that the landowner (Mr Jones) had attempted to level the site in order to fill in a nearby hollow. In 1952, a trial excavation was due to take place but was never undertaken.

Either side of the monument, along the west-facing ridge, are extensive Neolithic lithic scatters. On Vowchurch Common, some 4.5km to the south-east, are up to eight separate lithic scatters which have been found to date between the Mesolithic and Bronze Age. Along the same ridge to the north-west, a total of seven Mesolithic and Neolithic lithic scatters are present. Furthermore, later prehistoric lithic scatters are found to the west of the monument on nearby Cefn Hill.[33]

During the Neolithic, Cross Lodge Long Barrow would have been visible from the valley floor and also from the large settlement of Dorstone Hill (SO 3260 4230), approximately 1km to the north. The settlement site lies between Arthur's Stone and Cross Lodge Long Barrow, and was discovered during the 1960s. The positioning of settlement and monuments on either side appears to be a deliberate act.

Arthur's Stone and Cross Lodge Long Barrow differ architecturally, suggesting that one predates the other. Arthur's Stone is probably the earliest of the two as a small Mesolithic flint assemblage has been found, suggesting the site was already in use at the beginning of the Neolithic. The different architectural styles may, however, indicate different meanings. Cross Lodge Long Barrow is aligned with the valley, whereas Arthur's Stone may represent a valley-end territorial marker. More time and effort would have been needed to erect Arthur's Stone, judging by the size and weight of the uprights and capstone. Obviously, construction time would depend on the availability of suitable sandstone and the labour needed to transport these blocks across the landscape. In addition, the stone architecture of Cross Lodge Barrow remains unknown. One would assume that traits associated with the Cotswold-Severn monument group await discovery.

16. Dunseal Long Barrow, Dunseal
SO 39117 33845, EHL NO. 27502
County Reference Number: HRF 6

The mound at Dunseal (near the hamlet of Kerry's Gate) – intact and unexcavated – stands on a narrow ridge in the corner of a small field at around 175m AOD and was designated a Scheduled Monument in 1996. From this monument, are outstanding views that open out over the lower part of the Golden Valley and Black Mountains to the west. To the south and west of this monument is the River Dore which flows in a SSE direction. Within the vicinity of the monument are a number of Neolithic and Bronze Age lithic scatters; and approximately 4km to the NNW is an intense series of lithic scatters that date between the Mesolithic and Neolithic. Interestingly, and in common with other monuments within the

The unexcavated Dunseal monument, looking south-east

area, very little Neolithic activity is found to the east of the monument. All monuments and lithic scatters are concentrated on the west-facing slopes that overlook the Black Mountains.

The date of construction and use of the site remains a mystery, although the Scheduling description describes the mound as a bowl barrow – a monument type that is extremely uncommon in this part of the British Isles. The few surface finds (from ploughing) suggest a Neolithic and/ or Early Bronze Age date. The current mound measures approximately 27m x 14m, and 2m in height, suggesting a long mound-type monument. The mound may once have been circular, pointing towards a two-phase (or more) monument. Its location, high on a west-facing ridge with panoramic views, especially to the south and west, suggests strongly that Dunseal is a Neolithic long barrow, rather than as a bowl barrow (as per the Scheduling description). My interpretation of this site is further supported by the dimensions of the monument, a site visit and LiDAR evidence.

This monument and the location of the nearby Parkwood chambered tomb (SO 356 334; now possibly destroyed) mark the southern extent of Neolithic activity in the Golden Valley and the south-eastern extent of the Black Mountains Group.[34]

The first farmers appear to have used this and other monuments within the group to define a territory, controlling the landscape and, in the process, establishing an identity (e.g. Renfrew 1976). In this case, the landscape that includes the lower southern sections of the Dore and Ecscley, Olchon Valleys (forming the south-east hinterlands of the Black Mountains) and the Grey Valley to the south-east would have been ideal locations for Neolithic burial-ritual activity. In fact, Dunseal and other suspected monuments nearby close the circle with extant monuments that occupy the Welsh and north-eastern Herefordshire hinterlands, such as Arthur's Stone and Cross Lodge Long Barrow to the north with Garn Goch to the west.

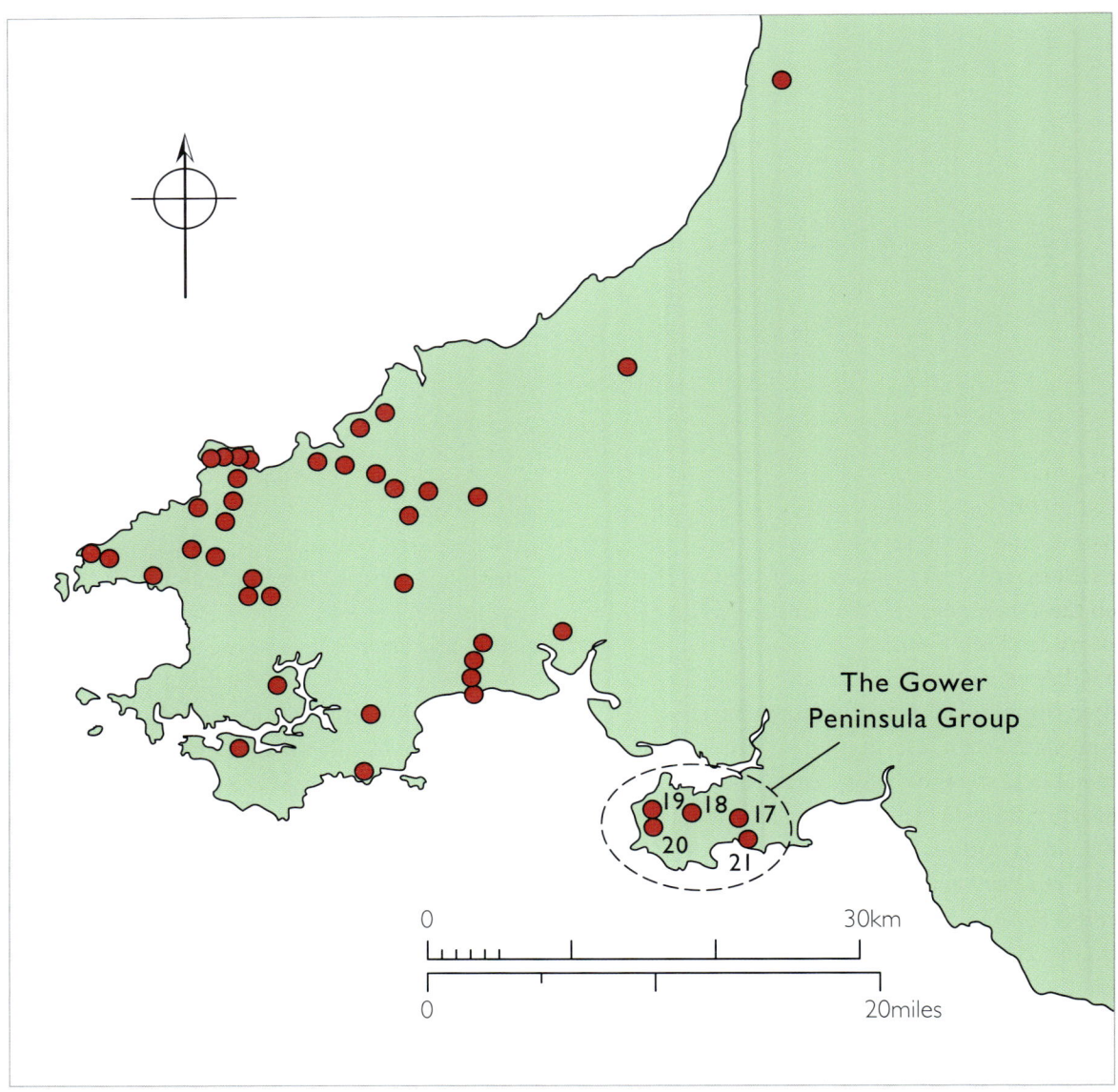

17 Parc-le-Breos-Cwm
18 Maen Ceti
19 Sweyne's Howes North
20 Sweyne's Howes South
21 Penmaen Burrows

THREE

The Gower Peninsula Group

This group, referred to by T.G.E. Powell (1969, 17) as 'the south-eastern Wales Coastal Group', consists of up to seven monuments, five of which are discussed in this inventory. Two monuments that are not on the Gower Coast but included within Powell's inventory are Tinkinswood (GLA 9) and Maes y Felin (GLA 10); both are included in the next chapter. Omitted from this inventory is the chambered long cairn at Nicholaston (GLA 11, SS 5075 8881) and the uncertain long mound at Upper Killay (GLA 12, SS 5848 9227). Monument distribution is concentrated in three areas: Rhossili Down, the central upland area of Cefn Bryn and the southern coastal area of Penmaen. Unlike the core areas of the Black Mountains Group and South-west Wales there are no geographical sub-groups recognised.

All monuments from this area possess very different architecture, varying from the classic hybrid Cotswold-Severn form of Parc-le-Breos-Cwm (GLA 4) to the large capstone dolmen of Maen Ceti (Arthur's Stone, GLA 3). The landscape setting for each monument is also very different. Maen Ceti dominates Cefn Bryn and, unlike many other monuments on the Gower, has extensive views. Sites such as Parc-le-Breos-Cwm and the Nicholaston monument are hidden away on or within secluded valleys, while the Penmean Burrows monument (GLA 5) was until recently hidden within a dune system overlooking Pennard Pill.

Judging by the different architecture of the monuments on the Gower, it is highly likely that they were constructed and used at different points in time during the Neolithic. However, the Maen Ceti and Sweyne's Howes monuments (GLA 1 and GLA 2) and possibly the Penmaen Burrows monument may have been in use at the same time. Each has a series of uprights supporting a large capstone to form a chamber. The Parc-le-Breos-Cwm monument and possibly Nicholaston are contemporary in construction and use. The now shapeless mound of the Nicholaston monument revealed a central chamber that may be of a similar hybrid shape and construction to the Parc-le-Breos-Cwm monument. If this is the case, both date from the Early to Late Neolithic transition, around 3,000 BCE.

The majority of the Neolithic sites on the Gower coast have within their view a large number of Late Neolithic/Early Bronze Age and Bronze Age monuments, including standing stones, ring-cairns and circles (RCAHMW 1976, 43–120). The cairns, ring-cairns and stone circles lie on the ridges of these upland areas.

To the east of the Gower Coast and located in an undulating landscape, are the truly megalithic monuments of Tinkinswood and Maes y Felin. Both stand less than one kilometre apart and represent Cotswold-Severn monuments, each possessing simple terminal chambers which are set within long mounds. Excavation has shown that the Tinkinswood monument has a distinct trapezoidal mound, similar to that of Parc-le-Breos-Cwm. It should be noted that other monuments located on the Gower Coast also possess terminal mounds which may once have been trapezoidal in plan, such as the two Sweyne's Howes monuments; however, many of these are now denuded, due to the rigours of time.

17. Parc-le-Breos-Cwm, Penmaen
SS 5372 8983, SM NO. GM122
County Reference Number: GLA 4

Parc-le-Breos-Cwm (also known as Giant's Grave) is one of only a handful of tombs in Wales that have been excavated by antiquarians in the nineteenth century, and subsequently by archaeologists in the twentieth century, followed by restoration. The monument, standing at around 31m AOD, is located on the floor of a hidden, narrow, dry limestone valley with no visual access to the sea, approximately 2km to the south. The drystone walling that forms the skin of the monument visually dominates both the valley floor and the surrounding limestone hillside. The landscape potential, however, is limited, with visual access from the south only. Similarly, Ty Isaf (BRE 5), another Cotswold-Severn hybrid, is set within a small, isolated valley and also appears to be deliberately hidden. A series of freshwater springs are located a few metres south of the monument, that flow into Pennard Pill. Approximately 1.8km to the SSW is the Penmean Burrows monument (GLA 5).

Parc-le-Breos-Cwm, although thought until 1937 to be enclosed within a circular barrow, is in fact trapezoidal in form and resembles a number of Cotswold-Severn tombs found in Gloucestershire and Oxfordshire, such as Belas Knap (GLOU 1) and Notsgrove (GLOU 4). The site was discovered and excavated in 1869, after the northern part of the cairn had been used as a quarry for road construction. The following year the southern end of the monument was excavated by John Lubbock and Lord Swansea. A funnel-shaped forecourt, passage (gallery) and four side-chambers were revealed. The opinion for

The façade entrance of Parc-le-Breos-Cwm, looking northwards towards the upper part of a dry valley

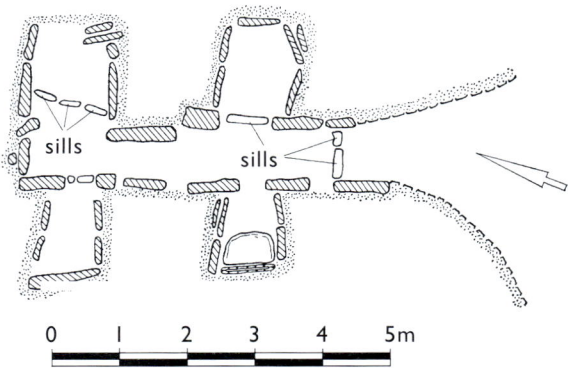

Parc-le-Breos-Cwm passage and chamber arrangement (after Daniel 1950)

many years was that this layout represented a gallery grave with 'two pairs of transepts' (Daniel 1950, 210). At least 24 skeletons that were 'much broken and in no regular arrangement' were also found. However, Lord Swansea wrote:

> Each set of bones was found in a small, confused mass, just as would be if a body in a sitting position had collapsed, as it were, vertically within its own area, (1887, 198).

The bone piles, although overlying each other, suggest that a crouched-burial tradition prevailed. The bones found represent three children aged 8–10 years old, and at least 19 adults, both male and female, aged between 25 and 45 years. Two other skeletons were aged over 45. The human remains from this monument suggest that this may have been a corporate monument serving the community as a whole, rather than special individuals within it; although the interred may represent a dynasty that used the monument over a long period of time. Some of the human remains, originally found in the NW and SW chambers, were radiocarbon-dated by Whittle and Wysocki (1998), with a date range of between 3,705±55 bp (OxA-6495) and 4,875±55 bp (OxA-6491). The bones of a badger and large undulate, possibly an auroch found in the passage area, possessed much earlier dates of 7,665±65 bp (OxA-6499) and 10,625±80 bp (OxA-6500) respectively (see Appendix 2). Also recovered from the first excavation was a small assemblage of pottery, including two rim sherds of Western-style pottery.

The second excavation, undertaken by R.J.C. Atkinson in 1960, showed that the cairn at the southern end of the monument was constructed of limestone rubble (Atkinson 1961). The passage, measuring 5.25m in length, and the chamber walls were made of locally quarried limestone slabs and

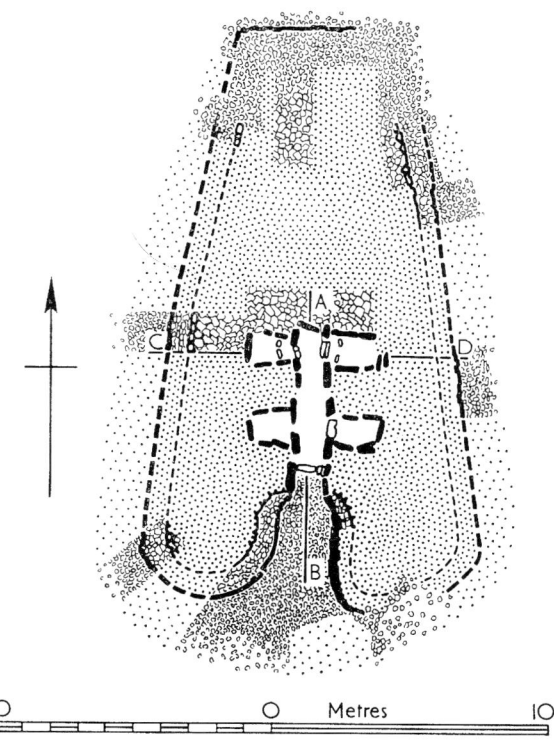

Plan of the Parc-le-Breos-Cwm site showing excavated areas in 1960 (after Atkinson 1961)

drystone walling. Between the two horns, a deep, funnel-shaped forecourt led to a small passage (oriented SSE–NNW). Both horns and inner forecourt were of rough drystone walling. Unlike other hybrid tombs of this size and form, Parc-le-Breos-Cwm had no false portal and may form part of a sub-group that includes Tinkinswood (GLA 9) and Maes y Felin (GLA 10). Instead, an entrance leading to a passage and four side-chambers was revealed. At the entrance, a low sill-stone formed the threshold. Three of the four rectangular chambers have sill-stones of a similar size, each measuring around 0.9m x 0.9m. Interestingly, many monuments of the type possess polygonal rather than rectangular chambers,

The door sill (threshold) into the realm of the dead at Parc-le-Breos-Cwm

Two of the five distinct rectangular chambers of Parc-le-Breos-Cwm

18. Maen Ceti, Llanrhidian
SS 4913 9055, SM NO. GM167
County Reference Number: GLA 3

Maen Ceti, also known as Arthur's Stone, Cefn Bryn and Coetan Arthur, is located 147m AOD on the northern slopes of Cefn Bryn, a central upland area extending along the spine of the Gower Peninsula (from Rhosilli Down in the west and the western outskirts of Swansea in the east). The site is not on the highest point within the landscape but is in full view of the Bristol Channel and Afon Llwchwr (River Loughor) inlet. To the west, located on the same ridge are two cairns which are Bronze Age in date. The RCHMW record up to 14 cairns/barrows and ring-cairns along the Cefn Bryn ridge (1976, 50–1). It is conceivable that the Bronze Age cairn builders acknowledged the presence of Maen Ceti.

This monument, classified by the RCHMW as a double-chambered megalithic tomb, is one of a handful in Wales that have never been fully

such as Notgrove (GLOU 4) in Gloucestershire, but a similar sill arrangement is found at Hetty Pegler's Tump (GLOU 14) and Nympsfield (BERKS 1). The chamber floors may have been cobbled (Daniel 1950, 35). Evidence for the capstone (or capstones), which may have measured up to 7m x 5m, has long since disappeared.

In the 1960 excavation, finds included several pieces of undecorated Neolithic pottery, described by Lynch (1969b, 171) as hard, clinker-like and possibly influenced by Abingdon and Ebbsfleet wares (Corcoran 1969, 102). Similar pottery has been recovered from Ty-Isaf and a number of other Welsh tombs (Peterson 2003).

As part of the final phase of the monument, the entrance, forecourt and external limit of the outer cairn were filled in with limestone blocking material. This probably occurred during the Late Neolithic/Early Bronze Age when the cairn appears to have been finally abandoned (this was not uncommon with other trapezoidal monuments in Wales and western Britain).

The capstone, surrounding cairn and mound of Maen Ceti, looking north

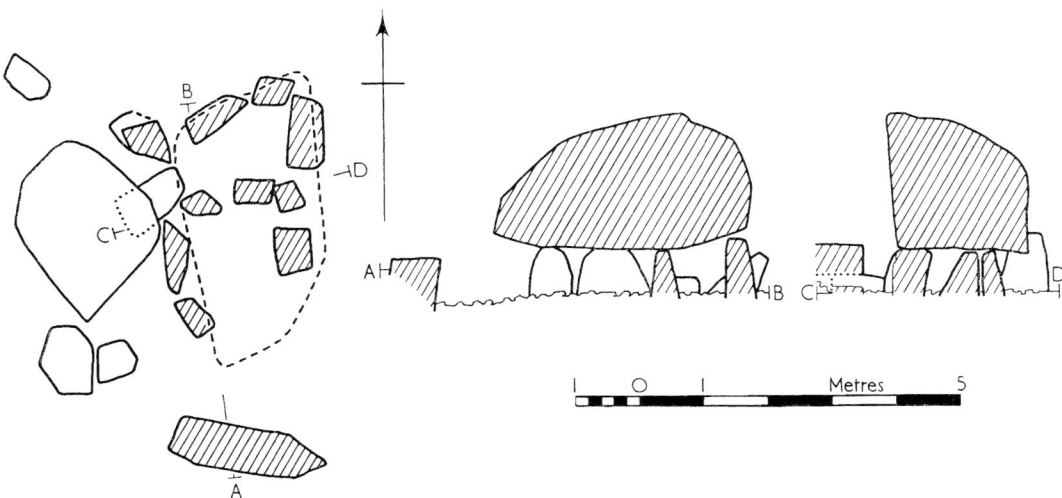

Plan and section of the architecture of Maen Ceti (after RCAHMW 1976)

investigated (1976, 31; Rutter 1949). The capstone – described as an unshaped glacial boulder (Castlelden 1992, 382) – is estimated to weigh between 30 and 35 tons, originally measuring 4m in length by 3m in width and 2.25m in thickness. A large angular slab, partially submerged in a hollow at the southern side, may have broken off from the capstone, possibly leading to the abandonment of construction (ibid. 382). The monument may, therefore, be unfinished. The RCHMW (1976, 31) suggests that the capstone derives from a nearby source, being made from local conglomerate and containing quartz.

Observations made by the author suggest the monument is set within a circular cairn, with the northern chamber being covered by this massive capstone. The chamber measures 1m x 1.8m and is delineated by four uprights. Between this chamber and the southern chamber are a further three angular uprights which separate both chambers.

Immediately west of both chambers are a number of large stones that probably once formed various sections of the chamber architecture, including a misplaced capstone measuring 2.2m x 3m. The uprights and surrounding cairn appear to be set in a hollow, which may have provided some of the cairn material. The hollow is around 15m in diameter and infilled with loose cairn, and is usually seasonally water-logged. The depth of the hollow is unknown although the bedrock may lie close to the present surface. Further remains of the chamber could, however, exist. The extent of the cairn that once covered the chamber architecture is circular in shape and measures approximately 23m in diameter (RCHMW 1976, 31). It has been suggested that the cairn would have covered the capstone that stands around 3m above the existing ground level (ibid. 31). However, the upper section of the capstone appears to be more weathered than the lower section, thus suggesting that the upper section may have been exposed during its use.

Corcoran (1969, 17) suggests that only one simple chamber is present. The southern chamber, forming the larger of the two chambers and measuring 1.2m x 2.3m, is rectangular in shape. This chamber is delineated by six uprights, five of which support the massive capstone. The southern extent of the chamber is open and probably has up to three uprights missing – presently forming a gap of around 1.2m. This gap may have formed a doorway into the chamber.

The capstone appears to have been raised during the sixteenth century and is quoted by the *Myvyrian Archaeology of Wales* (1870) as 'one of three mighty achievements of the Isle of Britain'. In 1695, Edward Lhuyd, who uses the English name of Arthur's Stone, noted that the site was used by 'the common people' as it stands on common land and was (and is) accessible to anyone.

The chamber section of Sweyne's Howes North

19. Sweyne's Howes North, Rhossili
SS 4211 8991, SM NO. GM027
County Reference Number: GLA 1

The Sweyne's Howes North monument, located about 140m AOD on the eastern slopes of Rhossili Down, is set within an open heath landscape. Neighbouring Sweyne's Howes South (GLA 2) appears to have once been oval in form and built of local sandstone conglomerate (RCHMW 1976, 30). Each monument, however, has been robbed and heavily disturbed, leaving an extensive cairn rubble spread around the remains of both chambered monuments.

According to Wendy Hughes (1999, 35), the name *Sweyne* derives from a legendary Viking warrior; the word *Howe*, meaning *mound*, has Norse origins. Legend has it that Sweyne is buried here. However, place-name evidence suggests that the name actually means 'swine's houses', coined because of its (Sweyne's Howes North's) similarities with a pigsty.

This northern monument is roughly similar in size to its southern neighbour, measuring 18.3m x 13.1m with a cairn height of 0.6m. This monument also has two possible phases of construction: an inner and outer cairn. A much-denuded rectangular

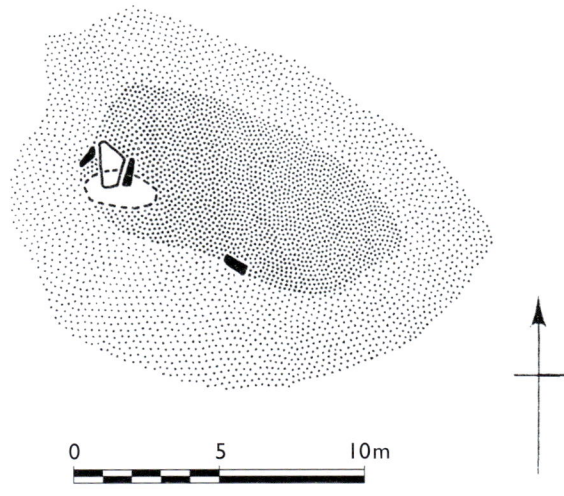

Plan of Sweyne's Howes North's chamber and mound (after RCAHMW 1976)

chamber, measuring 1.1m x 2m, is located on the north-west side of the monument, and consists of three uprights which are partially covered by a small capstone. The uprights measure 1.3m in height. Within the chamber area are a number of loose stones that may have once formed cairns.

The site, along with its Neolithic neighbour, was surveyed in detail by the Clifton Antiquarian Club in 2007 (Nash et al. 2007). The results revealed the two Sweyne's Howes' monuments occupy a distinct part of the Rhossili Down landscape that faces inland. Associated with both monuments were several possible standing stones that are found c.250m to the south.

20. Sweyne's Howes South, Rhossili
ss 4209 8981, sm no. gm027
County Reference Number: gla 2

The Sweyne's Howes South monument is located at around 136m AOD and is arguably constructed similarly to Sweyne's Howes North (GLA 1), 100m to the north (Nash et al. 2007). This monument along with its neighbour are laterally chambered. Based on a description in the RCHMW and observations made during the Clifton Antiquarian Club landscape survey in 2007, there is no clear evidence of a passage.

Sweyne's Howes South, the more disturbed of the two monuments, was first investigated in 1869–70 by the antiquarian Gardiner Wilkinson. The cairn, of possibly two phases of construction, measures 20.7m x 15m x 0.7m and is oval in form. The cairn material appears to be locally sourced, made from sandstone conglomerates. Contained within the inner cairn, are a number of loose and earth-fast boulders. One of the boulders may represent part of a capstone. The inner cairn is delineated by a series of possible kerbstones. The RCHMW (ibid. 30) suggests that the inner cairn may be wedge-shaped. Within the north-west area of the cairn are the remains of a possible chamber, represented by five recumbent slabs.

Both monuments stand 1.3km east of Rhossili Bay. Although close to the coast, they appear to ignore the

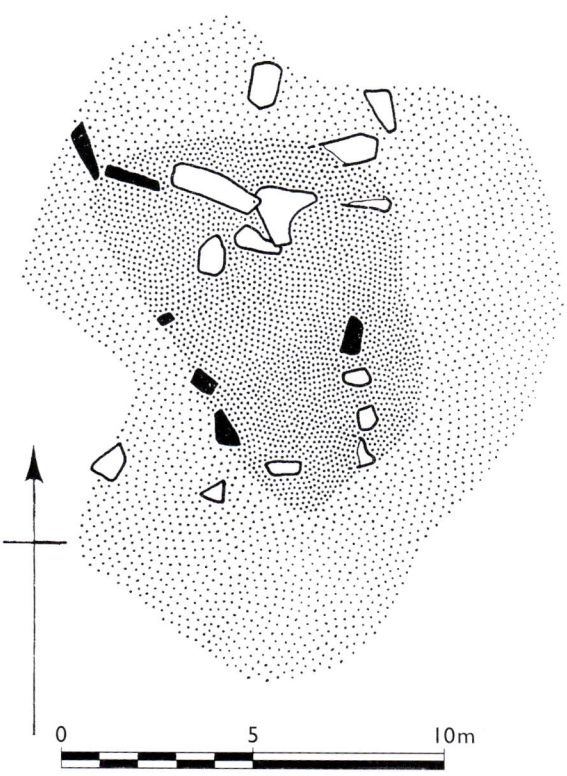

Plan of the partly-destroyed chamber and mound of Sweyne's Howes South (after RCAHMW 1976)

The much-disturbed chamber architecture of Sweyne's Howes South

The Sweyne's Howes South monument set within the heathland landscape of Rhossili Down

The capstone and chamber of the Penmaen Burrows monument

sea, purposely to shelter them from prevailing winds (Daniel 1950). Alternatively, I would suggest that the location of both monuments is typical of Neolithic burial-ritual sites found elsewhere (i.e. deliberately hidden away from certain landscape vistas, including the sea). Above both monuments and occupying the ridges of Rhossili Down, are a number of circular cairns that date from the Bronze Age.

21. Penmaen Burrows, Tilston
SS 5315 8813, SM NO. GM123
County Reference Number: GLA 5

This denuded monument, located 46m AOD among sand dunes, consists of two rectangular chambers with supporting uprights, and an entrance passage. The chambers seem to be constructed differently. The construction materials include limestone, sandstone and sandstone conglomerate. The use of these different stones may have socio-symbolic importance (see below).

The site was investigated in 1860 and later in 1881 by W.L. Morgan (1894, 1–7). The remains inside the chambers and surrounding the monument were removed during excavation in 1893, when the original ground surface was exposed. This disturbance resulted in several stones, possibly kerbing, being removed. Since then, the site has been covered by wind-blown sand, which has predominantly increased the protection of the monument.

The excavation revealed the height of the chambers to be 1m, so rituals would have been performed with the participants crouching (RCHMW 1976, 32). It appears that the passage was slightly lower, the height decreasing at the entrance. The passage, opening out towards the east, measures around 2m in length and, like other passage graves, it is narrow at the entrance, increasing in width and height as it approaches the chamber area. Powell suggests that the chambers are transepted terminal chambers, similar to those at Parc-le-Breos-Cwm and originating in South-west Wales (1969 16–17). This is also supported by Castleden, who suggests the monument is of the Cotswold-Severn tomb type. Despite the fact that the site has not been fully excavated, Corcoran (1969) argued that the monument was not trapezoidal.

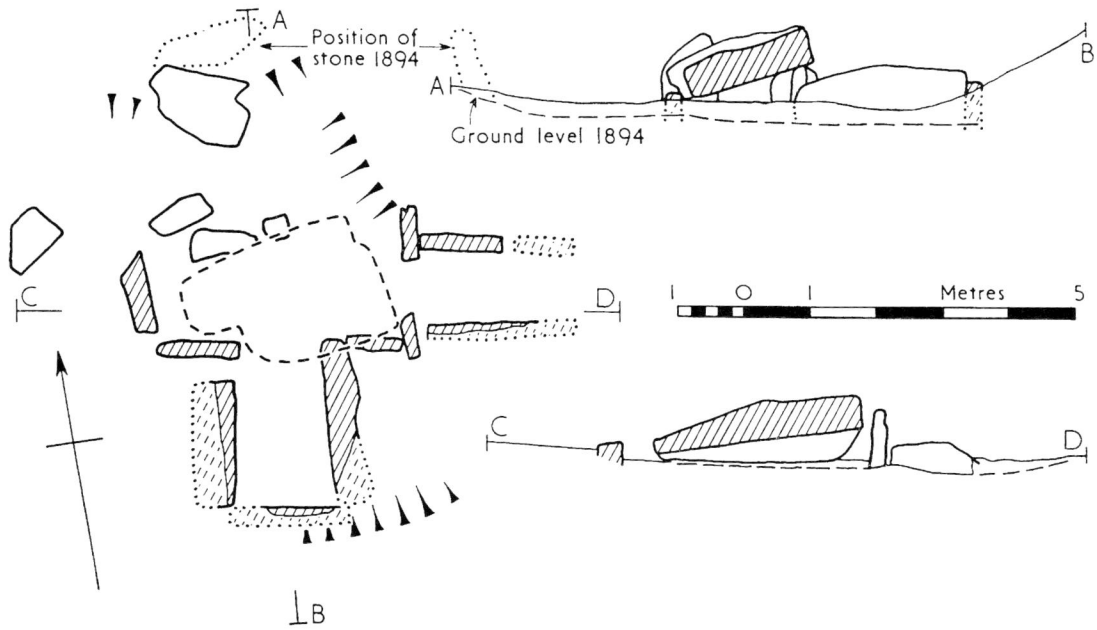

Plan and section of the complex passage and chamber areas of Penmaen Burrows (RCAHMW 1976)

The southern chamber, measuring 1.2m x 2.3m, constructed of three uprights, is rectangular in form. The western chamber, rectangular in plan, is constructed of two transverse uprights that open out into a passage to the east. There appears to be no trace of any sill-stones that would have delineated the space between the chamber and passage. The capstone appears to be dislodged (RCHMW 1976, 32). It is possible that a third chamber may have existed to the north of the western chamber and passage, thus forming a cruciform-shaped chamber alignment. However, this cannot be proven until further excavation takes place. A number of loose stones are present within this area of the monument, that probably represent cairn or blocking material.

Artefacts that were recovered from the two minor excavations, which were restricted to the southern chamber, included a fragment of a human mandible, animal bones and a fragment of a bone tool handle. The mandible probably represents the remnants of a human burial. This assemblage was located within a series of residual deposits that underlay a wind-blown accretion of sand. A further bone assemblage was found beneath two paving slabs, along with a small selection of 'brown pottery'. It is probably the latter material that is contemporary with the monument's use.

Concerning the architecture of the Penmaen Burrows monument, I would argue that it belongs to the passage grave tradition which was in use during the early part of the Late Neolithic, and has some similarities with nearby Parc-le-Breos-Cwm (GLA 4) and the Sweyne's Howes monuments on Rhossili Down (GLA 1 & 2).

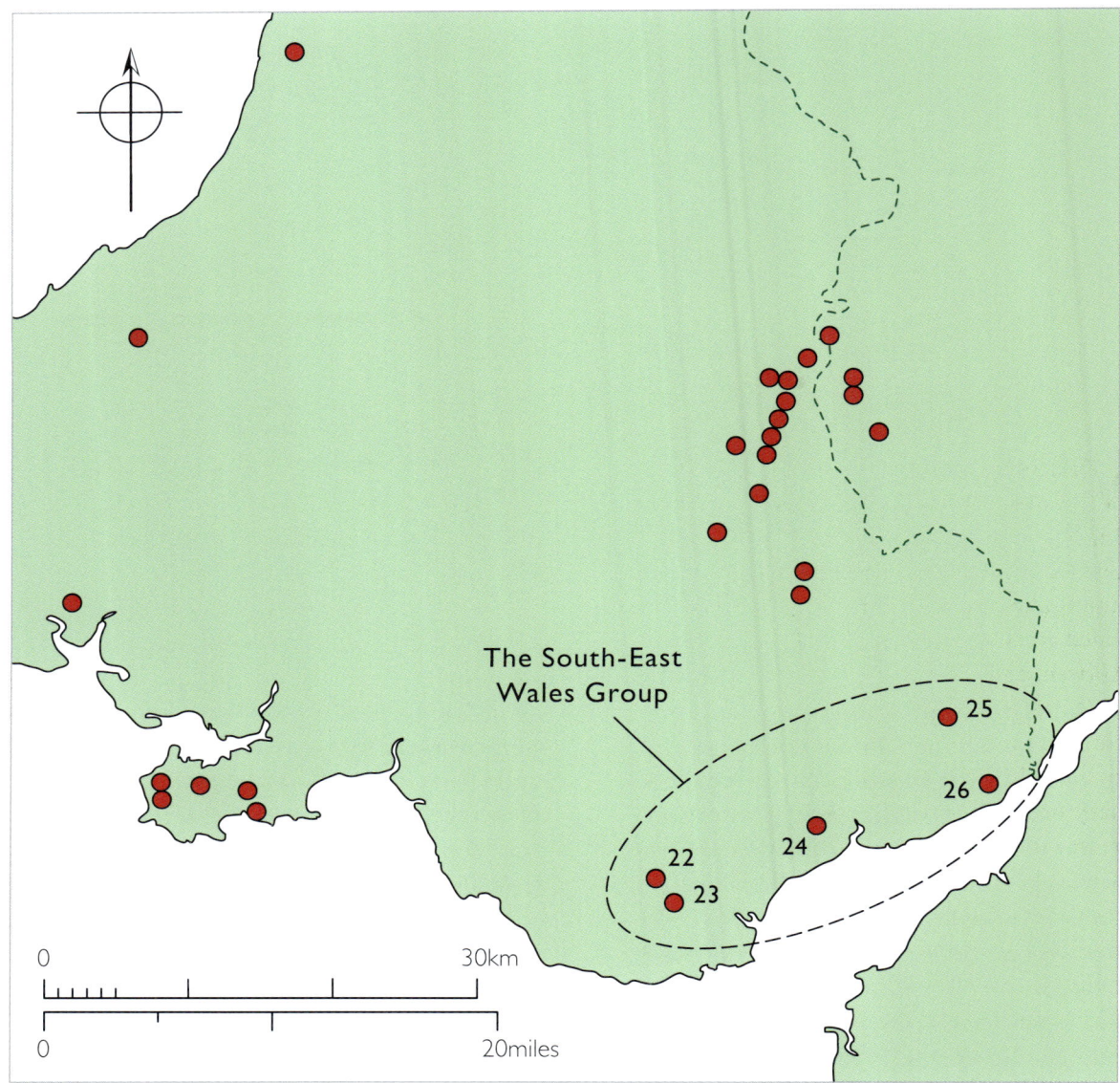

22 Tinkinswood
23 Maes y Felin
24 Cleppa Park
25 Y Gaer Llwyd
26 Heston Brake

FOUR

The South-East Wales Group

WITHIN THIS CHAPTER, the South-East Wales group is limited to five monuments: Tinkinswood (GLA 9), Maes y Felin (GLA 10), Cleppa Park (MON 1), Gaer Llwyd (MON 2) and Heston Brake (MON 3). Others that have not been included are: Cae-yr-Arfau, Coed-y-Cwm, Pen-yr-Alltwen, and the recently discovered Thornwell Farm (MON 4).[35]

Three of the four monuments, all in Monmouthshire, are located close to the Severn Estuary/Bristol Channel, whilst Gaer Llwyd lies some way inland, within the hinterlands between the Gwent Levels and the uplands of the south Wales Valleys. Unlike the core areas of the Black Mountains Group and South-west Wales, there are no geographical sub-groups recognised.

Each of the monuments, including those in Glamorgan, has been constructed using stone taken from local quarries, the predominant materials used in construction being Old Red Sandstone and sandstone conglomerate. Although the sandstone conglomerate is a weak material, Neolithic builders must have seen the importance of lustre, texture and colour when using this type of stone for capstones and uprights. The white quartz, set into red and brown sandstone, must have had a desired effect on the people who constructed and used these monuments. Even the greyness of the Gaer Llwyd monument would have dominated the landscape within its immediate setting. The absence of a covering cairn or earthen mound does not diminish the powerful colour statements these monuments were making.

The lack of monuments should not detract from this area being seen as an important core area. Associated with these monuments are a number of stray finds that include prestige items such as axes. Also found have been a number of small flint scatters.

From the south and east of the area are a series of single prestige finds that indicate possible trading alliances or seasonal expeditions. These high status goods, 12 in total, consist mainly of polished stone and flint axes. At least two examples from southern Sweden are known. A south Scandinavian flat-butted axe was found in Benchwood, an eastern suburb of Newport (SO 33 88). An identically shaped axe was also found within the root system of an old yew tree on the Great Doward, close to the Monmouthshire border with Herefordshire. Further axes originate from outlying areas as far away as Cornwall and Cumbria. An axe from the Scafell Pike axe factory in Cumbria was found on English Newton Common (SO 52 15), whilst two fine examples of Greenstone axes, originating from the Penzance area of Cornwall, were discovered close to the M4 Motorway, north-west of Newport (SO 30 88). A further three axes were discovered in Newport as a result of housing development (SO 29 86).

The Monuments – MON 1 to MON 3 – have been discussed by a number of antiquarians and eminent archaeologists over the past two centuries, but the Thornwell Farm monument (ST 539 916; SM NO. GM206) is very much a recent discovery and deserves some comment here.

The Thornwell Farm monument is located 0.4km west of the Severn Estuary and occupies the western banks of the River Wye, and was discovered through a housing development and excavated in 1990. The monument, having a similar landscape position as nearby Heston Brake, presently lies within the middle of a housing estate, marked by a large, 300-year-old oak tree. Tantalisingly found within the monument were the remains of four adults and two children and associated grave goods dating to the Early Neolithic. The human remains appeared to have been disarticulated. Also discovered was a large assemblage of bones from birds of prey. Within the rectangular chamber was a stone slab arrangement with a carved-out 'porthole'.[36] This architectural device, found elsewhere in a number of Cotswold-Severn monuments, may have divided the chamber into two areas (Hughes 1996). There was a substantial blocking deposit and evidence of secondary deposition in the form of two Early Bronze Age cist burials. The burials consisted of two crouched male burials with associated grave goods, including a barbed and tanged arrowhead and a corded-ware Beaker pot. Several Bronze Age barrows exist close by, suggesting burial continuity through time and space.

The state of preservation of a site like the Thornwell Farm monument is considered rare in this part of the British Isles. The three other monuments (MON 1–MON 3) – two of which are classified as Portal Dolmens and the other a possible gallery grave – lie in various states of destruction.

Concerning the sites of Tinkinswood and Maes y Felin (GLA 10), these lie with several kilometres of each other and are intervisible. Both monuments are truly megalithic in stature, with Tinkinswood arguably having the largest capstone in Wales (Castleden 1992). The present state of Maes y Felin, consisting of three large uprights which support a rectangular capstone, reminds the author of its similarities with the court tombs that are found in Cornwall and southern Ireland. However, when in use, Maes y Felin would have been covered with an enormous mound, similar in shape and design to those found within the Cotswold-Severn region of south-west England. Tinkinwood, which was restored by Ward during the early part of the twentieth century, still retains much of its architecture and is one of only a handful of sites in Wales where one can get an insight into how the architecture may have interacted with the ritual performances of the Neolithic and Early Bronze Age periods.

22. Tinkinswood, St Nicholas
ST 0921 7331, SM NO. GM009
County Reference Number: GLA 9

This monument and nearby Maes y Felin (GLA 10) are similarly placed within a slightly undulating landscape; Tinkinswood standing on a small rocky knoll. Located at around 75m AOD, it lies on a south-westerly slope at the head of the River Waycock. The monument appears to have been investigated prior to 1875, when Lukis claims that the 'contents of the

Tinkinswood chamber had been thrown out many years ago' (1875, 171). Lukis goes on to say that he dug in the debris outside the monument to find human teeth, unburnt bone and 'rude pottery'.

The monument was excavated and carefully restored in 1914 by the archaeologist John Ward (1915, 1916, 242–64). The excavation revealed a number of phases that included construction, utilisation, abandonment in the forming of a blocking deposit in front of the eastern chamber, and later secondary use. The monument consists of a chamber constructed of five uprights supporting a huge capstone at the eastern end of a large rectangular, E–W mound measuring 40m x 17m. A small stone cist or drystone walled pit, roughly 3m square and lined with nine upright slabs, was also incorporated within the cairn fabric at the northern end of the mound. This structure appears to date from after the construction of the mound and may be Late Neolithic or Early Bronze Age in date. Within this cist, the Ward excavation found a large quantity of domestic animal bone, including horse, cattle (*Bos primigenius*), sheep or goat and pig, which may represent a purpose-built repository for feasting remains, probably utilised during ceremonial funerary rites (Grimes 1951, 33). Also found was a small assemblage of wild animal bones, indicating a mixed economy.

The wedge-shaped mound is supported by a drystone revetment wall, which, according to Ward, was well laid, and appears to be of locally quarried limestone. The mound rubble also consists of locally quarried limestone and mudstone blocks, the largest of which lie close to the eastern chamber. At the western-end of the monument are up to seven

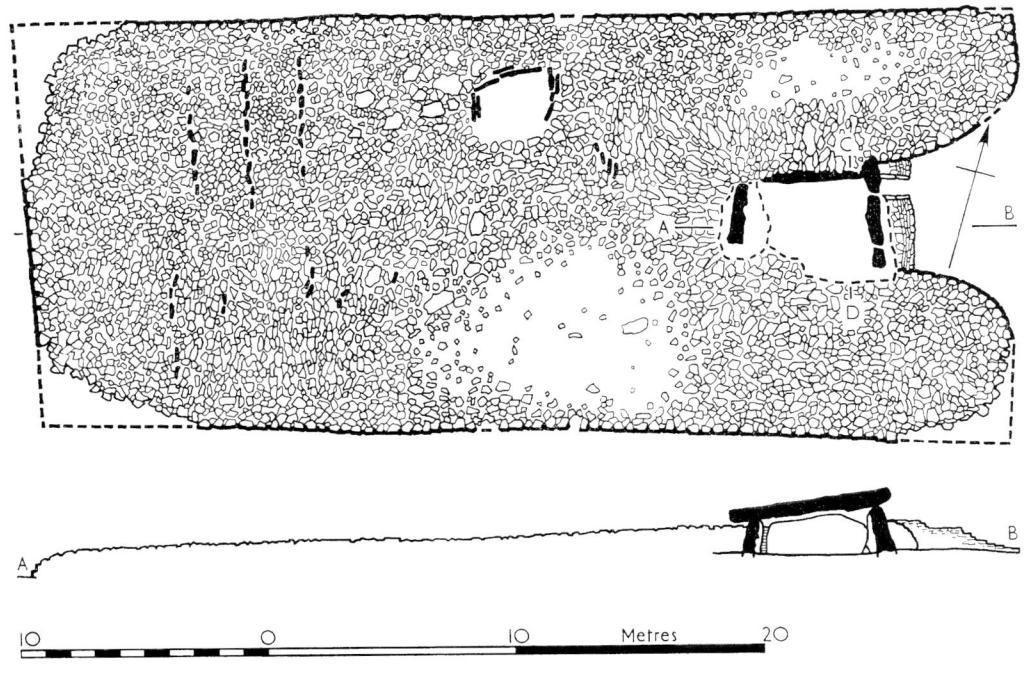

Plan and section of the Tinkinswood monument (after Ward 1915)

The chamber and capstone of Tinkinswood, looking north

The reconstructed façade and the main chamber of Tinkinswood

upright stone alignments which originally formed three or maybe four linear stone settings, oriented N–S, their purpose unknown.

The monument also possesses the distinctive horns associated with all trapezoidal monuments in Wales, forming a cuspate forecourt (Corcoran 1969, 43). The horns are located north and south of the main chamber. The eastern chamber, rectangular in plan, is constructed of five unworked stone uprights and measures 5m x 3.6m. Constructed between the uprights is drystone walling. The chamber is covered by a very large capstone, estimated to weigh 40 tons (Grimes 1951, 31), and partly supported by an inserted pillar. The original height of the chamber was 1.5m, suggesting that ritual activity could be conducted standing up. Between the horns, the forecourt area and the chamber, there would have been a narrow passage, possibly measuring around 1m in length, which leads to the entrance. The entrance is constructed of a large door-stone, flanked by two smaller uprights separating the chamber from the forecourt area.

Ward's reconstruction tastefully extends the stone revetment in front of the portal stones, a feature not seen on any other trapezoidal monument that has a chamber within the forecourt area. The idea that portals are covered by a revetment wall is also supported by Corcoran (1966, 43). The monument prior to excavation appears to have been robbed for building stone.

The excavation produced a remarkable assemblage of bone and associated artefacts, with the remains of at least 50 people found in the chamber: 21 women, 16 men, eight children and a number of unidentifiable remains (Grimes 1951, 152–3). These individuals were disarticulated and found within three distinct areas of the site: the chamber, the forecourt blocking and within the southern section of the cairn fabric of the mound. According to Sir Arthur Keith (in Ward 1916) the remains represented people aged between a few months and 70 years. A large assemblage of Late Neolithic pottery was also recovered, some of which was found on the floor of the forecourt in front of the entrance. All the pottery from this period consisted of round-bottomed bowls, much of it found embedded in the floor of the forecourt. Ward (1916, 260) rightly suggested that the pottery and the human remains were contemporary. The Neolithic pottery from this site was identical in type to that found in other Cotswold-Severn tombs (Grimes 1951, 32). Fragments of a Beaker vessel decorated with alternating bands of continuous chevrons and

Reconstruction of a Neolithic burial-ritual ceremony at Tinkinswood, sketched by Alan Sorrell, 1949

The chamber and faint mound of Maes-y-Felin, looking north-west

straight lines were also recovered, suggesting that the monument was in use during the Late Neolithic period and the Early Bronze Age. A large flint assemblage included a finely worked leaf-shaped arrowhead – or what Grimes (1951, 330) calls a 'lance head', which lay beneath the original surface of the cairn, in a trench, some 8.5m from the western end of the barrow.

The monument appears to have been used, possibly as a shelter, during the early Iron Age and Romano-British and medieval periods. A selection of artefacts, including a bone gaming die and associated pottery from the three periods, were found.

23. Maes y Felin, St Lythans
ST 1009 7230, SM NO. GM008
County Reference Number: GLA 10

This monument, also known as Gwal-y-Filiast and Llech-y-Filiast (by Rees in 1815) is located on a small knoll within open pasture, and has intervisibility with Tinkinswood (GLA 9). This monument (along with Tinkinswood) were first compared with the Cotswold-Severn monuments by W. Greenwell (1877), whose work helped extend the geographical range of the Cotswold-Severn classification, developed in the last century by Thurnam and refined by Daniel (1950). Daniel identified a number of tombs with terminal chambers in this area, including Maes y Felin, which he labelled the 'Tinkinswood-Manton Down type'.

The site was examined by J.W. Lukis in 1875, who reported finding fragments of unburnt human bone and coarse pottery outside the chamber (Lukis 1875). This material may represent a clearance dump, formed when the contents of the tomb were cleared away to make room for further burials (Daniel 1950). However, it is more than probable that the clearance dump represents antiquarian activity or stone robbing during the recent past.

This unexcavated single-phase tomb stands 70m AOD on a gentle north-western slope near the head of Waycock Valley, where the soils are light and easily worked. Tombs in this area are usually located close to the boundary between areas of freely drained soils and those with impeded drainage (Corcoran 1969).

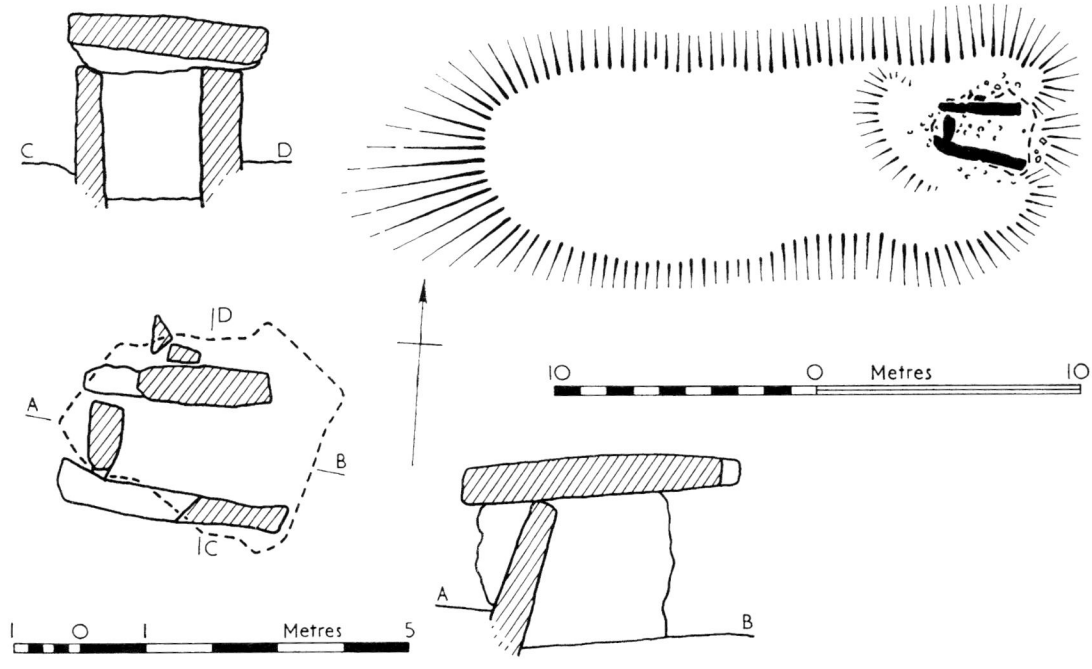

Plan, section and mound of Maes-y-Felin (after RCAHMW 1976)

A rectangular chamber is set at the eastern end of an eroded long mound, measuring 27m x 11m x 1m and oriented roughly E–W (RCHMW 1976, 39). The precise form of the mound is unclear, but is probably rectangular or even trapezoidal (similar to nearby Tinkinswood, although there is no trace of a revetment wall). According to a plan of the site published in the RCHMW (1976, 39), the mound may have resembled Parc-le-Breos-Cwm (GLA 4), with horns either side of the uprights within the eastern section of the mound. The mound was reported to have been severely eroded in the early 1990s, and as a result a Neolithic and pre-cairn land surface was exposed and artefacts including a polished stone axe recovered (Driver 1992). A subsequent limited excavation around the chamber area was undertaken in 2011 (see Coflein).

The chamber measures 2.6m x 1.3m and consists of three large unworked uprights that support a large capstone which is roughly 4.5m x 3m. The chamber is set on top of a small platform within the fabric of the mound. Traces of the cairn mound lie close to the uprights of the chamber. The chamber appears to be cut some 0.7m into the surrounding geology. There is no trace of any door-stone between the chamber and eastern side of the mound. In my opinion there would have been a small forecourt that would have been flanked by horns, similar in design and size to Parc-le-Breos-Cwm and Tinkinswood. The capstone, measuring 4.2m x 3.3m by 0.7m in thickness, is of mudstone, the same material used for the capstone at Tinkinswood. To the north of the chamber are two further uprights that may represent further chamber architecture.

24. Cleppa Park, Coedkernew
ST 2740 8571, SM NO. MM022
County Reference Number: MON 1

Cleppa Park, also referred to as Gwern-y-Cleppa and Gwern-y-clepai, is located on a south-east facing ridge and stands at around 43m AOD. This monument, named after a nearby farm, has been classified as a Cotswold-Severn long-chambered tomb. The form of this monument is much disturbed, but there are still traces of a long mound, approximately 40m long and oriented roughly E–W.[37] The remains consist of one fallen capstone and six other stones, three of which are uprights; the largest of these standing over 1.3m in height. A possible fourth upright, now dislodged, measures around 1.5m in length and lies underneath a siliceous grey sandstone capstone that measures approximately 2.5m by 1.7m. The uprights are made from locally quarried conglomerate sandstone or millstone grit.

One of the more useful accounts of this and other monuments in Monmouthshire is that by O.G.S. Crawford (1925, 151–2). The chamber, according to Daniel (1950, 67), forms the remains of an eastern lateral chamber that is rectangular in plan. It was reported in 1897 that three uprights were in place, forming what may have been a simple terminal chamber (Bagnall-Oakeley 1897, 11–12). Two of the uprights appear still to be in position. It is in this chamber that the fallen capstone lies and partly buries what was once a large, chambered area. A plan of the site, made by Bagnall-Oakeley, suggests that the three uprights form a rectangular chamber.

Cleppa Park may once have formed part of a ritual landscape that incorporated a nearby Early Bronze Age standing stone (ST 2430 8347). Other monuments, now long since destroyed, would have dominated the lower Usk Valley. This slightly undulating landscape is similar to that of the nearby

The Cleppa Park monument, looking east

Tinkinswood (GLA 9) and Maes-y-Felin (GLA 10) monuments (Glamorgan). The monument is positioned between the mountains and the flood plain of the lower Usk valley to the east, the alluvial flats to the south and the Severn estuary/Bristol Channel beyond. The Bristol Channel, approximately 4.8km away to the south, cannot be seen from the monument. The uplands of south-east Wales are in view to the north and west. The M4, running E–W here, blocks the view of the Severn estuary. The Afon Ebbw flows south-east into the River Usk. Today, there is woodland to the north and south-west.

Two kilometres to the north-east at Gaer, within the city boundary of Newport, are several Neolithic find-spots. These find-spots, along with others located either side of the River Usk, suggest that the river estuary and its hinterlands were probably utilised for settlement. Indeed, according to the regional HER (held by Glamorgan-Gwent Archaeological Trust), a small number of Mesolithic and Neolithic find-spots are present within Newport's boundaries. The find-spots suggest the economic importance of the hinterlands that surround the River Usk.

25. Y Gaer Llwyd, Shirenewton
ST 4476 9678, SM NO. MM013
County Reference Number: MON 2

This monument, also known as Gaerllwyd and Garnllwyd (meaning 'grey cairn'), stands at approximately 209m AOD on well-drained soils, to the north of the village of the same name. The monument, classified by Powell et al. (1969, 288) as a possible Portal Dolmen, is located within a small area of rough scrubland and bushes, close to a hedge boundary, and is now much disturbed.[38] The hedge boundary, which is of unknown date, may have served to preserve some of the monument's architecture. However, the road, located on the other side of the hedge boundary, ironically may have destroyed the south-western part of the mound. According to an unpublished account:

> ... that road cut into the field in which the cromlech stood, and which itself bounded on its eastern side, by the old trackway from Shirenewton over Earlswood Common, by Mynydd Bach to the great camp further to the north called Gaer-fawr. Until that new road was made, the cromlech lay entirely secluded and out of the way of tourists, or indeed of any ordinary communication; and though the Gaer-fawr is described by early writers, the cromlech appears to have been long unknown to, or unrecognised by, archaeologists.

The plan and form of Y Gaer Llwyd, and, in particular, two transverse portal stones, suggest that it is linked to a western architectural tradition – possibly the Irish Sea group of monuments (Houlder 1978, 139). The remains comprise a series of uprights, three of which support a large collapsed capstone (measuring 3.2m x 2.5m). Two of the uprights demarcate an entrance or divide two parts of a rectangular chamber (Corcoran 1969, 21). Around the chamber area are a series of fallen uprights that possibly demarcate a now-destroyed passage/entrance area. Several stones from this monument have been incorporated into nearby modern buildings (Castelden 1992, 386).

Similar to other monuments within this group, Y Gaer Llwyd occupies a unique setting. According to the regional HER, very little in the form of monuments and find-spots contemporary with this monument have been found. However, 3km to the south on Gray Hill, are a series of Early Bronze Age monuments, including two stone circles and a standing stone (ST 438 935). To the south-east and within Wentwood are several Bronze Age mounds located at ST 415 946 and ST 417 946 (Webley 1961; Children & Nash 1996, 52).

The historical evidence for this site dates to at least 1613, when it was first described as Garne Lloyde. This place-name formed part of a survey of the parish of 'Sherenewton' (Crawford 1925, 157). According to Crawford, the site is first mentioned by a Mr Wakeman who, in 1846, produced a woodcut engraving of the site (1846, 277);[39] an engraving

The Y Gaer Llwyd monument, looking north-east

reproduced in C.F. Cliffe's *The Book of South Wales* (1848). According to the engraving, the morphology of this monument has changed little since, although two further uprights are shown, and what can be suggested as a circular enclosure made from loose stones. However, it is more than probable that these loose stones are the result of historical disturbance. Cliffe adds that a trench and bank were present around the site; Crawford suggesting that this feature was the remains of a fossilised field enclosure. In addition to the observations and Crawford's notes, Mrs Bagnall-Oakeley in 1915 observed the presence of a mound within the north-eastern part of the site which, according to Crawford, would have been oriented NE–SW, with the chamber at the north-eastern end. Subsequently, the outer cairn has been destroyed by road-building and stone-robbing.

26. Heston Brake, Portskewett
ST 5052 8865, SM NO. MM018
County Reference Number: MON 3

Heston Brake forms one of the Cotswold-Severn group of monuments, as identified by O.G.S. Crawford (1925, 153–55). Later, Powell et al. (1969, 289) noted that this denuded monument was possibly constructed in two phases.

The monument, standing at around 35m AOD, is located on the upper terracing of the Gwent Levels and has views of the Bristol Channel to the south. The soils surrounding the monument are associated with the flood plain of the River Severn and, during the Neolithic, these soils would no doubt have been used to grow crops. Similar to nearby Tinkinswood (GLA 9) and Maes-y-Felin (GLA 10) monuments, Heston Brake is set within an undulating landscape, with the Severn estuary in the middle distance and the Cotswolds beyond.

The place-name appears not to have a Welsh origin. A Mr J.G. Wood, commenting in Crawford's volume (1925, 155), suggests that Heston Brake, along with Harpson Barn, are corruptions of a settlement known as Herberdston; translated to:

A Welsh knight's fee, which was held within the lordship of Striguil, 13th century in date (Matthew Daneband of Portskewet and Herberdson).[40]

The plan made by Mrs Bagnall-Oakeley, an active member of the Monmouthshire and Caerleon Antiquarian Association (MCAA) in 1888, suggests that this monument may be a gallery grave and, therefore, one of probably only two in Wales. The plan clearly shows evidence of a door-stone – stone 6 – and a kink between stones 14 and 15, located halfway along the stone alignment.

The entrance area of the Heston Brake gallery grave

THE SOUTH-EAST WALES GROUP

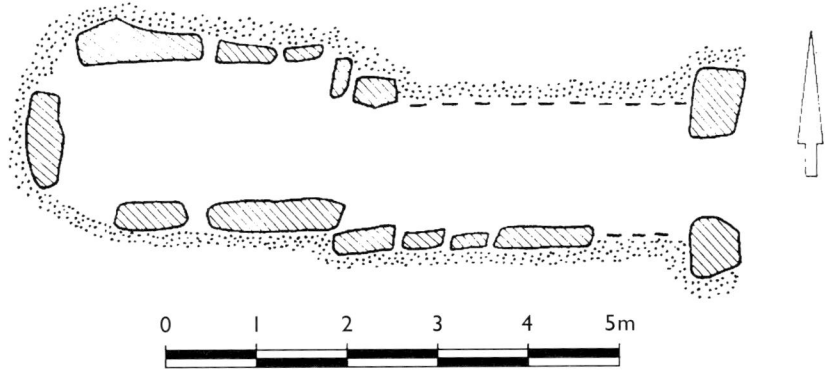

Plan of the gallery upright arrangement of Heston Brake (adapted from Crawford 1925)

The chamber was exposed on August 22, 1888, by members of the MCAA and the Clifton Antiquarian Club. Notes of the investigation were made by Mrs Bagnall-Oakeley, who made a plan of the chamber and passage. She recorded that the largest upright within the monument – stone 1 – was located at the entrance to the passage, and measured 1.3m in height. This and other stones were made from conglomerate sandstone (cf. Children & Nash 1996, 35). According to Crawford (1925, 153), stones 2, 3, 4, 10, 12 and 19 were missing when the initial investigations were undertaken; therefore, the plan by Bagnall-Oakeley of these stones is purely conjectural. Crawford appears to be concerned about the investigation of this monument and feels that Heston Brake had been excavated by antiquarian enthusiasts rather than a desired expert.

The human remains recovered from the east corner of the western chamber included teeth and finger bones. Also noted within the same area were some bones of an ox and two smooth stones. Bagnall-Oakley (1889, 18–20) states that:

On the north side of the mound, the workmen came upon three pieces of broken pottery; one of these was black and soft burnt, easily cut with a knife; another was grey, hard burnt, with lines upon it and near them lay a small piece of burnt bone. A third piece of pottery was very hard red ware, somewhat like Roman Samian ware.

Also found were part of a shaft of a human femur and part of a jaw of an unspecified animal. It was noticed during the investigation that the mound had been opened previously. Crawford suggests that the site may have been used for secondary burial. Found within this context was a sherd of medieval green copper-glazed pottery.

The supposed chamber and passage are set within a long cairn that is aligned E–W; the cairn measuring roughly 23m in length. The chamber (3m x 1.4m), now without a capstone, is set within the eastern section of the mound; chamber and passage, forming an eastern lateral structure. Formed from nine upright stones, the chamber lies off-line in relation to the passage. Two uprights mark the point of transition between the passage and the chamber entrance – both of which are 1.5m wide. The width of the chamber and passage is roughly 1.4m. However, the passage entrance is demarcated by two large uprights that measure 0.9m apart. The width of the chamber plus the kink in the internal arrangement of the chamber/passage alignment may suggest some form of restricted visual access between outside and inside the monument. The merging of the chamber and passage suggests the monument may be a gallery grave. In terms of architecture, the builders of Heston Brake and Y Gaer Llwyd (MON 2) may have been influenced by a western style, rather than the Cotswold-Severn tradition (Houlder 1978). Similarities with the chamber of Ffostyll South (BRE 4) in the Black Mountains have been noted (Corcoran 1969, 45).

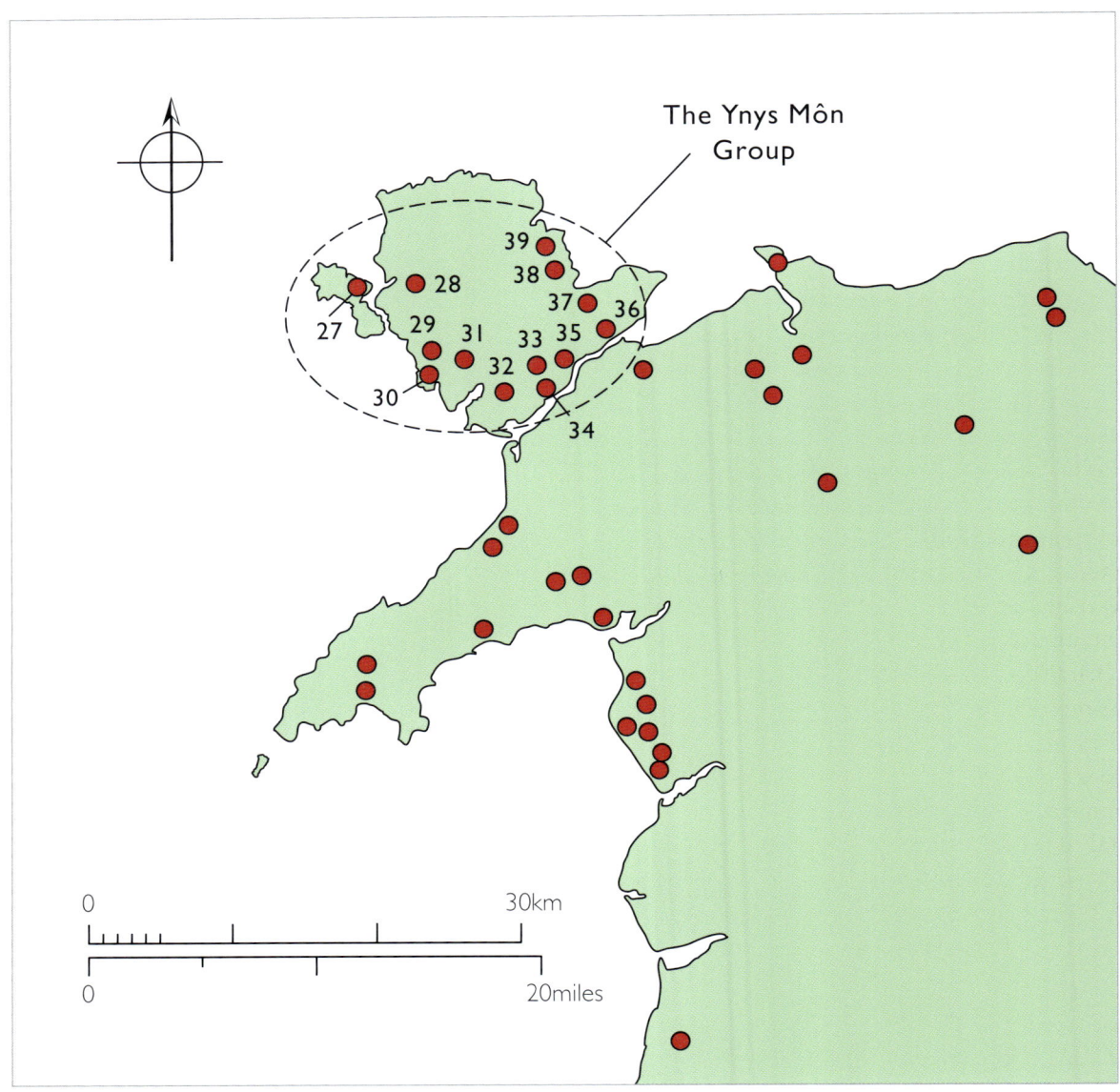

27	Trefignath	32	Bodowyr	37	Hen-Drefor
28	Presaddfed	33	Bryn Celli Ddu	38	Pant y Saer
29	Ty Newydd	34	Bryn yr Hen Bobl	39	Lligwy
30	Barclodiad y Gawres	35	Plas Newydd		
31	Din Dryfol	36	Ty Mawr		

FIVE

The Ynys Môn Group

Ynys Môn (Anglesey), lying north of the Llŷn Peninsula and separated by the Menai Straits from the North Wales mainland, covers an area of roughly 310sq km Topographically, the island can be described as undulating, but possessing a rugged, mountainous coastline, especially in the north-west. Large domes of rock outcropping are found across most of the island. According to Lynch (1969, 108) little or no significant change has occurred to the coastline since the Neolithic.[41] The majority of monuments in Ynys Môn lie within a 5km-wide coastal zone (see Appendix 2). Inland are a number of marshy areas, which may have some ritual-symbolic association with nearby monuments, especially the vast expanse of marshland that lies in the south-west of the island, referred to as Malltraeth Marsh.

Where monuments are sited, the soils are divided into two main types: slowly permeable, seasonally waterlogged Palaeozoic fine loamy soils, which occupy the north-west of the island; and deep well-drained Palaeozoic coarse loamy soils found in the central and south-eastern areas (*Soil Survey of England & Wales*, 1983). Interestingly, the majority of sites are located in the south-eastern part of the island, where the soils are much deeper and where monuments are usually sited on the lighter soils (Grimes 1945). It is highly likely that settlement lay close by.

According to Lynch, the Ynys Môn Group comprises at least 29 sites, 13 of which have been classified as either lost, damaged or doubtful (Lynch 1969a, 108–24, 1970; Powell et al. 1969, 296–300; Skinner 1802).[42] Importantly, antiquarians, such as the Reverend John Skinner in his *Ten Days Tour in Anglesey* of 1802, noted and sketched a number of monuments which have since been destroyed or damaged. Given the number of monuments that were in use, this Neolithic core area has the highest concentration of monuments per square kilometre in Wales.

For this volume, I have chosen sites that have a diverse architecture and a unique dating range, and therefore include the following sites: Trefignath (ANG 1), Presaddfed (ANG 2), Ty Newydd (ANG 3), Barclodiad y Gawres (ANG 4), Din Dryfol (ANG 5), Bodowyr (ANG 6), Bryn Celli Ddu (ANG 7), Bryn yr Hen Bobl (ANG 8), Plas Newydd (ANG 9), Ty Mawr (ANG 10), Hen-Drefor (ANG 11), Pant y Saer (ANG 13) and Lligwy (ANG 14). Possibly associated with the Ynys Môn Group are up to three monuments that are sited on the Welsh mainland, within the coastal hinterland of Caernarvonshire: Sling (CRN 5) and the doubtful sites of Bryn (CRN 16) and Coetan Arthur (CRN 17).

Dominating this group, both in their architecture and size, are the two passage graves of Barclodiad y Gawres and Bryn Celli Ddu. Associated with both monuments (and the Calderstones in Liverpool), is a unique megalithic art style, which consists of pecked chevrons, cupmarks, spirals and zigzag lines. According to Savory (1980, 222), the architecture is believed to have originated on the Iberian Peninsula during the fourth/fifth millennium BCE, later spreading northwards along the Atlantic coast of Europe to Brittany and Ireland, before arriving in North Wales. Roger Joussaume suggests that both monuments, similarly constructed, date to the Middle Neolithic and are associated with the Breton and Irish passage grave tradition (1985, 71). Lynch argues that both monuments date to the Late Neolithic and, along with the sub-megalithic chambered tomb of Lligwy, are the last of the megalithic structures to be constructed in Ynys Môn (1969a). However, despite the passage grave tradition being a late phenomenon, Bryn Celli Ddu has an earlier phase, in the form of a henge monument which is delineated by the ditch of the outer extent of the later passage grave phase. Further, passage graves in Brittany and within the Channel Islands have much earlier dates for construction and use. I am inclined to suggest that the passage grave tradition in North Wales, occurring sometime after, say, 3,200 BCE, is the last bastion of this way of constructing large corporate monuments and burying the dead in this part of the British Isles.

Despite the presence of the two passage graves, much earlier monuments exist on the island, including the excavated sites at Din Dryfol, Perthi Duon and Trefignath (Smith & Lynch 1987, Nash, James & Wellicome 2015). These early monuments (their use extending possibly into the Late Neolithic), along with other Neolithic monuments, suggest that there was a continuous Neolithic presence in Ynys Môn for some 2,000 years. Whether the island experienced culturation or acculturation is not clear. However, Ynys Môn appears to lie at the centre of a complex contact/exchange area whereby ideas as well as commodities were moving around the core areas of the Irish Sea Province.

27. Trefignath, Holyhead Rural
SH 25860 80547, SM NO. A011
County Reference Number: ANG 1

The Trefignath monument, one of the most complex and important chambered tombs in Wales, is also one of only a small number of Neolithic monuments to have been completely excavated in Wales using modern excavation techniques. It is also one of only a handful of monuments that has produced secure radiocarbon dates. The following description of the site is taken from the most recent source: Christopher Smith's comprehensive excavation report and monograph (Smith 1981, 1987). Lynch (1969a, 114) proved that this is a composite (or multi-phased) monument, whose complexity was similar to that of Dyffryn Ardudwy (MER 3).

The name Trefignath is derived from a nearby farm of the same name and means 'the settlement in the marshes [plural]'. The site is located at around 19m AOD, on a headland close to the port of Holyhead, 'over a cleft in a knoll of outcropping rock' (Lynch 1969a, 113). The site was described, prior to C.A. Smith's excavation, as 'one of three long graves' [in Ynys Môn] (ibid. 113). The monument was once thought to be a continuous gallery grave, possibly associated with the Scottish court cairn tradition. Masters (1981, 107–8) suggests that within the western area of the monument is a small passage grave which is set in a small circular cairn.

The multi-phased, chambered Trefignath monument, looking west

The antiquarian history of the site is extensive. The site was visited by John Aubrey in the mid seventeenth century (either 1656 or 1660) and the monument is described in *Monumenta Britannica* (1695). The description by Aubrey is the earliest on a megalith in Ynys Môn.[43] The description of the monument states:

> In Anglesey, about a mile from Holyhead, on a hill near the way that leads to Beaumaris, are placed certain great rude stones much after ye fashion of this draught here ... There is about a mile from Holy-H[ea]d a monument wch I conceive to be yt meant in yr paper of great rough stones about 20 stones in number & about 30 paces from one of ye roades leadinge from Holy H[ea]d to Beaumaris, between 4 & 5 foot high, at ye Northern End where of stand two stones on End, about two yards high above ground. The fashion of them can hardlie be exactlie described, by the reason some are sunk deep & some fallen flat w[hi]ch are almost overgrown w[i]th earth & grasse.

A later description of the monument, utilising Audrey's text, is made in Gibson's edition of *Camden's Britannia* (1695). Many years later, the site was visited by Nicholas Owen who first drew attention to the state of preservation[44] and noted the morphological complexity of the site:

> ... some rude stone monuments supposed to have been three cromlechs; they join each other, though the upper stones are now fallen off their supporters (1775, 33–36). [This comment predates Lynch's assumption by 210 years!]

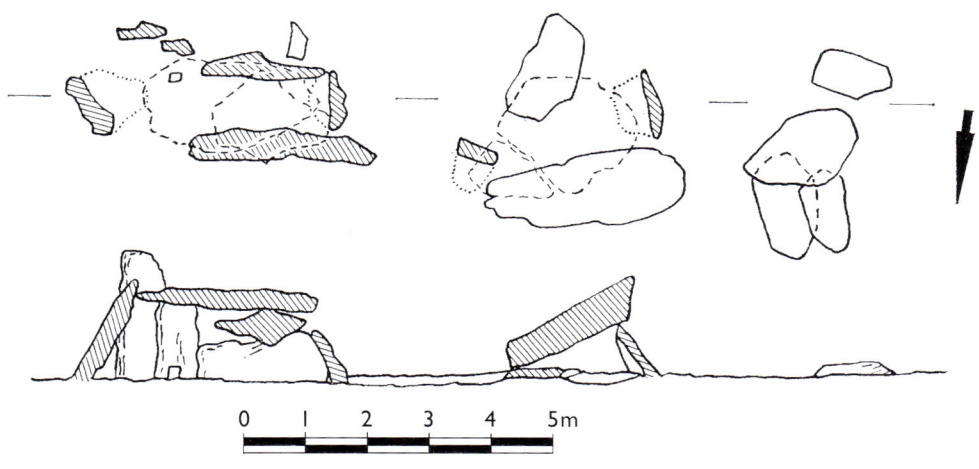

Plan and section of Trefignath (after Lynch 1969)

THE YNYS MÔN GROUP   99

Photograph of the chamber by J.E. Griffith, taken in 1900

During this period the site was something of an enigma, its morphology not being fully understood. Then in 1789, Richard Gough, following Gibson and Lewis Morris, supported the idea that the site consisted of two or maybe three cromlechs: in other words, three separate chambered tombs. In many respects this assumption was partially correct. It was not until 1870 that W.O. Stanley recognised not three cromlechs, but three chambers (1870, 58). If there were three chambers, then there may have been three phases of construction and use. However, it should be noted that this early phase of the assessment of the tomb's complex morphology, was also carried out at the time when the monument was under the greatest threat of destruction. According to Stanley, much of the cairn and some of the uprights had been removed by the late eighteenth century. Complete destruction of the monument was averted by the intervention of Lady Stanley in around 1790. Between the publication of Stanley's engraving in 1874, and 1971, the monument had changed little.

The monument was classified by E.N. Baynes in 1910 as a gallery grave and this description remained current until 1971 when revised by Lynch, who had always expressed reservations regarding this view of the monument (Lynch 1987). It was in 1971 that the extent of the damage to the monument was fully understood, when the capstone over the central chamber collapsed. As a result, the site was temporarily restored. However, by 1976, a timber support used to prop-up the capstone had begun to rot away. Following this, a decision was made to restore the monument comprehensively; but prior to this it was felt that a full excavation should be undertaken – the first conducted on any Neolithic monument in Ynys Môn with full, modern rigour.

The excavation was directed by Christopher Smith and took place over three seasons between 1977 and 1979 (Smith 1981). Following the excavation, a post-excavation programme and consolidation of the monument followed, up until 1982. The excavation programme initially concentrated on the eastern chamber and its forecourt (1977). A year later, in 1978, the central chamber and cairn either side of the eastern chamber were excavated. Smith also excavated the western section of the site in order to establish the extent of the cairn mound. The final excavation season concentrated on the western chamber and its forecourt, and determined the northern and southern limits of the cairn. The cairn

The western chamber of Trefignath

once covering the three chambers had, within the recent past, been robbed, probably for building stone.

From the excavation, Smith recognised three building phases as well as a further four activity episodes. The full sequence included pre-cairn activity (Phase I, 1a), followed by the construction of the western chamber which was within a circular cairn (Phase II 1b); the construction of the central chamber (Phase II 2a); the use of both chambers (Phase II 2b); construction of the eastern chamber and the closure of the central and western chamber (Phase II 3a); closure of the eastern chamber (Phase II 3c); and finally, the abandonment of the monument (Phase III).

Excavation detail

The pre-cairn ground surface was sealed by the primary cairn, and a radiocarbon date of 5,050±70 bp was obtained from this surface, from a charcoal sample. Scattered across the surface was a large selection of pre-monument artefacts including chert and flint tools and debitage, pottery, a sandstone disc and a chert hammer stone. These artefacts may suggest the presence of a small temporary settlement in existence prior to the construction of the monument (ibid. 11). In contrast, it may be the case that these domestic items are derived from the phase of preparation of the ground prior to construction of the monument, therefore suggesting ritual rather than domestic deposition. The association between death, burial and ritual, and domestication, appears to be a common denominator in many monuments, probably linking death with the concept of food preparation for the dead (see for example Nash, Brook and Wellicome 2020). The flint from this phase, according to Elizabeth Healey, possibly dates to the Late Neolithic (1987, 12), which confusingly is not consistent with the radiocarbon dates associated with the same phase.

The three chambers and cairn that form the Trefignath monument

The burial chambers within Phase II were not considered to be contemporaneous. The western chamber was the earliest structure and was originally incorporated in a circular mound. A post-mediaeval road surface had damaged much of the cairn. It was noticed by the excavator that this phase consisted of a small, simple passage grave and that little time had elapsed between the deposition of charcoal found within the pre-cairn surface and the construction of this chamber. This phasing is consistent with a date range of between 3,750 and 3,500 BCE for its construction.

Based on pollen evidence, Smith suggested that a considerable span of time had elapsed between the first use and subsequent abandonment of the western chamber, and construction of the central chamber. This chamber, rectangular in form and measuring 2.8m x 1.25m, had an entrance which opened towards the east. The uprights stood directly on the underlying bedrock, lodged in natural fissures, which gave some stability. During this phase, the cairn mound was completely re-planned, being modified from a circular-shaped mound to a wedge-shaped one. To the east of the central chamber was a deeply recessed forecourt area, the walls constructed of drystone walling. Incorporated into this architecture were horns, constructed to either side of the forecourt and entrance. The southern side of the forecourt was, according to Smith, nine courses high, measuring up to 0.3m in height (ibid. 21). Petrological evidence suggests that the stone was locally quarried. Smith postulated that the Phase II cairn had architectural similarities with the trapezoidal cairns at Capel Garmon (DEN 3) and Carnedd Hengwm North and South (MER 5 & 6), themselves having architectural affinities with the Cotswold-Severn Group of monuments. The demise of this monument phase is witnessed with a carefully laid blocking.

Due to the poor state of preservation, very few Neolithic deposits were found within the central chamber. Neolithic pottery was, however, located in the vicinity of the chamber, which was dated to the earliest phase (Phase I). Later historical disturbance in the chamber was proved by the discovery of a sherd of medieval pottery. It is thought that human remains were removed from the chamber in around 1790. The dating of the chamber was based on a number of small Neolithic pottery sherds found on stone ledges in the walls of the chamber. The pottery consisted of Irish Sea carinated ware, which dated to the fourth millennium BCE.

The third and final phase of construction consisted in the erection of the eastern chamber and associated portal arrangements. Pollen evidence from underneath the cairn suggests that the environment at the time of construction was an open landscape. This chamber, rectangular in form and measuring 2.5m by 1.1m, is the best preserved of the three and is constructed of two large capstones. The chamber opens towards the east. The portal arrangement consists of two sets of stones: one inner set standing around 1.2m in height, while the outer set stands around 2m high. According to Smith, the cairn surrounding this chamber may not have covered the capstones. The cairn, supported by drystone revetted walling, would have extended further to the east, north and south. The shape of the final phase cairn has similarities with other horned monuments in North Wales.

Located within the central area of the eastern chamber forecourt were four post-holes, which were arranged in an arc and may have had some ritual significance. Evidence was also found of a fire that dated to the first millennium BCE. A Romano-British coin was also recovered. This later disturbance suggests that the eastern chamber was open and was probably being used during later prehistoric and early historical times.

28. Presaddfed, Bodedern
SH 34757 80890, SM NO. A010
County Reference Number: ANG 2

South of a marshy lake (Llyn Llywenan) and within a gently undulating landscape, are two polygonal burial chambers, some 2m apart, forming the Presaddfed monument. This monument stands on a small rise at around 20m AOD. The site was recorded and sketched by the Reverend John Skinner in 1802, when on Tuesday 12 December, 1802, he described it thus:

> ... turning off into a field to the left we approached one of the finest and most finished cromlechs we have yet seen in the island, the cap stone measuring four yards and a half long, four yards wide and two yards thick, its three supporters each about a yard and a half high. Indeed, there is a fourth nearly of the same height, but it does

The double-chambered monument at Presaddfed

not touch the stone above. Under this cromlech we were informed a whole family who had been ejected from their habitation sought shelter during the last winter. There was another cromlech close at hand, but the cap stone had been forced down and rests in a slanting direction against the supporters; the top stone of this measured three yards long and two yards and a half wide and its supporters nearly two yards high.

According to Daniel (1950, 146) this monument has affinities with those found in Brittany and the Iberian Peninsula. I would also suggest that it has architectural similarities with the chambered tomb at Plas Newydd (ANG 9), and with the now-destroyed double dolmen at Trefor. Each monument possesses double polygonal-shaped chambers.

The south chamber (the larger of the two) has four uprights supporting a large capstone (approximately 3.3m x 2.5m) which slopes slightly to the south. The northern chamber has two uprights which support a probable capstone measuring 2.8m x 2.2m. The uprights and the capstone that form the chamber have collapsed inwards. Although the mound has disappeared, it seems it may originally have been oriented N–S.

Presaddfed has been listed as an unclassified monument (Lynch 1969a, 123) but it appears to be a double dolmen of the Dyffryn Ardudwy type. Others have suggested the monument is actually two passage graves which face east (Daniel 1950; Powell et al. 1969); Wheeler (1925). In his research into Welsh megalithic tombs, Wheeler has categorised this monument, along with Longhouse (PEM 18) and the Hanging Stone at Burton (PEM 24), as part of the polygonal and circular dolmen group. However, in Lynch's plan (1969a, 123) the chambers appear to be rectangular.

The RCAHM report for Anglesey (Ynys Môn) postulates that Presaddfed represents 'a much-ruined

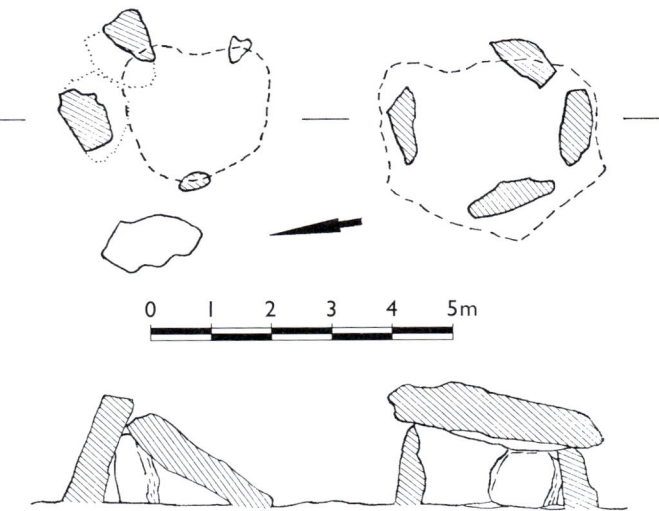

Plan and section of the double-chambered monument at Presaddfed (after Lynch 1969)

gallery grave', similar to that of nearby Trefignath (1937). I would suggest that Lynch's theory, that it belongs to the long mound tradition, similar to monuments those on the Llŷn Peninsula, is plausible. Daniel (1950, 59) identifies the monument as a round barrow, which may suggest a later date. However, no trace of this mound survives. Moreover, the linearity created by the two chambered dolmens would suggest an elongated or oval/kidney-shaped mound that is more akin to an Early Neolithic burial-ritual monument.

29. Ty Newydd, Llanfaelog
SH 3442 7386, SM NO. A013
County Reference Number: ANG 3

This monument, lying approximately 3km north-east of Barclodiad y Gawres (ANG 4), is sited on the northern slope of a broad ridge, around 37m AOD. The sea is in full view to the west.

The site was visited by the Reverend John Skinner on Monday 6 December, 1802, and described briefly:

Hence continuing our walk to the northward we passed through the parish of Llanfaelog and about half a mile beyond the church to a very perfect cromlech. The capstone is rather of an oblong shape and measured sixteen feet long, six wide, and three thick. It only rested upon three supporters each about three feet high although there were four placed in the ground. Near the cromlech were lying two large stones, the one seventeen feet long and three thick.

The monument consists of three large uprights supporting a large, sub-angular capstone (4m x 1.5m). During the mid twentieth century, two brick column supports were erected within the chamber area. According to the excavator, C.W. Phillips, the capstone had slipped to the north and did not cover the chamber area (Phillips 1936). The passage appears to be elongated, with a possible entrance at the south or south-east. Evidence of a fire of hazel wood

Ty Newydd, looking north (hiding the modern brick support)

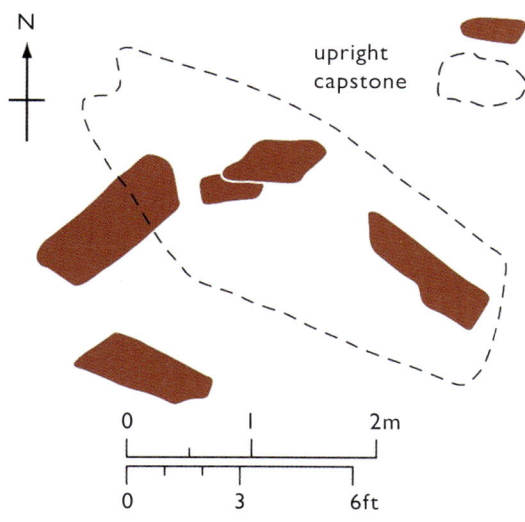

Plan of the chambers of Ty Newydd, drawn by Cadw

within this entrance area was also found. However, no firm dates could be ascertained at the time of the excavation.

The idea that this monument belongs to the passage grave tradition has been given strong support by the discovery of a low stone within the northern part of the chamber, which appears to form part of a passage approach (Lynch 1969a, 116). Skinner (1802) also mentions stone settings within the south-eastern part of the chamber. Lynch postulates that the chamber, in keeping with the passage grave tradition, was covered by a round cairn; which, given the monument's position, is a possibility. However, I am more inclined to consider this monument as a Portal Dolmen, given its surviving architecture and the outline of the mound.

When it was excavated by Phillips in 1935, the monument produced up to 110 fragments of broken white quartz, along with charcoal (Phillips 1936). These were found over the floor of the chamber, within a black humic earth 50mm thick, and may represent some deliberate ritual act that revolved around the whiteness of the quartz (it should be noted that quartz is naturally found in the vicinity). This fact does not exclude the possibility of the floor of the chamber being covered in white quartz. A fire-damaged barbed-and-tanged arrowhead, a polished flint axe fragment and a small assemblage of five tiny pieces of Beaker pottery were also found, suggesting either that the monument was constructed during the Late Neolithic or Early Bronze Age, or that it was in use during the Early Bronze Age. The pottery fabric is a typical fine, gritless ware with a course, sandy surface. One sherd was decorated with two finely impressed twisted cord lines. Also recovered was a small rim forming part of a Bell Beaker or Short-Necked vessel, of either the B3 or Cord Zoned class. I would tend to agree with Lynch that these artefacts are not primary in context but were deposited later. Other finds included a small chip from a polished flint axe. This could not be properly identified but may be similar to types found at Ty Isaf (BRE 5) in Breconshire and the passage grave cemetery at Loughcrew in County Meath, Ireland.

30. Barclodiad y Gawres, Llangwyfan
SH 3290 7072, SM NO. A032
County Reference Number: ANG 4

This passage grave, also referred to as Mynnedd Cnwc or Mynydd y Cnwc, lies 19m AOD on the southern part of a small promontory headland overlooking a small inlet known as Porth Trecastell. From the passage area, the monument looks over the rugged north-western coastline of Holy Island. To the north and east is a series of small undulating hills. Due to its proximity with Ty Newydd (ANG 3) and Din Dryfol (ANG 5), it is possible that these monuments may have had some contemporary association.

Aerial view of the Barclodiad y Gawres monument and the surrounding landscape (image by Andrew Beardsley)

The monument appears to have suffered the usual pillage of previous centuries. Used as a stone quarry in the eighteenth century, most of the contents, including archaeological deposits from the chambers, were removed. However, the monument did receive some archaeological recognition in 1799 when a note was published by David Thomas in the *Cambrian Register*, listing the Cromlechau or Druidical Altars of Ynys Môn. One of the first accounts of this monument was given by the Reverend John Skinner who, on Monday 6 December, 1802, described it thus:

> Instead of a cromlech at Mynnedd Cnwc we found the vestiges of a large carnedd; many of the flat stones of the cist faen or chamber are still remaining but the small ones have been almost all removed to build a wall close at hand. On another fork of the peninsula about a hundred yards distant we observed the traces of another carnedd of much smaller dimensions [This is now regarded as a Bronze Age cairn]. From the nature of their situation, the bay, the earth work &c. it is not possible to suppose that an engagement here took place with the natives wherein some principal officers were slain and interred on the spot.

In 1869, H. Prichard published a full description of the site, including a plan of the passage and part of the chamber, but also made reference to the destruction of the monument. It was photographed in 1900 by J.E. Griffith. In 1910, E.N. Baynes concluded that Barclodiad y Gawres was a small cairn, and it was not until 1937 that the full extent of the chamber area and the mound was exposed in the plan made by W.F. Grimes. In his research, Grimes concluded that the monument was a passage grave of the style 'of Newgrange and other Irish sites'.

Terrance Powell and Glyn Daniel excavated this large, impressive, now reconstructed, Late Neolithic passage grave – the only attested example of a cruciform type in North Wales – in 1953 (1956). The

Antiquarian photograph of 1900, showing the visible remains of Barclodiad-y-Gawres, including the chamber

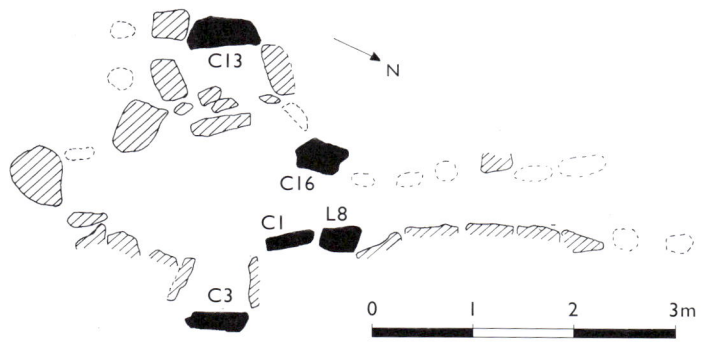

Detail of the chamber arrangement and the distribution of the engraved uprights of Barclodiad-y-Gawres

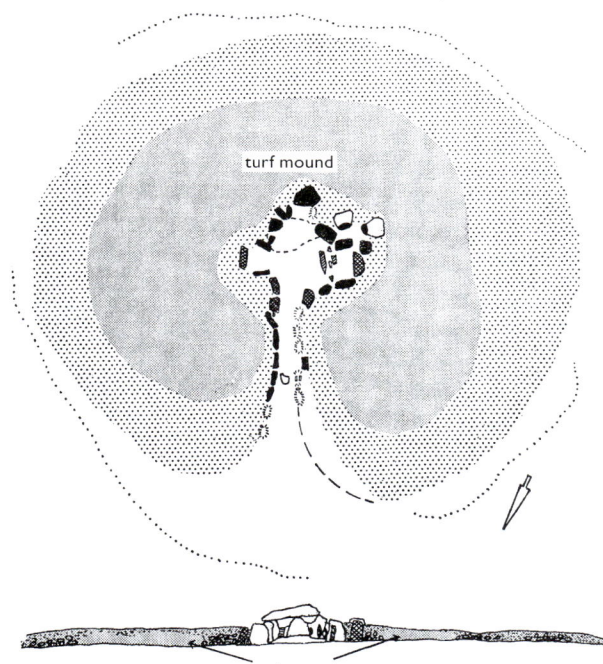

Plan and section of Barclodiad-y-Gawres (after Powell & Daniel 1956)

set within the reconstructed fabric is one of the most impressive decorated megalithic monuments in north-western Europe. The passage, measuring approximately 6m, leads to a cruciform passage which has a series of uprights decorated with engraved chevrons, lozenges, spirals and zigzag designs. These designs, which have been pecked rather than carved, are similar to those identified on decorated uprights found in association with the Bryn Celli Ddu (ANG 1) monument, and monuments found in the Boyne Valley of central Ireland (Lynch 1967, 1–22).

The southern section of the chamber with dipping capstone, as viewed from the passage

reconstruction sadly incorporates a concrete dome and drystone walling around the passage area. Set in a dramatic coastal landscape, the monument now has the appearance of an air raid bunker. However,

THE YNYS MÔN GROUP 107

CLOCKWISE FROM LEFT: Stone C3, forming the back wall of the eastern chamber, showing seven clear curvilinear motifs; Stone L8, showing faintly engraved geometric motifs; Stone C1, showing megalithic motifs and historical graffiti

FAR LEFT: The jacket illustration of stone C16, on the front cover of *Barclodiad Y Gawres* by T. Powell & G. Daniel (1956); LEFT: Stone C16, revealing, through oblique light, the geometric motifs that are indicative of megalithic rock art

Carved decoration occurs on Stones 5 (L8), 6 (C1) 8(C3), 22 (C13) and 19 (C16) (Shee-Twohig 1981, 229). On Stone 5 are lozenges and vertical zigzags; Stone 6 exhibits a conjoined circular motif, lozenges and vertical zigzags; on Stones 8 and 19 are a series of spirals and a series of unrecognisable motifs. Finally, on Stone 22 is a spiral, with supporting motifs, lozenges, a horizontal chevron band and a series of vertical zigzags. This particular stone bears some resemblance to the decorated Pattern Stone found at Bryn Celli Ddu. All five stones have their decoration facing into the chamber rather than being hidden, as found at monuments in the Boyne Valley.

Regarding the cruciform chamber area, it is likely that different strata of society were ritualistically deposited in different chambers; as, for example, male and female remains being placed in separate chambers. The chamber area was once covered by several enormous capstones. The chamber and passage architecture, prior to excavation, was partially exposed to the elements. However, when constructed it was probably covered by a large, turfed mound.

The forecourt area opens out onto views across the western coast of Ynys Môn Within the central chamber, a hearth was discovered, approximately 1m in diameter, which contained a mixture of charcoal and stone chips. Also recovered was an assemblage of shells, fish bones, and the remains of amphibia, reptiles and small mammals.

The profile of the passage appears to narrow as one progresses into the chamber area – an arrangement unlike passage tombs elsewhere. However, one should be cautious as the lines of both passage walls may no longer be in their original positions. It is clear that passages in all other passage graves provide some form of restricted visual access to the chamber area. One further missing element is the height of the passage uprights within the entrance area. It could be the case that these stones were set in such a way as to afford restricted visual access.

The cremated remains of two young adult males were found in the western chamber during the 1953 excavation. According to Powell & Daniel (1956),

THE YNYS MÔN GROUP   109

no primary pottery was found, but there was one artefact, which may be contemporary with the initial use of the monument. This was a bone or antler pin that was found with the cremation burials in the western side chamber: a pin similar to skewer pins found at Loughcrew and Fourknocks in central Ireland. The pin fragments were all burnt and would appear to be associated with the cremation. The location of a cinerary urn, above the collapsed roof area, also suggests that the deposition of the cremation was subsequent to the initial use of the tomb. The urn had a decorated, bevelled rim made up of a series of lines of plaited cord impressions.

It should also be noted that its impressive megalithic art has similarities with carvings on the Calderstones in Liverpool. Between 2004 and 2018, members of the Welsh Rock Art Organisation retraced and photographed the five decorated stones that occupy the chamber, and the space between the chamber and the passage (Nash 2020).

31. Din Dryfol, Aberffraw
SH 39562 72500, SM NO. A008
County Reference Number: ANG 5

This early Neolithic monument, excavated between 1969 and 1970, and again in 1980, is located in the south-western part of Ynys Môn and stands around 18m AOD. All that survives of the internal architecture is a rectangular chamber constructed of three uprights and a small capstone to the west; little of the cairn survives. It is highly likely that the cairn was robbed for building stone. According to Lynch, up to four chambers existed; all aligned roughly E–W. The arrangement of these chambers suggests a gallery-type monument (rather than a passage grave), similar in form to the much-damaged Cerrig Llwydion monument (CRM 10) in Carmarthenshire. If this

The denuded monument of Din Dryfol, showing a potentially complex chamber arrangement

is the case, Din Dryfol may also have similarities with the destroyed Llanymynech Hill monument in Montgomeryshire.[45] Further similarities are to be seen with the two- and four-chambered court tomb monuments found in Ireland. From the Lynch excavation report, there appears to be no formal division between the chamber compartments.

Situated some 6km from the south-west coast, this monument forms part of a small group, including Ty Newydd (ANG 3) and Barclodiad y Gawres (ANG 4). The monument is situated on a rocky south-west facing slope within a rocky landscape overlooking the Afon Gwna. Between the monument and Ty Newydd, approximately 4km to the north-west, is a large marsh area known as Llyn Padrig. To the south-west is a small lake known as Llyn Coron. It is probable that these two natural features would have had some ritual or economic significance at the time that the monument was in use.

The earliest reference to Din Dryfol was made by the Reverend H. Longueville Jones in 1865, when he suggested that it was two separate monuments, comprising a chamber to the north-west and a standing stone to the north-east. This interpretation remained current until the early part of the twentieth

The landscape surrounding the Din Dryfol monument

century. Later, Prichard (1871, 310–11) suggested the presence of two monuments on the basis of stone alignments. An engraving and plan of the site by Prichard shows a clear chamber. He also recorded the presence of two large holes (or depressions) which may represent the settings of two uprights. However, excavations by Lynch in 1980 did not find any evidence for these features. E.N. Baynes's survey *The Megalithic Remains of Anglesey* (1911), appears to propose that the two monuments at Din Dryfol are in fact one. He suggests that the menhir 'may have formed the end of a long chamber' (Baynes 1911, 75). Further, he compares the western section of the monument with Trefignath, classifying both as gallery graves. Daniel (1950, 186) also refers to the site it as a gallery grave.

According to the RCAHM inventory of Anglesey (1937), investigations revealed that a possible missing portal stone, approximately 2m north of the present standing portal, indicates that an unusually wide entrance existed, which may have formed part of a passage grave. Packing stones, according to Hemp (1935), were found in the location of the missing portal. Furthermore, investigations also showed that at some time during its use, possibly during the Early Bronze Age, the entrance was blocked, as cairn material was found in front of the portal area. However, this deposit turned out to be the remnants of a post-medieval trackway. Lynch agrees with Daniel that this monument is a form of gallery grave and is similar to tombs such as Cashtal-yn-Ard (MAN 1), Isle of Man and Trefignath (ANG 1).

The eastern and southern sections of the chamber (Lynch's Chamber 4) were excavated in 1969. In 1970 the capstone was lifted in order to fully excavate the chamber area. Further work was undertaken in 1980. The trenching, located in five areas which extended across most of the monument, showed that this was constructed over a rock shelf. In places, this shelf was exposed and that suggests that any stratigraphy within the area of the tomb was shallow.

The number of finds from the three excavation seasons was small, but included assemblages of Neolithic burnt bone, flint, pottery and stone implements from the chambers, and Romano-British ceramics, furnace slag and stone from inside and outside the cairn. The earliest pottery helped to provide a rough date for the monument of around 3,000 BCE. The absence of later pottery suggests that Din Dryfol was not in use during the Late Neolithic. Also recovered from each of the chambers was a small assemblage of bone, of which 12 fragments were identified as human. According to T.P. O'Connor, the human bone assemblage represented 2 individuals. Other identified bone included sheep/goat, pig and a large ungulate – either cattle or horse (1987, 129).

The monument itself consists of four uprights, two of which support a small capstone. The distance between the chamber and a large portal stone measured approximately 3m (Lynch 1987, 123).

Oriented roughly E–W, there appears to be little cairn present. The plan of the monument in some ways replicates the chamber and portal stone of Arthur's Stone in Herefordshire (HRF 1). Lynch (1969a, 114) suggests that there are some architectural characteristics in common with Hen-Drefor (ANG 11). Uncovered through excavation were the remains of a multi-chambered tomb with the eastern upright representing a door-stone to a chamber. Lynch suggests that chambers 3 and 4 are the earliest, followed by chambers 1 and 2 (1987, 123). This is partly based on two deliberately filled-in post-holes located either side of chamber 3. Chamber 3 may have been added after several generation's use of the original chamber (4) layout. Between chambers 3 and 4, Lynch uncovered blocking material, and to the east of chamber 3 was a possible façade that was partially delineated by uprights on the SE side of the chamber.

According to Lynch (1987, 123) this monument, classified as a long mound, has its architectural emphasis concentrated on the tall portal(s) around the entrance and the rectangular chambers. It also probably employed wood in its construction. These features are present in other monuments within the northern part of the Irish Sea province. Because of previous damage (especially during the Romano-British period and also during the nineteenth century), Lynch concludes that any full interpretation is inconclusive. However, it is multi-phased, though the number of phases are unknown.

The chamber arrangement of Bodowyr, looking east

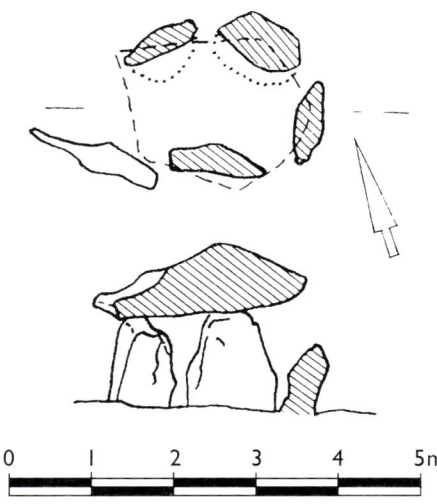

Plan and section of the Bodowyr monument (after Lynch 1969a)

32. Bodowyr, Llanidan
SH 46220 68165, SM NO. A007
County Reference Number: ANG 6

This monument, also referred to as Bodower,[46] is located 38m AOD on a lightly undulating south-eastern slope that overlooks the Menai Straits and the dramatic peaks of Snowdonia. Close to the monument and slightly later in date, is a series of standing stones that lie on the north-western slopes of the small valley of the Afon Braint. Both sets of monuments were once probably intervisible. Approximately 2km south-east of Bodowyr is Perthi Duon (ANG 17), located at SH 480 668.[47] It is probable that both these two monuments were in contemporary use during the Early Neolithic.[48]

In plan, the uprights of Bodowyr form a polygonal chamber, referred to by Daniel as a B-Dolmen (1950, 9).[49] Lynch has rightly suggested that this monument has close similarities with monuments such as the

Sketch of the Bodowyr monument by Skinner in 1802

Hanging Stone (PEM 24) at Burton, Pembrokeshire, and simple passage graves at Carrowmore, County Sligo (Lynch 1976, 75). I would suggest that Bodowyr is more likely to be a Portal Dolmen and is Early Neolithic in date.

This simple monument consists of four upright stones standing approximately 1.5m high, supporting a mushroom-shaped capstone measuring 2.45m x 1.75m. Located around the monument are the possible remnants of a mound. Two of the uprights towards the east of the monument form a possible entrance, while a single upright oriented N–E forms part of a possible passage, referred to as a sill-stone. An example of a sill-stone was also found, according to Hugh Prichard in 1873 (22–27), at Ty Mawr (ANG 10), also located close to the Menai Straits. The Reverend John Skinner visited this site and produced several sketches of the monument; one including the now demolished Bodowyr House and the other possibly showing himself sketching the monument. According to his sketches, little change has occurred to this monument since 1802. However, Skinner does show it to be located on a pronounced mound, of which little survives today. In his useful description, dated Thursday 2 December, 1802, Skinner remarks:

Here we were gratified of a very perfect cromlech standing in a field to the NW of the house [Bodowyr House]. The upper stone terminates in a ridge like the roof of a building and measures seven feet four inches long, three feet deep and four wide: this is sustained by three supporters, each three feet in height and nearly the same in thickness. That cromlechs were not always used (if they were at all) as altars for sacrifice I think may be demonstrated by the one before as its Pyramidical form is by no means adapted to the purpose. Indeed, there is a tradition amongst the Welsh that this rude memorial was erected over the grave of a British princess named Branwen ...

33. Bryn Celli Ddu, Llanddaniel-Fab
SH 50850 70175, SM NO. A002
County Reference Number: ANG 7

This monument, one of two known passage graves in Ynys Môn, can be considered one of the most important Neolithic monuments on the island. Located on a low ridge of glacial moraine at around 33m AOD and close to the Menai Straits, it has extensive views of the Snowdonia peaks. To the north and west is a slightly undulating landscape. Approximately 1.5km south-east of Bryn Celli Ddu is the large dolmen of Plas Newydd (ANG 9), while Bodowyr (ANG 6) and Perthi Duon (ANG 17) lie approximately 4km south-west of the monument.

Bryn Celli Ddu dates from the Late Neolithic, and probably has some temporal association with the nearby Bronze Age monuments, such as the standing stone that is located in a field some 200m west of the monument (SH 50632 70103). Also worth noting is the recent discovery of 26+ cupmarks on rock outcropping that lies roughly 250m north-west of Bryn Celli Ddu (at SH 50623 70240, Nash et al. 2005).

The mound kerbing and reconstructed entrance of Bryn Celli Ddu, looking west

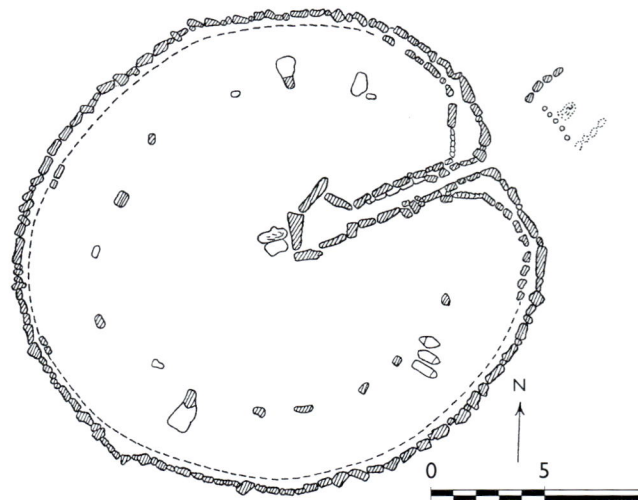

Plan of the Byn Celli Ddu passage grave (after Daniel 1950)

Within its recent history, the monument has been restored. However, one can get a glimpse of its original appearance by following the Reverend Skinner's account of his visit in 1802. He entered the passage and chamber on Friday, 3 December, and made a number of important, detailed (and sometimes rather quirky observations), which included the following account:

> But in this parish, we were fully recompensed for all our former disappointments by the site of the Carnedd at Bryn Celli. Accompanied by a young farmer who procured a lanthorn for the purpose we walked nearly a mile south east of the church to the spot where Mr Rowlands's time there were two carnedds remaining, having two rude stone pillars placed between them but these stones have been employed for the purpose of building a wall near this place as well as a great part of the western carnedd which is nearly destroyed for the same purpose about twenty years ago [1782] when the labourers went digging towards the centre discovered a flat pan about ten inches overturned bottom upwards and under it a wedge of gold the size of the heater of an iron with a piece of wire passing through the smaller end of it. The father of the young man who was with us happened to be one of the workmen employed at the time, but as what they found was immediately taken by Colonel Peacock the proprietor of the ground, the man could give no further account of the circumstance. I should imagine that what they called the wedge of gold was no other than one of the brazen celts or sacrificial instruments used in former times which have been discovered in great numbers in Cornwall and other parts of the kingdom. Whilst a farmer was removing some of the stones from the north east side of the larger carnedd to employ them in his repairs he came

Panoramic view of Bryn Celli Ddu and the landscape beyond, looking south-west

to a mouth of a passage covered with a square stone similar to that at Plasnewydd, anxious to reap the fruits of his discovery he precurred a light and creep forward on his hands and knees along the dreary vault, when lo! In a chamber at the further end a figure in white seemed to forbid his approach. The poor man had scarcely power sufficient to crawl backwards out of this den of spirits as he imagined however in a course of a few days instigated by the hopes of riches and the presence of many an assistance he made his second entrance into the cavern and finding the white gentleman did not offer to stir he boldly went forward and discovered the object of his apprehensions was no other than a stone pillar about six feet in height standing in the centre of the chamber. His former consternation could now only be exceeded by his eagerness to see what contained beneath the stone which he shortly overturned but treasure there was non, some large human bones lying near the pillar sufficiently testifying the purpose for which the structure was intended. This is the substance of the account we received from the young man whose father was one of Colonel Peacock's labourers and on the premises at the time of the discovery. The superstition of the common people still supposed this to be the habitation of spirits. Our two conductors seeming rather to complement each other about precedence, I took the lanthorn and crawling for about twelve feet long a narrow passage got into a more capacious chamber, my companions followed close at my heel and we assembled to the number of six in this singular sepulche. The passage by which we entered is about three feet high and a little more in breadth and was formed like that we noticed at Plas Newydd with flat stone stuck endways and covered with others of still greater magnitude laid across. I have still my doubts that if the former was further explored it might terminate in a similar vault to what we are now speaking of. The height of the chamber is nine feet, its form nearly triangular some of the sides being about three yards long and four or five feet high. The intermediate space up to the roof is filled with stones is placed one above the other in the manner they build walls but without any kind of cement. Two prodigious flat stones covered the whole one about three yards in length and two in breadth the other not quite so large. These are of a gritty substance not like any other stone found in the vicinity. The pillar stone lying in the cavern is a kind of freestone and seems to have been rounded by the tool.

Antiquarian engraving of 1847 showing a denuded passage and chamber of Bryn Celli Ddu

An antiquarian engraving by A.G. Hanlon (after H. Longueville Jones) of the site, published in *Archaeologia Cambrensis* (1847) portrays Bryn Celli Ddu as much ruined, consisting of a confused entrance and passage and an exposed chamber. There appears to be little or no trace of any mound. Therefore, much of the destruction had occurred sometime after Skinner's visit in 1802.

The site was first excavated by Captain F. du Bois Lukis in 1865. In letters to his brother, the Reverend W.C. Lukis, Captain Lukis describes how he excavated the chamber area and found a small piece of lead and a flint 'instrument'. After the death of his brother, the letters were obtained by the British Museum, who found among them a fragment of pottery, a strip of lead, a broken flint flake (possibly part of a tranchet arrowhead) and 'colouring matter' (c.f. Daniel 1950, 122). This 'colouring matter' was jasper which, according to Hemp, occurs frequently on the site (1930). Later excavations by Hemp between 1925 and 1929, revealed a complex history of the site. Beneath the mound was a possible circular henge consisting of 14 upright stones, some of which were broken, while others were leaning outwards, and within the centre of this was a pit that was covered by a recumbent stone slab. During excavation, socket holes were found which might represent the position of further uprights. Underlying some of these socket holes was evidence of cremation material, which perhaps suggests that the earlier henge monument may have deliberately included human burials during the period of its construction. Covering the area of the henge monument, but underlying the present mound, was a purple-coloured clay which Hemp suggests may represent a ritual floor. However, Lynch (1969a, 112) argues that it is a palaeo-turf line, the colour of which has been affected by drainage conditions from the overlying mound. This being the case, Lynch suggests that grass was covering the henge before the construction of the passage grave, indicating a time lapse between the abandonment and the construction of the henge (ibid. 112).

Lying next to the pit was the Pattern Stone. Outside the upright stones were the remains of a silted, flat-bottomed ditch that was approximately 6m in diameter and 2.2m in depth. It is this feature that is considered to be the remains of a henge and predates the passage grave mound. Within the entrance area of the passage grave phase were the sockets of five post-holes, that may represent a possible burial platform for human excarnation. Immediately behind this structure was a shallow pit containing the remains of an ox. Also within the entrance area were two hearths. The presence of the post-holes, the burial pit and the two hearths suggests that some form of ritual activity was being conducted within the entrance and forecourt area. The remains of the ox may suggest some form of offering for the dead to consume during their journey to the other world: an act widely recorded in the ethnographic record. However, this discovery was made before the advent of chronometric dating techniques, and therefore a date range was not possible.

Finds from the 1925–9 excavation were meagre but included a *petit tranchet* (transverse arrowhead) which is probably Late Neolithic in date. Also recovered was a rounded scraper (thumb-shaped end scraper), a small lithic assemblage numbering 20 pieces and a mudstone bead which was found within the turf line of the ditch, and south of the passage. According to Lynch, it is probable that this artefact belongs to the passage grave builders rather than the henge users (1969b, 160). However, previous antiquarian interest in this monument (dating to at least the early nineteenth century) has probably seen the removal of much of the artefactual evidence.

The mound, 26m in diameter, might have been larger, but during part-restoration by the Ministry of Works, the monument may have been severely altered. The entrance, with its two uprights (without a capstone/s), is located on the eastern side of the mound. It leads and into a slab-roofed passage approximately 7.5m in length. Intriguingly, the southern wall of the passage is straight, whereas the northern wall is not (Thomas 1988, 45). To the west of the monument and almost in line with the alignment of the walls of the passage is a standing stone, suggesting fore planning of the monument. The passage leads into a polygonal chamber roughly 2.5m across.[50] Between the entrance and the passage are two sets of kerbing, which suggests two phases of building during the passage grave phase.

Considering the design and the presence of an ox burial, Lynch suggests that this monument has a greater association with passage graves in Brittany than with monuments in the Boyne Valley in southern Ireland (1969a, 111). Within the chamber area is an undated single stone pillar, which has no structural use. It may therefore be considered to possess some ritual, or at least an aesthetic, significance; or was added sometime later after the original use of the monument.

LEFT: The early morning winter sun penetrating the passage and chamber of Bryn Celli Ddu, looking east; RIGHT: The early morning winter sunrise forming a distinct shadow on the western back wall of the chamber

Along with Barclodiad y Gawres (ANG 4), this monument has two decorated stones with megalithic art: one within a pit, the other in the chamber. Decoration of one of two stones includes an anti-clockwise spiral approximately 13cm in diameter. The other stone, known usually as the Pattern Stone, was found adjacent to a possible ritual pit in the centre of the monument. The stratigraphic relationship between this stone and the surrounding soil deposits suggest that it belongs to the henge phase of the monument, yet it has similarities with other decorated passage graves throughout north-western Europe, which are incorporated into single-phase monuments. It could be the case that the stone that formed part of the henge was left *in situ* while the passage grave was being constructed.

The complex decoration of the Pattern Stone, confined to three faces on the upper section of the stone, consists of a clockwise spiral which is linked

THE YNYS MÔN GROUP

The Pattern Stone, standing west of the chamber and belonging to the earlier henge phase of the monument

Outlying standing stone, to the south of Bryn Celli Ddu

Cupmarked surfaces of a natural rock outcropping, with Bryn Celli Ddu in the background

Cupmarked surface that forms part of the summit of a large rock outcrop that stands west of the monument

to a meandering curvilinear pattern, referred to by Shee-Twohig as a serpentine form (1981, 230), which covers both faces of the stone. Also present is a cupmark. There are also design similarities with the megalithic art of the uprights of the Calderstones, Liverpool. The simple spiral, located in the chamber, may have direct similarities with stone C16 within the chamber of Barclodiad y Gawres. However, this motif has been engraved using a metal tool, and is therefore of historic origin and not prehistoric.

Despite no archaeological investigations in or around Bryn Celli Ddu since Hemp's fieldwork during the late 1920s/early 1930s, a probable Bronze Age cairn was excavated by a team from the University of Central Lancashire between 2017 and 2019. The site is mentioned in John Skinner's *Ten Days Tour through the Island of Anglesey* in 1802, when the stone was used for road building. Prior to the recent excavation, the site survived as a shallow earthwork and was located on a low-lying knoll several hundred metres to the south of Bryn Celli Ddu.

34. Bryn yr Hen Bobl, Llanedwen
SH 5190 6900, SM NO. A006
County Reference Number: ANG 8

The name of this unusual monument translates as the 'Hill of the Old People'. It forms a kidney-shaped mound approximately 5.5m in height and 13.5m in diameter, and stands around 33m AOD. It has been classified as a passage grave and, although not similar to nearby Bryn Celli Ddu (ANG 5), it does share a similar landscape. The monument stands a few hundred metres from the Menai Straits. To the north-west, Bryn Celli Ddu is 1km away, while to the south-west and north-east are further Neolithic chambered monuments. Bryn yr Hen Bobl is also sited close to a series of standing stones running from north of Bryn Celli Ddu to the south of the Bodowyr monument (ANG 6). Prior to the monument being included within a late eighteenth-century walled parkland landscape, Bryn Yr Hen Bobl may have had even more outstanding views of the North Wales mainland, including Snowdonia, as well as views to the south which encompass the open sea.

The site was visited by the Reverend John Skinner on Friday 3 December, 1802, when he produced several sketches and remarked:

> From hence we pursued our walk across the park towards Lord Uxbridge's house, stopping on the way to examine a very large Carnedd or artificial hillock formed of loose stones but now overgrown with turf and trees. This remain is one of the most considerable in the island, measuring one hundred and thirty-four paces in circumference. On walking around, it we observed a square

The façade and entrance to the chamber at Bryn yr Hen Bobl, looking west

Antiquarian image of Bryn yr Hen Bobl, by J.E. Griffiths in 1900

opening on the south side which I entered on my hands and knees and found it about ten feet long, four wide and three high, the sides formed of three large flat stones placed edgeways in the ground supporting the roof, which consists of only two. I have endeavoured to be as exact as I could in my drawings of this cistfaen (which without doubt it was) and employed as the grave of some considerable personage in ancient times though Mr Rowlands appropriates the carnedd to a very different use and connects it with the religion of the Druids. In his time three skeletons were discovered in digging near the surface of the carnedd, which gave him an idea of its being a place of sacrifice; but he had never an opportunity of viewing the interior (the opening has been discovered within these few years) he was unable to speak with certainty on the subject.

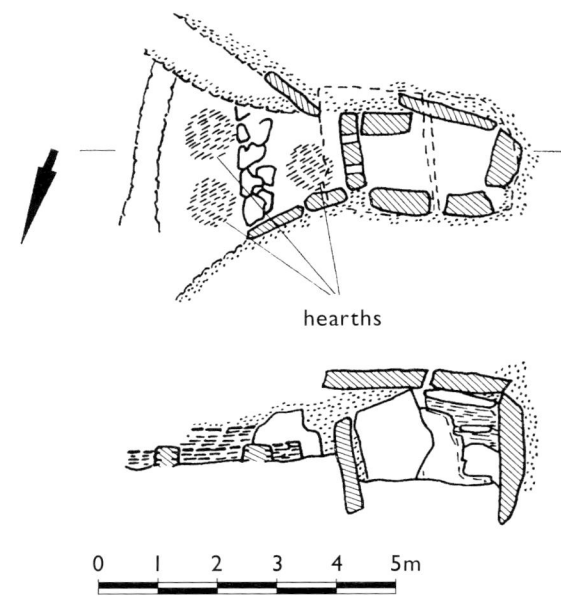

Detailed plan and section of the chamber arrangement (after Hemp 1937)

Currently, the monument consists of a damaged, stone-lined entrance that is incorporated into the mound on the eastern side. There are also several trees (one dead) extending from the mound. The burial chamber, measuring 2m x 1m and 1.6m high, is constructed of a series of uprights that support a large capstone. The remains of at least 20 individuals, including adults and children, were discovered in the chamber; all were disarticulated. There was also a small assemblage of burnt human bone, found outside the southern end of the terrace, which may be associated with a later Bronze Age urn burial connected with the monument (see below).

Bryn yr Hen Bobl was excavated by W.J. Hemp between 1929 and 1935 (Hemp 1935). The sides of the forecourt were found to be constructed of kerbstones and drystone walling. In front of the entrance was an extensive blocking deposit of large stones and soil. Lynch (1970, 47) suggests that the drystone walling was also used to block the forecourt. Within this blocking were fragments of Neolithic pottery, lithics and charcoal. The origin of these artefacts is unclear. However, similar deposition has been found in blocking material in the forecourt areas of other passage graves, and may represent some form of ritual activity. A few sherds of pottery were also found in three ritual fire pits in the forecourt area. In addition to the excavation of the chamber and forecourt area, Hemp also considered that a side chamber may have existed. However, this was never found.

Located around the southern part of the mound, and now almost undetectable, was a stone-revetted platform or terrace measuring 100m x 5m. This is referred to by some as the 'tail'. Excavators deduced that this was constructed after the mound and may have been part of an architectural trend that was associated with the construction of the horns, located either side of the entrance. The terrace, which is aligned N–S, had small pieces of pottery

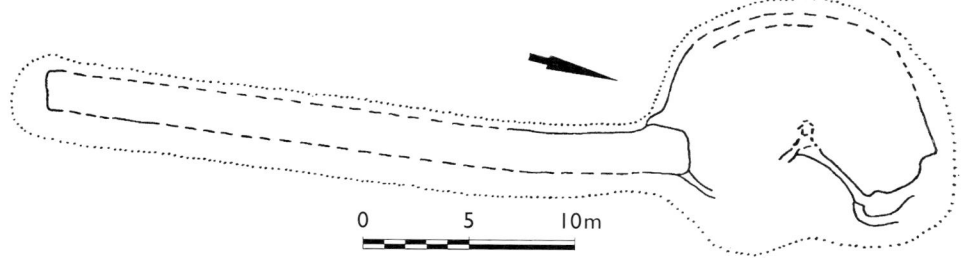

Plan of the mound and its associated avenue (after Lynch 1969a)

within its foundation material. This terrace was later replaced with a drystone wall. Beneath the foundation material, there appeared to be a specially laid primary deposit consisting of clay and charcoal. Remarkably, within this clay surface were a number of footprints probably belonging to the builders or users of the monument. The various suggestions as to what this platform may represent include Hemp's idea that it is a deliberate addition to the monument, which transforms the plan of the tomb and the surface into a phallus. However, this shape can only be viewed from above or in plan, and a more likely origin of the terrace is that it forms part of a 5m prehistoric field boundary which may pre-date the monument; or a causeway/procession route leading to the façade area of the monument (see Children & Nash 2001).

The finds from the ritual hearths and blocking material make Bryn yr Hen Bobl one of the richest pottery and flint sites in Ynys Môn. More remarkable is that the majority of these finds, according to Lynch (1969b, 161), are not associated with the actual monument, except for a broken bone pin which was found in the chamber.[51] The pin, not usually associated with the Irish Sea Zone long cairns, is nevertheless linked within the passage grave tradition, of which this monument is probably one. Concerning the pottery (of which there are decorated and undecorated types), it appears that the assemblage was not correctly provenanced, and it is now difficult to determine if the pottery came from the monument. Co-excavator Colin Gresham formally dissented from Hemp's findings and produced an alternative report on the pottery finds, offering a different account of their locations and associations in the site chronology.

The only location specifically associated with the mound was the south-eastern corner of the terrace (Hemp 1935, 269) where the fragments of two shouldered bowls were found. Other pottery from across the site included fragments of decorated Peterborough Ware and undecorated wares of Western Neolithic derivation. The Western Neolithic types were found beneath the main structures of the monument and both types were allegedly found within the chamber area. Up to six pots with slightly different fabrics were linked to the Western Neolithic pottery group (Peterson 2003). The most complete vessel was a lugged bowl (the fabric of which was very hard and pitted, and black to brown in colour throughout), which measured up to 25.4cm in diameter. The Peterborough Ware types comprised a series of sherds that included shoulders and rims decorated with whipped-cord and square-toothed comb designs. Also recovered was a single sherd which may belong to a beaker, suggesting that the monument was in use, or at least known about, during the Early Bronze Age. Along with pottery, there was

The mound of Bryn yr Hen Bobl, looking north

a comprehensive assemblage of lithics and stone, including scrapers, awls, leaf-shaped arrowheads, end scrapers and transverse arrowheads (*Petit Tranchet* derivative – type C1). Associated with the diagnostic lithics was a large assemblage of waste material, including stone flakes which are believed to come from polished stone axe production (Daniel 1950, 139). Probably the most interesting finds were four polished stone axes, three of which were recovered from the terrace and the other from the northern horn of the cairn. A roughed-out stone axe was also found at the base of the outer wall within the forecourt area. The three complete axes, with their pointed butts and convex cutting edges, appear to be made from local Ynys Môn dolerite, while the rough-out is made from Graig Llwyd diorite, and is almost certainly a product of the well-known axe manufacturing centre near Penmaenmawr, North Wales. Other finds included an Iron Age bead, which was found within the disturbed filling of the chamber, and two small balls – one of bone, the other of stone – which may be associated with the Irish Passage Grave tradition.

Located on top of the cairn was evidence of Iron Age or early medieval burials, again suggesting the monument's continuing sanctity as a place of burial.

35. Plas Newydd, Llanedwen
SH 52000 69720, SM no. A005
County Reference Number: ANG 9

This much-modified monument stands in front of the National Trust-owned property of Plas Newydd. During the Neolithic period, this monument may have enjoyed extensive views across the Menai Straits. It is located approximately 250m north of the shores of the straits, within an undulating landscape both to the north and west, and stands around 30m AOD.[52] Approximately 2km to the north-west is Bryn Celli Ddu (ANG 7). Further Neolithic activity is presumed both north-east and south-west of the monument, but whether or not these monuments were in direct association, either spatially or temporally, remains the subject of debate. Bryn Yr Hen Bobl (ANG 8) stands some 300m to the south-west of the Plas Newydd site. The architecture comprises 10 uprights that support two massive capstones which cover two chambers.

The double-chambered monument of Plas Newydd, standing north of a cricket ground

Although Lynch has described this monument as 'unclassified' (1969a, 123) due to the site being unexcavated, I would suggest that this monument has similar architectural traits to Trefignath (ANG 1) and Presaddfed (ANG 2).

Unsigned antiquarian engraving dated 1813, showing the northern elevations of Plas Newydd, looking south

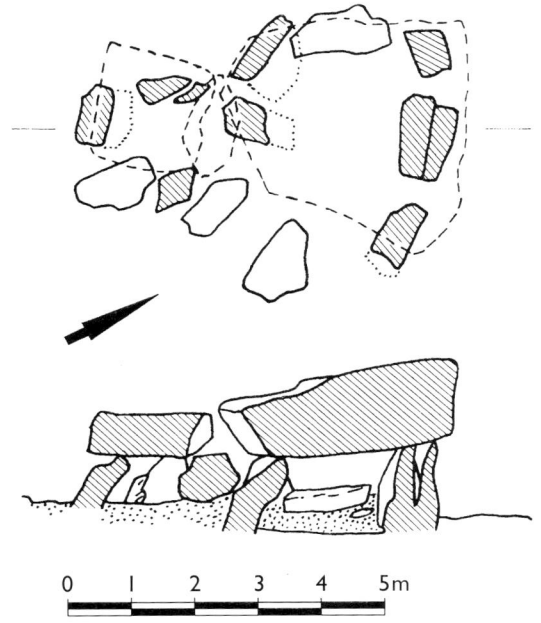

Plan and section of Plas Newydd dolmen (after Lynch 1970)

The Plas Newydd monument has functioned as a parkland folly for well over two centuries. The Reverend John Skinner, when visiting the site on Friday 3 December, 1802, remarked:[53]

> From hence we proceeded to look at a very large cromlech or Druidical alter preserved in the Park near his lordship's stables [which still stand] ... However, I made a drawing of the cromlech, which is nearly four yards long and above a yard thick, the supporters at the north end nearly five feet high; a smaller stone lying close to the other extremity measuring three feet long and two and a half thick has also its small supporters and is to all appearance intended as a separate cromlech.

The tomb consists of a large chamber measuring 3m x 2.7m, which supports a large capstone measuring 3.5m x 3m and 1m in thickness. It is considered that the entrance was located to the south-west where an antechamber with supporting capstone is located. Both chambers appear to be circular in plan and are separated by a large stone that restricts access between the two. The capstone of the larger chamber slopes towards the northeast, where three large uprights are aligned roughly E–W. It is probable that the central upright within this alignment was a closed portal similar to that at Pentre Ifan (PEM 5). Both the eastern and western sides of the large chamber are missing. It is more than likely that missing stones lie somewhere within the vicinity of the site, maybe underneath a cricket pitch located immediately to the north.

Due to the lack of excavation, one can only imagine what the monument may have looked like during the Neolithic. Hemp (1935) suggested that the monument consisted of a large, single chamber with associated antechamber or passage; whereas Daniel (1950, 57) suggests that the southern chamber is, in fact, a side chamber. The passage, according to Daniel, is located at the east. I am more inclined to think that both chambers, which are oriented on roughly a N–S axis, form a continuous chamber set. A cairn or turf mound would have covered the two chambers and it is probable that the two capstones were partially exposed.

36. Ty Mawr, Llanfair Pwllgwyngyll
SH 53855 72130, SM NO. A037
County Reference Number: ANG 10

This much-damaged monument, drawn by H. Prichard in 1873 (1873, 22–27), lies between Menai Bridge and Llanfairpwllgwyngyll, and has identical landscape affinities to those of nearby Plas Newydd (ANG 9) and Bodowyr (ANG 6), possessing outstanding views of the mountains of Snowdonia. The monument, standing around 73m AOD, overlooks the north-eastern reach of the Menai Straits (and the open sea of Conwy Bay beyond), whilst to the north-west is an undulating, marshy landscape. The location of this monument is interesting in that it sits on the interface between two contrasting landscapes – the sea and uplands.

Lynch (1970) has suggested that, although badly damaged, the capstone would formerly have been supported by three uprights, one of which stood up to 1.5m high. The capstone measures 2.5m E–W by 3m N–S and appears to slope from east to west. Between the two fallen uprights at the eastern-end is a sill-stone measuring 0.75m in height, believed to be one of the architectural traits associated with the short passage grave tradition. However, I am firmly of the view that it is a Portal Dolmen-type monument.

It is suggested by Lynch (1969a, 117) that Ty Mawr, along with Bodowyr, represents a simple passage grave type similar to those found at Carrowmore, Co. Sligo and Burton, Pembrokeshire (the Hanging Stone, Site 91). When visiting this site in early 2024, no particular architectural form could be discerned. Although much of the monument may have been removed (including its mound) one could be looking at a simple earth-fast type monument. No uprights to the west of the capstone are present, unless they have either been removed or are buried.

The ruins of Ty Mawr, showing the capstone and several uprights, looking north

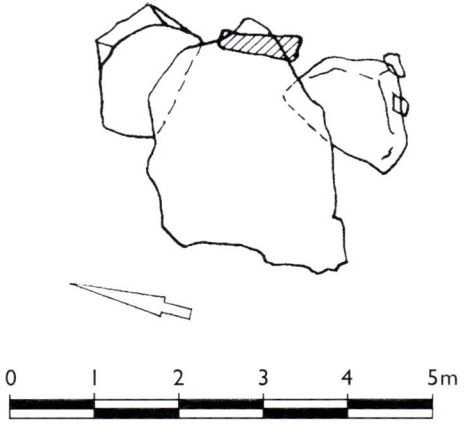

Plan of the Ty Mawr chamber (after Lynch 1970)

37. Hen-Drefor, Llansadwrn
SH 55095 77322, SM NO. A025
County Reference Number: ANG 11

Hen-Drefor is located approximately 6km north-west of Bryn Celli Ddu (ANG 7) and is one of a group of monuments which appears to visually acknowledge the hinterlands of the Menai Straits. This monument, approximately 2.5km north of the Menai Straits, is located on the intermediate slopes of an undulating landscape, standing around 112m AOD. To the north and west is a series of marshy bogs and therefore this monument occupies the interface between two distinct landscapes. Similar to other chambered tombs within the Menai Straits area, Hen-Drefor lies close to a number of Early Bronze Age monuments, including four standing stones. Despite its present appearance, Hen-Drefor would have been a striking visual monument during the Neolithic.

The monument was first described in 1783, when Thomas Pennant, in his *Tours in Wales*, noted that it was a 'sad monument'. In 1802, Hen-Drefor was visited by the Reverend John Skinner, who expressed a similar opinion.

Today, the monument consists of two groups of what are termed by Lynch (1969) as 'fallen stones', clustered roughly 8m apart. Included in the eastern group of stones is a tall portal stone. Close to this portal stone are a recumbent capstone and a possible upright. Lynch (1970, 34) suggests that the western group may have formed a rectangular chamber. According to the literature, there appears to have been no evidence of any stone in antiquity between the two groups. If this is the case, one can assume that this is a double-chambered monument similar to that of Dyffryn Ardudwy (MER 3) in Gwynedd, nearby Din Dryfol (ANG 5) and Trefignath (ANG 1); it may even represent two separate monuments. However, surrounding the monument are slight traces of a

The ruined remains of Hen-Drefor, looking south

cairn. According to Lynch (1969a, 115), Hen-Drefor had collapsed at some time within the last two centuries.

The site is difficult to assess because of its condition. Lynch (1969 & 1970) places Hen-Drefor within the long-mound tradition. However, Daniel (1950, 150) goes further and suggests that it belongs to a terminal-chambered long barrow related to the Irish Sea group of monuments; even suggesting that it is a gallery grave without forecourt or side chambers, similar to that of Bedd yr Afanc (PEM 27), Pembrokeshire, and Trefignath (ANG 1). What is clear is that the two piles of stone represent chambers. It is also clear that these chambers are incorporated into a mound, traces of which are still visible. It is probable that each chamber would have been entered either via a passage or forecourt. This being the case, the appropriate classification is that the monument belongs to the long-mound tradition (in other words, of Cotswold-Severn type); and that, if passages or entrances were present, the site conforms to a group of monuments which are indigenous to North Wales and Ynys Môn.

38. Pant y Saer, Llanfair-Mathafarn-Eithaf
SH 50967 82405, SM NO. A004
County Reference Number: ANG 13

Pant y Saer, located 0.75km north of the Glyn monument (ANG 12) and within the town of Benllech, encompasses dramatic views west over north-east Ynys Môn and east over The Wirral and Conwy Bay. The monument, standing around 99m AOD, occupies a ridge of a limestone escarpment, close to a small stream on uncultivated ground. It is one of a group of three chambered tomb monuments that appears to be typical of this part of the Ynys Môn coast. Recent development of the area has partly obscured the landscape vista of this monument and the nearby Glyn monument at SH 5142 8172,[54] and a doubtful burial chamber[55] at Benllech (ANG 26), at SH 5190 8267.[56]

Pant y Saer has a rectangular chamber which opens on its south-eastern side. The chamber consists of a rock-cut pit measuring 4m x 3m x 1m, and has three uprights. It is covered by a large capstone measuring approximately 4m x 4m, and is set within a kidney-shaped cairn mound, presumably similar in form to that at Bryn yr Hen Bobl (ANG 8). The cairn is defined by a low limestone and gritstone block wall. At the north-eastern end of the monument, excavation has revealed an original edge to the cairn.

Lynch states that the 1875 excavations were primarily concerned with the chamber and its contents, and in doing so, may have destroyed a rectangular Beaker cist which was cut into an existing pit containing at least two crouched burials (1969, 119). It is probable that these burials, dating to the Early Bronze Age, were a secondary deposition. More discoveries were made by Scott, when the bones of at least 54 individuals were recovered, of which 18 were children (Scott 1933). Also included within this skeletal assemblage were at least nine full-term foetuses. Osteological analysis revealed that there were not enough skulls to match the long bones, which may suggest that human remains were being deposited from other sites, with Pant y Saer

The chamber at Pant-y-Saer, looking east

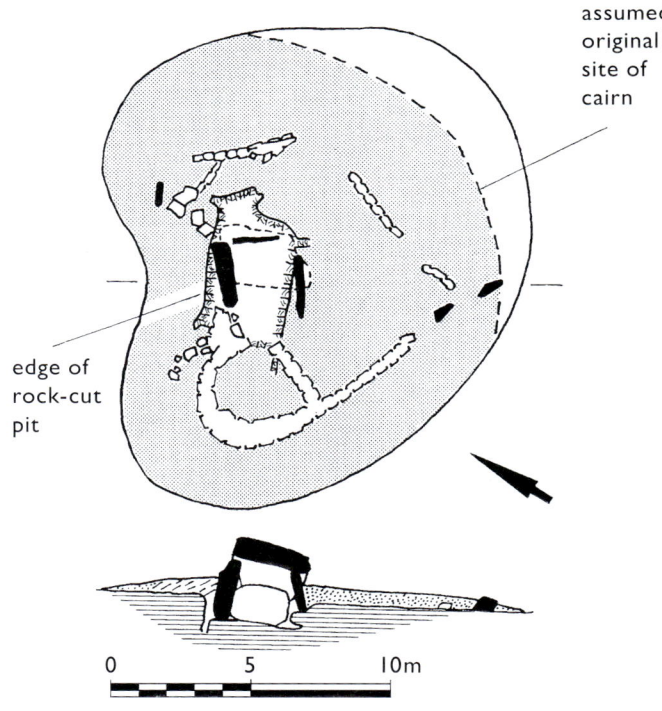

Plan and section of Pant-y-Saer (after Lynch 1970)

126 NEOLITHIC TOMBS OF WALES

acting as an ossuary. It could be the case, however, that bone material from the 1875 excavation had been mislaid. Alternatively, the deliberate removal of cranial material may have formed part of a religious act, similar to that observed with undisturbed material found at West Kennet Long Barrow in Wiltshire. The large number of people buried within the small chamber suggests that this monument was being used over a long period of time, either by high-status individuals; or it may be that a corporate approach to death was in vogue, in which all members of the community were interred together.

Other finds included an assemblage of Neolithic pottery, representing at least nine vessels of Western style pottery (Daniel 1950, 140). At the western end, between the horns and the cairn, were the remains of a forecourt area. Interestingly, there appears to be no direct entrance to the chamber from the forecourt area, and it is probable that one of the large uprights may have been periodically moved in order to deposit more remains. However, it should be noted, according to Lynch (1969a, 119), that serious disturbance caused by the excavators may have distorted the stratigraphy inside the chamber.

Pant y Saer revealed a typical homogenous Neolithic assemblage, which included undecorated or shell grit-ware pottery pieces. The majority of the finds came from within the forecourt area and the chamber. It is probable that the finds from the forecourt area are the result of the spoil, which was removed from the chamber during the 1875 excavation. However, based on the excavation by Scott in 1932, Lynch (1970, 46) mentions that within the forecourt there was a small assemblage of pottery, a scratched pebble and a section of human skull along with animal bone, which appears to have been a deliberate deposit, possibly an offering made in front of the tomb's entrance. Like most monuments, the deposit was covered by an extensive blocking deposit which is probably Bronze Age in date. Also included in the finds inventory was Beaker pottery, a selection of worked flint, including four leaf-shaped arrowheads, a lozenge-shaped arrowhead, scrapers, two stone discs and an antler-point. The largest arrowhead, made from chert, is believed to derive from a type found in Ireland, suggesting some form of contact/exchange network between Irish Sea Province communities. The pottery assemblages, which are very fragmentary, are interesting in that they appear to embrace pottery traditions that are both local and regional. Lynch (1969b, 172) suggests that the pottery has affinities with the Irish Sea traditions, as is seen with pottery from Dyffryn Ardudwy and from the Cotswold-Severn region. It is worth noting that a small nodule of pyrites was also found, believed by Lynch (1969b, 157) to be associated with burial activity, possibly dating to the Beaker phase.

As Lynch rightly points out (1970, 97), much of the upper stratigraphy of this monument was probably disturbed during the 1875 excavation, while what was then recorded was not fully understood. According to the excavators, Williams and Prichard, the rectangular stone cist covered by a capstone (measuring 2m x 0.75m) lay diagonally across the chamber and cut into earlier deposits. The cist walls were constructed of drystone coursing, while the floor was laid with a bed of shingle. According to Lynch, this type of architecture is unique (1969, 118). Inside the cist were two skeletons which, according to the plan published in *Archaeologia Cambrensis*, were arranged in a confused form (Williams 1875). The bones were crushed due to the collapse of the walling. However, it is interesting to note that the plan places the skeletal remains within the north-western part of the cist only; and, therefore, it is my belief that these remains had been deliberately moved to this area of the cist in order to make way for more human remains. Lynch states that no finds other than bone were discovered, and therefore dating these burials to the Late Neolithic/Early Bronze Age is difficult to substantiate (1969, 159). The later 1933 excavation, however, did uncover sherds from a long-necked beaker in areas of the cist which had not been disturbed by the earlier Williams and Prichard excavation.

39. Lligwy, Penrhos-Lligwy
SH 50130 86040, SM NO. A009
County Reference Number: ANG 14

This monument, in common with many similar genuine and spurious sites, is known as Coetan Arthur (Arthur's Quoit). It is located 1.5km east of Moelfre, and has extensive views across the North Wales coastline and the northern coastline of Ynys Môn. The monument, standing at 63m AOD, is located in an undulating landscape and shares a similar landscape position to two other monuments, Pant y Saer (ANG 13) and Glyn (ANG 12).

The site was visited by the Reverend Skinner on Saturday 11 December 1802, and he provides a brief sketch and a description, thus:

> Not far distant facing the ocean is a cromlech the upper stone six yards long, five yards and a half wide and three yards thick. One end rests upon a bank of earth and the other is supported by four or five small upright stones, leaving a hollow beneath about two feet high.

This chambered tomb is classified as a sub-megalithic monument that is considered to be a Late Neolithic or transitional development. Lynch's description suggests a structure that was not intended to be visually impressive, but which served

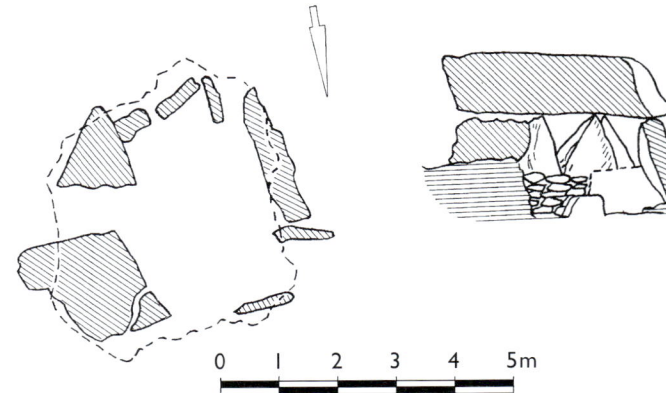

Plan and cross-section of the Lligwy monument (after Daniel 1950)

The subterranean chamber of Lligwy

Antiquarian photograph of Lligwy, taken by J.E. Griffiths in 1900

the purpose of providing a makeshift burial chamber with minimal effort. Both Daniel (1950) and Lynch (1970) suggest that this monument type appeared late in the megalithic sequence, and was a 'degenerate' form representing the waning of the megalithic tradition (other monuments within this classification include Glyn and Gop Cave, FLT 2). However, the monument is conspicuously megalithic, and is highly visible; while the size of the capstone, which weighs at least 25 tons, means that the monument cannot reasonably be described as makeshift or 'degenerate'.

The tomb comprises a massive capstone, measuring 5.5m x 4.5m x 1m, beneath which is a series of eight rough stones – some upright, others laid horizontally – and a rock-cut pit. The three supporting stones rest either on the edge of the pit or on drystone walling. The chamber is some 2m in height, measured from the underside of the capstone to the base of the pit. Lynch (1970, 52) suggests the entrance was on the eastern side and that the tomb never had a formal passage; and, although stones can be seen around the chamber, this is not taken as firm evidence for the existence of a cairn.

The chamber was partially excavated in 1908 by E.N. Baynes, who found, beneath a layer of sterile soil, an undisturbed burial deposit comprising two layers which were separated by a series of flat stones (Baynes 1909). Within the chamber he found the remains of up to 30 individuals, including men, women and children. The upper part of the deposit, which was covered by a layer of limpet shells, contained fragmentary unburnt human and animal bone, as well as black earth, some flint and several pottery sherds. More black earth and a greater quantity of bone was discovered in the lower layer, together with further pottery and flint, above a quantity of mussel shells. According to the excavator, Neil Baynes, many of the human bones had been deliberately broken and trampled. The later

Two budding archaeologists – John and Hannah sat on top of the Lligwy capstone

burials, located above the paving, probably date from the Late Neolithic or Early Bronze Age period – in other words, what Lynch refers to as Beaker in date (2,000–1,800 BCE).

During the Baynes excavation, there appears to have been no stratigraphic record of where 40 pieces of pottery were found, which is frustrating considering that this monument appears to have been in use during both the Neolithic and the Bronze Age. The pottery was subsequently analysed by Stuart Piggott in the 1930s, who found that all but two sherds belonged to a Western Neolithic pottery type, now referred to as Grooved Ware. Some were decorated with grooves, suggesting a Scottish connection (Lynch 1969b, 172), while others possessed cardium shell impressions, which came from above the paving. In general, the pottery showed marked affinities with sherds from Pant y Saer. Among the flint finds was a 'slug' (plano-convex) knife, said to resemble those found in the court cairns of Northern Ireland (ibid. 159). Also found was a polished bone pin that has been compared with examples from Loughcrew and Yorkshire.

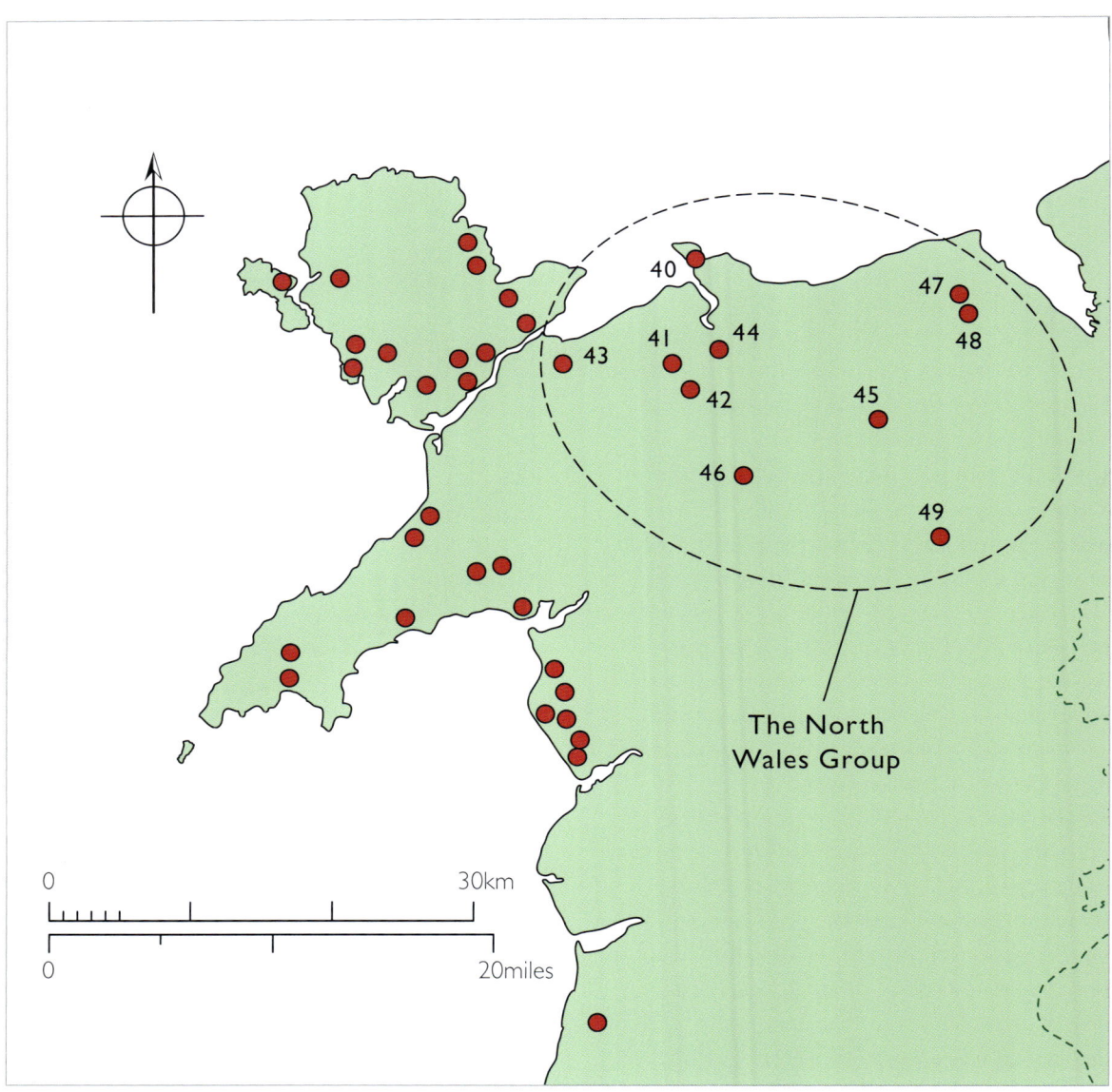

40 Llety'r Filiast
41 Maen y Bardd
42 Porth Llwyd
43 Sling
44 Hendre Waelod
45 Tyddyn Bleiddyn
46 Capel Garmon
47 Gop Cairn
48 Gop Cave
49 Tyn-y-Coed

SIX

The North Wales Group

Daniel (1950) has conveniently categorised the monuments based on what is present in each of the counties. I have attempted to do likewise, but I note that monuments within eastern Caernarvonshire and western Denbighshire are located close to the Afon Conwy. Further east in Flintshire, there is probably the largest and most impressive monument of all – Gop Cairn (FLT 1). In addition, there are a number of cave sites that have been used to house the Neolithic dead, including Gop Cave (FLT 2). Note that much of North Wales is underlain by limestone, and here numerous caves have been created over geological time. Arguably, and based on limited archaeological evidence, these cave sites appear to have a much deeper history that extends into the Mesolithic and Upper Palaeolithic periods.

Each of the ten monuments discussed here is located within a highly distinctive landscape setting. The group includes: Llety'r Filiast (CRN 1), Maen y Bardd (CRN 3), Porth Llwyd (CRN 4), Sling (CRN 5), Hendre Waelod (DEN 1), Tyddyn Bleiddyn (DEN 2), Capel Garmon (DEN 3), Gop Cairn (FLT 1), Gop Cave (FLT 2) and Tyn-y-Coed (MER 7).

Monuments in the eastern part of Denbighshire and Flintshire lie within secluded, undulating valleys, while inland monuments such as Capel Garmon (DEN 3) lie close to the mountains of Snowdonia. The Hendre Waelod monument (DEN 1), along with the Portal Dolmens of Maen-y-Bardd (CRN 3) and Porth Llwyd (CRN 4), lie next to or within the hinterlands of the Conwy valley.

The Gop Cairn (and neighbouring Gop Cave) lie some 8km south of the North Wales coastline, and have extensive views to the north, south and west. Its architecture, consisting of a large limestone-block cairn, is very different from the small chamber located within Gop Cave, some 100m below the cairn (RCAM 1912). The Gop Cairn is extremely visible within the landscape, although the cave and its surrounding rock outcrop is arguably hidden by visually merging with other rock outcrops in the immediate area.

Excavations in the late nineteenth century show that the cairn, which stands some 12m high and 100m in diameter, was constructed of limestone blocks. Close to this monument an occupation site was found, which had a series of finds indicative of the Neolithic, including leaf-shaped arrowheads and diagnostic flint scrapers and knives, as well as a flint borer and a large number of worked flint flakes. The visual impact of this monument along with nearby

Neolithic artefacts could suggest that Gop Cairn dates to the Late Neolithic at a time when the choice of position of monuments in the landscape was changing.

South-west of the Gop sites is the much-ruined site of Tyn-y-Coed (MER 7). This monument can be described as an inland site, lying as it does on the lower western slopes of the Berwyn Mountains, overlooking the River Dee. This monument lies within a fragmented Late Neolithic or Early Bronze Age landscape. To the south-east of Tyn-y-Coed is a stone circle, and beyond this are several cairns. Its situation is similar to that of Hendre Waelod (DEN 1), except that Tyn-y-Coed is classified as a Cotswold-Severn type monument (Lynch 1969a, 147).

Located close to the famous Palaeolithic cave site of Pontnewydd is Tyddyn Bleiddyn (DEN 2), which lies on the eastern slopes of Cefn Meiriadog. The site lies within a secluded valley oriented NW–SE. This laterally chambered Cotswold-Severn tomb, was excavated by Boyd-Dawkins in 1874, and is now in a poor state of preservation (RCAM 1914). Nevertheless, it occupies a typical valley situation, similar to that of a doubtful monument known as Maen Pebyll. To the south-west of this monument is an extensive upland area which forms the southern extent of the Snowdonia mountains. Arguably, Tyddyn Bleiddyn has a landscape affinity with the nearby Capel Garmon monument that lies some 19km to the west. Capel Garmon, located some 300m AOD, also occupies a valley location and is sub-megalithic in form, having extensive views to the north and west, but again is also hidden. In most examples, the visitor has to be in close proximity in order to see the form of the monument. During the Neolithic, most if not all monuments were covered with a mound or cairn; therefore, visibility would have been even more restricted.

40. Llety'r Filiast, Llandudno
SH 77062 82950, SM NO. C005
County Reference Number: CRN 1

Located within the central region of Great Orme's Head, a limestone headland, and close to the famous Great Orme Bronze Age copper mines, is the Llety'r Filiast monument. Standing around 165m AOD, this lies on the edge of a small depression and has restricted views of the immediate landscape. However, open sea to the east, north and west, plus the Conwy estuary to the south-west, are all within close proximity. According to Lynch (1969a, 140) the landscape location of Letty'r Filiast is similar to those of the Portal Dolmens in Ireland. Although, it is worth noting that its position – enclosed

The chamber and mound of Llety'r Filiast

within a restricted space – bears similarities to the small polygonal-chambered monuments found in southern Scandinavia (in particular, the monuments in Bohuslän, south-west Sweden) as well as several monuments in South-west Wales, particularly St Elvies (PEM 20) and Twlc-y-Filiast (CRM 6).

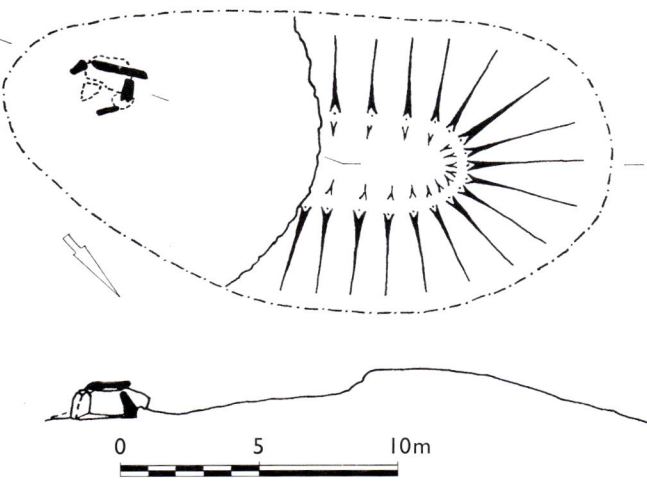

Plan and section of Llety'r Filiast, showing the extent of the mound (after Lynch 1969a)

The western landscape of Llety'r Filiast

The monument, described as a terminally chambered long barrow (Daniel 1950, 86), consists of an oval barrow approximately 25m in length. Near the southern end of the monument is evidence of recent quarrying. The chamber itself, originally rectangular in form, is set within the south-eastern part of the mound. The chamber comprises a dislodged and broken capstone which is supported by a series of uprights which may themselves have been dislodged. The uprights form a polygonal chamber with a large entrance located at the eastern end. The size of the entrance may be the result of an upright being removed. According to Lynch (1969a, 140), the chamber was probably rectangular in plan.

The site was visited by members of the Cambrian Archaeological Association in 1911, and was referred to as the 'Great Orme's Head site'. The meeting deduced that excavations had previously taken place. The objects found included a dark brown pottery sherd and a bone pin. It was later noted by Grimes (1936a, 106–39) that the mound was actually natural bedrock and that only excavation could reveal its full extent. It was also suggested by Grimes that it was likely that the whole 'barrow' was indeed natural. However, Lynch (1969a, 140) argues that the cairn has been 'greatly robbed' to reveal the natural bedrock. I would add that the site is on common land and would have been an ideal source for stone for roads and buildings.

41. Maen y Bardd, Caerhun
SH 74125 71892, SM NO. C027
County Reference Number: CRN 3

This Portal Dolmen is located near the village of Rowen. It was formerly known as Cwrt y Filiast (which translates as 'the kennel [or lair] of the greyhound bitch'), and is located on open grazing close to a track leading to Tal y fan and the mountains beyond. The track is arguably a Bronze Age route, and definitely on the line of the Roman road via Abergwyngregin to Canovium. It has extensive views across the eastern, northern and southern extents of the Conwy Valley. Maen y Bardd, sited on an exposed plateau at the foot of Tal y Fan, stands approximately 305m AOD. This monument is unusual in that it sits within the upland zone, unlike many Neolithic burial monuments in this area. Indeed, Maen y Bardd lies within a very much fragmented Late Neolithic/Early Bronze Age landscape. Several kilometres to the west and north lie a series of cairns and standing stones, including the 'Giant's Stick' (SH 738 717). According to Castleden (1992, 394), both the monument and the standing stones appear to be on a roughly E–W alignment. It is interesting to note that Mean y Bardd lies quite close to the Graig Lwyd Neolithic axe factory (centred on SH 717 750), some 3.5km north-west of the monument.[57]

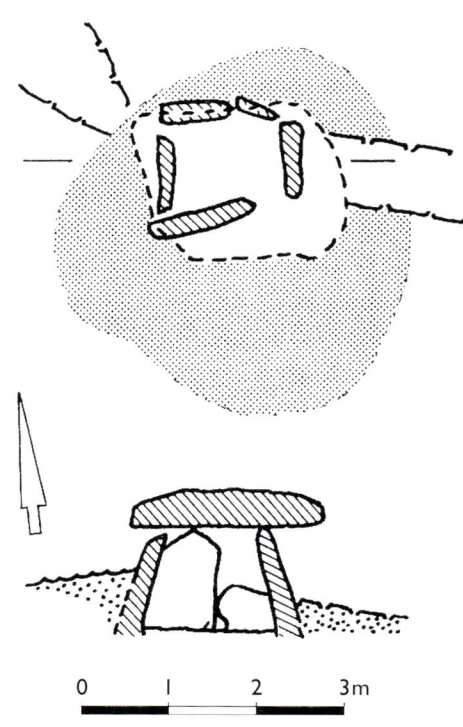

Plan and section of the Maen-y-Bardd Portal Dolmen (after Lynch 1969a)

The chamber of Maen-y-Bardd, looking south-west

The landscape vista of Maen-y-Bardd, and the later fossil boundary that incorporates the monument (foreground)

The monument, incorporated within a later field bank, consists of a large capstone which measures 4m x 2.2m x 0.7m, and is supported by four upright stones. The capstone dips up-slope, towards the north. The rectangular chamber and uprights sit within the traces of a long cairn; the entrance probably located within the western part of the chamber.

Daniel (1950, 191) notes that another monument – Rowen East (CRN 2), located at SH 7754 6604 – lies close to the Mean y Bardd site. This questionable megalithic site, approximately 18m east of Mean y Bardd, consists of an E–W oriented long barrow measuring approximately 10m.[58] A small rectangular chamber is located at the eastern end; also described as a cist (Besant-Lowe 1912, 40).

42. Porth Llwyd, Caerhun
SH 7703 6770, PRN: 1544
County Reference Number: CRN 4

Similar to Hendre Waelod, this much-ruined monument, once a possible Portal Dolmen, was sited within the Conwy Valley, approximately 8m AOD on the valley floor, close to Porth-llwyd Falls. The monument lay close to Dolgarrog on the western side of the valley, and may have had extensive views along the flood plain of the Conwy Valley to the north and to the hills to the east. It was one of a group of four monuments associated with the Conwy Valley and Creuddyn Isthmus. Others include Letty'r filiast (CRN 1), Maen-y-Bardd (CRN 3) and Hendre Waelod (DEN 1), in various states of poor preservation.

The site received attention in 1900 from J.E. Giffith, who photographed a number of cromlech sites in North Wales in *Portfolio of photographs of the cromlechs of Anglesey and Caernarvonshire, reproduced in collotype*. In a short description, Griffith writes the following about the monument:

Porth Llwyd Cromlech. Photograph by J.E. Griffith, 1900

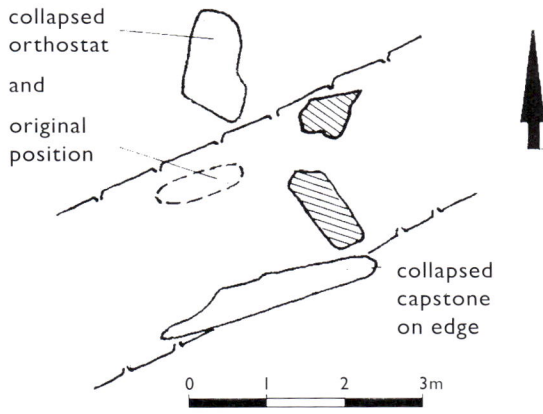

Plan showing the remnants of the Porth Llwyd monument (after Lynch 1969a)

This fine Cromlech is on the left-hand side of the road from Conway to Trefriw, on a farm called Porth Llwyd. The capstone has fallen down from its supports and is lying edgewise on the ground. There are still standing three of its supports. The one next to the road is five feet six inches long by three feet wide, and the one that faces the north-east is five feet long by three feet six inches wide, while the one nearest Conway River is six feet long by two wide. The other supports that belonged to it can easily be traced and are now serving as posts to a gate close by. The capstone lies on its edge close to the supports that are standing. It is ten feet long, and five feet wide at the end nearest to the road, and four feet at the other end, and it averages from twelve to fourteen inches in thickness. The space within what once formed the chamber is now full of debris and overgrown with briars. This Cromlech could easily be restored.

The monument consisted of four stones, of which three were incorporated into a field bank. One of the three remaining uprights was displaced by a flood in 1925, a result of the Dolgarrog dam burst. The largest stone is the capstone which sits on its edge, on the southern boundary of the field bank, whilst a recumbent stone lies within a field immediately north. The site is spread over a five-square-metre area. However, it should be noted that, according to Daniel (1950, 191), the surrounding fields were 'boulder strewn', which suggests that parts of the monument are scattered far and wide. However, Daniel, in the same paragraph, notes that much of the stonework of the monument was still in place. This is despite the Office of Works List of Scheduled Monuments recording the monument as 'presumed destroyed by the flood'.

As far as the author is aware, the J.E. Griffith photograph is the only image of the site, prior to the flood, that survives.

Lynch has considered that only two stones remain *in situ*, and these are understood to be uprights (1969a, 142). It is believed that the uprights were at least 1.5m high and may be similar in plan to the Carnedd Hengwm South chamber (MER 6). However, the upright arrangement suggests that the chamber may have resembled the chamber at Cist Cerrig (CRN 10). If the original position of the western upright is correct (as illustrated in Lynch, ibid. 142), the south-eastern upright may be a partition-stone dividing a rectangular chamber. It may also form an H-shaped entrance, leading into a former chamber located west of the *in situ* uprights. Crucially, the site was drawn by Bezant Lowe in his *The Heart of Northern Wales* (1912, 17), where it appears that the uprights formed a rectangular chamber. Later, the monument was recorded by the Office of Works *List of Scheduled Monuments* as presumed destroyed by flood. As a result of the flood event in 1925, the site was de-Scheduled in 1988. It has been assumed (probably correctly) that much of the site is now buried beneath an electricity pylon.

43. Sling, Llandegai
SH 6055 6696, SM NO. C119
County Reference Number: CRN 5

This much-ruined monument lies close to the town of Bethesda, within the village boundary of Tregarth, at around 210m AOD. The Sling tomb, also known as Yr Hen Allor (meaning *Old Altar*), is located

The collapsed chamber of the Sling monument

on a north-facing slope of Careg-y-gath. Standing west of the Afon Ogwen, it probably had extensive views across the North Wales coast between Bangor, Llanfairfechan and the southern coast of Ynys Môn. The upland peaks of Moel Wnion and Gyrn Wigau to the north-east may also have been within view. Today, the Sling monument is sited in scrub woodland.

Sling and the doubtful sites of Bryn (CRN 16), near Llanfair (SH 5154 6604) and Coetan Arthur (CRN 17), near Llandeiniolen (SH 5550 6485), form part of a series of Caernarvonshire monuments which face others along a southern ridge in Ynys Môn, between Brynsiencyn and Beaumaris.

The monument, standing around 220m AOD, consists of a large rectangular capstone, measuring 4.8m x 1.9m x 0.35m, and several uprights, one of which supports the capstone at its western end, and part of which is embedded in the ground. A recumbent stone found close to the capstone, appears to form the remains of a collapsed chamber (Lynch 1969a, 148). The chamber lies on the line of a collapsed historic boundary wall, which may have assisted in its survival during recent times.

A rectangular cist containing a human burial, probably Bronze Age, was found near the site in 1885 underneath a 'heap of stones' (Flook 1993). Although unclassified by Powell et al. (1969, 301), the remains are probably those of a small Portal Dolmen. There is, unfortunately, no trace of a mound. However, Daniel (1950, 14) suggests that the monument is earth-fast (or sub-megalithic), in which case it would be unnecessary to postulate the existence of a mound. I would disagree with this interpretation, as no other earth-fast monuments are known in North Wales. The site is evidently disturbed, with much of the original structure, including any cairn material, probably removed for building stone.

44. Hendre Waelod,
LLANSANTFFRAID-GLAN-CONWY
SH 79290 74810, SM NO. DE125
County Reference Number: DEN 1

This monument, with its large capstone and cairn, occupies a north-west facing slope overlooking the mouth of the Afon Conwy, on the eastern side of the valley. Below the monument is an area of salt marsh and open pasture. West of the river are the mountains of North Wales, where little Neolithic ritual activity occurs. This monument, standing at 21m AOD appears to be strategically located, in that it commands extensive views of the mouth of the Afon Conwy and the mountains to the west. It also would have had extensive views of Great Orme's Head to the north. It should be noted that the Afon Conwy is tidal at this point and that a multitude of economic resources would have been available to the people using this monument and the surrounding landscape.

Hendre Waelod, also known as Allor Moloch (Molloch's Altar), comprises a short, rectangular

The chamber of Hendre Waelod, looking north

Plan and section of the chamber of Hendre Waelod (after Lynch 1969a)

Antiquarian engraving of Hendre Waelod by J.T. Blight (*Archaeologia Cambrensis* 1865)

chamber with an entrance at the south-east, flanked by two portal stones which stand to a height of around 1.7m. The chamber, which measures roughly 4.1m x 3m, is set within an elongated cairn. The cairn itself sits on a slight shelf in the hillside. The portal stones on the eastern side are embedded in the cairn material. The capstone, measuring 4m x 3.2m x 1.4m, is supported by three uprights on the southern side of the chamber. The arrangement of uprights and capstone found at Hendre Waelod and also at Gwern Einion has been termed a 'portalled A-dolmen' (Daniel, 1950, 150).

The passage consists of two uprights that are approximately 1.5m apart, and a series of scattered stones (not cairn material). Located south-east of the southern upright is a possible door-stone. This device is positioned between the two uprights and separates the passage from the chamber. How far the two uprights are embedded into the hillside is not known. It is probable, and consistent with other monuments, that this part of the monument is the entrance. To the north, a number of uprights appear to have been removed.

The landscape position of this monument is similar to that of Carreg Coetan (PEM3), with both monuments occupying a low altitude position, and being close to estuaries or the mouth of principal river courses.

45. Tyddyn Bleiddyn, Cefn
SJ 00732 72462, SM NO. DE007
County Reference Number: DEN 2

This sadly neglected monument is often referred to as a passage grave (Powell et al. 1969). With its mound aligned along the valley, it stands within a hilly landscape close to the Afon Elwy, at around 122m AOD. To the south-east and north-east of the monument is an extensive limestone rock outcrop.

This monument, regarded as the only true megalithic structure in the Clwyd Valley, has, like Capel Garmon, been linked with the Cotswold-Severn tradition owing to its lateral chamber arrangement. The present state of the monument is such that only one intact, wedge-shaped chamber can be identified at the north-western side of an ovate mound that is oriented NW–SE. The chamber measured 2.7m x 1.8m wide. Discovered between the passage and the chamber, was a partition which consisted of a series of transverse jambs and a sill slab, measuring 0.45m in height. The chamber, which contained the remains of at least 12 people, measures 4.5m in length and includes a short passage (measuring 1.8m in length and 0.6m in width) to the south-west. Both passage and chambers are constructed from locally quarried limestone slabs. However, Daniel regards the chamber as opening to the east (1950, 88). He describes the north-western chamber as having a projecting jamb and a septal slab which lies between the passage and chamber (ibid. 45).

The mound, constructed of a stony-earth cairn, measures around 26m in length by 12m wide by 0.8m in height. The chamber alignment sits in a hollow within the central section of the mound. The monument was saved from total destruction after the site became a quarry for road repair (Britnell 1991, 59).

When Boyd-Dawkins excavated the monument in 1869 and 1871, he identified a second chamber (referred to as the southern chamber), roughly parallel with the first and sharing a NE–SW orientation. The chamber measured 3m in length by 1.8m and was triangular in shape. A jamb or sill lay between the chamber and the passage. The passage was entered from the north and measured 3m in length and 0.7m in width. It was said to contain a large quantity of human bone, along with the bones of dog, pig and roebuck. Also present was an assemblage of unworked flint pebbles and numerous pieces of quartz, but no pottery.

The denuded monument of Tyddyn Bleiddyn, looking east

The monument of Tyddyn Bleiddyn, looking south-west

Both chambers, according to Boyd-Dawkins, were full of remains of 'people of all ages', many of whom were placed in a 'sitting posture', with their backs to the sides of the chambers (1901). This statement is indeed interesting in that the preferred method of interment with the Cotswold-Severn tradition was disarticulation. Furthermore, Britnell (1991, 60) suggests that the visible chamber is similar to the two opposed chambers at Ty Isaf (BRE 5) and the chambers at Penywyrlod (BRE 14).

46. Capel Garmon, Llanrwst Rural
SH 81785 54317, SM NO. DE001
County Reference Number: DEN 3

Capel Garmon lies within a natural hollow behind Tyn-y-Coed Farm, and stands at around 264m AOD. Specific features have persuaded some authors that this monument is a northern outlier of the Cotswold-Severn distribution (Grimes 1936b; Lynch 1969). It has little or no affinity with other monuments in the Conwy Valley. Its closest relative is the multi-phased monument of Ty Isaf (BRE 5) in the Black Mountains (Lynch, 1969a, 143). Both monuments possess a wedge-shaped cairn, transepted lateral chambers and a forecourt with blind entrance.

At Capel Garmon, this latter feature consists of two slate uprights forming a simple doorway set in a deep forecourt measuring 5m E–W. Access to the chamber is from the south side of the mound, through a curved passage 4.5m in length and just over 1m in height. Despite the monument possessing horns, the location of the chamber within the wedge-shaped mound suggests that it has more in common with western monuments such as King Orry's Grave (MAN 2) on the Isle of Man (Daniel 1950).

In 1924 the Ministry of Works decided to excavate this monument, as the site was in such a poor state of preservation, with trees growing out of the mound. W.J. Hemp, who excavated the monument in 1927 in order to secure the chamber from further damage,

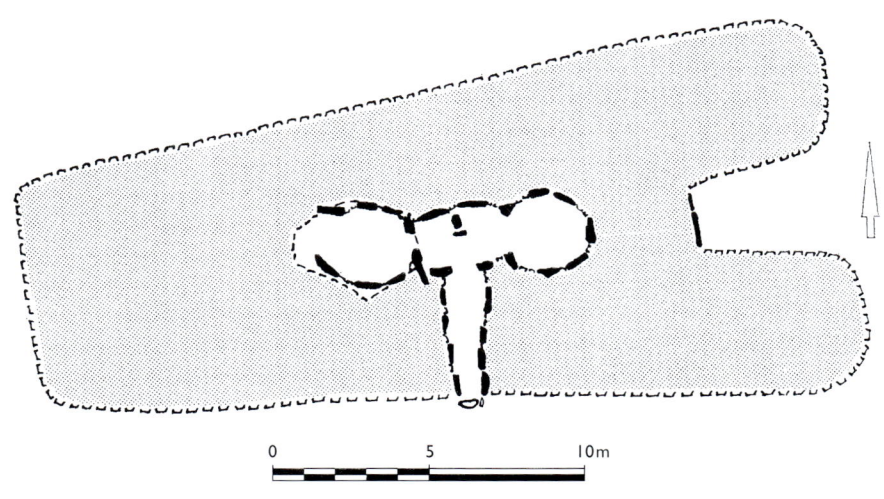

Plan of the trapezoidal mound and chamber arrangement

found the corbelled passage to be blocked, and took this to indicate that the tomb had been used once only and then sealed. According to Hemp, some of the stone in the chambers was dressed (Hemp 1927).

A small excavation south of the western chamber was undertaken in 1989. The excavation area measured roughly 2m x 2m (Yates & Jones 1991, 1), in which three broad phases of activity were recognised: pre-monument activity, monument construction and post-construction disturbance. A single fragment of human skull was found within a well-sealed context underneath the monument, and may be associated with the construction process (ibid. 4).

The outline of the monument is similar to that of other Cotswold-Severn monuments. However, the passage and chamber layout are not too dissimilar to Ty Isaf (BRE 5). The passage leads to a tripartite chamber arrangement, emerging into a rectangular central chamber roughly 3m x 2m and flanked by two circular chambers. The central chamber is partially divided by slabs projecting from the north wall and separated from the other chambers by door jambs. One of the chambers was in use as a stable in

The western chamber section of Capel Garmon

1853. As a result of measures to clear the chamber, the remaining two chambers were discovered. Today the site has only one original capstone covering the chamber.

As at Bryn Celli Ddu (ANG 7) and Bryn yr Hen Bobl (ANG 8) the floors of the chambers were found to be of 'prepared clay' extending beyond the kerbing. Grimes (1950 41–2) argued that the builders did not see the kerbing as the termination of the barrow area. In all three sites, the revetment material was firmly embedded into what Grimes refers to as the prepared clay floor.

The majority of the mounds of long-chambered monuments in Wales are oriented N–S. However, the mound of Capel Garmon is aligned E–W, suggesting that local landscape features played an important role in the siting and alignment of these monuments.

The cairn measures 27m x 12m and narrows towards its western end. The wider eastern end consists of a horned forecourt area. A false portal consisting of two uprights is located between the two horns. This architectural trait features prominently within the Cotswold-Severn group of monuments.

Regarding finds, a single rim-sherd of Ebbsfleet pottery was found in the passage (Grimes 1951, 35). There were also traces of small fires, an unworked flint flake and human bone. Five sherds belonging to two Late Neolithic/Early Bronze Age beakers were also discovered, suggesting either periodic or continuous use of the monument for at least 1,500 years.

Lynch (1969a, 139) suggests that Capel Garmon has no connection with monuments further down the valley, such as Maen y Bardd (CRN 3), Porth Llwyd (CRN 4) and Hendre Waelod (DEN 1). This fact suggests that Capel Garmon is very much isolated, and that penetration of the Conwy Valley and the subsequent settlement and construction of the lower Conwy Valley monuments was very much self-contained. Savory (1980, 222) tenuously suggests that the rounded transepts imply that the builders of this monument were influenced by the Boyne Valley passage grave tradition in central Ireland. However, I believe that the design is essentially a Cotswold-Severn trait with local idiosyncratic additions in order to place a community 'signature' on to the monument and to differentiate it from others nearby.

47. Gop Cairn, Trelawnyd
SJ 08657 80162, SM NO. FL007
County Reference Number: FLT 1

Gop cairn, also referred to as Gop-y-Goleuni (which translates as 'well-lit summit' – a reference to its being less densely-wooded), lies within an extensive Neolithic landscape. Close to the cairn and within fields to the north and west, a large assemblage of Neolithic flint has been found, including a number of leaf-shaped flint arrowheads, scrapers, knives, a flint borer or awl, as well as a large number of worked flint debitage. Many researchers consider that this enormous cairn, located on the brow of Gop Hill, is either Late Neolithic or Early Bronze Age in date (Britnell 1991, 61). However, its sheer size, which is unlike that of any other Bronze Age cairn in Britain, suggests a Neolithic date.

The cairn has outstanding views in all directions but appears to dominate the landscape to the south. It is approximately 12m in height and 100m in diameter, and stands around 250m AOD. At the base of the cairn is an extensive scree deposit, which is probably the result of continuous slope deposition. On top of the cairn is evidence of antiquarian excavation – forming a large and pronounced doughnut-shaped indentation. Recent disturbance around the southern base of the cairn has revealed a section of a limestone revetment wall (Britnell 1991, 62). It could be the case that this wall is contemporary with the construction of the cairn. A similar revetment wall, constructed of chalk blocking, is present at Silbury Hill in Wiltshire.

Northern view of Gop Cairn, one of the largest Neolithic structures in the western British Isles

The cairn was excavated in 1886–7 by Boyd Dawkins, and this revealed that the mound was constructed of a limestone rubble core. The excavation cut a single vertical shaft and two galleries. A large bone assemblage, including ox and horse, was uncovered within the mound's core, but there was no trace of any human remains. However, its English counterpart, Silbury Hill, while considerably larger, also showed similar finds and deposition, possessing a dating range of around 2,145 ± 95 BCE (Britnell 1991, 61). It is suggested by Castleden (1992, 372) that the cairn may house a passage grave which is comparable to passage graves in Ynys Môn and within the Boyne Valley in Ireland. However, the Boyd Dawkins excavation revealed no evidence of any passage or chamber architecture. His excavation tunnelled to the bedrock/cairn interface.

It is highly likely that the Gop cairn, whatever function it once fulfilled, is directly associated with nearby Neolithic activity within the Gop Cave system; and what one is probably looking at is a complex Neolithic landscape which encompasses both burial and ritual practices. The extensive flint scatters would also suggest that a Neolithic settlement was close by.

48. Gop cave, Trelawnyd
SJ 08642 80077, SM NO. FL067
County Reference Number: FLT 2

Two limestone caves,[59] located on the south-facing slopes of Gop Hill, have outstanding views to the south, and stand around 215m AOD. Approximately 35m north of the caves and up-slope, is Gop Cairn (FLT 1). The south-eastern cave was excavated by Sir William Boyd-Dawkins in 1886.

Immediately in front of the cave entrance is an extensive lip that partially hides the cave from

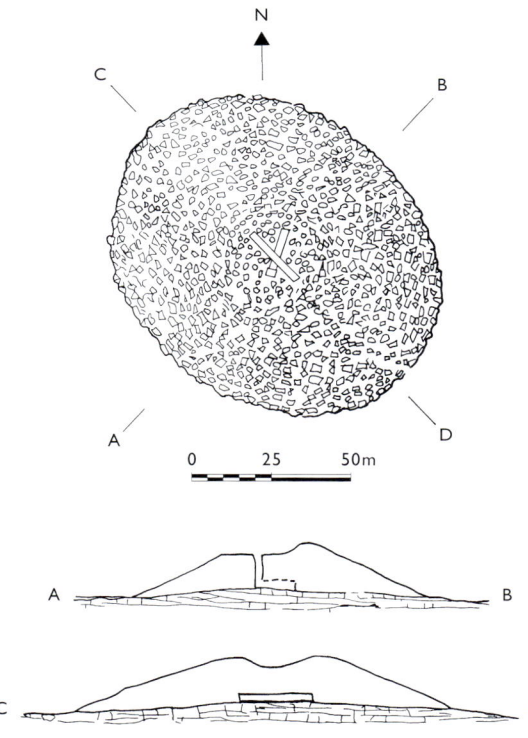

Plan and cross-section of Gop Cairn (after Boyd-Dawkins 1901)

The entrance to Gop Cave, looking north

THE NORTH WALES GROUP

sight when viewed from the base of the valley. It is difficult to assess whether this lip forms part of the natural topography or was constructed during the Neolithic, or is merely spoil from the nineteenth-century excavation of the site. Daniel regards the cave, which he classifies as a sub-megalithic tomb, as the only authentic Neolithic burial site in Flintshire (1950, 196). I would add that the Gop Cave site is one of a number of cave sites within north-east Wales, in which Neolithic burial has taken place.

According to the excavation report, inside the cave were several significant features and structures that date from the Neolithic, including a burial chamber. Excavation revealed the remains of at least 14 individuals, some of which were placed in a crouched position. Found in the assemblage of skeletal material were a number of decorated pottery sherds with a herring-bone pattern, possibly of the Peterborough type. Also recovered was a polished stone axe from the Graig Lwyd axe factory near Penmaenmawr. This important artefact was located close to the entrance to the cave. Other finds included a large assemblage of broken and burnt domestic animal bone, a discoidal polished flint knife, some white quartz pebbles and the possible remains of a jet slider or necklace (Boyd-Dawkins 1901, 330). The jet slider, although illustrated in the Boyd-Dawkins report, is now lost. Also found was a possible Beaker-type dagger, allegedly sold by one of the workmen to a visitor!

The burial chamber, rectangular in form, is constructed with three stone walls; the fourth wall being part of the northern wall of the cave. The roof of the chamber was likewise formed from the roof of the cave. The chamber lies some 2m inside the cave entrance and overlies a series of cave earth deposits. According to Boyd-Dawkins, the chamber was buried in (natural) spoil that completely covered the cave entrance.

It is probable that the site belongs to a Late Neolithic burial tradition, referred to by Britnell (1991, 64) as sub-megalithic in character. Daniel (1950, 153) regards Gop Cave, along with Glyn and Lligwy, as late, degenerate types of the Gwynedd group, due to its sub-megalithic nature. This later date is reinforced by the enormous cairn that lies above the cave and is roughly of the same date. Other cave sites in Flintshire, such as Perthi Chwarae (Llanarmon) and Rhosddigre (Llandegla), both in the Alyn Valley, have yielded similar burial assemblages that date from this period.

49. Tyn-y-Coed, Llangar
SJ 04760 39622, SM NO. ME048
County Reference Number: MER 7

This much-ruined monument is located close to the valley floor of the Afon Dyfrdwy (River Dee). The monument lies approximately 154m AOD on a west-facing slope. Directly behind the monument are the Berwyns, a range of mountains which extends to the east and the south. To the west are the hinterlands of the mountains of Snowdonia.

The monument is located outside the village of Rhyd-y-Glafais, and lies close to two doubtful sites known as Branas Uchaf and Maen Egryn. The monument sits within an elongated cairn, 30m in length, with a capstone lying at one end, embedded within cairn material (Bowen & Gresham 1967). The capstone measures 3m in length by 0.45m in thickness and is supported by at least one upright. Britnell (1991, 60) suggests that the chamber was entered via a passage, possibly measuring around 3m in length. Also present is a single upright. This site is clearly a terminally chambered monument, indicative of the Cotswold-Severn group of monuments. According to Bowen and Gresham

The chamber of Tyn-y-Coed, which is set within a large cairn mound

there is a possible passage leading to the chamber area from the side. However, Lynch (1969a, 147) suggests that this may be a result of extensive disturbance.

This monument can be regarded as unusual in its geographical location, due to little other monument evidence being present within the inland area of central and North Wales; although its position within the landscape is typical of other Neolithic monuments *per se*. Lynch has suggested that this monument is significant in that it may have been constructed by people from the Cotswold-Severn area who may have used the route over the Berwyns (1969a, 147). However, as suggested throughout this book, it is not people who were moving but ideas, and it is more likely that the long cairn design 'blueprint' was transmitted between groups. This monument, along with Gwern Einion (SH 587 286), Mean-y-Bardd (SH 741 718) and Porth Llwyd (SH 770 677), is located along a large river valley. Colonisation of this area would have probably come via the exploration of the streams and river valleys by hunter-gatherers or early Neolithic groups.

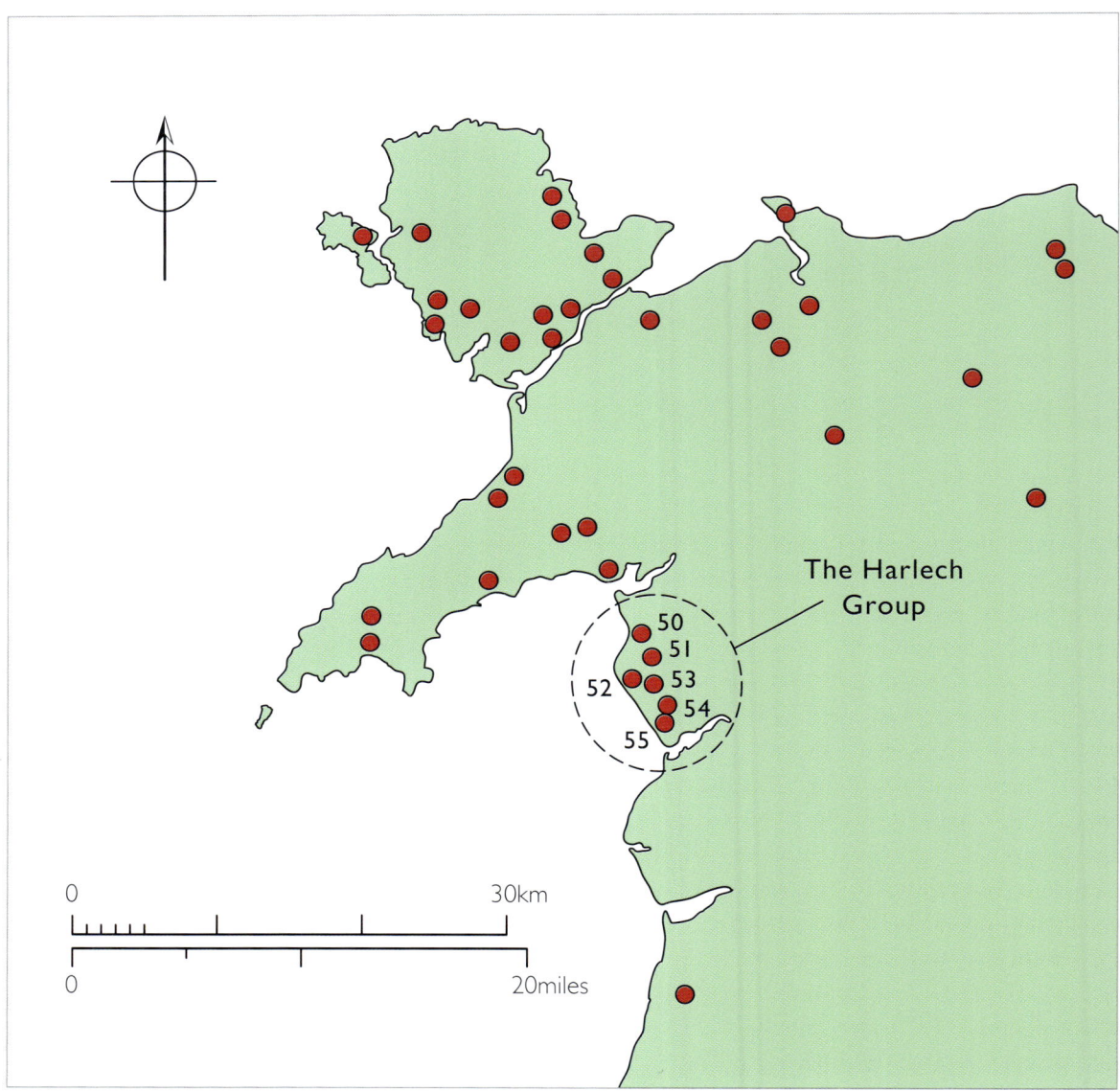

50 Gwern Einion
51 Bron-y-Foel-Isaf-West
52 Dyffryn Ardudwy
53 Cors-y-Gedol
54 Carneddau Hengwm North
55 Carneddau Hengwm South

SEVEN

The Harlech Group

Located south of the Llŷn Peninsula – between Traeth Bach and north of the Afon Mawddach – are seven monuments that lie on the western intermediate slopes overlooking Barmouth and Harlech. The six monuments listed within this inventory are architecturally diverse and all lie in different landscape settings. The sites include: Gwern Einion (MER 1), Bron-y-Foel-Isaf-West (MER 2), Dyffryn Ardudwy (MER 3), Cors-y-Gedol (MER 4), Carneddau Hengwm North (MER 5) and Carneddau Hengwm South (MER 6). One other site in this group, Bron-y-Foel-Isaf-East (SH 608 247) has been reclassified as of probable natural origin. All the other sites, with the exception of the two Carneddau Hengwm monuments, are Portal Dolmens. The Carneddau Hengwm monuments, with their surviving cairn long mounds, are regarded as belonging to the Cotswold-Severn group (Lynch 1976, 69). I would add that due to their isolation, little damage from antiquarians, archaeologists and farming has occurred to either site.

The orientation of all these monuments appears to be roughly consistent, in that their (Portal Dolmen) chambers and long mound axis are oriented approximately in the same direction, roughly E–W; thus the façades/entrances pointing to the sea and the terminal ends towards the mountains. This emerging pattern, repeated elsewhere within the coastal Neolithic core areas of Wales, has potentially significant ritual-symbolic ramifications (see Tilley 1994; Cummings 2002; Whittle and Cummings 2004).

The most northerly of this group is the monument of Gwern Einion. This classic Portal Dolmen, incorporated into a farm wall, lies on a plateau that has no view of the sea, although this only lies approximately 1.75km to the west. Although just the chamber of the monument survives, it is probable that the orientation of the wall delineates the alignment of the mound. Lying close to this site is further evidence of Late Neolithic/Early Bronze Age activity. This includes, on the western slopes of nearby Moel Goedog, two stone circles (SH 610 324). Between Gwern Einion and the stone circles, are several standing stones that occupy the eastern slopes of Moel Goedog and Moel y Sensigl. Given their position, there may be a monument association, albeit tenuous, between Gwern Einion and the standing stone and stone circles.

The Gwern Einion monument appears to be deliberately located in order to occupy the uplands that dominate the Harlech landscape.

The site of Bron-y-Foel-Isaf-West, lying north of the cairn circle at Tal y Ffynonau (SH 609 239), has been classified as a Portal Dolmen, and today is much ruined (Powell et al. 1969, 303). The site lies on the intermediate slopes of Moelfre, that rise to a height of 589m AOD, and is at the same elevation as the two Carneddau Hengwm monuments. Within local proximity to the Carneddau Hengwm monuments is Dyffryn Ardudwy and Cors-y-Gedol, each sited down-slope towards the coast.

The double-chambered monument at Dyffryn Ardudwy is approximately 1km to the west of the Cors-y-Gedol monument. This double-chambered tomb is classified as a Portal Dolmen. Both chambers are incorporated into a stone cairn. The monument lies at the interface between the uplands and the coastal hinterland and was constructed over several phases.

The Cors-y-Gedol tomb is located approximately 2.2km to the north of the Carneddau Hengwm monuments. Although much smaller, it nevertheless shows similar architecture. Despite being regarded as a Portal Dolmen, it is incorporated into a long mound and probably shares some architectural traits with the Cotswold-Severn classification.

The Carneddau Hengwm monuments lie on the western slopes of Mynydd Egryn, close to a number of upland streams and bogs. They also lie within an extensive Late Neolithic to Early Bronze Age landscape. To the east and north of these monuments are a series of cairns and standing stones together with two stone circles: Ffridd Newydd North (SH 616 213) and Ffridd Newydd South (SH 616 213; Burl 1976, 370). Unlike the two Carneddau Hengwm monuments, the Bronze Age sites are usually located on top of the highest points within the landscape, as typified by the Llanaber cairn, at a height of 515m AOD.

50. Gwern Einion, Llanfair
SH 58730 28597, SM NO. M011
County Reference Number: MER 1

This monument is incorporated into a field and sheep enclosure wall. The monument is a classic Portal Dolmen, which has been linked morphologically with other early forms in the area, such as the west chamber at Dyffryn Ardudwy. Hidden among local rock outcrops, this monument is sited 106m AOD on an intermediate plateau above the Afon Artro. It lacks intervisibility with the nearby tombs of Bron-y-Foel-Isaf West and Dyffryn Ardudwy and the sea, 1.9km away. Behind it, and dominating the view to the east, is the peak of Foel Ddu (473m AOD).

The closed chamber, oriented NW–SE, consists of a sharply-sloping capstone supported by two portal stones standing to around 2m, and resting at its western end on a third upright about 1m high. The portal blocking slab rises to about 1.3m. Grimes (1936a, 120) suggests the chamber may originally have extended further back than at present. Since the first edition of this book in 2006, the drystone wall that abutted either side of the chamber has been removed. It is likely that the construction of this drystone wall did much to protect this monument. The wall (and its foundations) probably cut into a former mound.

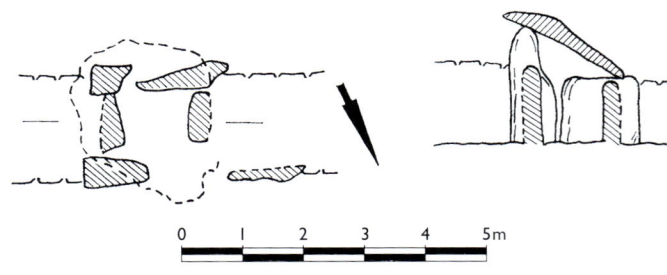

Plan and section of the Gwern Einion monument (after Lynch 1969a)

Image taken by the author in 1991 of Gwern Einion, showing the continuation of a post-medieval drystone wall. The wall probably saved the monument.

The chamber of Gwern Einion, with the drystone walling now removed

Late nineteenth-century engraving, published in *Archaeologica Cambrensis*, labelling Gwern Einion as 'Werneinion'

The mound, probably made of cairn, would have concealed much of the current visible architecture.

Both to the south and the north is a series of monuments, including standing stones and stone circles with associated settlements. This high concentration of sites dating from the Neolithic and Bronze Age, suggests the presence of a ritual landscape along the intermediate slope zone. Gwern Einion possibly marks the northern extent of this group of monuments.

51. Bron-y-Foel-Isaf-West, Llanenddwyn
SH 60795 24585, SM NO. ME065
County Reference Number: MER 2

Bron-y-Foel-Isaf-West, with its doubtful neighbour Bron-y-Foel-East,[60] stands on an upland plateau known as Moelfre, and has uninterrupted views of the sea to the west and the mountains to the east. To the east of this monument is the peak of Moelfre, which rises to 589m AOD. The monument – whose

View of the chamber area of Bron-y-Isaf, incorporated into a post-medieval drystone walled boundary

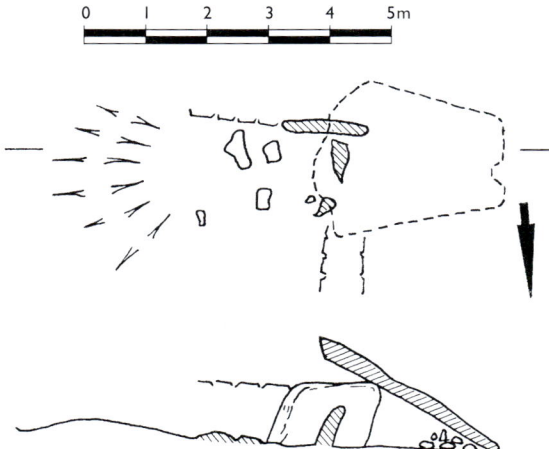

Plan and section of the Bron-y-Foel-Isaf-West monument (after Lynch 1969a)

name means 'The Lower slope of the Bare Hill' – is located within a probable early post-medieval (or earlier) field system. The farms of Bron-y-foel-ganol and Bron-y-foel-uchaf lie close by.

Cors-y-Gedol (MER 4) and the cairns of Carneddau Hengwm (MER 5 & 6) are sited on the same plateau. In addition to the Neolithic presence, this landscape is also occupied by monuments that date to the Bronze Age, and include a series of burial cairns, standing stones, a stone circle and evidence of associated settlement. Although these monuments occupy prominent locations, the siting of this tomb is such that it cannot be seen from the valley below.[61]

Bron-y-Foel-Isaf-West and Cors-y-Gedol are separated by the Afon Ysgethin from the two Carneddau Hengwm monuments to the south. This natural boundary may explain the change in tomb morphology between the two sets of monuments.

Bron-y-Foel-Isaf-West, oriented E–W and intervisible with both Dyffryn Ardudwy (MER 3) and Cors-y-Gedol, is sited on higher ground (at around 214m AOD) and located several kilometres further inland. The monument, initially classified as a laterally chambered long cairn, originally consisted

View of the fallen capstone of Bron-y-Foel-Isaf, looking south-east

of a closed portal with a rectangular chamber which was set into a mound measuring perhaps 18m x 9m. The chamber capstone is 3m x 2.5m and rests on an upright at the south, and on the ground to the west, and could be construed as being earth-fast in form. The height of the closed portal is about 1m: roughly the same as that of its nearest neighbour, Cors-y-Gedol, but only half that of Gwern Einion. As with Gwern Einion, the chamber has been incorporated within a field boundary wall. At present, only three uprights of the chamber remain, whilst loose stone litters the area where the chamber was once sited. Two of the uprights appear to form an H-chamber setting, and it is probable that the smaller upright, oriented N–S, forms a doorway which led into the chamber from the west. Immediately to the east of the field boundary, there may have been a forecourt area. A low crescent-shaped bank, 3.5m in front of the chamber, has been linked with similar features at Dyffryn Ardudwy and Cors-y-Gedol (see below) and considered 'a uniting element between these three tombs' (Lynch, 1969a, 127).

It is highly likely that the later field boundary has done much to preserve various elements of this monument.

52. Dyffryn Ardudwy, Llanenddwyn
SH 59135 22740, SM NO. ME003
County Reference Number: MER 3

The Dyffryn Ardudwy monument, lying within the village of the same name, is one of the largest within the Harlech group, and, because of its meticulous excavation in the 1960s, has received much attention. This is the only tomb within the area that is located on the edge of the coastal plain. Because of its landscape position, it seems unlikely that there was any direct intervisibility with other monuments of the known group. The earliest part of the monument, the western chamber, resembles other Portal Dolmens within the group, such as Gwern Einion (MER 1). In addition, its landscape position is similar to that of Cors-y-Gedol (MER 4) in that both are close to fresh running water – in this case, the Afon Ysgthin, which flows south of Dyffryn Ardudwy. The architectural elements of this and other monuments within the group also have affinities with Portal Dolmens that are found within the eastern part of Ireland. This again suggests a contact/exchange network existing between the two regions of the Irish Sea Province.

The monument stands on a western slope at around 50m AOD, and consists of two Portal Dolmen-type chambers that face up-slope to the east. The chambers are set within a well-defined cairn which is roughly rectangular in shape and aligned SW–NE. While the sea is only 1.8km away, and is clearly visible from the site, the monument forecourts are oriented inland and appear visually to ignore the coastal zone completely.

According to the excavator, T.G.E. Powell, two clear construction phases are evident, each phase consisting of a chamber and associated cairn (1973). It has been said of Portal Dolmens that their most striking components are monumentality and restriction of chamber access (Kinnes, 1992, 122). At Dyffryn Ardudwy, the original monument seems to have been a relatively modest structure, comprising a rectangular stone chamber 2.5m x 1m, closed off with a blocking slab. A V-shaped forecourt converged on two portal stones and contained what seems to have been a shallow ritual pit. Within the pit were found sherds of several fine Neolithic vessels, constituting a single context and comparable in overall form with finds from the Neolithic settlement of Carn Brea in Cornwall. Pottery from the chamber consisted of a single stamped Beaker sherd, assumed to represent secondary deposition.

The monument was enclosed in an oval cairn 8.5m x 9m. The western chamber was superseded by a second, larger chamber, built about 10m to the north-east. This partitioned structure comprises a western compartment measuring 2.3m x 2m, and an eastern entrance area containing sloped blocking stones. Lynch suggests that a gap in the north chamber wall provided a side entrance which could be easily reopened for the insertion of burials after the formal entrance had been blocked (Lynch, 1969a, 134–5).

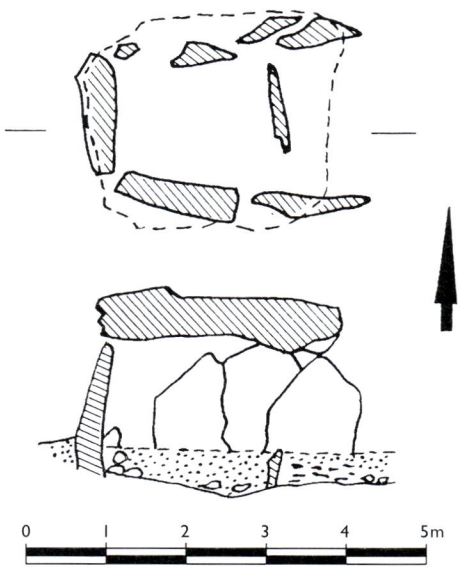

Plan and section of the east chamber of Dyffryn Ardudwy (after Lynch 1969a)

The western chamber of Dyffryn Ardudwy, originally forming a single-phased Portal Dolmen monument during the early Neolithic

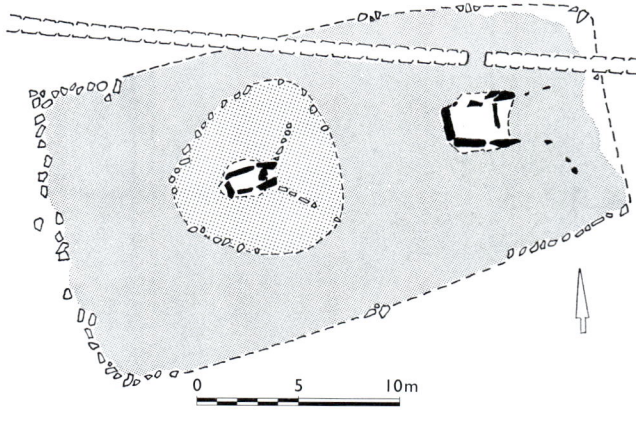

Plan of the Dyffryn Ardudwy monument (after Lynch 1969a)

Antiquarian engraving of the Dyffryn Ardudwy monument by Edward Barnwell (*Archaeologia Cambrensis* 1969)

Uprights to the east and south-east of the southern portal stone have been interpreted as a vestigial forecourt (ibid. 134). A rectangular long cairn (28m x 15m) enclosed both chambers and the original oval cairn. The deposition of the chambers and blocking revealed that the site, crucially, had not been disturbed and, therefore the cairn's stratigraphy lay intact (Powell 1973).

View showing both chambers, looking west

Pottery deposited in the forecourt and blocking area post-dates the construction of the western chamber. Largely undecorated sherds from the disturbed eastern chamber context itself have been compared with examples from Lough Gur in Limerick, southern Ireland. Other fragments decorated with fingernail impressions may again indicate the spread of Beaker influence into the area, as do small pieces of polished slate or schist, possibly belonging to a Beaker wrist-guard. A leaf-shaped arrowhead was also found beneath the cairn edge near the eastern chamber.

53. Cors-y-Gedol, Llanddwye-is-y-craig
SH 60280 22810, SM NO. ME038
County Reference Number: MER 4

The much-ruined monument of Cors-y-Gedol has been described by Daniel as a terminally chambered long barrow (1950, 86), with the remains of a Portal Dolmen located at the eastern end of the mound. This site has received much attention, especially from antiquarians up until the late nineteenth century. William Stukeley sketched both it and the Bron-y-Foel-Isaf (MER 2) monuments in the eighteenth century (Stukeley 1778). Crawford (1920, 98) notes that a possible drawing of the monument was made in 1800 (now housed in Devizes Library).[62]

Antiquarian engraving of Cors-y-Gedol by Edward Barnwell (*Archaeologia Cambrensis* 1869)

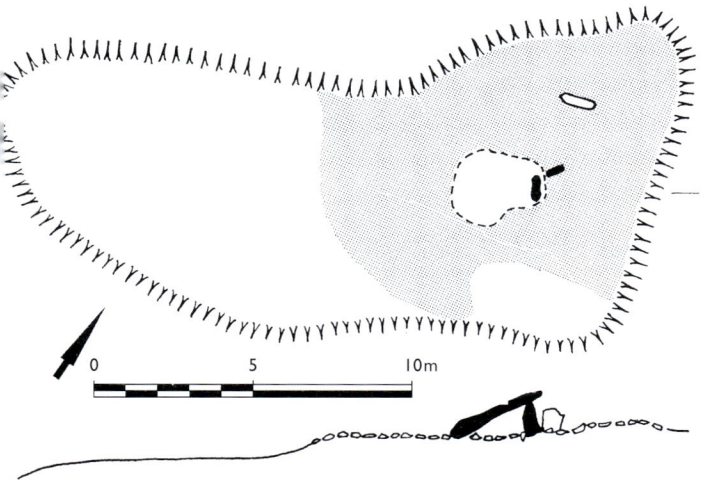

Plan and section of the Cors-y-Gedol monument (after Lynch 1969a)

The irregular, much-denuded cairn mound and ruined chamber are all that remain of this monument. The site lies on the slopes of Moelfre and has been classified by Lynch (1969a, 127) as a Portal Dolmen. It forms one of many belonging to the Irish Sea Group of monuments (Daniel 1950, 150).

The position of the capstone, which measures roughly 3.5m x 3m, has its western end resting on cairn material. The extent of the mound is roughly 25m x 12m. Approximately 0.4m of the original cairn material remains. The height of the upright supporting the capstone is about 1.5m. The present position of the capstone, resting on a single upright, gives the impression that it belongs to the earth-fast group of monuments; however, it is probable that the capstone has slipped off the two uprights, which once formed the northern section of the chamber. The chamber appears to be polygonal in plan, although it is impossible to determine its size from the position of the two remaining uprights. The general orientation of the chamber, which is located at the eastern-end of the cairn, appears to be NE–SW. The upright located NE of the capstone may in fact be part of an entrance or forecourt area that opened out

The chamber and cairn deposit of Cors-y-Gedol

towards the east, similar to that of nearby Dyffryn Ardudwy. Sited on the same plateau as Bron-y-Foel-Isaf and the two Carneddau Hengwm monuments (MER 5 & 6), this monument is the lowest at 191m AOD. It has a clear view of the coastal plain, the sea to the west, and the mountains – in particular the peak of Graig y Grut at 588m AOD, to the east. It also lies 200m or so from the Afon Ysgethin to the south.

A few kilometres to the east and in front of the mountain peaks, are a series of standing stones and cairns, together with the Iron Age settlement of Craig y Dinas. The monument is located, as are others within the group, on the interface between deep, well-drained fine loamy, silty soils and the more, shallow soils found on the slopes (*Soil Survey of England & Wales* 1983).

54. CARNEDDAU HENGWM NORTH, LLANABER
SH 61325 20575, SM NO. ME007
County Reference Number: MER 5

The two Carneddau Hengwm monuments are sited on an upland plateau and overlook the Llŷn Peninsula, standing around 283m AOD. The translation of the monuments name is simply 'Cairns of the Old Valley' (Olding *pers comm*). This monument, along with its neighbour (the individual monuments are spaced some 35m apart), forms one of a limited group of monuments which form a pair. Other pairs include Ffostyll North and South (BRE 3 & 4), the Eithbed Cemetery Group (PEM 31), the Garn Wen cemetery (PEM 7–9) and Morfa Bychan (CRM 2–5).

The Carneddau Hengwm monuments are constructed similarly and mark the southern extent of the Harlech group. To the east of both monuments is the dramatic peak of Graig y Grut (588m AOD).

Carneddau Hengwm North lies close to the top of a small river gully running roughly E–W. Between the monuments and the coastal zone, some 2km to the west, are extensive rock outcrops. Meanwhile, to the east of this site, at a point where the mountains and upland plateau merge, is a series of Bronze Age ritual monuments including several cairns, a cairn circle and standing stones. To the north-west is a small Iron Age enclosure known as Pen y Dinas (SH 6070 2081), at the highest point within the immediate landscape.

Carneddau Hengwm North is smaller than its neighbour. It has been extensively robbed and cannot be reconstructed with any certainty; the cairn being used for nearby drystone walling. However, two lateral chambers are visible and open from opposite sides of the cairn. The mound, oriented E–W and measuring around 33m x 18m, is much denuded and cairn material possibly spreads beyond the limits of the original cairn walls.

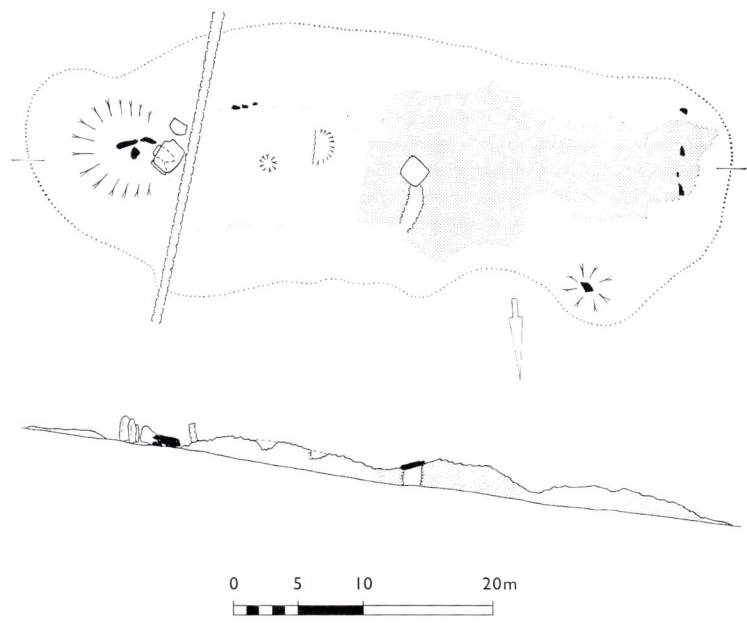

Plan and section of Carneddau Hengwm North

THE HARLECH GROUP 155

The chamber arrangement is rather complex and in some ways is replicated within the mound of the Carneddau Hengwm South monument. Three or perhaps four chambers are present within the mound. A recent site visit by the author confirmed that all the chambers are visible, with the two eastern lateral chambers appearing to mark the end of the mound. Each chamber is delineated by a series of uprights that are oriented N–S and measure around 1m x 1m in plan. The chambers are spaced 6.7m apart. Between the chambers are up to three uprights, which may indicate either a third chamber, or the possible denuded remains of a passage that may have led to the central chamber.

To the west of the two lateral chambers and within the centre of the mound, is a drystone-walled circular feature which Crawford (1920, 129) believed was another chamber. At present, cairn material has fallen into this void, preventing identification. At the western end of the mound is a probable capstone that may have belonged to the central chamber. This large slab, measuring approximately 3.7m x 2.2m, overlies cairn material. Daniel (1950, 197) also claimed that the slab overlies a chamber. If this is the case, a lateral chamber, possibly forming a Portal Dolmen, exists at the western end and it is probable that an entrance and forecourt area is present beyond this proposed chamber. Alternatively, the monument may be multi-phased, with a similar construction history to nearby Dyffryn Ardudwy.

Corcoran (1969, 103) suggests that the remains of a drystone wall, running E–W at the north-western end of the mound, could indicate a cairn revetment, and possibly reveals Cotswold-Severn or Wessex Culture influence. Corcoran (ibid. 103) goes on to say that if the mound is trapezoidal in shape, then this site may have been influenced by monument construction in Ireland – in particular, sites located within the Audleystown area, Co. Down.

Interestingly, the chamber arrangements of the monument are the opposite of those at Carneddau Hengwm South. This arrangement may have had significant implications with winter sunrise and sunset, in that light from the sunrise would enter the eastern chamber of the Carneddau Hengwm South monument, whilst light from the sunset would have illuminated the western chamber of Carneddau Hengwm North. However, it is unclear whether both monuments were in use at the same time.

Western view of the chamber and cairn mound of Carneddau Hengwm North

The chamber of Carneddau Hengwm North, looking north-east

55. Carneddau Hengwm South, Llanaber
SH 61305 20480, SM no. ME007
County Reference Number: MER 6

This monument and its neighbour, Carneddau Hengwm North (MER 5), should be regarded as one of the most important monument groups in North Wales. This apparently contentious conclusion is mainly based on two factors: landscape setting and the monument's state of preservation. The site was described both by William Stukeley and Thomas Pennant (in 1783). Pennant (Vol II, 262–3) remarks:

> Half a mile south of these, on the side of a hill, are two carnedds, of a most stupendous size, containing an uncommon assemblage of druidical customs, or religion, in the form of Cromlech, Maen Hir, Cist Vaen. Both are of an oblong form, and composed of loose stones: the largest is fifty-five long, and twelve [feet] high, in the middle. At the east end is a great Cromlech, composed of two sloping stones, one placed over the edge of the other, upon five upright stones, seven feet high in one part, and four feet ten in the lowest. About eight yards from this, is the upper stone of the Cromlech, lying flat on the carnedd, without the appearance of any support. Eleven yards farther, is another great heap of stones, and in it a large Cromlech, supported by upright stones. It is now converted into a retreat for a shepherd, who has placed stone seats within, and formed a chimney through the loose stones above. In the same carnedd, a little farther on, is another magnificent Cromlech, whose incumbent stone is twelve feet by nine; four vast columns, or maeni hirion, three now fallen, and a third erect. The columns are from the height of ten feet four, to that of twelve feet eight; and each between four and five feet broad.

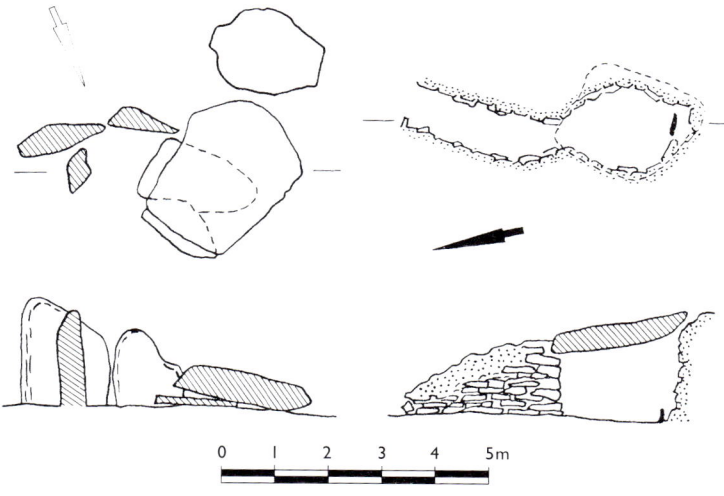

Site 55 Plan and section of the Carneddau Hengwm South monument (after Lynch 1969a)

Today, located close to a beaten track, the isolation of both monuments has probably dissuaded many an antiquarian from excavating this site. The landscape setting of this monument is identical to that of its neighbour, although Carneddau Hengwm South is at a slightly higher elevation (around 283m AOD) and has a post-medieval drystone wall oriented N–S incorporated into the eastern section of the monument.

Carneddau Hengwm South appears to be a two-phase monument comprising, in its present form, a closed Portal Dolmen at the eastern end of a long, irregular mound; and a lateral chamber with a passage and chamber located towards the centre of the cairn (Lynch 1976, 70; Masters 1981, 109). The phasing of the monument is based on the difference in cairn material, with small to medium stones being used in the initial construction. Lynch (1976, 69) suggests that the initial mound may have measured only 16.5m in length. Distinctively, larger cairn material is found within the remaining 27m of the mound.

The eastern chamber is now partially collapsed. However, this originally consisted of two overlapping capstones supported by five uprights, including the closing slab or door-stone. Pennant describes two capstones as being present, probably still in their original position (Pennant 1783). Other antiquarian reports, compiled in the eighteenth century when the chamber was still standing, suggest 'the great cromlech altar' stood about 2m high at its eastern end, sloping down to about 1.2m at the western end. The chamber, described by Powell et al. (1969, 304) as a ruined Portal Dolmen, measures around 3m x 2m (probably rectangular in plan). The surviving uprights once formed an H-shaped doorway; two of these lie underneath the capstone.

It is probable that the eastern section of the chamber formed part of an east-facing forecourt. The plan published by Lynch (1976, 68, Fig. 4) shows that this monument did not possess horns, which is unusual for a monument of this type.

A central rhomboid chamber, measuring 2.5m x 2.5m, may have been constructed during the phase of cairn enlargement, which extended the overall length to 57m. This chamber is formed partly of drystone walling. A roofing slab stands to a height of 1.5m, and a passage measuring 3m x 0.9m curves northwest from the chamber to the edge of the cairn. The passage narrows to 0.5m towards the chamber entrance, suggesting restricted visual access (see the discussion of Arthur's Stone, HRF 1). Pennant spoke of this chamber as having been taken over by a shepherd and used as a shelter during the post-medieval period (Pennant 1783). He believed that, in spite of some degree of rebuilding (Hemp, 1936, 29), the chamber was essentially as it had been at the time of construction, complete with a 'carefully worked recess in the southern wall and, possibly, a low bench of stone set into clay'.

TOP: The eastern section of Carneddau Hengwm South, looking west; MIDDLE LEFT: The carin mound, looking west; MIDDLE RIGHT: the side chamber; BOTTOM: The forecourt area

Several depressions between the central and eastern chambers may suggest further contemporary structures or stone robbing. Within the same area of the mound and located along the southern extent of the cairn, is probable evidence of mound kerbing. This kerbing, now consisting of three stones, is oriented E–W and probably delineates the extent of the mound.

Located at the western end of the monument and incorporated into the secondary phased cairn, are up to four stones. These are set in a N–S line and may either be further kerbing or the remnants of a small cist-type structure, similar to those found within the eastern section of Carneddau Hengwm North.

Earlier references speak of additional chambers in the body of the cairn – one to the east of the central feature, another to the west (Pennant, 1783). However, little evidence remains of these today.

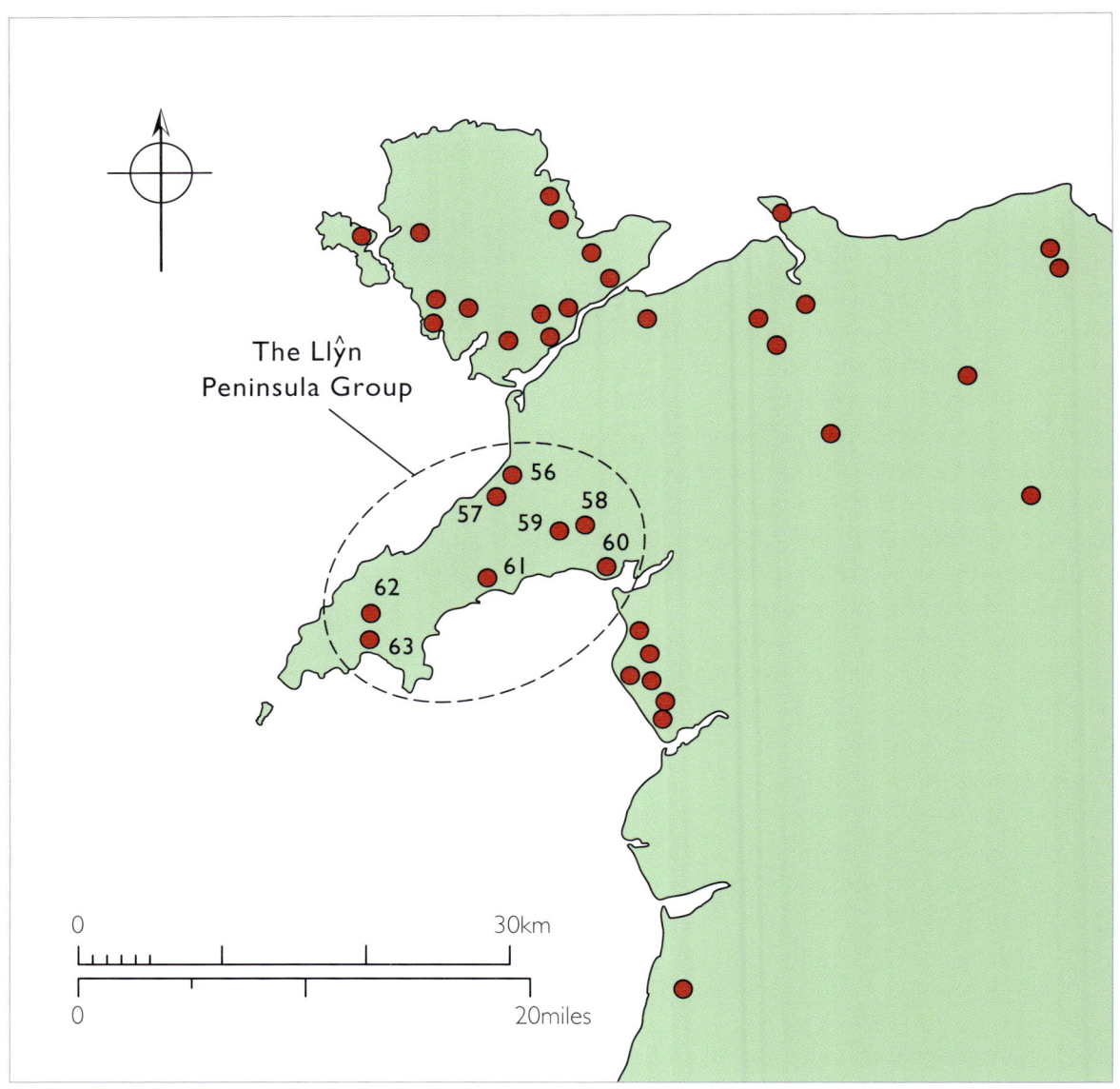

56	Penarth	59	Cefn Isaf	62	Mynydd Cefn Amlwch
57	Bachwen	60	Cist Cerrig	63	Tan-y-Muriau
58	Ystum Cegid Isaf	61	Four Crosses		

EIGHT

The Llŷn Peninsula Group

The Llŷn Peninsula is one of the major Neolithic core areas in Wales. Lynch (1969a, 109) has included monuments within the Dolgellau area – between Barmouth and Porthmadog, with monuments on the Llŷn Peninsula (referred to as the Llŷn-Ardudwy Group). However, each area has monuments with distinct architecture, and is separated by a 10km corridor between Llanfair and Porthmadog; which, according to the Gwynedd Archaeological Trust Historic Environment Record (HER), has little or no evidence of Neolithic activity. One must, therefore, keep these two groups separate.

There are three distinct environments present: coastal, coastal plateau and uplands. The upland zone, which in places exceeds 300m AOD, is spread along the western coastal fringes and along the central spine of the peninsula. The coastal plateau lies immediately north-east of the upland zone and rises to around 150m AOD. The coastal zone does not exceed 100m AOD. The majority of the Llŷn monuments occupy the coastal and coastal plateau zones, and appear to encompass – and visually acknowledge but not encroach upon – the upland zone.

Most of the 13 Llŷn Peninsula monuments are classified as Portal Dolmens (GAT HER; Lynch 1969a, 108). Some sites in this group are classified as either lost, possible or doubtful (Daniel 1950, 191–94; Powell et al. 1969, 300–8). Of the 13 monuments within this group, the eight discussed in this inventory include: Penarth (CRN 6), Bachwen (CRN 7), Ystum Cegid Isaf (CRN 8), Cefn Isaf (CRN 9), Cist Cerrig (CRN 10), Four Crosses (CRN 11), Mynydd Cefn Amwlch (CRN 12) and Tan-y-Muriau (CRN 13). Unlike other core areas, such as those found within the Black Mountains Group and South-west Wales, there are no geographical sub-groups recognised; they all appear to be evenly spread throughout this rugged landscape.

These monuments have been discussed by Daniel (1950), Lynch (1969) and Cummings & Whittle (2004). Lynch has concentrated on the morphology of each monument, and has made an extremely useful synthesis concerning the architectural similarities and differences between various monuments within this group and others in North Wales. However, little or no recent intrusive investigation into these monuments has been undertaken. Cummings & Whittle have tended to concentrate on the landscape setting of each monument; in particular their orientation and visuality (what is referred to as viewshed analysis).

The majority of the Portal Dolmens appear to conform to a series of basic rules. All have either rectangular or polygonal chambers. All have, or have had, a capstone, and all occupy one of two geographic locations, either on the valley floor or on the intermediate slopes located within the coastal plateau. It is only the site of Ystum Cegid Isaf (CRN 8) that has been identified as a passage grave with a large polygonal chamber (Powell et al. 1969, 301).

Monuments such as Cae-Dyni (CRN 14),[63] located within the coastal zone east of Criccieth, have in the past been considered as cists, and therefore wrongly classified as belonging to the Bronze Age (Powell et al. 1969, 306–7). I would suggest, however, that monuments of this size (which include a chamber measuring 1.3m x 0.80m) can still be considered megalithic and therefore valid in the context of Neolithic burial. The chamber is also set within a (denuded) rectangular mound measuring around 13m x 8m. Other monuments of this size and form found elsewhere within the core areas of Wales, such as Carn Besi (CRM 20), Bedd Taliesin (MER 11) or the Eithbed complex (PEM 31), are given megalithic status, and usually ascribed to the Late Neolithic. It is probable that Cae-Dyni conforms with this date range, although there is no direct dating for any of these monuments. A Late Neolithic date is supported by the discovery of up to 14 cupmarks found in 2007 (Nash, George & Waite 2007, 34–8).

56. Penarth, Clynnog
SH 42992 51072, SM NO. CN078
County Reference Number: CRN 6

This monument is one of two megalithic monuments within the parish of Clynnog. The Penarth tomb is located in a field (called Cae'r Goetan) between a road and the mouth of the Afon Desach, roughly 0.5km from the coast. It is one of a number of monuments along the Llŷn Peninsula that have similar landscape affinities to monuments found in South-west Wales. Penarth lies on the northern slopes of Bwlch Mawr. The nearby Bachwen

Western view of the Caer-Dyni monument, near Criccieth, with its slipped capstone

The much-disturbed Penarth monument

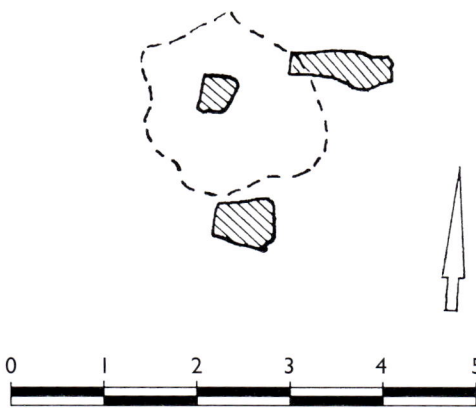

Plan of the Penarth monument (after Lynch 1969a)

monument (CRN 7) is located on the lower slopes of this impressive mountain, and both have some architectural associations.

The remains of the monument stand around 26m AOD on a gentle slope overlooking Caernarfon Bay. The site comprises three uprights, which define the plan of a chamber. A capstone, resting on two of the uprights, measures approximately 1.8m x 1.6m and may have been dislodged from its original position. The shape of the chamber is difficult to ascertain, but the three uprights could form a small rectangular or polygonal chamber, which would have been oriented roughly NW–SE (thus facing the sea). Surrounding the ruinous monument is a large stone cairn deposit that is the result of successive field clearance.

Lynch (1969a, 130) has suggested that due to the ruinous state of this monument, no classification can be applied. Nevertheless, it is probable that Penarth forms a small Portal Dolmen that was once laterally located within a long mound, although there is no evidence of any visible cairn surviving (Daniel 1950, 192).

57. Bachwen, Clynnog
SH 40770 49487, SM NO. CN008
County Reference Number: CRN 7

This Portal Dolmen is located approximately 200m from the sea, and stands at around 24m AOD. The monument is sited on the lower north-western slopes of Bwlch Mawr. As with the nearby Penarth monument, Bachwen would have had an affinity with the sea and its economic resources. It is probable that the location of the monument may have had an association with earlier hunter/fisher/gatherer communities that would have been economically drawn to the various coastal, marine and terrestrial resources found hereabouts.

The monument comprises a large capstone that is supported by four uprights that are incorporated into the traces of a shallow mound. Scattered around the monument are a number of loose and embedded stones which would once have formed a cairn or

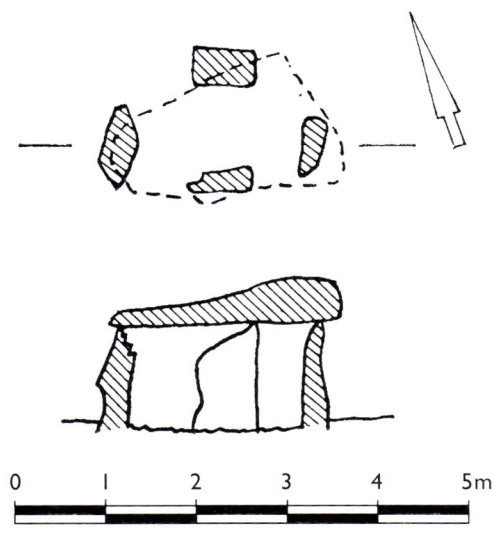

Plan and section of the Bachwen monument (after Lynch 1969a)

drystone infill between the uprights. For many years, the monument has been protected from livestock by an iron fence.

Lynch (1969a, 130) has suggested that drystone walling was used to infill the spaces between the four uprights. Each upright stands over 1m high and supports a wedge-shaped capstone. The capstone, measuring 2.4m x 2.7m, is aligned E–W, in order that the orientation of the capstone dips towards the sea. It is probable that the covering mound, measuring approximately 14m x 7.5m, was constructed of cairn and would have been similarly oriented. Probable traces of this mound can still be seen. It has been suggested that further chambers once existed (Hemp 1926, 429), but the idea of a multi-chambered cairn is difficult to sustain. The notes of antiquarian observers, however, do suggest that traces of kerbing were visible in 1783 (Pennant 1783, ii, 387–8).

The site was investigated by Barnwell, who describes in detail a large number of cupmarks that have been carved into the capstone (Barnwell 1867,

152). In the same year (1867), James Simpson described the site, albeit in a short summary. In his account, Simpson refers to the monument as 'Clynnog Fawr Cromlech' (Simpson 1867, 25).[64] Despite this mid nineteenth-century description, the rock art is also described in 1772 by Reverend J. Llwyd (from Caerwys, Flintshire) who describes the rock art thus:

> a near hundred shallow cavities running in oblique but almost parallel lines along its surface, three much larger than the rest in a triangular position; it is supported by four strong bearers (uprights), and in length four cubits, in beneath three, its inclination towards the setting sun [over the Irish Sea].

Based on a site visit in 2005, up to 110 cupmarks, each measuring roughly 5cm in diameter and 2cm in depth, are present on the capstone. They are similar to those found on the upper section of the capstone at the Trellyffaint monument (PEM 2) near Newport, Pembrokeshire (Barker 1992, 19; Nash et al. 2020).[65] Two shallow grooves on the upper surface of the capstone link three cupmarks together. Up to eight cupmarks are located on the northern ridge of the capstone, while the rest are on the southern side, facing the mountains to the south and east. Similar groupings are found on Bronze Age rock art panels in South Wales and northern Britain (Beckinsall 1999; Sharkey 2004). The eroded upper surface of the capstone does give support to the argument that capstones remained exposed during the period of use of the monument. It is even probable that the cupmarks date from the Bronze Age and represent a form of graffiti or 'statementing' of an ancestral monument by Bronze Age communities. Alternatively, the cupmarks on the capstone may have been hidden and were for the eyes of the ancestors only, as suggested for art found within the chambers

Southern view of the Bachwen monument

at Barclodiad-y-Gawres in Ynys Môn. What is noticeable is that the cupmarked area is located on the southern side of the capstone, the artistic endeavour extending to the central ridge. Limited rock art occurs on the northern side of the capstone. Interestingly, and looking east, the capstone appears to mark a north–south divide between the rolling hills to the north and the mountainous region of the Llŷn Peninsula to the south.

58. YSTUM CEGID ISAF, LLANYSTUMDWY
SH 49875 41330, SM NO. CN029
County Reference Number: CRN 8

This monument is also referred to as Coetan Arthur (Arthur's Quoit) and Ystumcegid (Bend in the [river] Cegid) Cromlech. It is located 0.7km east of the Afon Dwyfor, within a marshy area, and has a similar landscape position to the nearby Cefn Isaf monument (CRN 9). However, Ystum Cegid Isaf is very much larger. The monument, standing around 99m AOD, commands dramatic views of the uplands to the north and west.

Engraving of the Ystum Cegid Isaf monument
(*Archaeologia Cambrensis* 1869)

A sketch by Richard Farrington, published in *Snowdonia Druidica* in 1769, suggests that several large stones to the north are the remains of the passage. The drawing clearly shows further uprights and capstones ('triple cromlechs' as Pennant describes the stones in 1783), suggesting Ystum Cegid Isaf was indeed originally a passage grave. According to Lynch (1969a, 139) there was, during

Edward Pugh's painting of Ystum Cegid Isaf in 1816
(*Cambria Depicta*)

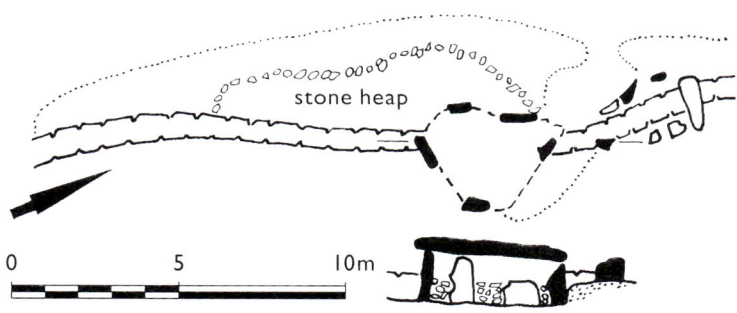

Plan and section of the Ystum Cegid Isaf monument
(after Lynch 1969a)

THE LLŶN PENINSULA GROUP   165

Side view of the chamber of Ystum Cegid Isaf

Ystum Cegid Isaf incorporated into a drystone wall

the eighteenth century, a 5m-long passage to the north of the chamber, which was made of seven uprights supporting two capstones. The remaining chamber appears to have been rebuilt sometime in the recent past. J.G. Williams (notebook published in *Archaeologia Cambrensis* in 1903) records that the capstone was dislodged in 1863, and Barnwell's sketch of 1869 shows the chamber in a ruined state (Barnwell 1869). It is clear, therefore, that the chamber has been renovated since that date. The position of the passage is indicated by the location of a drystone wall, and it is probable that the lower section of the passage is incorporated within the wall.

The monument is located within an E–W drystone field boundary. In the field to the west of the site are the remains of a rubble stone heap, partly a result of modern field clearance. However, beyond the rubble is evidence of a possible long mound that was oriented E–W. The drystone field boundary appears to cut through the centre of the mound. If this small rise does represent the mound, then the chamber is laterally positioned. The chamber, possibly polygonal in form, has five uprights that stand approximately 1.1m high. These uprights support a large capstone measuring 4.8m x 3.9m.

The monument has been compared, in terms of its morphology, with Bryn Celli Ddu (ANG 7) in Ynys Môn, which is regarded as 'the best example of a passage grave in England and Wales' (c.f. Daniel 1950, 55). Monuments of this size with a passage are usually incorporated into a circular mound (Grimes 1936a, 128–9), although one cannot rule out other architectural scenarios.

59. Cefn Isaf, Llanystumdwy
SH 48365 40875, SM NO. CN003
County Reference Number: CRN 9

In terms of landscape position, this monument stands close to an area of marshy land between the Afon Dwyfach and the Afon Dwyfor, at around 90m AOD. Approximately 0.75km to the east of the Afon Dwyfor stands the monument of Ystum Cegid Isaf (CRN 8). Both monuments have extensive views to the north and west – the upland rock outcrops of

The Cefn Isaf chamber, looking west

Photograph of Cefn Isaf by J.E. Griffith
(*Archaeologia Cambrensis* 1904)

Bwlch Mawr and Garn Goch are clearly visible some 3.5km from the mouth of the Afon Dwyfor and the coast, and may have landscape association.

Cefn Isaf, also referred to as Rhos-y-Llan and Rhoslan, comprises a substantial capstone measuring 3.4m x 2.5m, which is supported by three of four fine-grained sandstone uprights. The site, classified by Powell et al. as a Portal Dolmen (1969, 301), has been damaged. The north-western side of the monument appears intact and is formed by a single stone lying on edge. However, on the south-eastern side the monument has been destroyed, with all traces of uprights gone (RCAHMW 1960). The chamber, rectangular in plan, appears to be oriented NE–SW, and was probably covered by a mound which was also oriented NE–SW. The entrance to the chamber may have been from the north-east via a portal stone which is located between the north-eastern upright and the large slab which runs along the western wall of the chamber (Lynch 1969a, 129). However, this stone slumps in towards the chamber and appears to fit awkwardly if standing upright. Immediately west of Cefn Isaf is an historic field drainage ditch. Supporting the banks of this and other drainage ditching around the field are

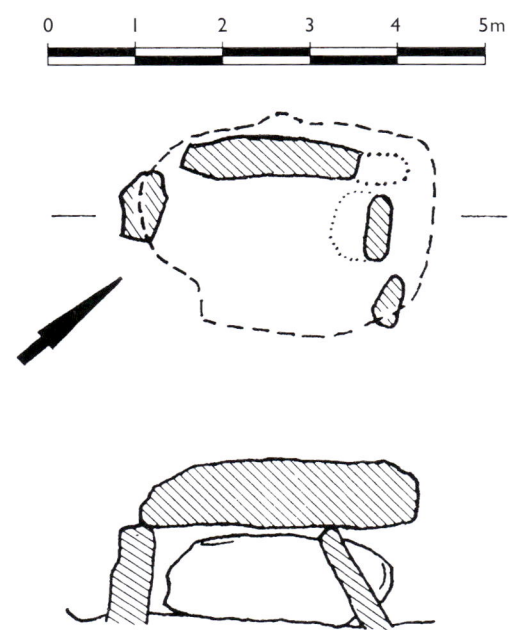
Plan and section of the Cefn Isaf monument
(after Lynch 1969a)

THE LLŶN PENINSULA GROUP   167

large quantities of stone, some of which may have originated from this monument.

It is suggested by Lynch (1969a, 129) that this monument, along with Four Crosses (CRN 11), is located close to a trading route which runs across the Llŷn Peninsula. I would further suggest that the Afon Dwyfach and the Afon Dwyfor would have served as approaches to these sites. It is worth considering that the marsh areas around this and the nearby Ystum Cegid Isaf monument would have restricted physical access to the monuments during use.

60. Cist Cerrig, Treflys
SH 54330 38397, SM NO. CN118
County Reference Number: CRN 10

This monument, also known as Cist Gerrig, stands on the lower slopes of Moel-y-Gest, close to Porthmadog. It is architecturally similar to Hendre Waelod (DEN 1), Gwern Einion (MER 1), Bron-y-Foel-Isaf (MER 2) and Cefn Isaf (CRN 9). Approximately 3km to the south-east are the sandbanks of the Afon Dwyryd, Afon Glaslyn and Tremadoc Bay, and these would have been economically important to Neolithic communities using this monument. The monument stands within an enclosed valley at around 73m AOD. Exposed rock outcrops located 0.75km to the north were utilised during the Iron Age and form the Moel-y-Gest hill enclosure.

The monument consists of two uprights and a possible door-stone. The largest of these stands 2.2m above the present ground level. Although in a ruined state, it is possible to suggest that a rectangular chamber once existed, based on the existing H-shaped plan of the door-stone and associated uprights. Alternatively, this may be a false portal of a former Cotswold-Severn monument, which now survives as an upright. This stone may have separated a large chamber from the entrance/façade; however, only excavation will answer this. Lynch (1969a, 129) has suggested that the three stones once formed a

The site of Cist Cerrig, minus its capstone, looking north-west

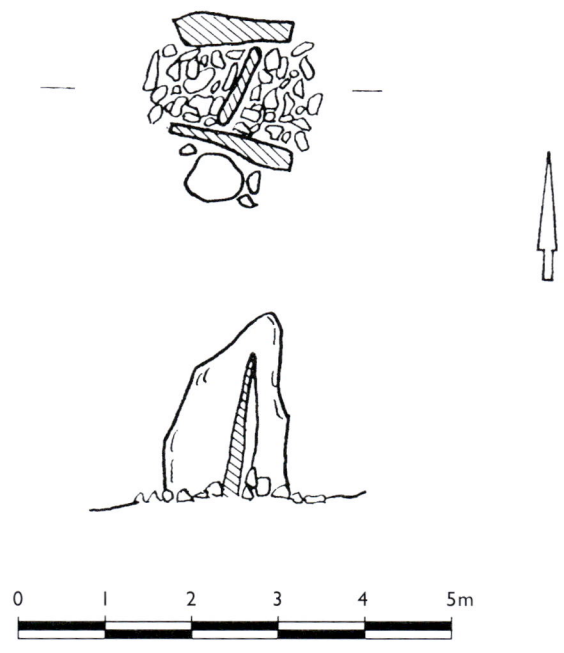

Plan and section of the Cist Cerrig monument (after Lynch 1969a)

Cist Cerrig and the rugged landscape to the north

A large glacial erratic boulder standing north of Cist Cerrig

61. Four Crosses, Abererch
SH 39897 38492, SM NO. CN095
County Reference Number: CRN 11

The monument stands in open pasture on a small ridge to the west of the Afon Erch at around 66m AOD. Close by, to the south of Rhyd-y-gwystl, are two standing stones each approximately 1.7m high (SH 400 389 and SH 400 388). The ridge was utilised to avoid extensive areas of marshland to the east, and provide the best route across the Llŷn Peninsula (Lynch 1969a, 129). This monument forms part of a small megalithic group within the area, that also includes Cefn Isaf (CRN 9) and the small coastal megalithic chamber of Cae-Dyni, east of Criccieth (CRN 14). Daniel (1950, 89) suggests that these monuments are similar in plan and can be linked architecturally to other Portal Dolmens in North Wales: for example, at Hendre Waelod (DEN 1), Gwern Einion (MER 1), Bron-y-Foel-Isaf (MER 2) and Cefn Isaf (CRN 9). All these surviving structures have a single capstone, which is supported by either three or four uprights, delineating a rectangular or polygonal chamber. Despite the state of *in situ*

small Portal Dolmen with a chamber to the west, facing uphill, 'since this is a very consistent feature of tombs of this class in North Wales' (ibid. 129). Inside the chamber area is an extensive rubble deposit, which may be the result of field clearance or rubble packing. No evidence of a cairn or capstone survives.

Cist Cerrig is one of nine megalithic monuments in Wales associated with engraved cupmarks. These do not occur on the monument itself, but on a natural rock surface 23m to the south-east, and comprise a vertical line of 12 cupmarks (Hemp 1938, 141).

The site was surveyed by members of the Clifton Antiquarian Club (Bristol) in 2006/7 (Fenn, Nash & Waite 2007). Through an extensive fieldwork survey, the team identified a number of rock outcrops that contained cupmarks. It soon became clear that the ritual landscape associated with Cist Cerrig is extensive.

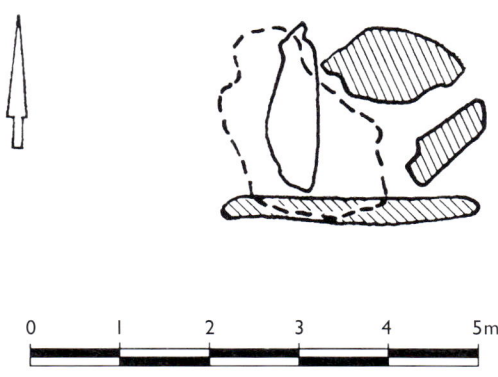

Plan of the Four Crosses monument (after Lynch 1969a)

The badly-reconstructed Four Crosses monument, looking north

preservation of the Cefn Isaf monument, the uprights and capstone are of the same geology: that of fine-grained sandstone.

Based on the RCAHM(W) inventory for Caernarvonshire (1964, Volume III, West), observations made by Richard Farrington in 1772 suggested that a possible approach of some form of processional route may have been in place. Farrington notes, 'to the north some remains of erected stones [are] visible'. Later, in 1877, it was remarked that a 'curious avenue of stones, 138 feet in length by 16 feet in average width, by which it is approached, and some of which appear to have formed at one time smaller cromlechs of their own'. My inspection of the area around the monument, showed no evidence of this potential stone avenue, although two standing stones are erected close by.

A plan of the site was made by Barnwell in 1869, which depicts the monument prior to its restoration in 1936 by the owner, Mr William Evans. It appears that prior to restoration, the western upright had fallen on its side under the capstone. Nothing was found within the chamber area of the monument during the restoration (Daniel 1936a). A site visit in January 2006 showed that the uprights are set into concrete. Moreover, the southern upright may be the capstone, and when reassembled, Mr Evans was not quite sure of the original morphology of the monument. The shape and size of the capstone is roughly similar to that of nearby Cefn Isaf (CRN 9).

Although regarding the monument as a typical Portal Dolmen, Lynch suggests that the siting of tombs within this area indicates the inland movement of people from the coast, probably using streams and rivers flowing northwards into the hinterland of the Llŷn Peninsula. Lynch further postulates that by the time the Four Crosses monument was constructed, the original architectural inspiration for this and other monuments had been lost (1969a, 129). I would further suggest that this monument has architectural similarities with nearby Cefn Isaf. Both monuments, although classified generically as Portal Dolmens, have short uprights which support horizontally placed capstones, unlike Hendre Waelod (DEN 1) and Gwern Einion (MER 1).

The monument consists of a small enclosed rectangular chamber measuring approximately 1.3m x 0.8m x 1.48m, which would have once stood within a covering mound. The current capstone, measuring 2.3m x 1.4m x 0.6m, is supported by three uprights, with an entrance probably located on the north-eastern side of the monument. A fourth upright stands short of the capstone by 0.2m.

62. Mynydd Cefn Amwlch, Penllech
SH 22975 34540, SM no. CN002
County Reference Number: CRN 12

Standing on the north-western slopes of Mynydd Cefn Amwlch, this tripod dolmen (Daniel 1950, 52), also known as Coetan Arthur and Tref-y-garnedd, shares a similar location to that of the

Penarth monument (CRN 6). It lies approximately 2km from the sea at around 99m AOD. The Afon Soch flows to the east and would have provided a direct route between this monument and that at Tan-y-Muriau. According to Lynch (1969a, 132), there are nineteenth-century accounts of destroyed monuments within the surrounding area, suggesting that the Neolithic ritual landscape in which the Mynydd monument stands, may once have been conspicuously richer.

Lynch has also suggested that the area around Mynydd Cefn Amwlch was probably unpopulated (ibid. 131). However, it was clearly an important symbolic area and has one of the greatest concentrations of Portal Dolmens in North Wales. It is more than likely, though, that settlement was concentrated in the valleys and close to the estuarine areas where resources were abundant.

This much-ruined monument consists of a large capstone measuring 3.5m x 2.5m, which is supported by three uprights, all of fine-grained sandstone. Located within the north-western area of the chamber is a possible recumbent sill-stone, which probably would have allowed periodic access to the chamber. The original shape of the monument is unknown. However, the chamber, regarded by Lynch (1969a, 131) as featureless, may have been laterally placed within a long mound – similar to other dolmen-type monuments in the Llŷn Peninsula. Castleden (1992, 394) states that the chamber is rectangular in form and speculates that the stone elements of the monument were incorporated within a circular mound measuring 8.5m in diameter. However, the mound's shape and size are difficult to determine. The present architectural form is similar to Bachwen (CRN 7), Llech-y-Tribedd (PEM 1) and Carreg Coetan Arthur (PEM 3), both the latter two being located within the Newport group in South-west Wales. Daniel (1950, 193) notes that a large flat stone, possibly belonging to another chamber, exists immediately west of the monument. This stone, made from white quartz-veined sandstone, is large enough to be a capstone. However it is more likely to be later field clearance; it seems unlikely that it forms part of the monument architecture.

The chamber of Mynydd Cefn Amwlch

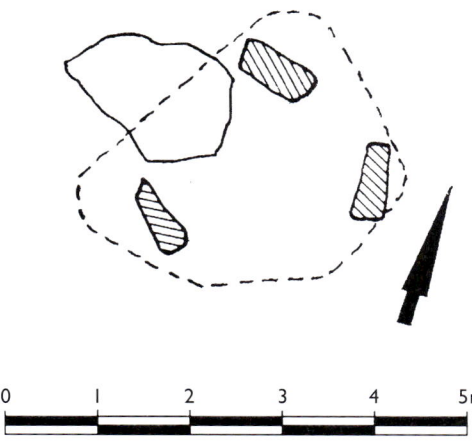

Plan of the Mynydd Cefn Amwlch monument (after Lynch 1969a)

THE LLŶN PENINSULA GROUP 171

63. Tan-y-Muriau, Rhiw

SH 23770 28765, SM NO. CN026
County Reference Number: CRN 13

This complex site is regarded as one of the Llŷn Peninsula's most important surviving monuments, and stands on the eastern slopes of Mynydd Rhiw at around 132m AOD. It has extensive views across the eastern part of the peninsula and the northern coastline of Cardigan Bay. At the foot of Mynydd Rhiw, on which Tan-y-Muriau stands, is a large area of marshland. Beyond this are many small streams running off the mountain, which feed into the nearby Afon Soch. During the Neolithic, these natural spaces may have been significant, perhaps dividing the landscape into social and symbolic areas.

The monument, classified as a laterally chambered long mound, consists of a Portal Dolmen-type chamber at the western end. The mound may once have been trapezoidal in form. Morphologically, Tan-y-Muriau may be similar to monuments belonging to the Cotswold-Severn group. It is possible that sometime during the early part of the Late Neolithic there was a need to alter the form of existing monuments, and Tan-y-Muriau may exemplify this process of architectural change. Similarly, elsewhere, at Ty Isaf (BRE 5) in the Black Mountains, the original round mound with central chamber and passage was later incorporated into a large trapezoidal monument.

The survival of this monument is mainly due to it being incorporated into a large field bank. This field bank, coupled with the mound, runs down a 10-degree slope, the unorthodox N–S zigzag line of the field boundary shows the probable extent of the monument. During its construction and use, the mound must have measured some 43m in length and 15m in width.

This monument, described by J.G. Williams in 1871 (*Archaeologia Cambrensis* 1903, 260) notes three chambers as being in a N–S line, 20 yards (9.5m) from each other.

The northern chamber consists of a large capstone measuring approximately 3.6m x 2.9m x 0.7m, supported by four uprights (RCAHMW 1956). The chamber floor, rectangular in plan, appears to be cut into the natural slope of the mountain. The centrally placed upright at the northern end of the chamber

One of two chambers belonging to Tan-y-Muriau, and the dramatic landscape in which it sits

The northern chamber of Tan-y-Muriau

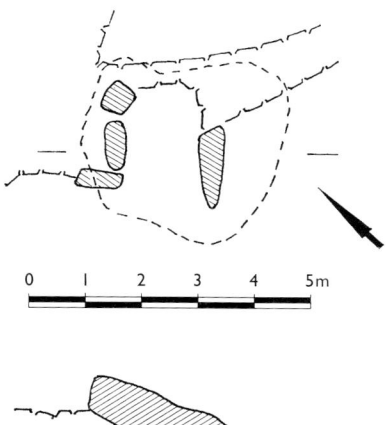

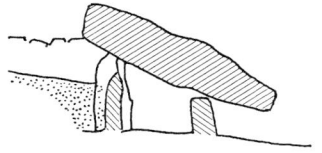

Plan and section of Tan-y-Muriau's northern chamber (after Lynch 1969a)

possibly forms a door, which was periodically moved in order to allow ritual deposition of human remains into the chamber area.

Approximately 7m south-east of the northern chamber, and incorporated into the mound, is a smaller chamber, which Castleden refers to as a side chamber (1992, 394). This consists of a capstone measuring 2.3m x 1.5m, leaning against two uprights. Located outside the western area of the chamber, within the mound, is an extensive rubble spread, which possibly represents a passage. The plan reproduced in Lynch (1969a, 131) suggests that the small chamber is centrally located within the mound, and would have been entered via the passage from the west. The large chamber at the northern terminal is believed to have formed part of an earlier monument, which may have been circular or oval in form. Lynch (ibid. 133) associates the architectural form with other monuments, such as Carnedd Hengwn South (MER 6) and Dyffryn Ardudwy (MER 3). Approximately 10m north of the southern end of the barrow was, according to Daniel (1950, 193), a heap of large stones which may have formed part of another chamber.

Plan and section of Tan-y-Muriau's side chamber (after Lynch 1969a)

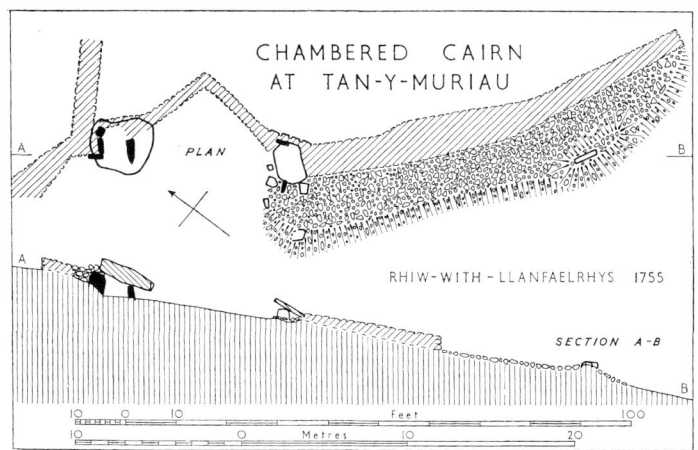

Plan and section of the Tan-y-Muriau monument, showing the location of the two chambers (after Lynch 1969a)

THE LLŶN PENINSULA GROUP 173

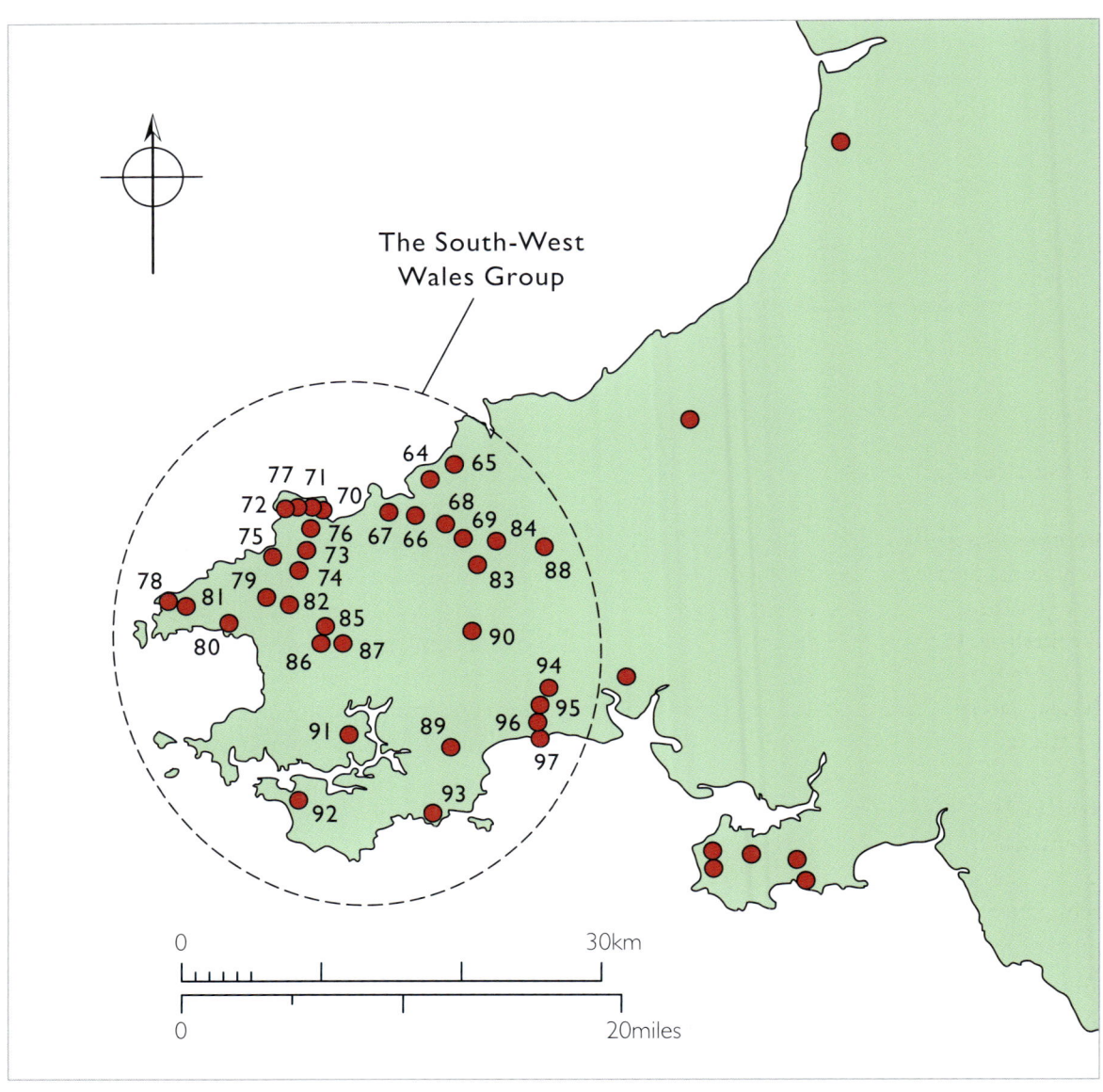

64	Llech-y-Tribedd	73	Ffyst Samson	82	White House	91	The Hanging Stone
65	Trellyffant	74	Trewalter Llwyd	83	Gwal-y-Filiast	92	Devil's Quoit
66	Carreg Coetan	75	Carreg Samson	84	Mountain	93	King's Quoit
67	Cerrig y Gof	76	Ffynnondruidion	85	The Altar	94	Morfa Bychan A
68	Pentre Ifan	77	Parc-y-Cromlech	86	Garn Turne	95	Morfa Bychan B
69	Bedd-yr-Afanc	78	Coetan Arthur	87	Parc-y-llyn	96	Morfa Bychan C
70	Garn Wen Cemetery	79	Treffynnon	88	Carn Besi	97	Morfa Bychan D
71	Carn Wnda	80	St Elvies Farm	89	The Cuckoo Stones		
72	Garn Gilfach	81	Carn Llidi	90	Eithbed Cemetery Gp		

NINE

The South-West Wales Group

BY FAR THE largest Neolithic core group in Wales is that comprising the 50 or so extant monuments found in South-west Wales.[66] These sites are located within the counties of Cardiganshire, Carmarthenshire and Pembrokeshire. In the recent past these have been discussed in detail by Barker (1992), Children & Nash (1997; 2002), Cummings (2002), Cummings & Whittle (2004) and Kytmannow (2008). Up until 2004, only one site in this area – Carreg Coetan (PEM 3) – had been dated using radio-chronometric methods (see Appendix 2). There is, therefore, a problem in assessing the chronology of architectural phasing of monuments within this group (Kytmannow 2008). However, based on the limited artefact evidence, it is probable that the Portal Dolmen group, of which Carreg Coetan is one, is the earliest, and the earth-fast style monument the latest. No one monument group appears to have been in use throughout the Neolithic, the duration of which spans 1,700–2,000 years. In addition to morphology, the landscape position of each monument type varies through time and geographical area. Due to the size and distribution of these monuments, I have organised them into a series of geographical sub-groups.

The South-West Wales Group of monuments can boast the most diverse architecture, itself incorporated in a variety of landscape settings. In particular, ideas from central and southern Ireland appear to have reached the builders of some of the monuments, creating an Irish Sea Portal Dolmen tradition. It would appear the some form of alliance, through contact and exchange, was ongoing throughout the duration of the Neolithic (and beyond). Also important to this group are the three axe factories located around and on Mynydd Preseli, which encouraged the trade and exchange of exotic imported items, including axes, some of which were deposited in a number of burial monuments (Figgis, 2001). One should also remember that Mynydd Preseli is additionally the area in which the Preseli blue stones of Stonehenge fame originate.

The location of many of the monuments is based on the relationship with the sea: many monuments have extensive views of the sea, and arguably the Neolithic package, which includes burial monumentality, may also include farming the sea. A similar geographic location is found in other core groups, such as Ynys Môn and the Harlech Group. Tilley (1994), David & Williams (1995) and Children & Nash (1997) have suggested, further, that monuments were deliberately positioned in order to be visually associated with various local landscape features. In South-west Wales, features may have included mountains, spurs, naturally constructed cairn heaps and water courses, boggy areas and estuarine locales.

Many monuments in South-west Wales are also sited within extensive rock outcropping, thus hiding the monument within the landscape. It appears that all monument classifications are represented, in particular by a group of Late Neolithic monuments referred to as 'earth-fast'. This is probably the only area in Wales that has earth-fast monuments. Unlike many monuments within this part of Wales, these probably did not possess a covering mound.

This group includes some of the largest megalithic sites in Wales. The sites of Pentre Ifan (PEM 3), Garn Turne (PEM 11) and Carreg Samson (PEM 18) all possess massive capstones and large chamber architecture. The Garn Turne capstone weighs in excess of 60 tons. The size and weight of such stones would probably have required inter-communal co-operation. Indeed, this area contains two Neolithic settlements, Clegyr Boia and Coygan Camp, which have allowed researchers to associate settlement activity with burial activity. Throughout the rest of Wales, there are many upland and lowland lithic scatters which could be deemed as settlement sites, but Clegyr Boia and Coygan Camp both have the remains of house structures.

Since publication of the first edition of this book, I have directed several excavations at the Trefael standing stone (Barker's ref: 52) and the impressive Trellyffaint double-chambered stone monument, both north of the Pembrokeshire coastal town of Newport (Barker 1992). Although Trellyffaint is included within my inventory, Trefael is not, and it therefore deserves a few words due to new information that was revealed during the excavation programme.

Cupmarks on the Trefael Stone

The excavation of Trefael (SN 1030 4030), between 2010 and 2014, exposed a number of significant features and structures. Until 2012, the Trefael Stone (also known as Trefoil) was classified as a standing stone, and was probably of Early Bronze Age date (c.2,500 BCE). The site is located east of the Afon Nevern Valley, and shares similar landscape affinities with nearby Llech-y-Tribedd and Trellyffaint. In terms of an archaeological context, the site was first recorded by W.F. Grimes in his *Pembrokeshire Survey* (1929, 31 & 277). Grimes was the first to record the presence of cupmarks. He also considered it to be a capstone, possibly belonging to a Neolithic burial-ritual monument. Based on historic Ordnance Survey mapping, Trefael and a nearby standing stone were known during the latter part of the nineteenth century. Until recently, up to 45 shallow cupmarks were recorded on the surface of the stone. The team traced the stone surface in 2010 and increased the number to 75 cupmarks of varying quality and size (Nash, Brook & Wellicome 2012). Following an initial geophysical survey, a targeted excavation programme continued for the next four years. From this fieldwork, we ascertained that the standing stone was the capstone of a small Portal Dolmen, the remains of which were uncovered during the latter stages of the excavation programme. From this excavation, we also managed to extract the remains of a cremation burial that dated to 3,653 ± 45 BP (SUERC–45386).

Due to the large number of extant monuments within this region, I have created up to nine sub-sections that collate burial-ritual sites based on geographic distribution. The main reference used is Christopher Barker's impressive inventory. This identifies not only 46 extant monuments but also lists a further 88 destroyed, forgotten, lost and questionable sites (Barker 1992). The majority of the 46 extant monuments discussed in Barker are included in the following chapter.

The Newport Group

The Newport Group comprises six monuments – Llech-y-Tribedd (PEM 1), Trellyffaint (PEM 2), Carreg Coetan (PEM 3), Cerrig y Gof (PEM 4), Pentre Ifan (PEM 5) and Bedd-yr-Afanc (PEM 27) – that encompass an area either side of the Nevern Valley of around 40km². Other monuments may have existed, but due to intensive agricultural activity over recent centuries they are now long gone.

The area has a continuous early prehistory dating back at least to 6,000 BCE. Flint from the Late Mesolithic has been found all along the mud flats of the Afon Nyfer (Nevern) estuary. Between the estuary, the coast and the mountains, Neolithic mortuary structures occupy the intermediate slopes. Above these slopes, and all along the northern extent of the Mynydd Preseli overlooking Newport, Bronze Age and Iron Age activity is also represented.

Domestic life for Neolithic communities in and around the Nevern Valley seems to have been generally favourable. A choice of economic resources would have been available, ranging from coastal and riverine fishing, hunting and gathering, to limited animal husbandry and crop cultivation. Samples of wood discovered within the inter-tidal peats of the Nevern estuary (-0.6m OD) have been dated to 6370±150 BP, suggesting the environment in and around Newport was wooded. Indeed, this and similar samples from Cardigan Bay originate from part of a now-submerged forest. The area within the estuary would, therefore, have been foraged by large mammals such as red and roe deer.

For each of the tombs in this cluster, the primary landscape focus seems to be the rocky outcrop of Mynydd Carningli, at the north-eastern extent of the Preseli Mountains. Three of the monuments – Pentre Ifan, Carreg Coetan and Llech-y-Tribedd – all have capstones with a shape that appears to replicate the summit of the outcrop, drawing the landscape within the architecture of the tomb (Tilley 1994; Children & Nash 1997).[67] Similar ideas concerning monument/landscape replication have been proposed by Tilley & Bennett (2001, 336), who suggest that the capstones of Portal Dolmens from the Penrith Peninsula in Cornwall mimic natural phenomenon known as tors. The idea of monuments adding new meaning to a (hunter/gatherer) landscape has been promoted by Bradley (2000), and it seems possible that mimicry forms part of the legitimisation whereby monuments partially complement the form of the land.

What we see today is only the *skeleton* of the monument (the stone). During the Neolithic, this skeleton would have possessed *flesh* – a covering earthen mound – although in each case the capstone may have been partly exposed in order to emphasise the symbolic association with Carningli. Also gone is the façade area and any ritual associated features, such as pits and (wooden) platforms.

Apart from the gallery grave of Bedd-yr-Afanc, which probably dates from the latest phase of the Neolithic, the remaining Newport tombs – despite their damaged and, in some cases, ruined state – probably embody a process of replication and control which seeks to establish and perpetuate a sense of identity between the group and its landscape. Tombs belonging to clusters elsewhere in South-west Wales tend to confirm these observations, revealing a similar pattern of landscape orientation. The chamber at St Elvies Farm (PEM 20), St David's, for example, is angled down towards a small coastal valley, an inlet of the River Solva.

However, given this general association with Carningli, individual monuments of the Newport Group are nevertheless sited within diverse landscape settings, ranging from coastal locations to inland valley floor sites. Apart from Cerrig y Gof and perhaps Carreg Coetan, tombs appear to ignore the draw of the sea. Indeed, the two monuments of Llech-y-Tribedd and Trellyffaint, although only 0.5km from the coast, appear to be deliberately hidden from the sea, being constructed on east- and south-facing ridges overlooking the Preseli Mountains. This pattern recurs throughout the South-west Wales Peninsula.

Due to the diversity of architectural forms, the dating of individual tombs is difficult. One cannot say with certainty that all the tombs in this group were constructed about the same time, although they were probably all in use during the middle and later phases of the Neolithic. It has been suggested that simple Portal Dolmens, such as Carreg Coetan and Trellyffaint, are the earliest monuments in this area

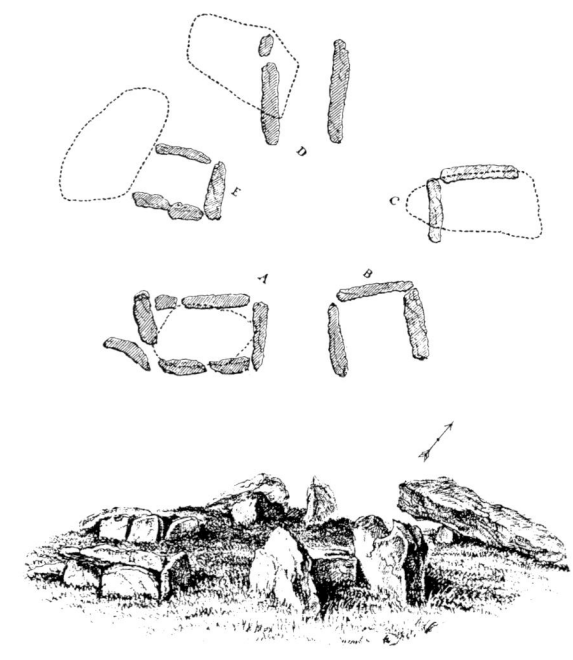

Antiquarian engraving of Cerrig y Gof (*Archaeologia Cambrensis* 1890)

(Rees 2012; Barker 1992; Nash et al. 2020). This type of monument architecture, incorporating a small chamber, originally housed a single burial, probably that of an important figure in Early Neolithic society. Following burial, the tomb may have continued to function as a significant place within the landscape, changing its symbolic significance through time (as witnessed through the different ways of burying the dead). Indeed, towards the latter part of the Neolithic and the Early Bronze Age, there is evidence for monuments in this area becoming political statements within the landscape – their identity changing, but not their form. For instance, at Trellyffaint, the tomb ceased to be a monument for the dead. The 75 cupmarks on the capstone, possibly Bronze Age in date, indicated a transformation of the ideology associated with the tomb. It is suggested that these cupmarks act as a rejection of the old Neolithic order (Children & Nash 1997). An equivalent today might be redundant Nonconformist chapels being reused as workshops and dwellings. Here, the building has changed its meaning, but not its architectural form. Alternatively, it could be the case that inscribing single or multiple cupmarks onto a monument was part of a ritual package that is incorporated into the construction and early use of a monument (Nash 2021).

Of the six monuments, Bedd-yr-Afanc stands apart and has been classified as a Late Neolithic gallery grave. Its construction, location and orientation suggest a change in monument ideology. Located inland, and oriented E–W along the valley floor, the tomb ignores Carningli, the sea and other monuments. Gallery graves follow a similar pattern elsewhere. Compared with earlier monuments, they are smaller, less intrusive and sometimes actually hidden. With its covering earthen mound, Bedd-yr-Afanc would have merged with the valley floor. Without specialist ritual knowledge, the tomb would have been invisible, with access restricted to members of the local group.

64. Llech-y-Tribedd, Nevern
SN 1005 4319, SM NO. PE049
County Reference Number: PEM 1

This monument, also referred to as the Altar Stone, Llech-y-Drybedd and Samson's Quoit, commands one of the most outstanding views of any tomb in the area, and draws in the whole extent of the north Preseli Mountains (Tilley 1994, 105). Legend has it that St Samson originally threw the stones for the monument from the summit of Mynydd Carningli.

The monument stands around 188m AOD, and comprises a single, large capstone supported by three uprights, and is classified by Lynch as a Portal Dolmen (1972, 77–8). The uprights, derived from locally quarried sandstone, are arranged in a tripod form. Another is located close by, suggesting the chamber was once rectangular. Indeed, in 1695 it was reported by Lhuyd that this fourth upright was in place and supported the capstone. Daniel claims that the fourth upright lay close to the monument in a prostrate position in 1950 (1950, 198). There is no evidence of any covering mound, but there is some potential cairn material in and around the chamber area. It should also be noted that the surrounding field boundaries are constructed of turf and stone, and it is probable that cairn material may have been reused within the boundary fabric.

The massively thick capstone, triangular in shape and measuring 5m x 3m, points towards Mynydd Carningli, a focal point for nearly all the tombs in this area. Indeed, the south-eastern point of the

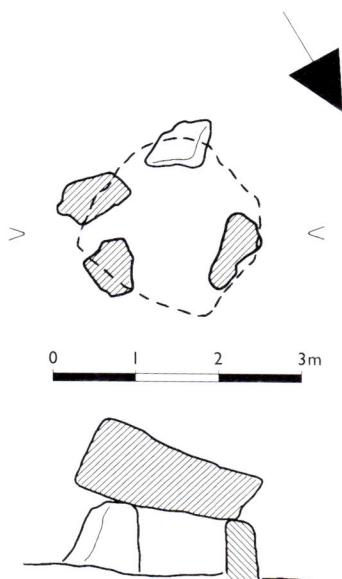

Plan and section of the Llech-y-Tribedd monument (after Barker 1992)

capstone appears to replicate its summit. By contrast, Llech-y-Tribedd is completely hidden from the sea, although located on a south-east-facing ridge only 0.6km from the coast (ignoring any view of the sea appears to be a common trait among monuments within this part of Wales). The monument is also 1.75km north-east of the Trellyffaint monument (PEM 2) but not intervisible.

The eastern side of Llech-y-Tribedd, showing cairn material that once formed a mound

The eastern side of Llech-y-Tribedd (photograph in Daniel 1950)

A small pipeline trench, aligned E–W, was excavated by Cambria Archaeology (PRN 1121), and located approximately 10m north of the chamber area, in October 1977. According to the report, no prehistoric artefacts were recorded.

Several recent visits by the author confirmed that one of the uprights on the western side of the monument has a severe vertical hairline crack. This crack is currently being monitored by Cadw.

65. Trellyffaint, Nevern
SN 0822 4252, SM NO. PE041
County Reference Number: PEM 2

This much-ruined burial monument is also referred to as Trellyfant or Trellyfaint, and stands approximately 1.75km south-west of the Llech-y-Tribedd monument at around 137m AOD. Lynch (1969a, 131) describes Trellyffaint as a Portal Dolmen. Originally, the chamber seems to have been rectangular in plan; and Daniel, writing in 1950, gave a height of 1.8m, with an opening to the south-east. The chamber is constructed of three large uprights, with a fourth stone acting as a back-stone. According to Lynch (1972, 78), the voids between the uprights may have been infilled with drystone walling. The capstone appears to have been oriented NW–SE, and measures 2.1m x 1.8m.

To the north of the main chamber is a small, square feature – possibly another chamber – measuring approximately 1.5m x 1.7m; in which case it would make Trellyfaint a double-chambered tomb (RCAM 1925, 760).[68] This chamber would have possessed a small capstone, and Lynch (1972, 79) suggests that a cairn or earthen mound would originally have covered both chambers, traces of which are still visible and were confirmed by an earthworks survey undertaken by the author (Nash, Brook & Wellicome 2020).

There is evidence of later prehistoric ritual defacement on the upper surface of the capstone. Thirty-five cupmarks were identified by the recorder for the RCAM inventory, and later illustrated by Lynch (1972, 78–9) and Barker (1992, 19). The cupmarks may be of Bronze Age origin and associated with the appropriation and re-use of the tomb by people seeking to alter its meaning – perhaps transforming what was once principally a mortuary structure into a monument marking the site of exchange transactions or political gatherings. Such acts may be interpreted as attempts to subvert remote and irrelevant beliefs. The authenticity of the Trellyfaint cupmarks, however, has been questioned. The RCAM (1925) argued that, owing to the random size and distribution of the marks, they should be regarded as natural. Daniel, however, believed these 'pitted' cupmarks to be genuine and some of the finest in southern Britain. The author, who traced the capstone (with Carol Brook) in 2018, regards the cupmark arrangement as genuine. The traced surface of the capstone revealed 75+ cupmarks, with

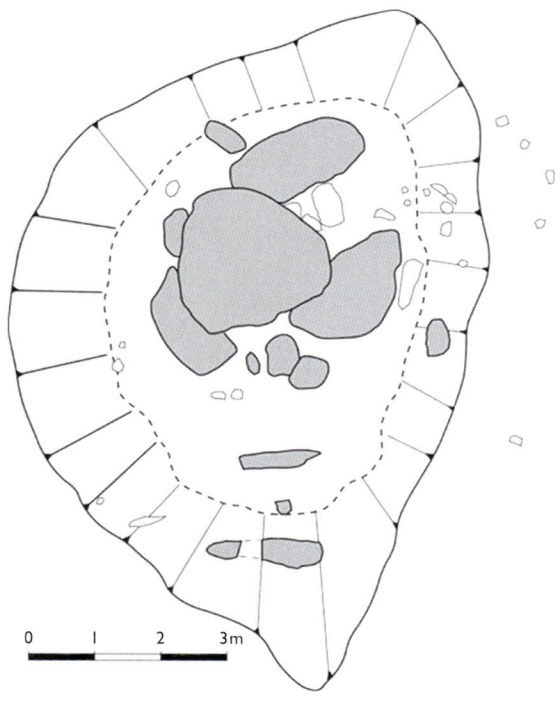

Plan and section of the Trellyffaint monument (after Nash 2020)

The Trellyffaint monument, looking east towards Mynydd Carningli

THE SOUTH-WEST WALES GROUP

Section of the capstone belonging to Trellyffaint, revealing multiple cupmarks through the use of oblique lighting

some appearing to be organised in a linear fashion. Cupmarks present on the capstones of Neolithic chambered tombs are considered a rare occurrence and are present on only nine monuments in Wales (Nash 2021).

About 3km to the south-east of Trellyffaint burial chamber, further cupmarks are visible on a large rock slab known locally as Trefael,[69] which Daniel believed was the capstone of a destroyed megalithic chamber. The site was excavated between 2010 and 2014 by Nash, Brook, Wellicome & Rees (2020).

Following a geophysical survey within the field in which the Trellyffaint monument stands, a small, targeted excavation was undertaken to the west of the site, over a potential henge measuring *c*.12m in diameter. Traces of this anomaly, along with other subsurface features, were exposed during the geophysical survey. The excavation revealed a Neolithic land surface which was cut into by three distinct features, two of which were circular pits; the other, a small section of the henge bank. Within

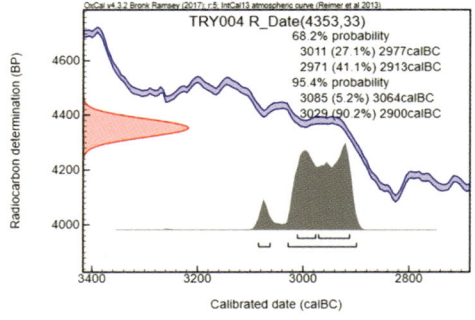

TOP: Excavation of a shallow pit within a small henge monument, 15m north of Trellyffaint; MIDDLE: One of 35 sherds of Neolithic Grooved Ware pottery excavated at Trellyffaint; BOTTOM: Dating graph showing the date range of pottery residues from Trellyffaint

Trench 1, a shallow pit was excavated. Within the pit and dispersed among a small assemblage of stone were 35 fragments of Grooved Ware pottery. Many sherds were encrusted with food residues. The Department of Chemistry at the University of Bristol analysed the residues and concluded that they originated from dairy products. The pottery probably represented the remains of a single pot. The lipids extracted from the residues were uniquely dated to 3064 cal. BCE (Nash et al. 2021). Along with the pottery, a small assemblage of worked flint and stone implements were also recovered.

As a footnote, the medieval Welsh historian and geographer, Giraldus Cambrensis (Gerald of Wales), believed that Trellyffaint ('Toad's Hall') was so named because a chieftain who was buried inside the tomb had been devoured by toads. The author adds that when viewed from the east, the capstone and the flanking uprights do resemble the mouth and head of a toad!

The chamber and mound of Carreg Coetan, looking north-west

66. Carreg Coetan, Newport

SN 0602 3935, SM NO. PE054
County Reference Number: PEM 3

This monument, also known as Coetan Arthur (Arthur's Quoit) and Carreg Coetan Arthur, is classified as a small, chambered Portal Dolmen: one of a number that are present along the coastal stretches of Pembrokeshire.

One of the earliest accounts of this monument was by Wyndham, who in 1775 said of the monument:

> In a small field, between Newport and its harbour, is another monument, still larger, and quite perfect, of the same kind [Cerrig y Gof]; the upper stone is shaped like a mushroom and is upwards of nine feet in diameter.

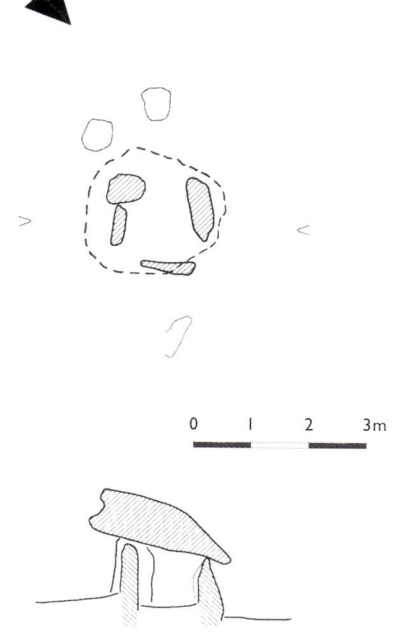

Plan and section of the Carreg Coetan monument (after Barker 1992)

THE SOUTH-WEST WALES GROUP

Early twentieth-century antiquarian image, showing several side wall stones dispersed across the eastern side of the mound

This monument did not receive a full appraisal until a plan of the site was published by Frances Lynch in 1972. Prior to this, the monument had been briefly commented on and sketched by Gardner Wilkinson in 1871, and engraved by Barnwell in 1872. According to Christopher Barker (1992, 19), there has been little or no change to the monument since then.

One of the lowest-lying tombs in Wales, Carreg Coetan stands just 8m AOD, close to the Afon Nyfer estuary and 0.5km from the coast. The estuary and Dinas Head lie to the west; while to the south, and rising to a height of 350m, the summit of Carningli provides the obvious topographical focus for the tomb. Legend has it that the stones forming Carreg Coetan were thrown from the summit of the mountain. When aligned with the peak, the capstone appears to replicate its profile, drawing the landscape into the fabric of the tomb.

Carreg Coetan is often described as a 'tripod dolmen', consisting in fact of four uprights, two of which support a massive sloping capstone. Lynch (1972) also classifies this monument as a Portal Dolmen, whereas Grimes describes it as a simple polygonal chamber (1936a, 132). I see it as a Portal Dolmen with a polygonal chamber. A number of outlying stones belonging to the tomb have been identified, together with traces of a covering mound. Littered within the vicinity, and concentrated about 2m in front of the chamber, is possible evidence of blocking material or the remains of a mound, oriented roughly E–W. During the 1979/80 excavation carried out by Sian Rees (Rees 2012), it became evident that a build-up of plough soil, in places over one metre thick, lay around the uprights. This being so, Carreg Coetan would originally have appeared much taller than it does today.

When excavated, the much-disturbed chamber revealed traces of 'powdery, cremated bone' along with two sherds of corded Beaker and three rim sherds of Grooved Ware. Large amounts of pottery (enough for two pot reconstructions) and more cremated bone lay deeper within the chamber stratigraphy. Charcoal beneath an upright socket was radiocarbon-dated to about 4700 ± 80 BP or 2700 BCE. Other uncalibrated dates were taken from underneath the mound which showed a similar date range. However, the construction method suggests a much earlier monument, possibly Early to Middle Neolithic in date.

The fact that both cremated bone and charcoal are present in the chamber suggests that bodies were not deposited in the tomb immediately after death; a more elaborate burial method may have been used. I tend to favour the idea that the dead were exposed to the elements – in what is termed excarnation – possibly on wooden platforms like those used by the north-west American coastal Indians, and seen within the archaeological record at Gwernvale (BRE 7) and Wayland's Smithy in Berkshire (BERKS 1). Here, the body would decay, the flesh devoured by wild animals, to leave only a skeleton. The tomb would have acted as the final resting place after the body had lost its flesh and could not be recognised as human.

67. Cerrig y Gof, Newport
SN 0365 3890, SM NO. PE050
County Reference Number: PEM 4

Also known as Cerrig Atgof, this unusual coastal tomb stands between Dinas Head and the Nevern River, at around 46m AOD. Affinities with tombs in Ireland and Scotland have been noted, and it has been suggested that architectural influences may have been transmitted along Irish Sea trade routes (Castleden, 1992). Daniel (1950) includes the tomb within his Irish Sea cultural province, as a late innovation of the local Dyfed group.

There are many antiquarian accounts of this monument, the earliest by Edward Lhuyd, who in 1695 noted:

> In Newport-parish there are five of these Tablesor Altas placed near each other, which some conjecture to have been once encompass'd with a circle of stone pillars, for that there are two stones yet standing near them. But these are nothing comparable in bigness to the Gromlech [Pentre Ifan] here described, and not raised above three foot high; nor are they supported with pillars, but stones edgewise ...

A later antiquarian report by Fenton gives a more detailed description of the monument, including details of an excavation that he undertook in 1810. In one of the earliest written accounts in Wales of an excavation (1811, 554–5), he states that:

> ... I come to a singular cluster of Cistvaens, which, having provided myself with labourers, I was prepared to open, permission being politely granted me for that purpose by George Bowen, Esq. of Llwyn gwair, on whose property they were. This group, consisting of five placed in a circle, radiating from a centre once occupied by a denominated Cromlech, long since overturned, stood on a gentle rising in a field to the right of the road, and was almost hid, being overgrown with weeds and briars, and, by several upright stones still to be traced, seemed to have been surrounded by an extensive circle of such, forming a mysterious precinct. Having removed the lid stones of the cists, and digging down about a foot through fine mould, I came to charcoal, and soon after discovered pieces of urns of the rudest pottery, some particles of bone, and a quantity of black sea pebbles. I opened them all, and with a very trifling variation of their contents found them of the same character. In the vacant space between each Cistvaen, as well as in the centre over which the Cromlech had been raised, I likewise dug, but found nothing indicatory of sepulture, furnishing a strong presumption that it was for a very different use. The largest lid stone was thirteen feet three inches in length, nor were the others much less, and the whole group was in circumference 42 yards.

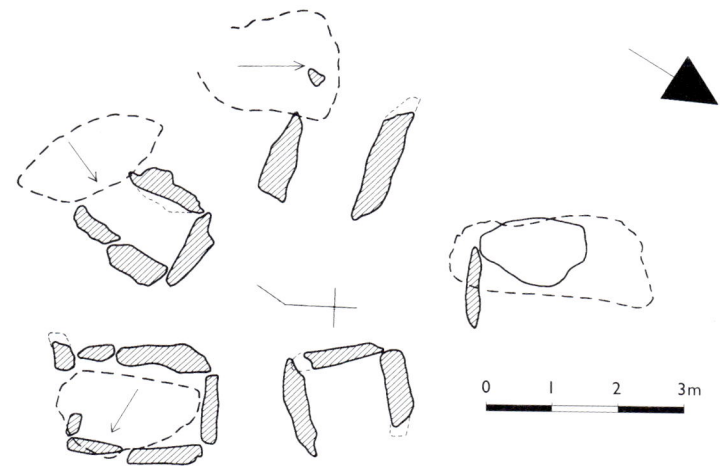

Plan and section of the Cerrig y Gof monument (after Daniel 1950)

TOP: Western view of Cerrig y Gof, with Strumble Head in the background; ABOVE: The north-east chamber: one of five that form a circular monument, with traces of a mound; LEFT: Cupmarked standing stone, located 90m south-west of Cerrig y Gof

Fenton believed a central cromlech originally completed the complex, but this hypothesis is disputed because the central area is too small to accommodate a chamber of a size similar to the other five.

The tomb is possibly transitional, suggesting Bronze Age burial practice in its use of multiple cists, or small, stone-lined burial chambers, within an oval mound. Close by and to the south of Cerrig y Gof is arguably a dense Bronze Age landscape consisting of cairns, hut circles and enclosures. Furthermore, a possible Bronze Age hillfort, one of only two in Wales, is sited on Carningli.

What is undisputed is that the mound measures 9m N–S and 8.2m E–W, and contains five square and rectangular chambers lacking passages.

Certain prominent topographical features in the surrounding landscape seem to be acknowledged by the tomb's architecture. The north-west chamber encompasses Dinas Head and Newport Bay; the south-west, Mynydd Dinas; the south-east, Mynydd Melyn; and the eastern chamber, Carningli. All of these areas have yielded evidence of intense Bronze Age activity. By indicating significant features, Cerrig y Gof encompasses the whole of the surrounding landscape. I disagree with the idea put forward by Lynch (1972), that the chamber settings are 'a haphazard agglomeration which must be the local answer to the need for more burial space within a tradition of single compartment monuments'. On the contrary, each chamber appears to be deliberately positioned. Furthermore, each chamber may have housed more than one body. Family members may, over many generations, have been deposited as disarticulated remains or even as cremations.

Approximately 120m to the west of the monument, within the south-western corner of the field, is a cupmarked stone – possibly a recumbent standing stone or an engraved rock outcrop. Similar with other Neolithic burial-ritual monuments in this part of Wales, landscape monuments, such as standing stones, are never too far away. This cupmarked stone may have acted as a processional marker, whereby communities visiting Cerrig y Gof would have walked through the landscape in a proscribed way. Alternatively, the stone may have delineated the extent of the ritual area of Cerrig y Gof.

68. Pentre Ifan, Nevern
SN 09940 37022, SM NO. PE008
County Reference Number: PEM 5

Pentre Ifan, one of the most impressive, chambered tombs in Wales and standing at around 145m AOD, consists of a tilted capstone, dipping towards the Nevern Valley to the north, and perched upon three tall, upright megaliths or uprights. The resulting chamber is 3m long, 2m wide and 3m high. It was originally cut about 40cms into the ground surface and lined with drystone walling, but has been infilled. The blocking stone (doorway) in the forecourt area was packed with small stones around the base. On the outer face of the blocking stone, a single cupmark and ring have been identified (Lynch 1974, 120). Later, Morris (1989, 87) noted the cupmark as a spiral, although I failed to recognise any such regular patterning on this stone.

The monument is located on the eastern side of Mynydd Carningli and has extensive views of the lower Nevern Valley and the sea. It is also intervisible with Carreg Coetan (PEM 3) and Llech-y-Tribedd (PEM 1), which lie off the western side of the Nevern Valley. The chamber and the cairn mound were, during historic times, incorporated into several field boundaries that would have protected the façade/entrance area and the chamber, and the central spine of the mound. Remnants of the field boundaries can be traced using LiDAR.

Eastern side-on view of the chamber of Pentre Ifan

Early seventeenth-century woodcut print of Pentre Ifan

Early nineteenth-century engraving of Pentre Ifan, set within a woodland vista

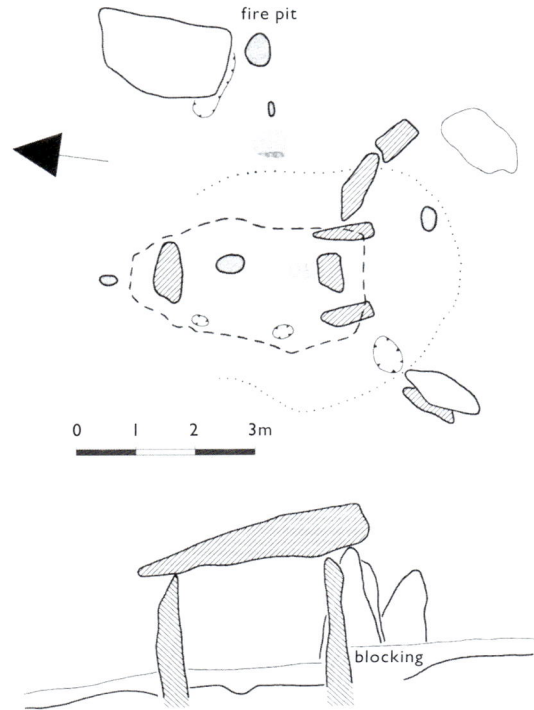

belonging to the chamber are visible. The capstone is dipping towards the west, and through the chamber is Carningli.

According to Barker, this monument is an impressive example of a terminally chambered long cairn, with a semicircular forecourt set in the broad southern end of the barrow – a model 'Closed Portal Tomb' (1992, 23). It is possible that the chamber and forecourt were freestanding, and any enclosing

Plan and section of the Pentre Ifan monument (after Barker 1992)

There are many antiquarian accounts of the site, the earliest dating from 1603:

> An other thinge worth the noteinge is a stone called Maen y gromlegh upon Pentre Jevan lande: yt is a huge and massie stone mounted on highe and sett on the toppes of iijee other highe stones, pitched standinge upright in the grounde, yt farre passeth for giggnes and height Arthurs stone in the waye between Hereford and the Haye, or Legh yr ast near Blaen Porth in Cardiganshire, or anye other that ever I saw … (George Owen, British Museum Manuscript No. 6250)

The site appears to have changed since the early to mid nineteenth century, when Richard Tongue painted it in 1835. In this painting, some of the stones

A sketch elevation plan of the 'Cromlech' of Pentre Ifan, dated 1884

mound was added later, but alas this remains unproven (Barker *pers comm*). Daniel compares the forecourt at Pentre Ifan and other chambered tombs in the region with the so-called 'horned cairns' of Carlingford in Ireland, arguing for colonisation by people of the Carlingford culture. He further suggests that the more easterly Cotswold-Severn tomb group is derived from the Pentre Ifan-type.

Lynch (1972) has suggested the tomb was built in two phases. Phase one may have consisted only of the chamber, uprights and capstone, with a low square cairn. Phase two would have seen the construction of a low mound, perhaps with the capstone left exposed.[70] However, according to the excavation report by Grimes (1960), it is very difficult to find evidence for two phases of construction. Indeed, I would suggest that any phasing of this monument was restricted to ephemeral changes; possibly the use of materials that have degraded over short periods of time.

Grimes, who excavated the tomb in 1936/37 (1948, 3–11) and again in 1958/59 (1960) for the Office of Works, described the forecourt, where ritual feasts may have been held, as consisting of two uprights placed either side of an entrance, itself blocked by a massive upright (what is referred to as a door-stone). Daniel disputes the argument that these blocked chambers, found also at Capel Garmon (DEN 3) and Dyffryn Ardudwy (MER 3), prevented the tomb being fully reopened after the mound had been piled up with human bone (Hemp, 1927). Hemp's belief led him to propose the theory that tombs were constructed to house the remains of 'great chieftains', and that the other individuals found in the chambers had, in life, been relatives or attendants who had sacrificed themselves on the death of the great man. The chambers would therefore have been used once only by high-ranking members of a stratified society, and would not have been intended for communal use. Daniel, however, argued that, 'chamber tombs were for the most part used collectively on a number of occasions' (1950, 146). This is interesting in that the doorway is firmly set into the ground, and I would suggest was opened only on special occasions. Rather than fresh bodies being placed into the tomb, collections of bones would be stored elsewhere before being deposited en masse in the chamber. This hypothesis challenges Barker's idea (1992) that the doorway was a permanent feature, otherwise known as a false portal, which occur in hybrid Cotswold-Severn tombs such as Ty Isaf (BRE 5) and Pipton Long Cairn (BRE 8) in the Black Mountains.

The mound itself does not survive, but may originally have measured 40m long and 17m wide. Traces of possible stone kerbing have been identified, delineating the long sides of the barrow. However, their alignment does not match precisely the orientation of the barrow, and they may be linked instead with possible ritual pits found beneath the mound and predating its construction.

The chamber (photo by the author in 1989, now infilled)

THE SOUTH-WEST WALES GROUP

Pentre Ifan yielded a small number of flint flakes and fragments of Welsh (Western) pottery. These are similar to artefacts from the excavated chambered monument of Pant y Saer (ANG 13), North Wales. It is highly likely that the pottery from both monuments derived originally from a single cultural source. As a result, pottery was traded and replicated within the different Welsh Neolithic core areas. Interestingly, this mundane artefact, used for cooking and storage, has become a grave commodity. Grimes (1960) distinguishes between the pottery of the western megalithic groups, with its flattened, expanded hammer-head rims, with pottery from the south and east of England. Lynch (1969) has noted similarities of form, but not of fabric, between the neck of an open bowl discovered in the chamber at Pentre Ifan and fragments recovered from the Dyffryn Ardudwy monument in Gwynedd.

69. Bedd-yr-Afanc, Meline
SN 10800 34592, SM NO. PE122
County Reference Number: PEM 27

Bedd-yr-Afanc, also known as Bryn Berian, is located at 142m AOD at the centre of a dramatic U-shaped valley, on a slightly raised oval-shaped plateau made up of gravels. It is surrounded by a raised bog, and is the only definite example of a gallery grave in Wales. The plateau on which the monument stands, according to the RCAM (1925, 681), measures around 21.3m by 8.2m and is 0.6m in height. Around the monument is a large stone scatter; some are loose, others partially buried. These stones may be associated with possible cairn material which covered the mound. Architecturally, the monument is quite different from its nearest neighbour, Pentre Ifan (PEM 5), which lies 3.8km to the north-west.

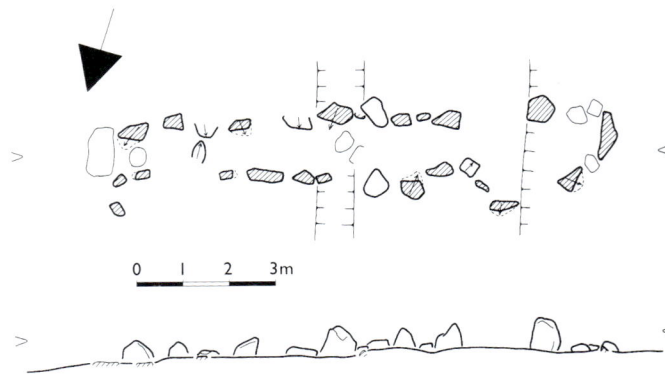

Plan and section of the Bedd-yr-Afanc gallery grave monument (after Barker 1992)

The Bedd-yr-Afanc gallery grave and the landscape in which it is sited

Lacking side chambers and forecourt, the tomb was originally covered by an oval barrow consisting of 22 small upright stones arranged to form a gallery 10.5m long and 2.5m wide, oriented roughly E–W, and blocked at its western end. The orientation of the tomb may be governed by the E–W alignment of the rising and setting sun, as well as symbolising the life and death cycle; the west being seen as relating to the termination of life.

The monument was surveyed in 1936, and later excavated in 1938 by W.F. Grimes (Grimes 1938). He noted traces of two lines of stones or kerbing(?)

(Grimes 1939b, 258), possibly defining the extent of the mound. Some of the excavation scarring is still visible, and shows that little change to this monument has occurred over the past 80 years. There are traces of a slab or flagged stone floor located within the gallery area, at the eastern end of the monument. According to the RCAM (1925, 681) the monument is much disturbed, which leads to the question of whether the gallery was divided into a series of chambers; a number of gallery graves being subdivided using a portal stone.

Grimes had suggested that the monument represented a 'passage' some 30ft in length (9.15m) and was slightly wedge-shaped in plan, widening to 1.8m at the western-end, and thus similar to those found in Ireland and the Isle of Man (1939b). However, he abandoned this idea after his excavation. According to a conversation between Barker and Grimes in 1986, there were no finds from this site. However, a section of a palaeosurface, located 5m away from this site, revealed several undiagnostic flint chips (Barker 1992, 40).

The tomb is sited on an exposed (raised) ancient land surface. Its axis is oriented along the marshy valley, the location suggesting an intimate affinity with topographic features to either side (especially Cnwc-yr-Hydd, Cerrig Lladron and mountains to the south). During the Neolithic, the tomb may have witnessed seasonal water-logging. Like a moat, this would have set up both a physical and psychological barrier, maintaining the exclusivity of the site and safely containing the dead within the confines of the tomb, and the raised plateau on which it stood. Settlement would probably have been confined to the intermediate slopes, away from the damp valley floor. To the east of the site, and occupying the ridges of the valley, is possible evidence of an axe factory, and a series of potential quarry sites that would have been used to supply the bluestones at Stonehenge.

THE FISHGUARD GROUP

This group consists of ten monuments: Garn Wen (PEM 7–9), Carn Wnda (PEM 13), Parc-y-Cromlech (PEM 14), Garn Gilfach (PEM 15), Ffyst Samson (PEM 16), Trewalter Llwyd (PEM 17), Carreg Samson (PEM 18) and Ffynnondruidion (PEM 28). Nearly all appear to conform to the same architectural rules and landscape positioning, embracing the fertile lowlands of Strumble Head, and nearly all located close to rock outcropping. With the exception of Carreg Samson, all are small, hidden, unobtrusive monuments.

At least seven of these tombs may be considered earth-fast: Garn Wen (comprising three separate monuments), Carn Wnda, Garn Gilfach, Parc-y-Garn and Ffynnondruidion. Tombs of this type have one end of the capstone deliberately placed on the edge of an earth-cut pit, rather than being supported by an upright stone. They are also sited on the intermediate slopes, amongst extensive rock outcropping, and it is suggested that they were never totally covered by an earthen mound. Daniel (1950) believes a shallow cairn may have been banked up against the side of the chamber in order to conceal the burial. This being the case, each tomb would have merged with the surrounding rocky landscape, with users relying on local ritual geographic knowledge in order to locate it.

All the earth-fast tombs concentrated to the north of the Fishguard Group take the sea as their main visual focus, even though each is locally oriented. The dramatic landscape of St David's Head to the west is an important focal point for the five southernmost tombs.

The largest tomb in the group is Carreg Samson, which is similar in size to Pentre Ifan (PEM 5) in the Newport Group. Its landscape setting is also comparable, as the monument looks towards the fertile lowlands and sea beyond, while acknowledging the jagged rocky outcropping along Garn Fawr, Garn Gilfach and Garnwnda to the north-east.

The jagged peaks of Garn Fawr, Garn Gilfach and Garnwnda form a natural barrier which divides the coastal plain of Strumble Head from the rest of northern Pembrokeshire. It is along these ridges that a series of chambered earth-fast and rock-cut monuments are located; all probably dating to the Late Neolithic (Nash 2008a). Three of these monuments, including the Garn Wen cemetery, appear to be equally spaced, oriented roughly E–W. The other two monuments include Carn Wnda and Parc-y-Cromlech. Oriented on the same E–W line but located on the western side of Strumble Head, is the rock-cut chambered site of Garn Gilfach. However, this monument, unlike the other three sites, is located on the southern side of the outcropping. This monument would have been intervisible with Ffyst Samson, itself standing close to the summit of an exposed rock outcrop. Could it be possible that other equally-spaced monuments once stood between Garn Gilfach and Parc-y-Cromlech?

The three sites of Garn Wen, Carn Wnda and Parc-y-Cromlech are separated by around 700m. The distance between Parc-y-Cromlech and Garn Gilfach is roughly 1,400m, suggesting a possible monument may be sited at around SM 921 392, north of Pontiago Farm. Fieldwork and documentary research by the author has identified a lost site within the vicinity of Pontiago Farm, known as Y Garn (Barker 1992; Nash 2008a). The monument, sited on historic mapping but presumed lost or destroyed, does in fact survive as a ruined monument, between Garn Gilfach and Carn Wnda. Using predictive modelling, there are, however, a further two areas along the spine of Strumble Head where monuments should be sited. Several other possible monuments are listed within the Strumble Head area and are commented upon by Barnwell (1872), and include Glynymel (SM 966 369), Man y Gromlech (SM 9438 3847).

70. Garn Wen (3), Llanwnda
SM 9483 3903, SM NO. PE030
County Reference Number: PEM 7–9

Above the fishing settlement of Goodwick is a line of at least three chambered tombs that, when constructed and in use, would have commanded views right across Fishguard Bay and Dinas Head. Alas, these are now obscured by several rows of houses that form the northern boundary of Goodwick. Nevertheless, the positioning of the tombs conforms to a pattern that is dominant

The central section of the Garn Wen Cemetery and the immediate landscape, looking north-west

One of the larger and intact chambers within the Garn Wen Cemetery

throughout South-west Wales: that is, the tombs acknowledge only part of the landscape. Blocking views immediately to the west is a large, deep-fissured rock outcrop (also known as Carn Wen). This cemetery group lies some 750m east of Garn Gilfach (PEM 15) and possibly forms a linear group of monuments that separates the coastal plain of Strumble Head from the inland landscape of north Pembrokeshire.

The three tombs, standing between 90m and 95m AOD, share a similar construction method. Each is partly rock-cut (sub-megalithic); and, according to Daniel (1950, 200), each was incorporated within a round cairn mound. However, Barker has intimated that the present ground surface around each of the monuments does not show evidence of cairn material (1992, 27). Each of the capstones, lying a few centimetres above the present ground level, is supported by low or collapsed uprights.

The northern site, located 5m north of the central monument, has a dislodged capstone that lies on top of a smaller slab. There appears to be no trace of any uprights, although the immediate landscape is overgrown and undulating. It is possible that cairn material and dislodged uprights exist underneath the present land surface.

The southernmost tomb, known locally as Carrig Samson, is the best preserved of the three. It comprises five low uprights around a small polygonal chamber (Barker 1992, 27). The capstone appears to be displaced, leaning on two uprights on the north-east side of the chamber.

Another two monuments appear to have suffered a similar fate. Fenton (1811, 16–7), who visited the cemetery site in the early nineteenth century, commented that:

> The most remarkable are three cromlechs in a line, one erect on columnar stones, the other two partly overturned.

It would appear that the cemetery had been 'investigated' sometime before the publication of Fenton's *An historical tour through Pembrokeshire* (1811).

I visited the site in 1993 and 2003 and noticed a possible fourth tomb of similar construction (with low supporting uprights) and in line with the other three, lying approximately 5m to the north of the northern monument. This possible monument would have had an identical landscape outlook. Up to nine monuments were reported by members of the Pembrokeshire Archaeological Survey (Laws & Owen 1897–1906). However, many slabs considered to be capstones may in fact occur as natural outcropping. Assuming that more than three monuments existed at this site, it appears that the surviving three monuments would have been sited symmetrically – in other words, all sited at an equal distance from each other. It is therefore probable that an additional monument existed between the surviving central and southern monuments.

Four of a possible nine chambers that form the Garn Wen Cemetery

71. CARN WNDA, LLANWNDA

SM 93310 39239, SM NO. PE031
County Reference Number: PEM 13

The rather inconspicuous monument of Carn Wnda (also known as Carreg Samson), standing at around 135m AOD and located on a north-facing rock outcrop, appears to form an alignment with several other monuments: Penrhiw (PEM 14), the Garn Wen Cemetery (PEM 7–9) and Garn Gilfach (PEM 15).

The monument is aligned NW–SE and situated on the northern slope of Garnwnda, a large, exposed rocky outcrop. Fenton eloquently describes both the landscape position and the form of the monument when he writes:

> Proceed to the village of Llan Wnda ... where, on the verge of the rocky eminence just above it, stands a Cromlech, resting obliquely on one stone about five feet high from the ground, whose dimensions are fifteen feet by nine, nearly of an equal thickness of two feet. (1811, 18)

The capstone, measuring 4.6m x 2.8m is earth-fast and rests on the edge of a rock-cut pit. It is supported at the north-western end by a single upright. As such, it is one of a number of sub-megalithic tombs that make use of what Daniel calls a labour-saving 'makeshift device'. Developing the argument, Daniel follows Grimes in doubting that covering mounds were ever a significant component of these tombs, suggesting that:

> They were probably originally surrounded by a low accumulation of stones sufficient to ensure that the chambers were efficient burial vaults and that they were not disturbed by beasts of prey. (1950, 48)

The earth-fast Carn Wnda monument, hidden within a rocky landscape, looking north

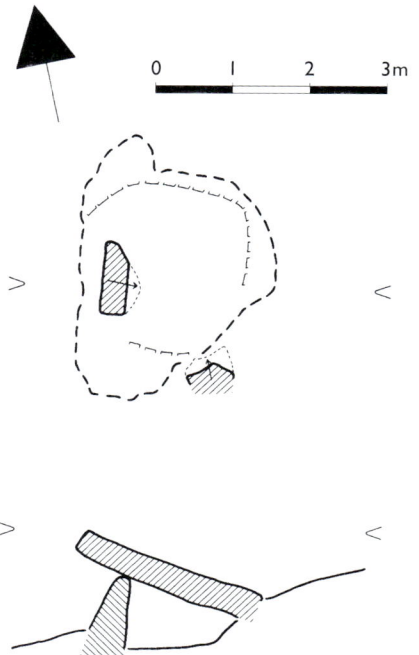

Plan and section of the Carn Wnda monument (after Barker 1992)

Grimes (1936a, 31) describes in slightly more detail this accumulation of stones, concluding that on the south side of the chamber are four courses of drystone walling. I would add that the drystone walling, seen from a distance, would further hide the monument within the immediate landscape. In addition, the ledge on which the monument stands, is too small to have supported a covering mound. This manner of construction would have ensured that the monument merged with its surroundings; a trait which is experienced with other monuments on Strumble Head.

An antiquarian excavation inside the chamber revealed evidence of a cremation, indicating a possible Late Neolithic or Early Bronze Age date for the tomb. The burial consisted of a small urn made from a coarse and crumbly fabric and containing cremated bone (Fenton 1848, 284). From the same reference, Fenton comments:

> From the quantities of red and black ashes mixed with portions of what seemed to be decomposed burnt bones and small fragments of rude pottery which I found ... in the hollow below, I felt no hesitation in forming the conclusion that it had been a place of interment. (Fenton 1848, 284)

The outlook of the monument takes in all of the northern lowland fertile soils of Strumble Head. There is, however, no intervisibility with any other tomb. It appears to be the only tomb oriented in this way; the rest point towards the east, south and west.

Some 250m to the south of Carn Wnda and located at the north-east foot of Carn Gelli, is a standing stone (SM 9336 3915). Whether or not this monument has an association with Carn Wnda is not known. Further standing stones are located to the south-west, close to the burial monuments of nearby Ffynnondruidion (PEM 28) and Ffyst Samson (PEM 15).

72. GARN GILFACH, LLANWNDA
SM 90895 38985, SM NO. PE032
County Reference Number: PEM 15

This much denuded burial chamber is also known as Carn Gyllwch, Gillfach Goch (Barnwell 1872), Gilfach, Carn Gyllych (Grimes 1936a & Daniel 1950), and, more recently, Garngilfach (Barker 1992). It is sited on a small ridge, halfway up Garn Gilfach, a large, jagged rock outcrop. The monument stands at around 183m AOD. However, it is very difficult to locate, the capstone being only a few centimetres above present ground level. Daniel (1950) suggests the chamber pit was cut and underpinned while the capstone, then probably a glacial erratic, lay *in situ*.

Garn Gilfach consists of a large, irregular, low capstone (4.6m x 2.5m) and is supported by four uprights. It is argued that other possible uprights are in fact the collapsed remnants of drystone walling (Barker 1992, 33). The tomb is sub-megalithic, in that the chamber is cut into the underlying bedrock. There is no evidence of a mound – the ridge appears to be too narrow and is similar in construction and landscape setting to others on the Strumble Head peninsula. An entrance into the main chamber

The Garn Gilfach monument, hidden within the rocky upland landscape of Strumble Head

appears to be located at the eastern end. Barker (1992, 33) remarks correctly that an 'unusually full account' was made by Richard Fenton in 1811, who notes that charcoal and pottery had been found at the site in 1800. He goes on to describe the monument in some detail:

> There is one more remarkable than the rest; a large unshapen mass of serpentine, fifteen feet by eight and a half average thickness; under the edges of it are placed nine or ten small pointed upright stones, embedded in a strong pavement, extending some way round. These small supporters are fixed without any regard to their height as only two or three bear the whole weight of the incumbent stone, one of which is so pressed by it, as to have become almost incorporated with it. On the upper surface of the Cromlech are three considerable excavations near the centre, probably intended to have received the blood of the victim, or waters for purification, if (as is the most general opinion) they were used as altars … This stone has a small inclination to the north-east. Its height from the ground is very inconsiderable, being scarce one foot high on the lowest side; and on the other only high enough to admit of a person creeping under it, though once entered, the space enlarges from the upper stones having a considerable concavity. The earth below is rich and black … I have since learned that the blackness I refer to, appears to have been chiefly the effect of fire, as many bits of charcoal and rude pottery have been picked up there. (Fenton 1811, 22–3)

Barnwell, in his account of 1872 (1872, 137), records that a Mr Blight made an attempt to get underneath the capstone. Here, he found one fragment of flint which, in his view, had been deliberately placed.

The views from this tomb recall those of nearby Ffyst Samson and Garn Wnda. All three possess commanding vistas of the dramatic rock outcrops on Strumble Head. Both Garn Gilfach and Ffyst Samson overlook the lowlands to the south and west, as well as St David's Head. It is probable that there is intervisibility between this monument and Ffynnondruidion (PEM 28) and Ffyst Samson (PEM 16), located 2.7 km and 4.1 km respectively.

The capstone of Garn Gilfach, looking south-east

73. Ffyst Samson, St Nicholas
SM 9059 3492, SM NO. PE044
County Reference Number: PEM 16

This monument is sited on the large rock outcrop called Carn Llys, and is one of the monuments that lie within the southern part of Strumble Head. Also known as Trellys Cromlech, Trellysycoed, Ffyst Samson and Samson's Quoit, Ffyst Samson is now much-damaged. It comprises a single capstone supported by two enormous uprights, each standing to a height of well over one metre above the present ground surface. The original chamber may have been rectangular. Small stones litter the floor, both inside and outside the chamber, indicating either the remnants of a cairn, or a stone-lined chamber. There is evidence around the tomb of a slightly raised, and possibly circular (Barker 1992, 33) or ovate mound. Indeed, the site was visited by Gardner Wilkinson in 1871, who described the chamber as being incorporated into 'a very slight mound'. The mound, which is aligned roughly E–W, is probably constructed from cairn, and appears to be truncated on the south-eastern side by a stone and turf wall.

Unlike other tombs in the locality, Ffyst Samson stands on a high point within the landscape. A few metres to the east stands an exposed rock outcrop which is also visible from the site of the Ffynnondruidion monument (PEM 28). Approximately 500m north-east of the site, at around 128m AOD, is a small tumulus and a standing stone (SM 913 355). It is probable that the standing stone, along with several others between the site and the Ffynnondruidion chamber, are contemporary.

To the south-west, Ffyst Samson is intervisible with the monuments of Cerreg Samson (PEM 18) and Trewalter Llwyd (PEM 17), and is also within full view of the sea and St David's Head to the west. This monument may therefore have been an important

The simple chamber of Ffyst Samson, located within the rugged upland landscape of Strumble Head

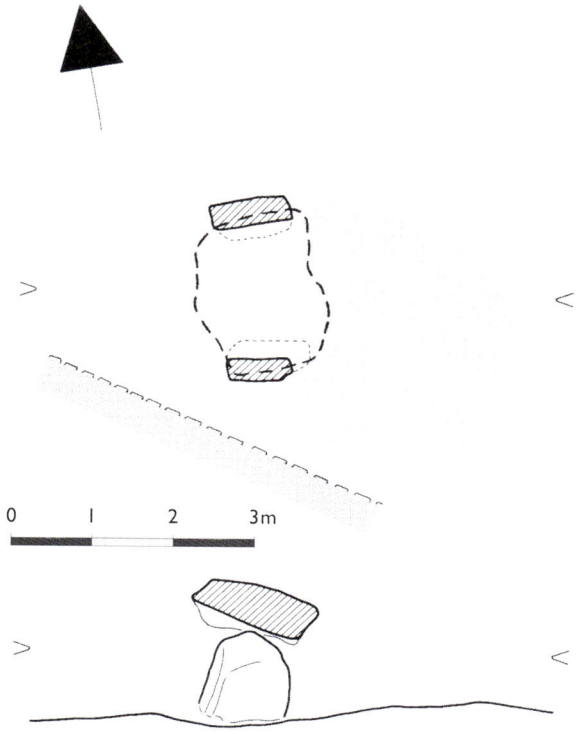

Plan and section of the Ffyst Samson monument (after Barker 1992)

focal point, given its location on such a dramatic rock outcrop. Yet, as the mound would have been constructed of local stone to merge with the exposed rock outcropping close by, the tomb was not so much a visual concept, but one constructed through ritual and symbolic knowledge. A similar idea can be promoted for Garn Gilfach (PEM 15), 4.1km north of Ffyst Samson; another monument that merges within its immediate surroundings.

To the east and beyond the small hill on which Ffyst Samson stands, is a large standing stone and cairn, again suggesting possible monument and landscape continuity through time and space. This small monument group (located at SM 9135 3550) is 1.1km north-east of Ffyst Samson and stands close to a Bronze Age mound. The site appears to conform to a N–E alignment with two other standing stones, each located close to other Late Neolithic chambered monuments.

74. Trewalter Llwyd, Mathry
SM 8682 3176, SM NO. PE037
County Reference Number: PEM 17

This chambered monument, also known as Parc-y-Garn, comprises a large, single capstone and one visible collapsed upright. Much of the southern section of the monument, including the chamber, is incorporated into a turfed bank field boundary; therefore, a sizeable portion of the monument may be undisturbed and preserved *in situ*. A single, partially collapsed upright is the only visible evidence of the northern section of the chamber. The capstone, measuring 3.99m by 2.68m and up to 1.4m in thickness, appears to be oriented NW–SE. The monument stands at around 124m AOD.

Now considered much damaged, Trewalter Llwyd would, in earlier times, have looked very much like Llech-y-Tribedd (PEM 1) or the White House monument (PEM 47); in other words, a tomb of true monumentality. However, this site has previously been considered nothing more than field clearance material by the Ordnance Survey Field Officer – in Barker's words, an 'unnecessarily harsh assessment' (1992, 45).

The enormous capstone of the collapsed Trewalter Llwyd monument, now incorporated into a field boundary

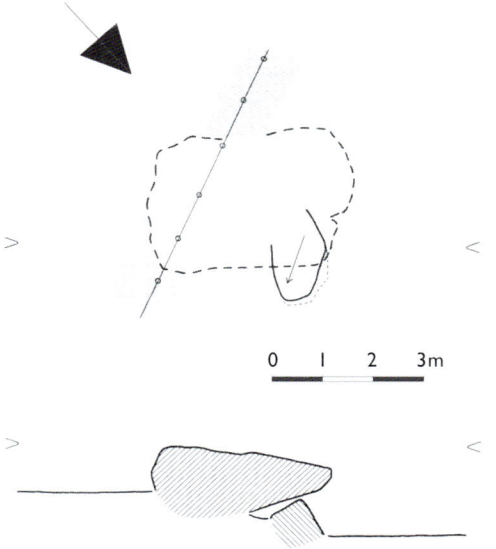

Plan and section of the Trewalter Llwyd monument (after Barker 1992)

The monument appears to form part of a group that includes nearby Carreg Samson (PEM 18) to the north, and White House (PEM 47) and Treffynnon (PEM 19) to the west. The four tombs may delineate the inland extent of a ritualised territory. It was reported by Fenton in 1811, and later by Gardner Wilkinson in 1871, that at least one other tomb may have existed close by, a monument referred to as Glandwr. Gardner Wilkinson (1871, 232), who sketched and recorded the site, noted that:

> I looked in vain for two cromlechs to the west of Mathry, and found only one [Trewalter Llwyd], half concealed in a fence [boundary], of which it forms a very efficient part. The capstone is 13ft long by 8ft 8in, and 4ft 5in thick, resting on one of its supporters, which is 5ft 5in high. Another fallen pillar [upright] measures 7ft 6in in length.

Daniel (1950, 201) describes the monument as: 'a collapsed chamber consisting of a capstone ... with a number of uprights lying underneath it.'

Trewalter Llwyd is sited within a slightly undulating landscape, and from the top of the capstone, the sea is visible approximately 4km away to the north. It also shares intervisibility with Carreg Samson, 3km to the north-west. In the far distance, to the west and north-east, are the jagged peaks of the St David's peninsula and Strumble Head.

75. Carreg Samson, Mathry
SM 8483 3350, SM NO. PE036
County Reference Number: PEM 18

Carreg Samson is one of the most impressive megalithic tombs in South-west Wales, second only to Pentre Ifan (PEM 5). This imposing monument, standing around 42m AOD within a dramatic landscape, was also known as Cerreg Samson, or The Longhouse. It was also known as 'the grave of Samson's finger', for it was believed that St Samson was the son of a sixth-century royal courtier who went on to become abbot of the monastery of Piro on Caldey Island, and who lifted the capstone into place with his little finger.

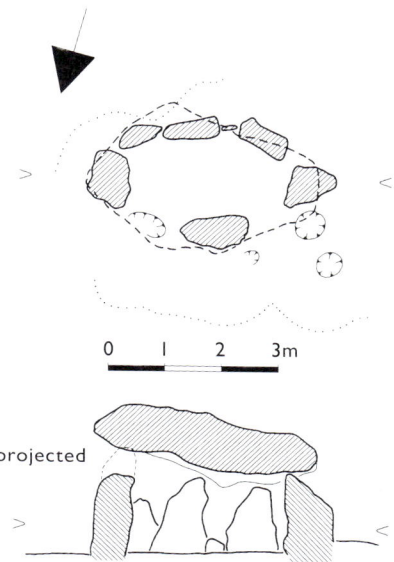

Plan and section of the Carreg Samson monument (after Barker 1992)

The monument as it was in around 1900, when it was incorporated into a drystone field walled boundary

THE SOUTH-WEST WALES GROUP

Carreg Sampson and the landscape to the north

The capstone dips towards the immediate bay and Strumble Head beyond. To the east and north-east, the landscape is dominated by the jagged peaks of Garn Fawr, Garn Gilfach and Garnwnda. On all three peaks there is evidence of Neolithic burial. To the south, another two tombs stand close by: Treffynnon (PEM 19) and White House (PEM 47). Hidden from view to the west are the jagged peaks of Carn Llidi, Carnedd-lleithr, Carnffald and St David's Head. Similar to many other monuments in this part of Wales, the monument, sited on a north-facing slope, is not on the highest point within the immediate landscape. Some 20m to the south-west of the monument, are a number of jagged, sandstone, conglomerate rock outcrops. Further outcropping is visible in the field north-west of a stone boundary wall that runs a few metres west of the site.

The monument is constructed from an enormous capstone measuring 5.3m x 3.6m, and is supported by three of the six large, locally quarried sandstone conglomerate uprights to form an oval/polygonal chamber (3.3m x 1.7m).[71] According to Barker (1992, 34), one upright is missing. Both the uprights and chamber have been erected over an irregularly-cut pit. The elongated shape of the chamber and capstone suggests that there was once a large rectangular covering mound, possibly comparable in size to that at nearby Pentre Ifan. However, no direct evidence for a mound or cairn survives (although a recent visit to the site in December 2022 has shown that cairn material may lie just below the surface of the field). It is also likely that the cairn has been incorporated into the nearby boundary wall.

The site was excavated by Frances Lynch during August 1968. Excavation revealed that a possible entrance was located within the south-western section of the chamber, with an approximately 2m-long passage leading from it (Lynch 1976, 74). This possible passage was delineated by a number of stone sockets. Also uncovered was a pit which was located on the northern side of the monument, similar to those found at Pentre Ifan. During the recent past, the chamber has been used as a sheep shelter, and some investigators have recorded drystone walling or packing between the uprights. I was not able to verify this when visiting the site, although there was a large number of stones littering the floor of the chamber.

The finds from the eastern side of the chamber were few, but did include fragments of burnt bone. Outside, a hemispherical bowl dating to the Early

Neolithic was recovered (Lynch 1976, 75). The chamber floor was lined with a yellow clay which had been subsequently disturbed by the excavation of three holes, possibly the result of antiquarian investigations.

76. FFYNNONDRUIDION, ST NICHOLAS
SM 9204 3679, PRN NO. 2498
County Reference Number: PEM 28

The exact location of this monument is difficult to substantiate, as not only do opinions differ, but the immediate area has, in the recent past, been severely disturbed. A chambered monument certainly stood within view of Ffynnondruidion Farm before 1830, and probably stood around 107m AOD. A short reference in *Archaeologia Cambrensis* (1872, 139) notes that the monument was demolished, leaving just one or two stones to mark the site where the chamber once stood. Fifty years earlier, in 1811, Richard Fenton had noted that a probable burial chamber once existed on the site. In 1950 Daniel noted that only a few stones exist 'which may be the remains of the site' (1950, 203). Yet the remnants of a possible capstone and uprights are just visible in an overgrown hedge bank. According to detailed Ordnance Survey data, the monument is sited within an extensive, naturally deposited cairn field; and certainly, many large stones are haphazardly scattered across a south-facing undulating landscape, some of which may have belonged to the monument. Cook (2004) notes that the area round the supposed site appears slightly raised, and at least one earth-fast stone slab was, in 2004, set on its edge. The possible remains of a broken capstone, measuring *c*.2.1m x 1.1m and 0.4m thick lie over a number of stones. The possible capstone has a probable charging hole drilled into it, suggesting the site had been destroyed using explosives. By 1920 the site comprised the remains of a capstone that was supported by 'two stout pillars' (Grimes 1936c); however, Daniel doubted its authenticity.

The landscape position of the monument is similar to others within the area. It has intervisibility with the sea (Fishguard Bay) as well as the southern extent of the Preseli Mountains. Also, it is not on the highest point within the immediate landscape, the land sloping upwards to the north. Therefore, the monument visually commands fertile, undulating lands to the south and west. Approximately 1.7km to the south-west is the upland rock outcrop of Carn Llys and the site of Ffyst Samson (PEM 16). However, no intervisibility probably existed between the two monuments: Ffyst Samson appears to be deliberately sited on the southern extent of the rock outcropping.

Despite its condition, Ffynnondruidion ('Druid's Spring') does have an interesting early archaeological past. In 1830, while levelling the site, labourers discovered two Neolithic flint artefacts: an axe (Celt) and a stone adze. It was believed axes were used for 'flaying victims, for which, in the opinion of a professional butcher to whom they were shown, they seemed admirably calculated' (Fenton 1811, 24). The polished stone axe (Tenby A8), made from gabbro, is now in Tenby Museum. If intact, the site together with the finds would have represented one of the richest Neolithic discoveries in South-west Wales.

Polished stone axe from the Ffynnondruidion monument

77. Parc-y-Cromlech, Goodwick
SM 9422 3907, SM NO. PE033
County Reference Number: PEM 14

Parc-y-Cromlech (also known as Penrhiw), now badly damaged, stands 142m AOD in a large south-facing field, away from the coast to the north and east. The site was first recorded by the RCAM in 1925, when the chamber was noted as being filled with 'field gathered stones. Further, the capstone has been overthrown and lies at the feet of its quondam supporters' (ibid. 548). In 1936, W.F. Grimes made a plan of the site before re-erecting the capstone (1936a).

This much-denuded site lies some 750m west of the Carn Wen complex or cemetery. The tomb comprises a single, large rectangular capstone supported by three uprights. The shape of the

The denuded Parc-y-Cromlech monument, looking west

capstone and the configuration of the three uprights suggest the chamber, too, was rectangular. Littering the inside of the chamber, and around the outside edges of the three uprights, are numerous stones. These are either cairn material or the result of extensive field clearance. It was noted on a visit to Parc-y-Cromlech that several large stones abutting the monument appeared to be shaped so as to form part of the tomb architecture, although this could be the result of frost shattering. Today, there is no evidence of any mound, although Daniel (1950, 201) suggested that there was a slight trace. However, if the chamber arrangement – in particular, the uprights – is in its original position, a mound could be suggested to the west of the present monument, with the eastern extent of the chamber exposed to form a forecourt. Unfortunately, the ploughing regime within this field has been severe.

Interestingly, this monument, along with the Garn Wen complex and the earth-fast monument of Garn Wnda, appears to be spaced equally at a distance of 750m apart. However, the landscape setting for each of these monuments is very different. Garn Wen is set in a rocky outcrop landscape, Parc-y-Cromlech within an enclosed field setting, and Garn Wnda set within a large rock outcrop facing the open sea.

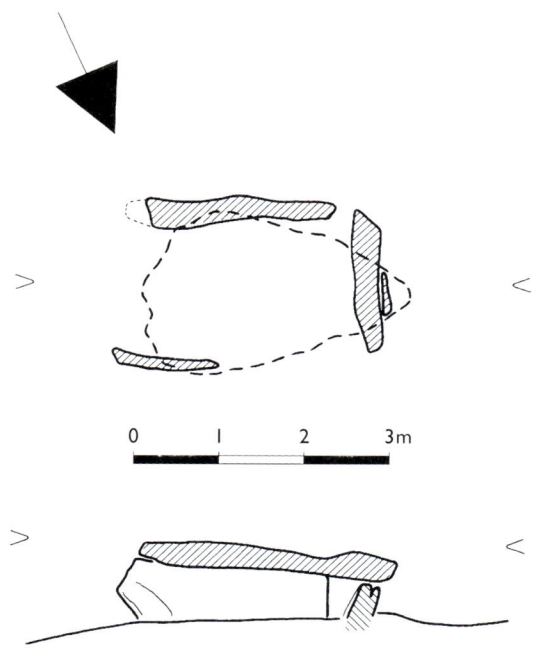

Plan and section of the Parc-y-Cromlech monument (after Barker 1992)

THE ST DAVID'S GROUP

The St David's group of monuments is sited within two distinct landscapes: one coastal, the other inland. The group comprises five monuments: Coetan Arthur (PEM 3), Carn Llidi (PEM 21 & 22), St Elvies Farm (PEM 20), Treffynnon (PEM 19) and White House (PEM 47). All are locally oriented so as to incorporate a variety of landscape features. The three coastal sites are all located close to or within exposed rock outcroppings, whilst the two inland sites are set within a slightly undulating landscape, usually close to medieval or post-medieval field banks. Not surprisingly, both landscapes appear to have influenced tomb design and construction. The coastal sites usually incorporate large capstones overlying low rectangular chambers, and two of these are classified as double-chambered monuments, and occupy similar landscape positions as those on Strumble Head – Carn Llidi (PEM 21 & 22), St Elvies Farm (PEM 20).

With the exception of the now much-damaged White House monument, all possess small chambers. Coetan Arthur and Carn Llidi are earth-fast monuments and resemble those on Strumble Head. Both are also located in similar rocky landscapes. These earth-fast tombs are probably a later architectural form, as they are less monumental than, for example, St Elvies Farm and Treffynnon. The White House site can be classified as a Portal Dolmen and would have been a truly megalithic monument, maybe standing over 2.7m in height.

Sited south of these tombs is Clegyr Boia, a probable contemporary Neolithic settlement. One could imagine the settlers of Clegyr Boia placing the remains of their dead in either of the two St David's Head monuments. The lack of architectural elaboration in these tombs should not detract from the idea that, towards the later Neolithic, the dead were considered special, and consequently special places were required in order to honour and bury them.

78. COETAN ARTHUR, ST DAVID'S
SM 72246 28025, SM NO. PE054
County Reference Number: PEM 23

Coetan Arthur is yet another iconic monument within the Neolithic of South-west Wales, though the architecture is relatively simple. It comprises a large capstone and several surviving uprights, and the remnants of a possible cairn mound. The site is set within a dramatic and evocative landscape that marks the extreme south-western edge of Neolithic influence in South Wales. It is at this and other iconic sites where the old ways of subsistence economy meet with a new concept – Neolithicisation.

Coetan Arthur and the St David's landscape beyond

Antiquarian engraving of Coetan Arthur
(*Archaeologia Cambrensis* 1868)

The site was visited by an antiquarian named G.W. Mamby in 1801, when he described the site as follows:

> At a little distance from St David's Head, upon a plain, is a famous Druidical altar, one of solid stone 12 feet long, 8 feet broad, and averaged at 2 feet thick; it formerly was supported by several stones, but now rests on one. (1801, 70)

Jones and Freeman gave a further description of the site in 1856, when they commented on the missing uprights (Jones & Freeman 1856). The site was also illustrated in several engravings, one by Longueville Jones in 1865 and another by Barnwell in 1872.

This much-denuded site, which stands approximately 38m AOD, was first excavated in 1898 by Baring Gould (1898). The results were poor, although the excavators did reveal traces of a drystone lining and a possible revetment associated with the chamber on the south-eastern side of the monument.

Grimes argued that Coetan Arthur never had a prominent mound (1936a), whilst Daniel in 1950 believed that just enough stones were used to ensure 'efficient burial vaults'. He argued for a round barrow as the original tomb covering, and has cautiously identified a passage leading west from the chamber. According to Daniel, there are traces of a passage and covering cairn. However, when visiting the site, I found no trace of a passage and little evidence of *in situ* cairn material.

The chamber, probably of Daniel's sub-megalithic earth-fast type, may have been formed by levering up one end of a stone lying *in situ*, and supporting this with a 1.8m upright. Others have suggested the chamber represents a collapsed conventional form, as two further uprights have been identified, lying beneath the capstone. Indeed, my visit suggests that Coetan Arthur may have been constructed with four or more uprights. If this is the case, then a substantial cairn mound would have surrounded the chamber. Faint traces of a possible circular cairn can be seen north of the chamber.

The capstone measures about 3.6m long x 2.5m wide and, interestingly, resembles the outline of the nearby rocky ridge of Carn Llidi. A few metres to the west of this monument is extensive rock outcropping, and from a distance Coetan Arthur appears to blend into the surrounding landscape. Nevertheless, it is intervisible with the double-chambered monument of Carn Llidi. Between both monuments, and hidden away in a small valley oriented NE–SW, are the remnants of a settlement and field system of unknown date. However, it should be noted that extensive Mesolithic and Bronze Age lithic scatters exist along the coastal fringes of St David's Head. Several hundred metres to the west of Coetan Arthur is an Iron Age promontory hill enclosure. A single cairn rampart orientated N–S, encloses six or seven well-defined hut circles. This settlement site, plus the presence of Mesolithic material, suggests a continuous sequence of prehistoric activity within this area for around 6–7,000 years. Moreover, the archaeological evidence over this long period of time indicates the interplay between burial-ritual and economic subsistence landscape use.

In May 2022, a heritage crime was reported when a fire was found to have been lit underneath the capstone and within the chamber area. The remains of a makeshift hearth were enclosed by stones that were taken from an unknown source, but probably originated from the immediate area of the site.

79. Treffynnon, Llandeloy
SM 85360 28655, SM NO. PE027
County Reference Number: PEM 19

Treffynnon stands 125m AOD on a slight, south-facing ridge, close to an eroded field bank. The surrounding landscape is slightly undulating, but the tomb does have views of the jagged peaks of St David's Head. Locally, a number of small rocky outcrops are also visible. The River Solva is located south of the monument at the base of the hill on which the monument stands.

This monument consists of a small, single capstone that now rests on one of three uprights. The chamber is rectangular (2.2m x 1.5m) and is open on the northern side. There are three uprights that are 1m high; the capstone appears to be dislodged, lying prostrate on the southern upright. According to the RCHM of 1925 (435), several flagstones, that may be associated with the monument, were uncovered during ploughing. This monument, like many others, has been used as a dump for field debris and stones, possibly cairn material, which litters both the chamber and the area around the monument. However, there is no trace of any mound. Grimes (1939) had suggested that Treffynnon is a simple, chambered monument, one of three in the locality. In plan and condition, it is similar to the Parc-y-Cromlech monument on Strumble Head (PEM 14).

Although much smaller than its neighbour, White House, Treffynnon may be considered megalithic in form. Its capstone is similar to a number of earth-fast monuments in the Pembroke group, including the Devil's Quoit (PEM 25), King's Quoit (PEM 26) and the northern chamber of the Hanging Stone (PEM 24).

The Treffynnon monument with its dislodged capstone

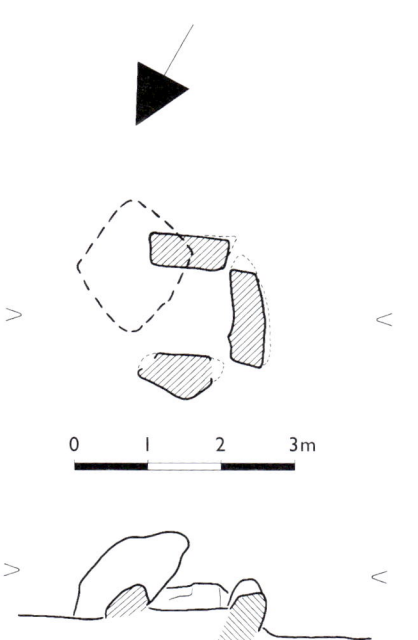

Plan and section of the Treffynnon monument (after Barker 1992)

80. St Elvies Farm, St Elvies
SM 81205 23945, SM NO. PE043
County Reference Number: PEM 20

Located on a north-west-facing slope, around 61m AOD, the tomb is one of three coastal burial sites in South-west Wales, which appear to have been purposely concealed from the sea. The tomb seems

Side-on view of the St Elvies Farm monument showing the two chambers, looking north

to have been intact in 1890, when it was described as a 'double cromlech'. Each capstone (the largest measuring 3.7m x 3.1m) is supported by two uprights. There are traces of a mound between both chambers and on the western side of the western chamber. However, today both structures are badly damaged. It has been suggested that large stones found in nearby walls may have been plundered from the monument. Certainly, during the latter years of the nineteenth century, a tenant farmer from nearby St Elvies Farm was asked to stop 'blasting' bits of the tomb structure away. Williams, when writing part of the *Pembrokeshire Archaeological Survey* between 1897 and 1906, remarked on:

> ... two cromlechs, both cap stones thrown down. Twelve years ago the tenant blasted and carried off two legs of the eastern cromlech, but at the request of the writer ceased this work of destruction. The cromlechau stand within two yards of each other. Each has only two legs left.

Although Daniel describes the tomb as 'morphologically indeterminate', the southerly chamber may be of his earth-fast type, with the western end of the capstone resting on the ground, and the eastern end supported by uprights and forming the chamber entrance.

There are a few other examples of multiple chambers in South-west Wales. One is the unusual five-chambered tomb of Cerrig y Gof (PEM 4); others include The Hanging Stone (PEM 24) near Pembroke, and Carn Llidi (PEM 21 & 22) standing on St David's Head.

Within the past, there have been several excavations in and around the monument. The first of these was undertaken in the early years of

Plan and section of the St Elvies Farm monument (after Barker 1992)

the twentieth century by Felix Oswald. According to Grimes (1936a, 13) and Daniel (1950, 143) these findings were insignificant. Investigations following the recent erection of fencing, in order to protect the western side of the monument, have revealed traces of a mound (Dyfed Archaeological Trust 1982).

Both chambers at St Elvies Farm are aligned NW–SE, with capstones dipping towards an inlet of the River Solva. However, due to disturbance it is not known if the capstones have been moved from their original position. For this reason, the plan of the chamber is difficult to discern.

81. Carn Llidi, St David's
SM 7352 2789, SM NO. PE042
County Reference Number: PEM 21 & 22

This monument, standing at around 122m AOD, commands one of the most dramatic views of all the monuments within South-west Wales. Sited on the rocky western slope of Carn Llidi, the tomb comprises two chambers. From here, there are views to the north, south and west; and the northern section of Ramsey Island and Ramsey Sound are clearly visible. Similar to other monuments of this type, Carn Llidi merges into its immediate surroundings, and is not easy to find. There is intervisibility between this monument and nearby Coetan Arthur (PEM 23), located some 1.2km to the west. Between Carn Llidi and Coetan Arthur is a settlement and an ancient field system, delineated by stretches of bleached and weathered drystone walling. According to the Regional HER, the settlement, known as Penlledwen, may have its origins within prehistory.[72]

The site was first recorded in the mid nineteenth century, when W.B. Jones adequately describes the site thus:

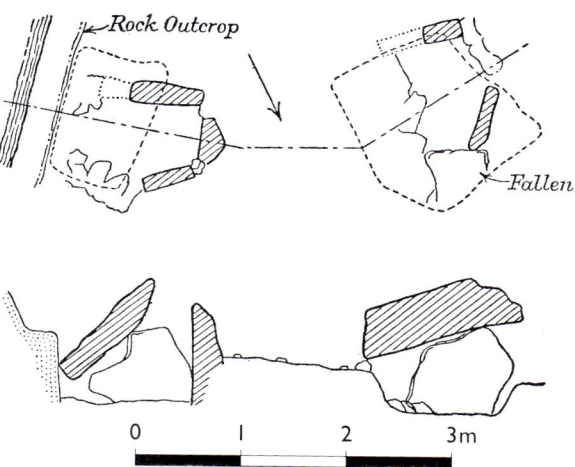

Plan and section of the Carn Llidi monument (after Daniel 1950)

A few days ago, in walking over Carn Llidi, the picturesque rock which towers over Whitesand Bay, to the north-west of St Davids. I discovered the remains of a double cromlech on the northern slope of the hill, and near the western extremity of its rocky portion. The two cromlechs, which stood side by side, differ in size: the larger one being on the northern side, and the other standing close under the rock. The capstones of both are dismounted: that of the former is some eight or nine feet in length, and the other considerably smaller. Three of the supporters of the lesser cromlech are in situ, and stand close together, presenting the appearance of a wall. (Jones 1863)

The site appears to have suffered some damage due to the construction of a Second World War gun emplacement. Modern brick fragments have been incorporated into what is possible cairn material surrounding both chambers. Between 2m and 3m south-west of the western chamber are a series of concrete platforms which are approached by a now much-weathered tarmacadam road. It is highly likely that this gun emplacement may have destroyed any ritual evidence associated with the site.

This double dolmen, which is similar in its architecture to other double dolmen sites in this part of Wales, conforms to a number of rules.

TOP: The western chamber of the Carn Llidi monument, constructed against a large rock outcrop; MIDDLE: The eastern chamber of Carn Llidi with its dislodged capstone; LEFT: Landscape view from the western chamber, looking north

Firstly, the monument stands close to rocky outcropping. Secondly, the chamber arrangement usually consists of one small and one large chamber (similar to the Hanging Stone, PEM 24; and the St Elvies monument, PEM 20). Finally, a cairn mound is usually present. The larger western chamber consists of a large capstone that is supported by a single upright and is set within an earth-fast rock-cut pit. The capstone, now 'dismounted', is described by Jones (below), who suggests that the site may have suffered antiquarian investigation prior to 1863. The northern section of the capstone rests on collapsed cairn or possibly a fragment of shattered capstone. The eastern chamber survives as three uprights that are set within a rock-cut pit. The capstone stands between the cliff-face and the southern upright. Daniel believes that the easterly chamber once had its capstone placed horizontally, with one side resting on the ledge of the rock outcrop and supported on the other three sides by uprights inside a rock-cut pit (Daniel 1950, 202). The smaller eastern chamber is sited at the edge of the rock outcropping.

There is no evidence of a covering mound at the site. Castlelden (1992) believes that a mound once existed, but I consider it unlikely as mounds were not an important component of the rock-cut tombs in this area. However, possible remnants of a cairn were recorded on a visit to the site in 2001 and 2003. Moreover, a plan produced by Barker (1992, 35) shows the remnants of a mound, located between the two chambers and to the west of the larger chamber. Grimes, who surveyed the monument in the mid-1930s, argues that:

> ... the mounds [of Carn Llidi and Carn Wnda] must have been small and could never have been elaborate. (1936a, 12)

82. White House, Llanhowell
SM 82545 28380, SM NO. PE159
County Reference Number: PEM 47

The White House monument, also referred to as Tresewig, is located within a fossilised field bank, and stands at around 91m AOD, in a gently undulating terrain with the peaks of St David's Head and localised small rock outcrops clearly visible. The surrounding landscape is very similar to that of the nearby Treffynnon monument (PEM 19).

As far as I am aware, the site has never been excavated, but offers considerable research potential. Much of the internal chamber and the immediate land around it appear intact and undisturbed. Grimes (1960, 11) describes the monument simply as 'a rectangular chamber with portal stones'. A more useful description is provided by Barker (1992, 48)[73] who wrote of the site:

> ... the remains of this burial chamber are incorporated in a modern hedge bank. They consist of a capstone 2.2 x 1.8 x 1.2m, resting on its side on one supporting stone. The latter is 1.5m high and 2.1, long. On the E side of the chamber opening are two 1.5m high upright stones. In and around the hedge lie several stones ... there is no trace of a barrow.

In the recent past, the tomb has suffered extensive damage through field clearance. Indeed, both Rees (1981) and Barker (1992) noticed field clearance debris piled against the tomb. Furthermore, plough damage is noticeable up to the chamber itself (Barker 1992). However, it is highly likely that the remnants of a mound outline exist as subsurface remains.

White House has five chunky uprights, but no trace of a covering mound. In between the two sets of uprights and within the chamber, is the capstone (measuring 2.3m x 1.8 x 1.2m). This has either been placed or has slipped from its original position, on its edge. The chamber, probably rectangular in form, now contains a substantial soil and stone deposit, possibly contemporary with the monument's abandonment. The size and original form of the uprights and capstone would have been very similar to The Hanging Stone (PEM 24), near Pembroke. This would have made White House a very substantial and highly visible monument, possibly standing over 2.7m in height (based on the length of the uprights and the thickness of the capstone).

The ruinous White Horse monument, set within a clear mound

In spite of the damage inflicted by post-medieval and modern farming practices, the White House monument may be classified as a Portal Dolmen. Although there are no traces of a mound, it appears that the surviving chamber forms part of a monument that was once oriented N–S, based on a comparison of the chamber plan with those of Carreg Samson (PEM 18) and Pentre Ifan (PEM 5). There may have been a doorway or entrance to the south, that could have led from a sizeable forecourt area (see plan and photograph).

THE INLAND ST DAVID'S GROUP

This group consists of at least eight monuments: Gwal-y-Filiast (CRM 1), Carn Besi (CRM 20), Mountain (PEM 6), The Altar at Colston (PEM 10), Garn Turne (PEM 11), Parc-y-llyn (PEM 12), the Cuckoo Stones (PEM 119) and the Eithbed complex (PEM 31). Each of the monuments within this group can be placed within different architectural styles. Gwal-y-Filiast, Mountain and Parc-y-llyn are possibly Portal Dolmens, which would have been located within a cairn or earthen mound; whilst The Altar and the Eithbed complex are considered short-chambered monuments (with short uprights supporting a low capstone). Carn Besi may also be placed in this category. The Garn Turne monument, the largest within this group, can be considered an opportunistic design in that it sits within a cairn field where stone would have been easily to hand. This monument, classified as a forecourt tomb, may or may not have possessed a mound.

Although listed by Children & Nash (1997) as one group, this collection of monuments is divided into at least two clusters. The most impressive cluster consists of Garn Turne, Parc-y-llyn and The Altar, all sited within a 2km-square tract of territory. In addition, Parc-y-llyn and The Altar are similar in size and architectural form. Their landscape setting is also similar, but they are dwarfed by the massive capstone and forecourt of Garn Turne. None of these monuments is intervisible with another, but it is suggested that they were constructed and in use at the same time. Garn Turne may have been utilised as the main burial place and a focus for non-burial activity by local communities. I say this because it would have required many people and hours of labour to construct and maintain this monument. Small family units were probably using Parc-y-llyn and The Altar, and it may have been the case that communities outside the immediate sphere of the three monuments also used Garn Turne. Similar nucleated monuments with associated satellite tombs exist elsewhere within South-west Wales.

Farther north, and close to the southern extent of the Mynydd Preseli, is the Eithbed complex. Here, three (or more) tombs are positioned in such a way that they face towards the south and St David's Head. Close by are the monuments of Carn Besi, the Gors Fawr stone circle, the destroyed henge monument of Meini-Gwyr and a number of standing stones. All are located close to, but never on, the Preseli Mountains. They may either be socially controlling the space around the south Preselis or, more importantly, establishing a boundary between familiar social space and the symbolic unknown of the mountains; or both. It is from this same area that the bluestones that form one of the inner circles at Stonehenge, originate.

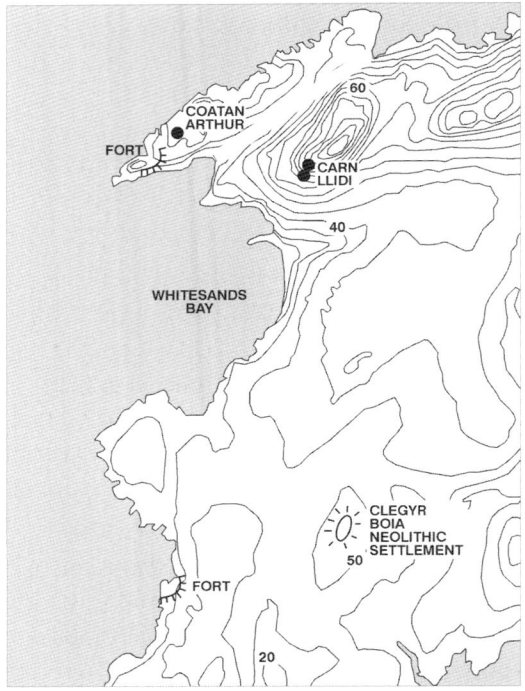

Distribution of Neolithic monuments on St David's Head

83. Gwal-y-Filiast, Llanboidy

SN 17045 25580, SM NO. CM031
County Reference Number: CRM 1

The Gwal-y-Filiast monument stands on the intermediate slope of a spur that overlooks the Afon Taf at around 100m AOD. The much-ruined, chambered monuments of Rhosfach (SN 1490 2555) and Meni-Gwyr (SN 1390 2650) are located 2.2km and 3.3km to the west respectively.[74] These monuments along with Cefn Brafle (SN 1957 2294), Carn Besi (CRM 20) and the Mountain site (PEM 6) may form a small cluster of monuments that occupy the southern hinterlands of the Preseli Mountains.

The earliest account of this monument was made by Lhuyd in 1695 (column 628), in which he describes the site thus:

> … rude stone [capstone] about ten yards in circumference, and above three foot thick, supported by four pillars, which are about two foot and a half in length.

This impressive monument, also known as Bwrdd Arthur and Dolwilym, consists of a large, single capstone supported by four uprights. The uprights appear to delineate a polygonal chamber. A fifth upright was recorded by Barnwell in 1872, suggesting that this formed an entrance (facing east, down the slope). On the eastern side of the chamber area are two uprights that stand 0.30m above the present ground level. Positioned away from the main chamber upright alignment, these appear to form a possible sill, and may in fact be the entrance into the chamber. The position of the sill and entrance perhaps suggests that a passage leading from the mound once existed.

Surrounding the monument, is a series of stones that may form the remnants of an earthen mound. Barnwell also claimed that a mound/barrow still

TOP: Plan and section of the Gwal-y-Filiast monument (after Barker 1992); MIDDLE: The chamber and the ridge on which it stands, looking south; BOTTOM: Western view of the chamber and ridge

THE SOUTH-WEST WALES GROUP

covered the chamber and capstone in 1872, and that at least 32 kerbstones were visible, which delineated the edge of the mound. This being the case, Gwal-y-Filiast must have suffered either large-scale vandalism or serious deterioration (or both) over the past 120 years. The position of the kerbing suggests that Gwal-y-Filiast possessed either an oval or circular mound; traces of possible *in situ* kerbstones are present within the northern and western areas of the site.

The capstone points towards the Afon Taff (to the west) and the eastern extent of the Preseli Mountains. However, views of the mountains are presently obscured by thick woodland (whether or not the valley was wooded during the Neolithic is unknown). At the point where the Afon Taff flows past Gwal-y-Filiast, the river becomes a violent rapid. This change in the river's character might have decided the tomb's location upon the ridge (Tilley 1994, 109). Other inland monuments in Wales follow a similar rule: Ty Isaf (BRE 5), Gwernvale (BRE 7), Cwm Fforest (BRE 9) and Garn Goch (BRE 12), all from the Black Mountains Group, and nearby Twlc y Filiast (CRM 6).

84. Mountain, Mynachlog Ddu
SN 16575 3285, SM NO. PE039
County Reference Number: PEM 6

This monument, also referred to as Llech y Gwyddon,[75] consists of a massive capstone (measuring 3.7m x 3.3m) incorporated within a field boundary. According to antiquarian accounts in Barker (1992, 26) by 1885, much of the monument had slipped into a modern ditch. When standing, the Mountain monument would have been an impressive tomb, similar to that of The Hanging Stone (PEM 24) in south Pembrokeshire, and probably standing over 3.5m in height (based partly on the dimensions of several prostrate uprights that lie to the west of the boundary).

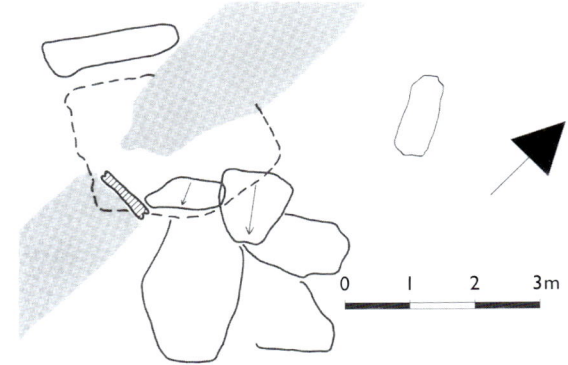

TOP: Plan of the Mountain monument (after Barker 1992); MIDDLE: Western view of the Mountain monument, a section of which is incorporated into a field boundary; BOTTOM: View showing the collapsed uprights (LEFT), and the large capstone (RIGHT) which is incorporated into the field boundary

Standing at around 236m AOD, The Mountain monument lies within the north-west corner of a waterlogged field. It is probable that the waterlogged area extended to the east of the monument and the boundary (thus, surrounding the site with water and creating an island for the dead). Lying prostrate around and underneath the capstone, are five large stones, probably collapsed uprights. Other smaller stones are also present, including one visible support for the capstone. Located within the fabric of the boundary is a probable chamber upright, oriented E–W. Lynch (1972, 81–2), who was the first to record this monument, suggests that Mountain is a Portal Dolmen that may have been centred within a round mound. The size of the recumbent uprights (one of which is over 3m in length) and the position of the capstone may indicate this. However, Barker (1992, 26) suggests that the site is too damaged to make any valued assessment.

Although the Mountain monument is very much damaged on its eastern side, the majority of the central and western chamber area is incorporated into a large, earthen field boundary, oriented N–S. Similar to many other monuments in this part of Wales, it is probably the case that the later field boundary has done much to protect this monument from destruction.

An extensive quantity of possible cairn debris was recorded by the author in 1997, now either incorporated into the field boundary or spread across the western corner of the field. It is probable that the chamber and uprights would have been covered by an extensive mound that was oriented roughly N–S, with an entrance to the east. On visiting the site, Rees (1981) remarks that there were traces of a 7m-wide, round mound that rose to a height of around 0.6m. However, a recent visit to the site suggests that the mound is probably oval or a long mound, measuring approximately 25m x 7–9m.

85. The Altar, Colston, Little Newcastle
SM 9828 2812, SM NO. PE025
County Reference Number: PEM 10

The Altar at Colston (also referred to simply as Colston) is the smallest monument in the group. Standing at around 102m AOD, this monument is located a few metres south of the Afon Anghol. Although The Altar is sited in a small valley, the southern extent of the Preseli Mountains is visible from the monument. Standing close by and forming a possible cluster, is Garn Turne (PEM 11) and Parc-y-llyn (PEM 12). All three monuments possess different architectural styles, and therefore may have been used at different times during the Neolithic.

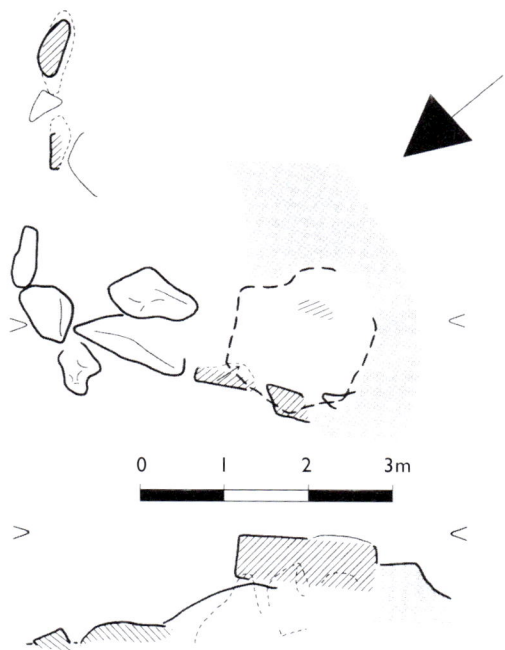

Plan and section of The Altar monument (after Barker 1992)

The RCHM inventory of 1925 (396) states:

> About half a mile south-east of Little Newcastle village, on the farm of Ffynnonau, is a small but perfect cromlech, and on its S side the ruined remains of a second [The Altar ?]. The first cromlech is separated from the road to Beulah bridge by a fence which is carried over the mound on which the stones are placed.

This significant but rather confusing account for this site suggests that a further megalithic monument existed during the early part of the twentieth century. Unfortunately, no other reference to the missing monument has been made elsewhere, not even within Barker's extensive inventory. One can only assume that the missing monument is Parc-y-llyn (PEM 12) or the Altar once possessed a second chamber that was located on the southern side of the field bank, or within the southern field bank on the opposite side of a narrow lane.

The tomb has suffered much cattle damage, especially on its northern side. However, the southern section of the monument forms part of a hedge boundary and probably remains intact. The monument consists of a small, rectangular capstone supported by two or more uprights. The two visible uprights support the western section of the capstone. The capstone, measuring 2.1m by 1.9m and 0.97m in thickness, is encased within the field bank. It has been suggested in Barker (1992, 28) that the shape of the mound has been much disturbed by the hedge and the road.[76] Several uprights, located to the north-east of the chamber area, may represent the remains of a forecourt area or even kerbing. These uprights are within an extensive spread of cairn material that must be the result of recent disturbance to the monument. Two of the slabs within the forecourt area, measuring over one metre in length, may have once formed part of the kerbing.

Based on early Ordnance Survey evidence, Barber and Williams (1989, 111) have commented that a possible second chambered monument exists 40m due south of this monument. However, I have yet to locate this. Furthermore, a single pointed stone stands 1m above ground level, but is hidden within the boundary hedge. I would tentatively suggest that this stone shares a landscape affinity with nearby Parc-y-llyn (PEM 12), and a group association with nearby Garn Turne (PEM 11), maybe as a marker between the monuments.

The Altar, partly incorporated into an historic field boundary, looking south

Detail showing the chamber and capstone of The Altar

86. Garn Turne, St Dogwells
SM 97935 27255, SM NO. PE061
County Reference Number: PEM 11

Garn Turne (also known as Carn Turne, Garne Tarne and Old Coldstone), the largest of all the inland monuments in Wales, is one of three megaliths clustered around the hamlet of Colston. All three stand approximately 10.5km from the nearest coastline. This monument, standing at around 137m AOD, consists of a chamber constructed of a series of uprights that support a capstone. Immediately east of the chamber is a large forecourt area. One of the earliest accounts of this monument is by Fenton (1811, 337–8), who writes:

> Repassing below Little Newcastle [nearby village] I turn to the right, and enter a field covered with detached fragments of broken rock, called Garn Twrne ... it appears to have been a great resort of the Druids, if to them are to be ascribed those monuments called cromlechs, of a dimension exceeding that of Pentre Evan [PEM 5], for it measured in length about sixteen feet and a half by thirteen and half in breadth, and from four to five feet five inches in thickness, and its circumference sixty-three feet eight inches. This immense incumbent stone and its three columnar props stood in a circle of upright stones, some of them yet standing.

The massive volcanic capstone (measuring 5m x 4.1m) is arguably one of the largest in the British Isles. It weighs more than 60 tons and is now collapsed, resting on a series of dislodged uprights. The unusual V-shaped forecourt is similar to that of Pentre Ifan and the Irish court tombs of southern Ireland; an architectural trait endorsed by Grimes as the 'Pentre Ifan type' (Grimes 1932, 92; 1948, 13). Here, Grimes refers to the forecourt area as an 'asymmetric funnel-shaped upright forecourt'. The forecourt arrangement is 'familiar with the general western family of long cairns'. This forecourt and entrance area, constructed of at least six uprights, faces north-east towards a large, rock outcrop. This may be replicated within the forecourt itself, as a large, pointed volcanic

The Garn Turne monument, with its horseshoe-shaped façade

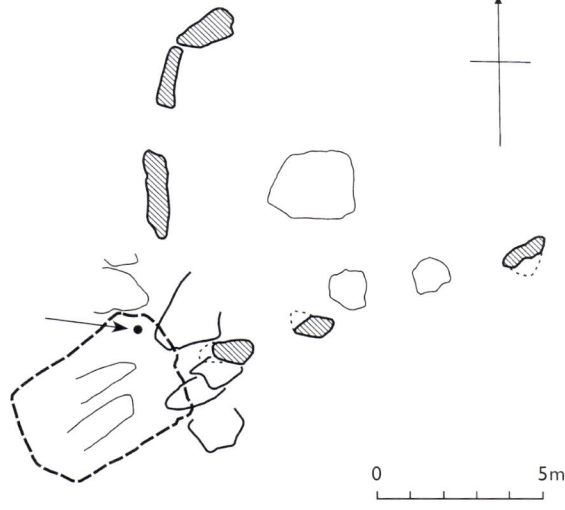

Plan of the Garn Turne monument, showing the location of the cup-and-ring mark on the capstone (after Barker 1992)

THE SOUTH-WEST WALES GROUP

Engraved cup-in-ring motif located on top of the capstone of Garn Turne

block is located within the central forecourt area, although it is not certain that this boulder was in place (and therefore in use) when the monument was being utilised. The northern forecourt arrangement, consisting of three uprights, appears to form an arc, thus enclosing the central and northern section of the forecourt area. However, on the southern side, three uprights are set in a straight line. The two lines of uprights are not symmetrical, and it is highly likely that a southern inward-sweeping arc was present. The two uprights located within the southern section of the forecourt area may have been re-erected at a later date.

Sited as it is, close to localised substantial rock outcropping, the tomb merges into its immediate surroundings. Indeed, so well is it 'hidden' within the landscape that, despite the monument's size, it is difficult to locate. Apart from the nearby rock outcrop, the surrounding landscape is gently undulating. Nevertheless, the southern extent of the Preseli Mountains is in full view. The question remains: how much of the stone construction of Garn Turne would have been visible? – was this megalithic structure once entirely concealed beneath an earthen mound? Barker (1992, 29) does not entirely agree that this monument is a portal tomb; rather, that it may be an earth-fast type. However, many of the earth-fast monuments within this region are located and constructed very differently. Furthermore, these monuments are small and unimposing. Others have suggested that the southern part of the monument, which incorporates the chamber and capstone, may have been part of a long cairn. However, I have found no evidence of this.

Grimes (1932, 92) and later Stenger (1982) have both claimed that a 'peristalith' arrangement (or kerbing) existed around the monument. My own observations have shown that outside the forecourt area, and 150m beyond the monument, is a ridge outcropping that may have provided construction material for the tomb itself. Either side of this rock outcropping, are marshy areas which may have contributed to the sacredness of the site.

Approximately 50m to the west of the monument and obscured by natural cairn field debris, is a large monolith standing at around 1.2m in height, possibly contemporary with the Garn Turne monument. If this is the case, Garn Turne and its surroundings represent an important and complex Neolithic landscape. Indeed, despite Grimes surveying this monument in 1932, there has been little interest in the area beyond the monument, and it is highly likely that further sites exist. Rees, on an inspection of the site in 1981 for CADW, has noted that a possible long cairn may exist among the natural rock outcropping.

In terms of its recent archaeological history, the author and a team from Bristol University discovered a cup-and-ring engraving and several cupmarks on the upper surface of the capstone in 2005 (Nash 2006). The cup-and-ring engraving comprises a natural cupule that was created by a clast indentation, and an engraved ring that is partially interrupted by a natural quartz vein.

In 2011, a team of archaeologists from the University of Central Lancashire excavated in and around the monument, and ascertained that the outcropping was quarried and was sited over the edge of an excavated pit (possibly the source). The pit contained evidence of 'intense' burning (Cumming and Richards 2011, 2014). Charcoal extracted from this area was radiocarbon-dated between 3702–3639 BCE. Radiocarbon material from a second pit included burnt hazel (sp. *corylus*) and provided a potential construction date-range of the monument of *c*.3787–3656 BCE or 3761–3643 BCE.

87. Parc-y-llyn, Ambleston
SM 9823 2659, SM NO. PE133
County Reference Number: PEM 12

Standing in the corner of a banked field, Parc-y-llyn seems to be hidden away within a small narrow valley. Although this monument appears to be small in comparison with nearby Garn Tune (PEM 11), it is nonetheless an important site, as part of it is hidden within a nearby field bank, and is therefore archaeologically undisturbed.

The monument, standing at around 128m AOD, is sited on a north-facing rise within the valley of the Western Cleddau. Constructed of a small, single capstone (measuring 2.5m x 1.8m) supported by four uprights, the monument has suffered from livestock damage in recent years. Many large stones, possibly belonging to a covering mound, are scattered nearby.

One of the earliest accounts of this monument was made by Gardner Wilkinson (1871, 224) who stated that:

The ruinous chamber and faint mound of Parc-y-Llyn, looking east

Plan and section of the Parc-y-Llyn monument (after Barker 1992)

Landscape view from the western side of the Parc-y-Llyn capstone

At Ffynnonnau ("The Wells") two miles west of the Roman Station, and a little beyond Carn Tarn, is a low cromlech, supported on three stones, having a capstone 8ft long by 6ft broad, and 1ft 6in thick; with many small stones lying about it.

Within the field boundary to the east is a possible second chamber with one supporting upright. Other large stones, which may be uprights, are located north of the monument. Other double dolmens of this size and form exist elsewhere in South-west Wales, including Carn Llidi (PEM 21–2), the Hanging Stone (PEM 24) and Trellyffaint (PEM 2). The RCHM inventory of 1925 adds that:

> In the hedge to the east, and largely concealed by it, is what may have been the capstone of a second cromlech … both remains stand on a slightly elevated platform of 180ft circumference.

According to Barker's plan (1992, 31), the entrance faces north-west, but appears not to be oriented to any particular nearby feature. However, 1km in the same direction is the Garn Turne monument. Very little of the regional landscape is visible. Similar landscape positioning is evident at The Altar, Colston, approximately 1.6km north of Parc-y-llyn. The chamber and the remains of the other possible chamber are aligned E–W. Barker suggests that both chambers were enclosed within an NW–SE elongated cairn perhaps up to 15m in length (ibid. 32). If this is the case, the entrance would probably be west-facing, and similar to other monument orientations within the British Isles.

88. Carn Besi, Llandyssilio East
SN 1560 2768, SM NO. CM049
County Reference Number: CRM 20

The denuded Carn Besi monument, also known as the Dolwilim Dolmen, stands a few metres north-west of the A487 at around 236m AOD. Carn Besi, easily the most unimpressive of all the monuments listed in this book, does, nevertheless, occupy a site with outstanding views over the northern and western extents of the Preseli Mountains. It stands 1.5km north of (and may be incorporated into) a Late Neolithic landscape that includes a burial chamber (SN 145 255), several standing stones (SN 137 255, SN 154 258 & SN 137 254) and a cairn circle (SN 142 267)

The capstone of Carn Besi and the Mynydd Preseli south-west

at Meni-Gwyr. The monument has been classified by Barker as 'a large capstone' (1992, 59),[77] while the RCAM inventory (1917, 321) describes it as a cromlech.

The monument consists of a small single capstone, measuring 2.5m x 2.1m and 0.35m thick, supported by a number of short or collapsed uprights that do not rise above the surrounding ground level. The chamber area is therefore partially submerged, cutting into the drift geology. The capstone, oriented E–W, appears to point towards the general area of the Gors Fawr stone circle, 2.7km to the west. To the south, west and south-east, there is much evidence of a Bronze Age landscape, with Carn Besi possibly marking the northern boundary of this symbolic landscape. Despite the fact that it is undoubtedly Neolithic, the monument would have played an important role in organising and controlling later prehistoric landscapes.

Its appearance suggests that Carn Besi, along with examples at the nearby Eithbed complex, should be classified as a single slab rather than an earth-fast monument. I would add that monuments such as this would have been known only to people who used the site, as it merges so completely into the surrounding landscape (Children & Nash 1997, 99).

89. The Cuckoo Stones, Carew
SN 06438 03903, PRN: 3523
County Reference Number: PEM 119

The remains of a chambered tomb, probably a Portal Dolmen. The site comprises two small uprights (standing 0.45m in height) and set at right angles. One of the uprights supports a large capstone which has slipped. Dispersed around the site are a number of loose and earth-fast boulders which probably belong to a cairn that once encased the chamber and formed a covering mound.

The site is located on the eastern side of a small hillock, north of the village of Sagaston. A large capstone, uprights and cairn material survive. The capstone, made from quartzite, measures 1.8m by 1.55m, and 0.65m thick. The capstone appears to have slid away from its uprights (also referred to as supporters or pillars). Indeed, the capstone is embedded into the earth on its western side. At the time of the publication of the Royal Commission account in 1925, four of its five uprights had 'fallen'. However, Barker's 1992 plan shows only two uprights lying prostrate – probably the result of collapse from the weight of the capstone. Based on the amount of loose and partially buried stone around the monument, it is probable that the chamber was surrounded by a circular or kidney-shaped mound. According to the RCAM (1925, 50), the site stood close to an ash tree (identified by Barker as a hawthorn bush). A photograph of the site in Barker (1992, 47) shows the site to be covered in vegetation. A recent visit (October 2023) confirmed that the site has been cleared. The Cuckoo's Stone monument can be seen from a field gate in the neighbouring field, 250m to the south-east.

In terms of an archaeological context, the site stands around 1.5km to the west of Neolithic and Bronze Age settlement activity that was identified

The damaged chamber of the Cuckoo Stones, looking north-west

during excavations by Cambria Archaeology in 2001. This activity was uncovered in advance of the construction of the Sageston to Redberth bypass section in the early 2000s.

The site was dismissed as not being a Neolithic burial-ritual site by an Ordnance Survey field officer in 1965, who characterised it is as being 'a collection of shapeless erratic boulders'. My recent visit (2023) confirmed the presence of the requisite architectural characteristics of a Neolithic chambered burial-ritual site. As far as I am aware, this monument has yet to be designated a Scheduled Monument.

90. Eithbed Cemetery Group (North, Central, South), Maenclochog
SN 07960 28635 (centred upon), SM NO. PE119
County Reference Number: PEM 31

The much-disturbed Eithbed Group of monuments comprises one of maybe three or four megalithic cemeteries in South-west Wales. Others include the Garn Wen Complex (PEM 7–9), the Llan Complex (PEM 30) and the Morfa Bychan Group (CRM 2–5). The original excavator, Done Bushell (1911), records three or four monuments within this complex – all are aligned roughly N–S.

One of several destroyed chambers that belong to the Eithbed Cemetery Group

The remains of the Eithbed monuments are located close to a series of natural springs that feed into the Afon Syfynwy. All once formed a complex multi-phased monument group, which includes a possible stone circle and enclosure.[78] Approximately 3km to the north of this monument group is the upland area of Cerrig Lladron, which stands at 468m AOD. Immediately to the north-east, the land forms a spur which rises to 427m AOD. This dramatic setting forms a typical backdrop to this and other inland monuments within this part of Wales.

Standing between 240 and 250m AOD, the Eithbed cemetery (North, Central and South) is located on the edge of a south-facing field. They are victims of recent clearance believed to have taken place between 1905 and 1909 (Done Bushell 1911, 303). The presence of large, irregularly-placed stone slabs, makes the actual identification of the monuments very difficult.

Gardner Wilkinson (1871, 227) provides the clearest account (along with engravings) of the precise location of the two of the sites:

> A little to the N [of Maenclochog] are two fallen cromlechs, or "Coetan", the capstone of the first being 8ft 4in by 5ft 3in, 6ft thick and one of the stones on which it stood 6ft high by 3ft 6in. Fifty feet N by E of this is a large fallen stone; and nine feet beyond it an upright slab, 5ft in height by the same in breadth; twenty nine feet from which is another fallen cromlech, with a capstone 11ft 6in long by 6ft 6in, amidst some fallen stones. Thirty-three feet from it to the W is a small stone circle, 21 feet in diameter; and about eighty yards to the NE, is a circular enclosure within a mound composed of earth, and once encircled by large stones, most of which have been taken away for fences [walling]. It is on the slope of the hill, its smallest diameter being about 170ft, and within the area on the S side is a spring of water.

Debate over whether three or four monuments exist at the site has continued for well over 150 years. Gardner Wilkinson (1871, 227) remarked that two (of the three) cromlechs were 'fallen'. Later, Done Bushell (1911, 300–1) recognised three capstones. Today, all are low-lying (almost at ground level), with little or no evidence of uprights or covering mound. They may all be similar in architecture to the Carn Besi (CRM 20) and Garn Wen (PEM 7–9) monuments.

The largest tomb of the complex recorded by Done Bushell and his son in 1911, was The Gorse Grave, enclosed within the north-east section of a possible stone circle. However, Done Bushell had doubts as to whether or not this was a burial chamber, stating:

The Gorse Grave, if it be a grave, is 20ft by 7ft. It was opened by my son, Mr Warin Foster Bushell, on April 26th, in the present year [1911]. He found within it, on the level of the external surface of the ground, a pavement of flat stone of no great thickness roughly fitted together, and underneath the pavement, in the centre of the barrow, a small amount of black ashes. The stones had been roughly shaped and were of considerable size, some of them being nearly two square feet in area (Done Bushell 1911, 305).

A visit in 1915 by officers compiling the RCHM, confirmed that the remnants of a cairn did exist, in particular the survival of three 'pillars', probably representing chamber uprights, plus two large slabs, possibly capstones, which were lying against a nearby hedge bank.

The monuments, plus the remains of burial chambers at Glandy Cross (Meini-Gwyr),[79] Carn Besi (CRM 20), Gwal-y-Ffiliast (CRM 1) and Mountain (PEM 6), appear to be deliberately placed around the southern hinterland of the Preseli Mountains. All of them could either delineate and encompass a social/political territory, including the mountains, or mark a symbolic frontier between what is known, and what is unknown and dangerous landscape (in other words, the Preseli Mountains). No monuments appear to be sited within the uplands of this mountainous area.

THE PEMBROKE GROUP

The Pembroke Group of monuments (with the exception of the Morfa Bychan cemetery, which is in Carmarthenshire), is located along the southern coastline of the county and occupies quite different landscape locations to monuments on St David's and Strumble Head. Based on monument distribution and different styles of monument building, it is probable that a continuous Neolithic influence stretched from Angle in the west to the Gower Peninsula in the east.

The seven monuments within this group – the Devil's Quoit (PEM 25), The King's Quoit (PEM 26), Morfa Bychan A, B, C and D (CRM 2–5) and The Hanging Stone (PEM 24) – are constructed and located according to a number of different architectural and spatial rules. They involve different chamber and capstone designs. The Hanging Stone, for example uses a large, rounded block for a capstone, whilst Morfa Bychan D uses an angular slab. This choice of stone is restricted to local availability. Many other differences include chamber size, shape and mound construction.

Despite these differences, there are several monuments that seem to share some common rules, both in architectural form and landscape setting. For example, The King's Quoit and The Devil's Quoit, although located in different landscapes, are similar architecturally. Both are arguably earth-fast, supported by a series of uprights at one end. Furthermore, the capstones of each monument are similarly shaped and are made from red sandstone.

The four tombs on Ragwen Point – the Morfa Bychan Group – are all constructed, located and oriented in the same way. Although close to the sea, all seem to ignore it, their chambers and possible passage alignments pointing inland: a pattern repeated in many of the coastal monuments of South-west Wales. The most obvious example is The King's Quoit at Manorbier. Here, the monument is just a few metres from the edge of the sea, but the capstone has been deliberately placed so as to point inland, towards the beach and headland. Other monuments, such as The Devil's Quoit and The Hanging Stone, are positioned in a more subtle way. Even so, although close to the coast, they share no orientation, and no relationship with the sea.

Three, perhaps four, architectural styles are used throughout this group, which may suggest either a localised building tradition, incorporating a symbolism unique to each monument, or, equally plausibly, different construction dates. Within the Neolithic core areas of western Britain, new trends affected a monument's identity through time and space. Thus, small polygonal chambers supporting large boulder-like capstones were succeeded by tombs having flat, wedge-shaped capstones overlying square or rectangular chambers of the earth-fast type. Each monument was probably constructed so as to acknowledge social (public) and symbolic (private) space.

91. The Hanging Stone, Burton
SM 9722 0822, SM NO. PE066
County Reference Number: PEM 24

The Hanging Stone forms part of a boundary between a field and garden, and is located just south of the village of Hill Mountain, at around 75m AOD. The surrounding landscape is gently undulating, with open fields to the north and east. Milford Haven Sound, approximately 3km to the south, is clearly visible from the top of the capstone. This monument can be considered as being in a reasonable state of repair. This may be partially due to its location within the bounds of a garden.[80]

Barnwell first illustrated the monument in 1872, and it was later described by Grimes (1936a), Daniel (1950) and Lynch (1976). Grimes (1936a, 131) suggested that the Hanging Stone may be a passage grave and may be more complex than previously considered. Lynch prefers to use the term 'chamber and passage monument' (1972, 26) – a term that conveniently fits with the Western seaways' tradition. There are certainly a number of similarities between this monument and Irish court monuments, but I

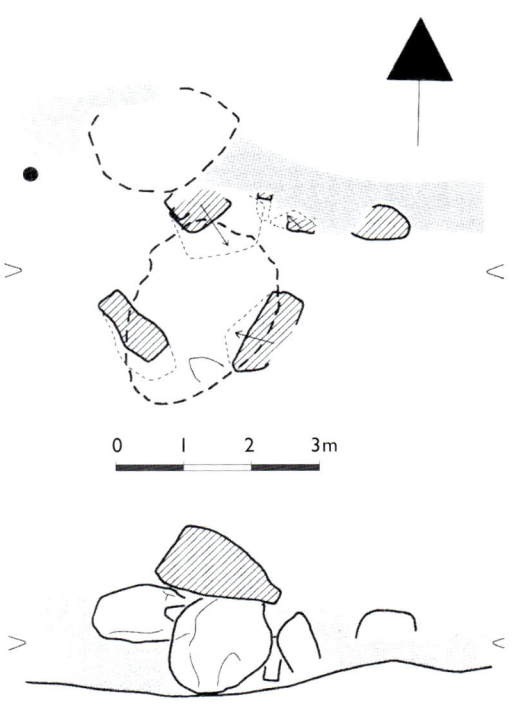

Plan and section of the Hanging Stone monument (after Barker 1992)

222   NEOLITHIC TOMBS OF WALES

The larger of two chambers that form the Hanging Stone monument

consider that there is little in the way to distinguish this monument with other passage graves in Wales, especially when no passage and little of the mound's form remains.

An anonymous account made in 1864 stated that the structure:

> ... at present consists of the remains of its supporters and a covering stone. A huge mass of rock lies touching part of it, which looks as if it had at one time formed a portion of the gallery or chamber. There is also the remains of original small, dry masonry, by which the gaps between the larger stones were always carefully filled up. Few traces of its former covering, or tumulus, could be made out (1864, 346–7).

Today, the tomb consists of two large, substantial capstones, one of which measures 3.1m x 2.6m. This capstone is supported by three uprights and forms the southern chamber, rectangular in shape. A northern chamber is partially incorporated into a large earthen boundary aligned roughly N–S. However, revised plans by Barker suggest that the capstone has been dislodged. A stone alignment, partially exposed within the earthen boundary lies north-north-east of the southern chamber. An additional stone setting was recorded by Lynch in 1975 (1976, 74). This alignment probably represents the uprights to the northern chamber. There is, immediately to the north of the boundary, a build-up of soil which may represent disturbed cairn or mound material, thus suggesting that the covering mound was oriented NE–SW (in line with the two chambers). The northern capstone is located 2.5m west of this alignment. The northern chamber is possibly smaller than its southern neighbour, with the top of the capstone reaching the height of the base of the southern capstone. A similar architectural trait is seen within the double-chambered monument at Trellyffaint (PEM 2).

The southern chamber appears to be polygonal; and, until 1864, it was reported that drystone walling was visible in between the uprights (anon 1864, 346–7). Also present was a substantial amount of possible cairn material. Alas, the drystone walling

Antiquarian engraving of the larger of the two Hanging Stone chambers (*Archaeologia Cambrensis* 1884)

Antiquarian engraving of the smaller of the two Hanging Stone chambers (*Archaeologia Cambrensis*) 1884

92. Devil's Quoit, Angle
SM 88655 00810, SM NO. PE020
County Reference Number: PEM 25

This monument, also known as Broomhill Burrows, is constructed of a large, rounded capstone supported at the western end by three uprights. At the opposite end, the capstone is set firmly into the earth. Daniel (1950) refers to this construction as earth-fast, a form found throughout the region. However, in his notes on this site, he refers to it as a collapsed chamber, to be compared with the Cors-y-Gedol monument in Merionethshire (MER 4; 1950, 203). I would agree with his initial interpretation of the site as being earth-fast, although Barker (1992, 38) suggests that, in this particular case, the term 'earth-fast' is misleading because the capstone sits on an earthen surface that may not be contemporary with the construction of the tomb.

The first account of this site was made by Richard Fenton (1811, 405) who eloquently describes the site and its surroundings thus:

and the vast remains of the covering mound have long since gone. However, in a nearby hedge there is a possible second capstone and two uprights. Both Grimes (1939) and Lynch (1975) suggest that these stones may represent the vestiges of a short passage.[81] I am of the opinion that the Hanging Stone and the nearby displaced second capstone and dislodged uprights are in fact two chambers forming a double-dolmen with the remains of a passage located at the north-eastern end of the monument. Other examples of multi-chambered tombs exist elsewhere in South-west Wales: for example, St Elvies Farm (PEM 20), Trellyfaint (PEM 2) and Twlc y Filiast (CRM 6).

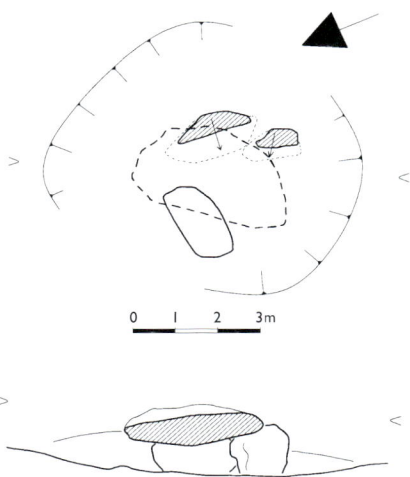

Plan and section of the Devil's Quoit monument (after Barker 1992)

A little further on, across an extensive tract of sandy burrows, in the centre of which stands a Cromlech resting on two upright stones, the third overturned. There seems to have been a low circular agger of earth raised around it, of no inconsiderable area. This is the only druidical relic of the kind I have observed in Castle Martin, such monuments being much less frequent in the lower part of the country than they appear to be near the mountains.

Several interesting comments derive from Fenton's observations. Firstly, the depression and 'low circular agger', suggest that some type of antiquarian investigation was undertaken prior to 1811. Secondly and more importantly, Fenton has started to understand the concept of deliberate landscape positioning of monuments. He notices that the Devil's Quoit is in an unusual place and should be 'near the mountains' (by 'mountains' I think he is probably referring to the jagged rock outcropping on, say, St David's Head and along Strumble Head).

The site was later recorded by Longueville Jones in 1865 (1865, 281) who noticed 'traces of a carnedd of stones', suggesting some subsequent damage to this monument. An engraving by Barnwell in 1872 (1872, 142), published in *Archaeologia Cambrensis*, claims to be a more actuate representation than the Longueville Jones engraving of 1865. Barker (1992, 38) recorded, on a visit in 1986, that a slab 'protrudes through the turf some 3m north-east of the chamber'.

The capstone, made from local sandstone, is similar in shape to the King's Quoit at Manorbier. There appears to be no trace of a mound, but the chamber is set within a shallow depression (Barker 1992), suggesting that the chamber area may be sub-megalithic. However, the depression, roughly 8m by 7m, may also be the result of continuous cattle or sheep trampling.

Although located on a small ridge at around 37m AOD, the tomb does not look out towards the open sea, but rather takes in a visual sweep of Milford Haven Sound, 5km to the north. Other burial monuments that similarly ignore the sea are Llech-y-Tribedd (PEM 1) and nearby St Elvies Farm (PEM 20).

Broomhill Burrows lies adjacent to Freshwater West, an extensive beach system where Mesolithic and Neolithic lithic activity has been recorded. The remains of a submerged forest dating to the Early Post-Glacial period (c.10–14,000 BCE) can be seen at low tide from this beach. Approximately 150m to the east of the Devil's Quoit, is an extensive sand dune system, possibly representing an ancient sea inlet (known as Kilpaison Burrows). And c.300m south-east of the Devil's Quoit is a probable Bronze Age mound (SM 8899 0060).

The earth-fast type Devil's Quoit monument

Antiquarian engraving of the Devil's Quoit (Edward Barnwell 1872)

93. King's Quoit, Manorbier
SS 05897 97267, SM NO. PE035
County Reference Number: PEM 26

The King's Quoit has one of the most dramatic landscape settings in South-west Wales, and is one of only a few monuments located on the coast. Others include Carreg Samson (PEM 18), Garn Wnda (PEM 13), Coetan Arthur (PEM 23), Carn Llidi (PEM 21–2) and the four rock-cut monuments of Morfa Bychan A, B, C, and D (CRM 2–5).

The monument, standing at 18m AOD is located on a small bank above a cliff face, and comprises a huge single capstone supported by two uprights; although there is a third upright located at the south-eastern end, which is now probably recumbent. The three uprights form a rectangular chamber.

In 1865, Longueville Jones noted its unusual landscape position, recording that:

On the south-eastern side of the little cove at Manorbeer ... is to be seen a cromlech ... it is curious from its position, because, instead of lying on an elevated or bare patch of ground, it is just under a ridge of rocks ... in this respect it resembles the cromlech near Llanwnda [Carn Wnda?] ... the cause in each of these cases has, no doubt, been the convenience of using large slabs from adjoining, or rather overhanging cliffs (1865, 282).

The King's Quoit and Manorbier Bay beyond, looking south-west

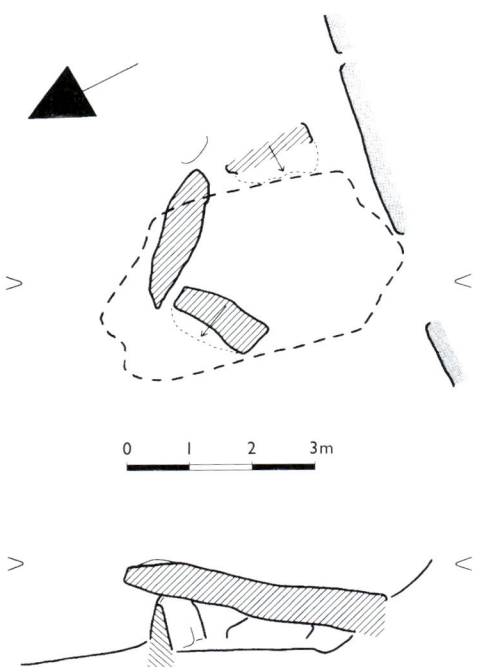

Plan and section of the King's Quoit monument (after Barker 1992)

Antiquarian engraving of the King's Quoit (*Archaeologia Cambrensis* 1872)

The monument may be regarded as earth-fast, belonging to the sub-megalithic classification (Daniel 1950). The capstone, made from local sandstone, points inland towards Manorbier Bay, suggesting that the King's Quoit is in some way ignoring the sea. Its builders and users are quite clearly orienting the monument inland.

The King's Quoit was once regarded as a natural 'accidental formation' of stone (Anon 1851, 315). Recently, Barker (1992, 38) has supported Daniel's earth-fast classification. In addition, I believe no covering mound would have existed during the Neolithic because the ledge on which the monument stands is far too narrow. This being so, the King's Quoit is similarly constructed to – and shares a comparable landscape setting with – both Garn Gilfach (PEM 15) and nearby Devil's Quoit (PEM 25). Recent observations by the author have revealed that the rear section of the monument has several concealed fallen uprights, and therefore one should dismiss the assigned earth-fast classification.

94–97. Morfa Bychan A, B, C, & D, Marros
SN 22172 07552 (centred upon),[82] SM NO. CM053
County Reference Number: CRM 2–5

The Morfa Bychan cemetery group consists of four monuments that stand between 75m and 120m AOD. These are sited among rock debris and merge into the surrounding landscape in what appears to be a deliberate act of concealment. During the Neolithic, only those with special ritual knowledge may have known the precise whereabouts of each monument. Similar monument locations are evident within other coastal headlands in this part of Wales.

The landscape seen from these monuments is extremely dramatic. All four tombs are aligned N–S, and all appear to face Gilman Point rather than the sea (like the capstone of the King's Quoit, Manorbier). Pendine Sands and the surrounding headland are clearly visible beyond Gilman Point.

In addition to the four monuments mentioned below, a possible long mound is located west, above the extensive rock outcropping between Morfa Bychan B and C (sited at SN 2213 0751). This site, described as a wedged-shaped long cairn, measures

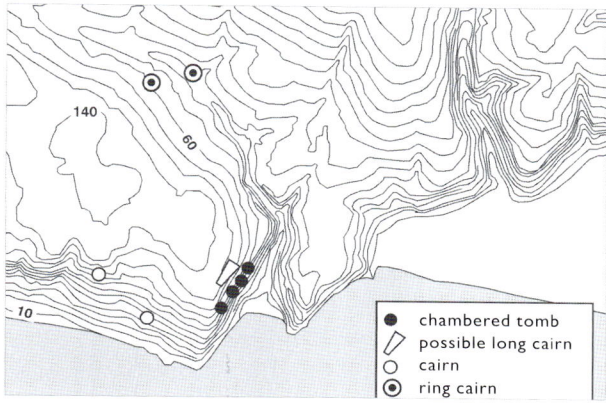

Plan of the Morfa Bychan group of monuments (after Barker 1992)

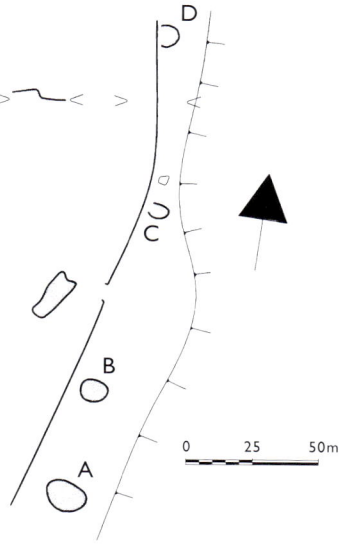

Morfa Bychan: plan showing the location of all the monuments

roughly 20m in length by 10m in width and is aligned NE–SW. The mound was first recorded by Treherne in 1926, and later by Murphy in 1985 (Murphy 1985). If it is a long mound, the size and, more importantly, its shape would make this the earliest monument within the cemetery group, and could be compared with monuments constructed within the Cotswold-Severn tradition, such as Parc-le-Breos-Cwm (GLA 4) and the Nicholaston monument (GLA 11), both on the Gower Peninsula.

Barker correctly refers to this series of monuments as the Morfa Bychan cemetery (1992, 10). The four monuments sited below the rock outcropping are oriented N–S. Morfa Bychan A, B and C are intervisible with each other, and all are similar in construction. Morfa Bychan D, a submerged monument set within the loose rock debris, lies closest to the outcropping.

94. Morfa Bychan A
SN 2213 0743, SM NO. CM053
County Reference Number: CRM 2

Morfa Bychan A is the farthest south of the group, and stands at around 75m AOD. It comprises a single capstone, now dislodged, which was originally supported by nine uprights. The stone material is local, possibly frost-shattered debris from the nearby cliff face. The chamber is rectangular (measuring 2m x 1.5m), with evidence of a passage (Castleden 1992). This, plus remnants of an oval cairn, place Morfa Bychan A in the passage grave tradition. Its landscape setting suggests the tomb could be compared with the Ynys Môn passage grave of Barclodiad-y-Gawres (ANG 4), albeit on a much smaller and less impressive scale. Castleden (1992) suggests that the other three Morfa Bychan monuments may also be passage graves. If this is the case, these monuments are

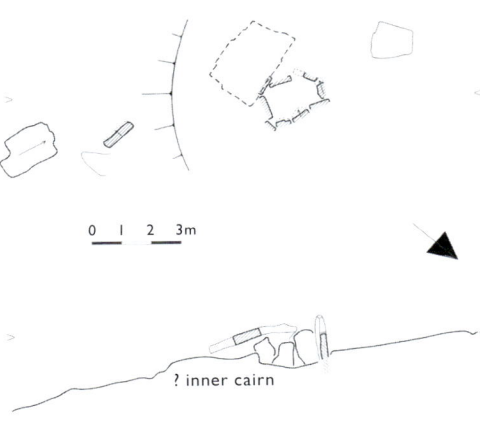

Plan and section of the chamber belonging to Morfa Bychan A (after Barker 1992)

Morfa Bychan A, overlooking Gilman Point and Pendine Sands

The squared capstone of Morfa Bychan A, looking west

possibly the only group within this part of Wales that conform to the passage grave tradition.

When recently visiting this monument, I saw little or no evidence of either a passage or cairn material. The whole area in front of the cliff face was littered with weather-shattered rock debris. I suggest the tomb's morphology represents a local tradition very much utilising local materials and applying a local/regional architectural style. The uprights and capstones are either cut or conveniently shaped by nature, rather than by design. In the case of Morfa Bychan D, there is evidence of a single passage upright, but this is by no means conclusive evidence that it is a passage grave.

This monument, along with Morfa Bychan B, C and D, was excavated and restored during the early part of the twentieth century (1910–1). A few artefacts were found in a stratified sequence within the chamber of Morfa Bychan A. In the southern part of the chamber, a small lithic assemblage was recovered, including scrapers and waste flake material. Also found were charcoal and a few fragments of bone (Ward 1910). The artefacts, according to Ward (1918, 69–70), overlay 'a rude pavement'. The presence of fragments of human bone probably reflects cremation burial deposition. The presence of cremated human remains suggests that this and other monuments along this upland ridge are Late Neolithic in date.

95. MORFA BYCHAN B
SN 2214 0748, SM NO. CM053
County Reference Number: CRM 3

Morfa Bychan B stands on a natural ledge about 50m north of Morfa Bychan A, at around 100m AOD. Here, there is clear evidence for a small cairn on the southern extent, but certainly no passage. Barker (1992, 12) questions whether or not this monument had a proper entrance. However, I suggest that a possible entrance may be located to the south, facing the open sea. A similar opening exists with Morfa Bychan A.

According to Gardner Wilkinson (1870, 42–3), the pear-shaped cairn was surrounded by kerbing. However, rock debris now covers any traces of such a feature. In the vicinity of the cairn are two large flat slabs, one of which is a possible displaced capstone. The chamber, now much disturbed, is pentagonal and consists of six or seven (confused) uprights that open out to the north-west. Some of the uprights have slumped into the centre of the chamber, probably as a result of dislodgement from antiquarian excavation. Further disturbance is found with a shallow depression extending around the chamber. To the west of the chamber are three uprights that may represent an E–W aligned passage. However, one of the uprights is oriented N–S and contradicts any apparent E–W passage alignment.

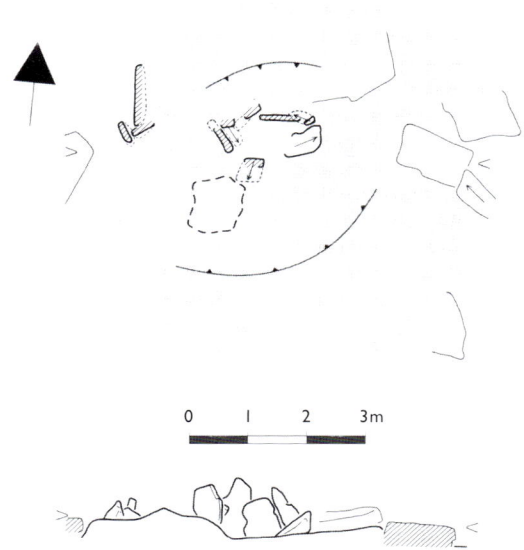

Plan and section of the chamber belonging to Morfa Bychan B (after Barker 1992)

Treherne, Gibbins, Clarke and Ward excavated the site on a single day (17 May, 1910). Apart from discovering previous excavation disturbance, three flint flakes were found (Ward 1918).

96. Morfa Bychan C
SN 2216 0754, SM NO. CM053
County Reference Number: CRM 4

Approximately 90m north of Morfa Bychan A is the third tomb, standing at around 110m AOD. Gardner Wilkinson first recorded the site in 1870 and described it as 'an irregular enclosure of uncertain time' (1870, 43). However, Treherne (1911), Ward (1918), Daniel (1950) and Barker (1992) have all speculated that this site is a megalithic burial chamber.[83] I would add that the morphology of this monument and its landscape setting is very similar to others within this group. According to Castleden (1992), this tomb, now much-damaged, consists merely of a collection of stones. I have noted a small section of what may be a capstone and at least ten uprights arranged as a polygonal chamber and passage, as well as traces of a low mound.

I have also noted that the chamber area is Y-shaped (in plan), delineated by a series of uprights and a possible sill-stone. These uprights, along with a number of recumbent stones, form the eastern corner of a large chamber and a possible passage approximately 2.5m long. In total there are 12 uprights. There is no trace of any entrance. However, the E–W alignment of six stones appears to terminate at the eastern edge of the cairn mound. The construction of passages elsewhere tends to favour this orientation. If this is so, one of the large uprights that forms the eastern section of the chamber may act as a doorway that was periodically removed in order to gain access to the chamber. It is also probable that the two recumbent stones within the chamber area are in fact dislodged chamber uprights.

An upright stone, located along the north-eastern edge of the mound, may be the remains of kerbing. It is probable that further kerbing underlies loose cairn material.

This monument marks the axis point whereby intervisibility exists between Morfa Bychan A and B, but not with D. Morfa Bychan A, B and C have definite landscape affinities that are seaward. However, Morfa Bychan D, although having intervisibility with the sea, is oriented inland. The three seaward monuments are constructed in a similar fashion.

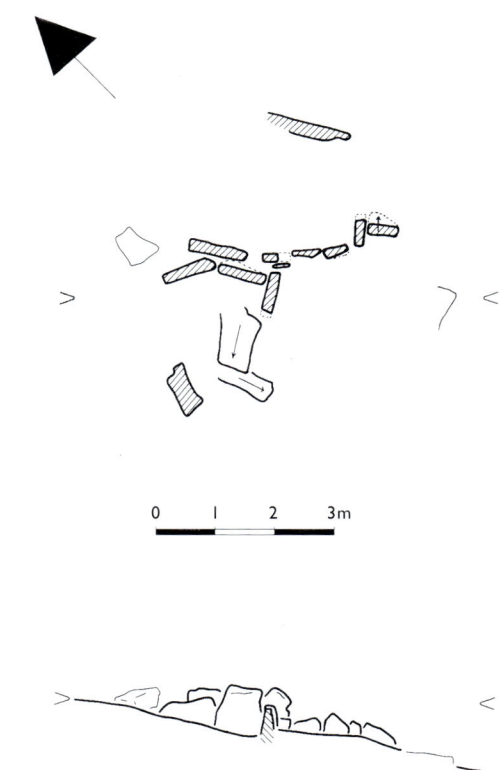

Plan and section of the chamber belonging to Morfa Bychan C (after Barker 1992)

97. Morfa Bychan D
SN 2216 0755, SM NO. CM053
County Reference Number: CRM 5

Four of the five tombs utilise the surrounding geology and are largely hidden within the immediate landscape. Several monuments are constructed of rock-cut chambers. The fourth monument within this group is possibly the most interesting. Again, located on a natural ledge just below the cliff face, Morfa Bychan D has a chamber submerged within the rocky soil. The position of this monument, constructed up against a rock face, is similar to sites such as Carn Llidi (PEM 21–2) on St David's Head and Garn Gilfach (PEM 15) on Dinas Head. With these and other monuments within the Morfa Bychan group, there appears to be a deliberate attempt to conceal the precise location of each monument. Indeed, the position of Morfa Bychan D is by far the most concealed of all the Morfa Bychan monuments, and cannot be seen from any position east of Ragwen Point.

The large capstone (almost at ground level) covers a rectangular chamber and is supported by at least 11 uprights, with irregular drystone walling set between each upright. Outside, there is a possible small, low earthen mound. The size of the mound is difficult to calculate but certainly extends some 2.3m around the chamber area. Cut into the mound, and – unusually – at the side of the chamber, is an entrance with a doubtful passage. Two uprights are positioned on the north-western cut. Immediately to the west of this cut is a large slab, which may be a passage roofing stone. The entrance looks out towards Gilman Point and Pendine Sands beyond.

The chamber appears to have been constructed by underpinning the large capstone with initially natural slabs. These appear to have then been replaced with purposely-placed uprights. The chamber is partially cut into the surrounding geology.

This tomb and others within the group were discovered by Treherne and Evans on 11 June, 1910, and excavated a few days later (Treherne and Evans 1911). The massive capstone (4.1m x 2.3m) and passage were partially covered by loose cairn rubble, whilst a thin slab blocked the chamber entrance. Inside the chamber was 'a considerable accumulation of brownish soil, on the surface of which lay bones of recent animals' (Ward 1918, 72–3). The excavation, conducted over two days, was halted when it was discovered that the capstone had become unsafe, and the chamber uprights had started to slip inwards.

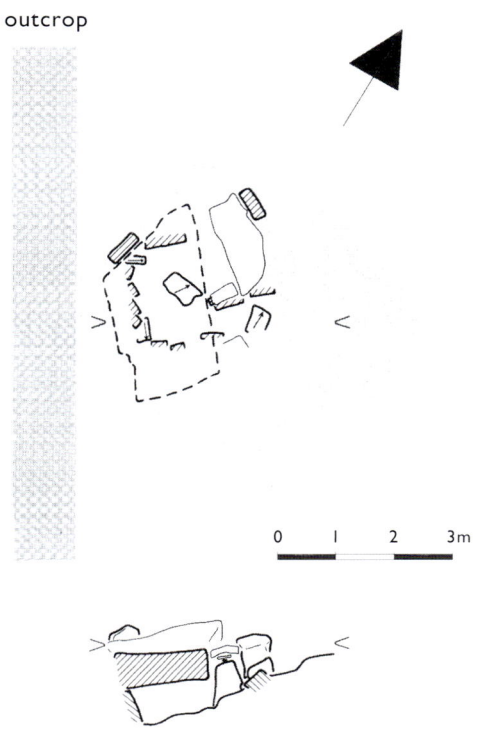

Plan and section of the chamber belonging to Morfa Bychan D (after Barker 1992)

The rock-cut monument of Morfa Bychan D, looking west

The excavators found the original chamber floor but no artefacts. Since Ward's excavation, three uprights within the northern corner of the chamber have been removed and the southern section of the probable passage has partially collapsed inwards.

TEN

Isolated Monuments

Most of the monuments discussed have fitted comfortably within a series of groups that are scattered throughout Wales. In the south-western and western regions, are a limited number of sites that can be considered isolated monuments. However, with further investigation, one comes across other enigmatic sites that are damaged, lost or unidentified. I have chosen three of the more well-known and intact sites from regional Historic Environment Records. There are probably many more that deserve recognition.

The Cerrig Llwydion (double) dolmen may be designated as an isolated monument, to the extent that its nearest definite neighbour is well over 20km away to the south (Twlc y Filiast); although Barker (1992) recognises a possible chambered monument 8km to the north-east – Yr Hen Llech. My analysis reveals that the mean distance between tombs in this part of Wales is between 2km and 3km. It is probable, therefore, that Cerrig Llwydion – and for that matter, Bedd Taliesin (MER 11), some 70km north, near Aberystwyth – would, at one time, have been part of a more concentrated distribution. It is highly likely that other monuments located around these sites have either been destroyed or are yet to be discovered. The extensive inventory in Barker's monograph (1992) is testimony to this, in which he identifies up to an additional 85 sites that are either lost, misidentified or possible sites. Several of these, including the Eithbed complex, are listed in this volume.

The Twlc y Filiast monument, again isolated from the main megalithic clustering in South-west Wales, can be considered a substantial monument, and unusual in that it is located away from the sea and close to a stream. Few monuments, even those that form the Inland Pembrokeshire Group, appear to conform to the landscape rules set by Twlc y Filiast. The nearest group of monuments with clear megalithic morphology is the Morfa Bychan cemetery, located some 13km to the south-west.

The rectangular chamber and large capstone of Twlc y Filiast resembles the capstone present on the Hanging Stone monument (PEM 24), but the latter is sited within a completely different landscape. The Twlc y Filiast monument is hidden within a narrow, secluded, steep-sided valley; its builders clearly having the desire to conceal the monument. Although it is not clear if the landscape around Twlc y Filiast was cleared, the mound and the surrounding rock outcropping would have hidden this most sacred place from certain individuals or strands within Neolithic society.

The Bedd Taliesin monument, located in the parish of Llanfihangel Genau-y-Glyn in central west Wales, is rather an enigma in that very little is known about it. It is not catalogued in any of the popular volumes of Welsh megaliths except by Barber & Williams (1989, 118–9). However, references (albeit fragmentary) are made to it in nineteenth-century accounts of the site in *Archaeologia Cambrensis*. Unlike other isolated monuments in Wales, Bedd Taliesin is sited within a typical monument location; that is, not on the highest point within the immediate landscape but at the same time possessing commanding views, in this instance to the north and west towards the Dovey estuary.

Although only three sites are mentioned in this chapter, there are clearly more. As stated earlier, Barker (1992) has done much to identify the potential number of monuments once distributed across the Neolithic landscape of South-west Wales, probably doubling the number of monuments that survive the archaeological record. The number of extant monuments surviving today can be doubled or even tripled in each of the ten core areas of Wales.

98. Twlc y Filiast, Llangynog
SN 3383 1608, SM NO. CM055
County Reference Number: CRM 6

Twlc y Filiast, also known as Ebenezer and Arthur's Table, is one of a handful of Megalithic monuments in total isolation from the main megalith clusters within South-west Wales; and yet it has a similar landscape setting to those that occupy the coastal zones in neighbouring Pembrokeshire. The monument, standing at around 124m AOD, lacks visibility with the sea, despite standing only 5.5km from the coast and around 4km from the Afon Taf and Tywi Estuaries. Its excavator, Hubert Savory, remarked that the site is hidden, lying in a steep-sided valley with a small stream running by (Savory 1956b).

This much-denuded monument has similar architecture to a number of monuments in South-west Wales: in particular Treffynnon, Llandeloy (PEM 19), Gwal-y-Filiast, Llanboidy (CRM 1) and the Hanging Stone at Burton (PEM 24). It is only the Gwal-y-Filiast monument that has not only similar architecture but also an identical landscape position, standing on the eastern banks of the Afon Taf.

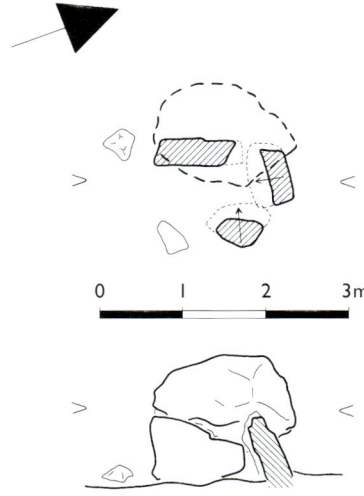

Plan and section of the Twlc-y-Filiast monument (after Barker 1992)

Twlc-y-Filiast dolmen, looking west

The tomb comprises a small, rectangular chamber of three uprights. A displaced capstone located outside the chamber, is supported by two of the three chamber uprights. These uprights stand in shallow sockets that are packed with small stones. At the southern end of the chamber is evidence of a sill, delineated by the setting of five small up-turned slabs. Houlder (1978) argues that the chamber is trapezoidal, but I would suggest that the shape is actually rectangular.

Early investigations found no trace of a covering mound (Daniel 1950). However, an excavation carried out in 1953 by the esteemed archaeologist Hubert Savory discovered the remnants of an elongated mound, measuring 18m by 9m, a possible antechamber and a series of ritual pits. Three shallow stone settings and a fallen slab delineated the antechamber, to the south of the main chamber. The mound is oriented NNE–SSW, following the axis of the valley, and one side of the mound has been eroded by the brook. Savory (1953, 225–8) suggests that this possible Portal Dolmen had an extensively damaged entrance area.

The 1953 excavation yielded very few artefacts. Nothing was found in the chamber except for a dark brown earth deposit containing fragments of charcoal. This deposit was cut into the clay floor, suggesting recent antiquarian disturbance. Indeed, Savory recovered from various overlying contexts up to 650 artefacts, including ceramics that dated to the post-medieval period. However, a small flint scraper, a stone pendant and a few fragments of unidentifiable pottery were recovered close by within the cairn. The stone pendant is said to represent a metal axe, suggesting that this artefact is either Late Neolithic or Early Bronze Age in date. Uncovered below the cairn was a charcoal-flecked clay surface that may represent pre-cairn activity, or the preparation phase prior to the construction of the monument. Within the area of stone settings were found flecks of charcoal and burnt bone. A selected human bone fragment from one of the pits within the chamber was radiocarbon-dated to the Middle Bronze Age (3214±70 BP). This late date suggests the monument was in use for a considerable amount of time.

On a recent visit to this site in 2023, I noted that perhaps seven stones appeared to delineate a possible narrow passage and forecourt area. Indeed, Savory records a curved line of stones south-west of the antechamber, which may demarcate the remains of a revetted forecourt area. If this is so, then the antechamber could actually be the remains of a passage (1956b). These additions could establish Twlc y Filiast as an important site, especially as it is located away from the main South-west Wales Group of monuments.

99. Bedd Taliesin, Llanfihangel
SN 67145 91180, SM NO. CD067
County Reference Number: MER 11

Bedd Taliesin, one of the most enigmatic and isolated monuments in central West Wales, stands on the west-facing slopes of Moel y Garn, north-west of the settlement of Tal-y-bont and the Dovey estuary,

Pre-excavation image, looking west and in an open landscape

ISOLATED MONUMENTS 235

at around 250m AOD. The site has been known for some time. Thomas Evans remarked in 1781:

> The spurious sepulchre of the Bard Taliesin, who flourished in the 6th century and one which stood near the highway, has, within these five years, been entirely plundered and the broken stones are now converted into gateposts (107).

Bedd Taliesin has a loose connection with the sixth-century poet Taliesin. Taliesin is considered to be the founder of a Welsh poetic tradition. The seventeenth-century antiquarian Edward Lhuyd recorded a local story about the monument, remarking that if one was to spend the night at Bedd Taliesin, you would wake up as a poet or a madman!

This monument, sometimes considered to be a Bronze Age round cairn, consists of a well-preserved central passage or long chamber, with a displaced capstone set within an oval or long-denuded mound measuring 12–13m in diameter and standing around 1.5m in height. The mound appears to be delineated by a series of kerbstones (Rees 1992, 55). The displaced capstone measures 1.75m x 1.2m and is 0.45m in thickness. Around the capstone and the chamber are a number of loose, sub-angular and angular stone blocks, which either form part of the cairn mound or may be fragments of another capstone. It seems likely that the capstone is not *in situ* and probably overlies further chamber or passage activity.

Surprisingly perhaps, there has been very little archaeological investigation of this site. It is certainly outside the major Neolithic core areas of Wales, but is close to important Mesolithic environmental sites along the Dovey estuary and within the marshlands of Cors Fochno, near Borth. Approximately 4km to the south-east of the site, are the remnants of a Late Neolithic/Early Bronze Age landscape, including a standing stone (located at SN 689 877). A large number of cairns are also located 2km to the north and east of the monument on Foel Goch, which overlooks the Dovey estuary.

According to the RCAHMW (1921), this monument dates to the Bronze Age. However, its sheer megalithic appearance suggests a Neolithic date, and in some ways it is similar to the sub-megalithic monument of Capel Garmon (DEN 3). If so, this monument may possess a trapezoidal mound with a horned forecourt and false portal, and with the chamber and passage alignment located within the centre of the monument; however, only excavation will tell.

Bedd Taliesin, showing the partly-collapsed chamber and dislodged capstone

Bedd Taliesin, showing the dislodged capstone, looking north

100. Cerrig Llwydion, Cynwyl Elved
SN 3738 3258, SM NO. CM047
County Reference Number: CRM 10

Cerrig Llwydion is a substantial tomb incorporating at least two chambers with a possible long mound, perhaps having similar dimensions to that of Pentre Ifan (PEM 5) near Newport. If this is the case, then other smaller tombs may have been located close by. There is certainly evidence of megalithic structures in woodland at Nant-y-ffin (SN 5527 3060) and the site of Yr Hen Llech (SN 4128 3602), located 17.5km and 4km to the east of Cerrig Llwydion respectively.[84] The presence of Bronze Age barrows and cairns in the vicinity indicates ritual and

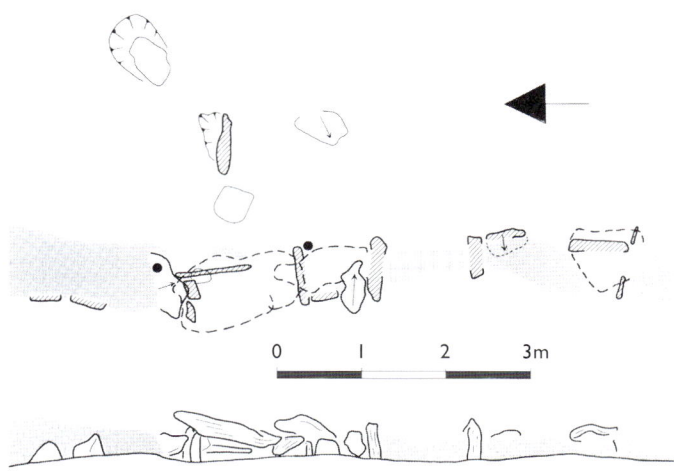

Plan and cross-section of the chamber arrangement at Cerrig Llwydion (after Barker 1992)

The northern chamber of Cerrig Llwydion, looking north-west

The western side of Cerrig Llwydion showing the remnants of the mound, looking west

symbolic continuity within the landscape. It could be suggested that the Cerrig Llwydion dolmen housed at least two members of a ranked society, with one burial per chamber. The erection of single burial barrows and cairns during the subsequent Bronze Age would have carried on the 'tradition' of high-status single burials. On this basis I suggest the monument was constructed and in use during the Late Neolithic and was possibly contemporary with the smaller earth-fast tombs farther south.

The denuded monument of Cerrig Llwydion, also referred to as Conwil Elvet, is one of a handful of monuments benefitting from the protection afforded by being incorporated into a stone and turf boundary wall. There appears to be little evidence of a covering mound. However, disturbance in the field to the east of the monument may represent mound material. Large stone blocking may be cairn material or even part of the chamber fabric.

This isolated monument, standing at 291m AOD, was first commented on as far back as 1811, when Carlisle describes the site thus:

ISOLATED MONUMENTS 237

On the side-land summit of a high mountain, facing the south, is a centre stone of a huge magnitude, from 10 to 15 tons, horizontal, oblong, two feet thick, supported by four uprights, one of which has declined from its original position, and sunk deeper into the ground. Four other similar, but smaller stones, of about four to five tons, surround it: but these have all slipped from their respective fulcra, and now lie in a shelving position. Scattered about, at various and irregular distances around, are several smaller stones, distributed and broken up by the masons building the house at Nant y clawdd ucha.

The description by Carlisle infers that the site has, in the past, been partially reconstructed and has suffered a similar fate to other stone monuments in western Britain, in that it has served to support late post-medieval road and industrial infrastructure. In 1877, Barnwell reassessed the site. His description indicates that little had changed since the early nineteenth century. Barnwell claims that there were traces of an oval mound measuring roughly 21.5m by 15.2m (Barnwell 1877, 82–6).[85] Later, Jones notes that the capstone had fractured by 1907 (Jones 1907, 141).

The large, irregular, elongated capstone is supported at the northern end by three uprights forming a small rectangular chamber. The capstone (and therefore the chamber) is, unusually, oriented N–S. Directly behind the main capstone is a smaller slab and what appears to be an extension of the main chamber. Approximately 3m behind the main chamber is a second chambered structure, comprising a capstone and five uprights (Barker 1992). Daniel (1950) classifies this monument as a large cist, whereas Houlder (1978, 175) has suggested that this monument is a segmented cist that is unique to Wales. Barker (1992, 17) tends to agree with this comment, but adds that probably more internal architecture existed. Although the architecture suggests a gallery grave-type monument, I firmly believe that Cerrig Llwydion was a double-dolmen of massive proportions.

Although isolated from other similar monuments, Cerrig Llwydion lies within a dense concentration of Bronze Age barrows. The landscape is bare, almost moor-like, the barrows dominating all of the high ground. However, the tomb is typical of megalithic monuments in this part of Wales, in that it is sited on a ridge, rather than the highest point in the landscape. It overlooks a river valley – the Afon Bele – and has dominant views to the south, towards the upper reaches of the Afon Duad valley and the eastern section of the ridge on which it stands.

CONCLUDING REMARKS

The introduction to this book aims to give some insight into how and why these monuments were constructed, used and later abandoned. However, there are still many questions that remain to be answered. Scholars such as Cummings & Whittle (2004), Tilley (1994), Thomas (1999), Whittle (2003), Darvill (2004) and Ray and Thomas (2018) have attempted to incorporate a number of socio-political mechanisms which use various conventional and philosophical approaches. Furthermore, and despite a near-complete lack of physical evidence, the detail of the drama, emotion and religious experience has been boldly proposed by Deveraux (2001), Dronfield (1996) and Bowen & Pritchard (2023), each of whom has looked at such thought-provoking topics as acoustics, shamanism and sublime experiences inside and outside chambered monuments. Each of these texts has gone some way to picture the ritual life and death of the Neolithic.

I have drawn together 100 monuments from nine distinct Neolithic core areas of Wales, as well as several monuments within the central Marches. It is highly likely that as many as three or four times that number existed during Neolithic times. The antiquarian accounts on Ynys Môn, for example, give testimony to the number of monuments that were either damaged or destroyed between the seventeenth and nineteenth centuries; and what we see today is maybe only a fraction of what was being constructed and used during the Neolithic. Antiquarian accounts in other Welsh core areas suggest similar scenarios. Given this, I think one has to be careful when making general assumptions on, say, the trends in site location or deposition of material culture (see Flemming 1999).

The 100 or so monuments discussed in this volume represent a 2,000-year social-religious movement during which the dead were as important as the living. I would say, at this juncture, that more sites could have been added to this book; however, many of these sites are either destroyed, partially destroyed, lost or of questionable origin (inasmuch as it isn't clear whether they are Neolithic or later).[86] As suggested throughout the volume, there appear to be many variations on a generic architectural theme. All monuments are constructed of stone; all possess a chamber; some have a passage; some with a façade; and nearly all have a covering mound or cairn. The Welsh assemblage has been chronologically classified into four main architectural groups – Portal Dolmens, long mounds, passage graves and earth-fast monuments. Portal Dolmens are considered the earliest, followed by long mounds, and so forth. The Irish Sea Province, identified and discussed at length by Lynch (1970) and more recently by Cummings & Whittle (2004), appears to have been a melting pot where many different types of architecture were being experimented with, resulting in multi-phased construction activity.

We can never know what people in our recent past must have thought of these enigmatic monuments. The fact that little or no destruction occurred up until the early post-medieval period suggests that they were tolerated or even revered. For example, the Breconshire monument of Ty Illtyd (BRE 6) was used as a hermitage for St Illtyd during the medieval period. Here, in great contemplation, St Illtyd carved a series of Christian symbols on the uprights of the chamber. His conviction to carve such symbols suggests he felt the need to establish his mark on a monument that had been known for many generations. Likewise, many of our monuments contain modern graffiti and, similar to the example of St Illtyd, we are creating our mark – our history on a series of artificially-constructed stones with an ancestral past.

Old ways, new ways

The transition from a hunting/fishing and gathering way of life to sedentism, agriculture and burying the dead in a certain way, would have been no overnight affair. The spread of agriculture, from the Fertile Crescent of the Middle East to north-western Europe took around 6,000 years. Was this (what I call *Neolithicisation*), an invasion of ideas or an invasion of people? Certainly, researchers such as Humphry Case (1969) have advocated that grain, pottery, cattle and, more importantly, new ideas came over with colonising groups via boats. However, many of the old ways of doing things – food production, gender roles and the celebration of the life stages – must have been maintained, at least in part during the early part of the Neolithic. If this were the case, the transition between the Mesolithic and Neolithic becomes more difficult to define; and, arguably, the transition period may have extended some 1,000 years. It is within this transition that the British Isles witnesses the construction of the first burial monuments.

Dealing with death

In the past, archaeologists have tended to draw a dramatic line between the Neolithic and the preceding Mesolithic. Essentially, the Mesolithic is a period based on economy and the Neolithic a period of death and burial. This unbalanced approach is based on the surviving archaeological evidence, and it is obvious that other things were going on during the Neolithic besides the treatment of the dead. Similarly, during the Mesolithic, and based on southern Scandinavian burial evidence, hunter/gatherers were symbolically burying their dead as well. The treatment of the dead appears to be a most important process in both societies. Certainly, during the Neolithic in Britain, it is not just the monument and how it is constructed that is important, but also the way in which the body was prepared and positioned within his or her final resting place, and the chosen landscape in which these sites were constructed.

In the case of the chambered monuments in Western Britain, the dead or their remains were usually placed within chambers, and sometimes in the passage area. From the sometimes-fragmentary evidence, three clear burial processes are in operation – disarticulation, excarnation and cremation. These burial processes appear to be very different from the cemetery burials of the Late Mesolithic sites of Skateholm and Vedbæk in southern Scandinavia. Here, male, female and child extended burials are accompanied with ornate grave goods. More interestingly, some burials appear to represent family groups, and all burials have been garnished with a light scattering of red ochre. The grave goods and the red ochre probably represent items that were to be taken with the deceased to the next life. Of course, parallels exist with the way in which the dead were treated during the Neolithic. It appears that the monument itself was an extension of the body; the chambers, façade, passage and the mound all have an intimate association with the way in which the dead were presented, treated and garnished before interment (Nash 2020).

Despite the archaeological evidence, it is now becoming clearer that chambered monuments were more than just repositories for the dead. They also appear to embrace many social and political attributes that are inextricably intertwined with the day-to-day life of the social elite. This volume has highlighted a number of traits, which display ostentatiousness of architectural design: an essential prerequisite for any social elite.

APPENDIX 1: SUMMARY OF SITE DATA

Site No.	County Ref. no.	Site Name	Grid Reference[87]	Metres AOD	Distance from open water (km)[88]
1	BRE 1	Pen yr Wyrlod	SO 2248 3986	251	54.0
2	BRE 4	Ffostyll South	SO 1789 3489	312	52.0
3	BRE 3	Ffostyll North	SO 1791 3495	312	52.0
4	BRE 8	Pipton Long Cairn	SO 1604 3727	145	55.0
5	BRE 5	Ty Isaf	SO 1819 2906	211	50.5
6	BRE 11	Croesllechau	SO 1672 3626	140	51.0
7	BRE 14	Penywyrlod	SO 1505 3156	253	48.0
8	BRE 6	Ty Illtyd	SO 0984 2638	215	53.0
9	BRE 10	Mynydd Troed	SO 16145 28417	258	51.0
10	BRE 7	Gwernvale	SO 2110 1920	69	46.0
11	BRE 12	Garn Goch	SO 2123 1771	84	45.0
12	RAD 2	Clyro Court Farm Long Barrow	SO 2123 4313	90	56.0
13	BRE 2	Little Lodge Barrow	SO 1822 3806	137	54.0
14	HRF 1	Arthur's Stone	SO 31885 43127	280	52.0
15	HRF 4	Cross Lodge Long Barrow	SO 33247 41697	180	50.5
16	HRF 6	Dunseal Long Barrow	SO 39117 33845	175	51.0
17	GLA 4	Parc-le-Breos-Cwm	SS 5372 8983	31	1.5

18	GLA 3	Maen Ceti	SS 4913 9055	147	2.2
19	GLA 1	Sweyne's Howes North	SS 4211 8991	140	0.8
20	GLA 2	Sweyne's Howes South	SS 4209 8981	136	0.8
21	GLA 5	Penmaen Burrows	SS 5315 8813	46	0.3
22	GLA 9	Tinkinswood	ST 0921 7331	75	6.6
23	GLA 10	Maes y Felin	ST 1009 7230	70	5.6
24	MON 1	Cleppa Park	ST 2740 8571	43	4.3
25	MON 2	Y Gaer Llwyd	ST 4476 9678	209	10.7
26	MON 3	Heston Brake	ST 5052 8865	35	1.5
27	ANG 1	Trefignath	SH 25860 80547	19	1.2
28	ANG 2	Presaddfed	SH 34757 80890	20	5.2
29	ANG 3	Ty Newydd	SH 3442 7386	37	2.7
30	ANG 4	Barclodiad y Gawres	SH 3290 7072	19	0.1
31	ANG 5	Din Dryfol	SH 39562 72500	18	6.0
32	ANG 6	Bodowyr	SH 46220 68165	38	3.2
33	ANG 7	Bryn Celli Ddu	SH 50850 70175	33	1.6
34	ANG 8	Bryn yr Hen Bobl	SH 5190 6900	33	0.3
35	ANG 9	Plas Newydd	SH 52000 69720	30	0.2
36	ANG 10	Ty Mawr	SH 53855 72130	73	0.8
37	ANG 11	Hen-Drefor	SH 55095 77322	112	5.5
38	ANG 13	Pant y Saer	SH 50967 82405	99	1.3
39	ANG 14	Lligwy	SH 50130 86040	63	1.1
40	CRN 1	Llety'r Filiast	SH 77062 82950	165	0.8
41	CRN 3	Maen y Bardd	SH 74125 71892	305	5.3
42	CRN 4	Porth Llwyd	SH 7703 6770	8	14.1
43	CRN 5	Sling	SH 6055 6696	210	3.5
44	DEN 1	Hendre Waelod	SH 79290 74810	21	5.0
45	DEN 2	Tyddyn Bleiddyn	SJ 00732 72462	122	11.5
46	DEN 3	Capel Garmon	SH 81785 54317	264	26.0
47	FLT 1	Gop Cairn	SJ 08657 80162	250	4.3

48	FLT 2	Gop Cave	SJ 08642 80077	215	4.4
49	MER 7	Tyn-y-Coed	SJ 04760 39622	154	37.0
50	MER 1	Gwern Einion	SH 58730 28597	106	1.9
51	MER 2	Bron-y-Foel-Isaf-West	SH 60795 24585	214	4.2
52	MER 3	Dyffryn Ardudwy	SH 59135 22740	50	1.8
53	MER 4	Cors-y-Gedol	SH 60280 22810	191	2.9
54	MER 5	Carneddau Hengwm North	SH 61325 20575	283	2.4
55	MER 6	Carneddau Hengwm South	SH 61305 20480	283	2.4
56	CRN 6	Penarth	SH 42992 51072	26	0.7
57	CRN 7	Bachwen	SH 40770 49487	24	0.2
58	CRN 8	Ystum Cegid Isaf	SH 49875 41330	99	3.2
59	CRN 9	Cefn Isaf	SH 48365 40875	90	3.6
60	CRN 10	Cist Cerrig	SH 54330 38397	73	1.9
61	CRN 11	Four Crosses	SH 39897 38492	66	2.6
62	CRN 12	Mynydd Cefn Amwlch	SH 22975 34540	99	2.0
63	CRN 13	Tan-y-Muriau	SH 23770 28765	132	0.5
64	PEM 1	Llech-y-Tribedd	SN 1005 4319	188	1.4
65	PEM 2	Trellyffant	SN 0822 4252	137	1.1
66	PEM 3	Carreg Coetan	SN 0602 3935	8	0.5
67	PEM 4	Cerrig y Gof	SN 0365 3890	46	0.8
68	PEM 5	Pentre Ifan	SN 09940 37022	145	4.2
69	PEM 27	Bedd-yr-Afanc	SN 10800 34592	142	7.9
70	PEM 7–9	Garn Wen Cemetery	SM 9483 3903	90–95	0.3
71	PEM 13	Carn Wnda	SM 93310 39239	135	1.0
72	PEM 15	Garn Gilfach	SM 90895 38985	183	1.9
73	PEM 16	Ffyst Samson	SM 9059 3492	128	2.3
74	PEM 17	Trewalter Llwyd	SM 8682 3176	124	2.0
75	PEM 18	Carreg Samson	SM 8483 3350	42	0.3
76	PEM 28	Ffynnondruidion	SM 9204 3679	107	3.4
77	PEM 14	Parc-y-Cromlech	SM 9422 3907	142	1.0

78	PEM 23	Coetan Arthur	SM 72246 28025	38	0.3
79	PEM 19	Treffynnon	SM 85360 28655	125	4.4
80	PEM 20	St Elvies Farm	SM 81205 23945	61	0.4
81	PEM 21–22	Carn Llidi	SM 7352 2789	122	0.9
82	PEM 47	White House	SM 82545 28380	91	4.1
83	CRM 1	Gwal-y-Filiast	SN 17045 25580	100	18.0
84	PEM 6	Mountain	SN 16575 32850	236	13.0
85	PEM 10	The Altar	SM 9828 2812	347	10.1
86	PEM 11	Garn Turne	SM 97935 27255	137	10.2
87	PEM 12	Parc-y-llyn	SM 9823 2659	128	11.1
88	CRM 20	Carn Besi	SN 1560 2768	236	15.0
89	PEM 119	The Cuckoo Stones	SN 06438 03903	32	5.9
90	PEM 31	Eithbed Cemetery Group	SN 07960 28635	240–250	11.9
91	PEM 24	The Hanging Stone	SM 9722 0822	75	2.9
92	PEM 25	Devil's Quoit	SM 88655 00810	37	1.0
93	PEM 26	King's Quoit	SS 05897 97267	18	0.1
94	CRM 2	Morfa Bychan A	SN 2213 0743	75	0.2
95	CRM 3	Morfa Bychan B	SN 2214 0748	100	0.2
96	CRM 4	Morfa Bychan C	SN 2216 0754	110	0.2
97	CRM 5	Morfa Bychan D	SN 2216 0755	120	0.2
98	CRM 6	Twlc y Filiast	SN 3383 1608	124	6.1
99	MER 11	Bedd Taliesin	SN 67145 91180	220	6.7
100	CRM 10	Cerrig Llwydion	SN 3738 3258	291	12.4

APPENDIX 2: RADIOCARBON DATES FOR NEOLITHIC CHAMBERED TOMBS[89]

Bryn Celli Ddu (ANG 7), Ynys Môn
    UB-7113   3320–2899 BCE   Human cranium

Carreg Coetan (PEM 3), Pembrokeshire
    CAR-392   4,830±80 BP   Charcoal sealed by stone kerb
    CAR-394   4,700±80 BP   Charcoal from socket hole of chamber
    CAR-391   4,560±80 BP   Old ground surface sealed by mound
    CAR-393   4,470±80 BP   Charcoal from within mound

Cathole Cave, The Gower Peninsula
    OXA-16605   3606–3365 BCE   Human cranium (burial?)

Garn Turne (PE 061), Pembrokeshire
    3702–3639 BCE   (beneath the capstone)
    3761–3643 BCE   (beneath the capstone)
    2464–2210 BCE   (within the forecourt area)
    2618–2470 BCE   (within the forecourt area)

Gop Cave (FLT 2), Flintshire
    OXA-22991   3318–2918 BCE   Mandible
    OXA-22992   3092–2912 BCE   Mandible
    OXA-29990   3082–2902 BCE   Human bone

Gwernvale (BRE 7), Breconshire
    CAR-113   5,050±75 BP   Pit F68 (pit below cairn)
    CAR-114   4,390±70 BP   Pit F58 (pit outside cairn)
    CAR-115   4,590±75 BP   Pit F47 (pit outside cairn)
    CAR-118   6,895±80 BP   Charcoal from Mesolithic pit

Llanfechell Burial Chamber (ANG 15), Ynys Môn
BETA-254971	3780±40 BP	Hazel nut (charcoal)

Lower Luggy Long Barrow (MNT 3), Montgomeryshire
BM-2954	4,830±45 BP	Charcoal from post hole in east ditch
BM-2955	4,710±40 BP	Charcoal from post hole at end of east ditch

Parc-le-Breos-Cwm (GLA 4), Glamorgan
OXA-6487	4,685±65 BP	Adult male, SE chamber
OXA-6496	4,850±65 BP	Adult, SE chamber
OXA-6641	4,690±55 BP	Adult, SE chamber
OXA-6488	4,780±60 BP	Adult ?male, SW chamber
OXA-6489	4,445±60 BP	Adult ?female, SW chamber
OXA-6493	4,875±55 BP	Adult, NE chamber
OXA-6494	4,645±60 BP	Adult, NE chamber
OXA-6490	4,660±60 BP	Adult ?male, NW chamber
OXA-6491	4,805±55 BP	Adult, NW chamber
OXA-6492	4,805±55 BP	Adult ?male, NW chamber
OXA-6495	3,705±55 BP	Sub-adult, passage
OXA-6497	3,750±55 BP	Adult female, passage
OXA-6499	7,665±65 BP	Badger (*meles meles*), passage
OXA-6500	10,625±80 BP	Large undulate, passage

Penywyrlod, (BRE 14), Breconshire
HAR 674	4,970±80 BP	Sample of human bone from Chamber NE II

Trefael (PEM 32), Pembrokeshire
SUERC-45386	3,653±45 BP	Cremated human juvenile bone

Trefignath (ANG 1), Ynys Môn
HAR 3932	5,050±70 BP	Palaeosol from underneath cairn
HAR 3933	2,210±70 BP	Deposit within eastern chamber

Trellyffaint (PEM 2), Pembrokeshire
BRAM 3041	4,353±33 BCE	Dated lipids extracted from dairy residues

Twlc y Filiast (CRM 6), Carmarthenshire
UB-6752	3214±70 BP	Human bone

NOTES

CHAPTER ONE

1. Early Bronze Age 2,500–1,600 BCE.
2. Glyn Daniel (1950), W.F. Grimes (1936a & 1951) and O.G.S. Crawford (1925); each recognised changes in architectural regionality.
3. Listed in Daniel (1970, 263) and arranged into the following site-type classification: (i) Randwick – Tinkinswood Group; (ii) Notsgrove – Parc-le-Broes-Cwm Group; and (iii) Belas Knap – Rodmarton Group. Other site-type classifications used for southern Britain are listed in Grinsell (1984, 11–7).
4. The forecourt area is also referred to as the façade.
5. For example, from the mid eighteenth century onwards, the corporate approaches to death had far-reaching effects on the communal burial practices and the allied trades that supported it.
6. One fine example where both Neolithic and Bronze Age activity co-exist within the same monument, can be seen at the Neolithic passage grave of La Hougue Bie, Jersey. Here, within the massive chamber area, is evidence of a rectangular cist that has been cut into the floor. Although no bone material was recovered (possibly as a result of later disturbance), it does suggest that this monument, which was used as a corporate burial monument, became a single status monument sometime between the Late Neolithic and Early Bronze Age. Other evidence includes a series of cupmarks, both within the chamber and along the 9m-passage; and most conclusive of all, is the extensive blocking of the monument and destruction of the entrance, which has been clearly dated to this transition period (Hawkes 1937; Patton 1995; Nash 1998).
7. See also Shee-Twohig (1981, 229).
8. Within the bounds of Graig Lwyd Farm.
9. Go to: https://archwilio.org.uk/wp/
10. Go to: https://coflein.gov.uk/en/
11. Lynch (1970, 46) mentions that nine full-term foetuses were found at Pant y Saer, Ynys Môn (see also Scott 1933, 224–7).
12. I would recommend the rather eclectic volume *The Ancient Stones of Wales* by Barber & Williams (1989) in which they discuss in some detail the antiquarian history and literature of some of the Welsh monuments.
13. Not to be confused with Penywyrlod (BRE 14), Talgarth.

CHAPTER TWO

14. This site is also known as Great Llanavon Farm (see Appendix A, 288 of Powell *et al* 1969).
15. Park Wood was reported in 1854 by George Clinch, and reported in O.G.S. Crawford (1925, 149–50).
16. The chamber originally measured 0.7m by 1.7m (RCAHMW 1997, 60).

17 It is believed that the two sherds formed part of a pot that would have been 0.16m in basal diameter (RCAHMW 1997, 61).

18 The RCAHMW inventory suggests that the coin may have been deliberately planted in order to confuse the excavators (1997, 62).

19 Found within the spoil were 72 teeth (see Crawford 1925, 62).

20 As a result of nineteenth-century quarrying and excavation, followed by ploughing close to the edge of the mound, the classification of this monument is difficult to assess. The RCAHMW (1997, 43) suggests the possibility that there may have been a further chamber located at either terminal end.

21 RCAHMW notes the bones that were deposited at the Royal College of Surgeons by Sir Arthur Keith, were lost during the Second World War. However, some survive at the British Museum, including a mandible (RCS 4901), and the National Museum of Wales. The latter have not been officially located.

22 It should be noted that very little of the mound fabric is present. All that is visible is a single, pointed upright stone, standing about 1.2m high.

23 Grimes states that there had been much reduction to this woodland between 1905 and 1936. Evidence to support this is seen with the presence of stools, a product of coppicing hazel (*corylus*) and alder (*alnus*).

24 Referred to as Chamber I (Britnell 1984, 5).

25 This structure is referred to as the Main Chamber. The eastern uprights to this chamber were partially exposed during quarrying.

26 This Early Neolithic four-post-hole structure was dated to 3,230 uncalibrated BC (4,100 BCE) and was in use prior to the construction of the monument.

27 Bach Neolithic Long Barrow (SO 2773 4294) is badly damaged at the northern end. Drystone walling can clearly be seen on the woodland side of the mound. The mound is oval-shaped, approximately 13m x 10m x 2m high. This tomb is the most north-westerly of the Golden Valley Group. Interestingly, Bach Long Barrow is sited on a north-facing slope, overlooking the upper Wye Valley towards the Clyro Court Farm monument.

28 A diagrammatic plan of this monument is published in Darvill (1982, 99).

29 On re-examination in 1975, only one red deer upper molar (M1) was recorded.

30 These items are now considered lost.

31 According to footnotes within the RCAHMW (1979, 53), Vulliamy presented the bone material to the Royal College of Surgeons in 1934. The assemblage was re-catalogued in 1955, registered as RCS 4.901–4.9015. Some of this assemblage was re-examined by Powers and Briggs in 1975.

32 I wish to thank Ruth Richardson for discussion concerning the morphology of this monument. Following our discussion, the author undertook an excavation within the field immediately north of Arthur's Stone Lane and the monument (Nash 2008).

33 During the late 1920s and early 1930s, the Golden Valley was extensively walked by Gavin-Robinson (1934).

34 According to Olding (2000), there are two further sites that have recently been discovered. However, their form has not been fully verified. Garway Long Barrow is located at SO 4395 2550, close to a television mast on Garway Hill, and stands around 335m AOD. According to Olding, Garway Long Barrow is well preserved. The oval mound is aligned E–W and measures 30m x 16m x 2m. A further possible long barrow may be present at SO 3440 4140 on Woodbury Hill, Peterchurch. This monument is located at about 287m AOD; the mound is approximately 1.8m in height. The barrow was discovered by Gavin-Robinson in 1936 and was later classified by Leslie Grinsell (referred to as Peterchurch I). When visiting the site in the late 1990s, Olding was informed that the site had been ploughed out. There were, however, a number of Neolithic diagnostic flint tools recovered within the vicinity of the monument. These potential additional monuments, along with

monuments at Bach, Dunseal, and Parkwood, further supports the idea that the Black Mountains massif was completely surrounded by Neolithic burial-ritual activity.

CHAPTER FOUR

35 I have labelled the Thornwell Farm monument as MON 4, continuing from Daniel's referencing system.
36 Port-hole is usually constructed of one or two pieces of rectangular-shaped stone from which a hole is cut. If two pieces are used, a semi-circular shape is cut out of each.
37 Crawford (1925, 151) suggests the length of the mound to be around 45m.
38 Also referred to in the same volume as a long cairn with a lateral chamber (Corcoran 1969, 20–1).
39 According to Crawford (1925, 157), a pencil drawing of the site was made by Sarah Ormerod, dated 9 August, 1837, and is located in the Library of the Wiltshire Archaeology Society in Devizes.
40 See Inquisitions Post Mortem of Roger, earl of Norfolk, March, 1306–7.

CHAPTER FIVE

41 James Scource of the School of Ocean Sciences (University of Wales Bangor) has suggested, based on radiocarbon dating of marine deposits, that sea-level rise inundated the present shoreline during the late Mesolithic (*pers comm*).
42 David Thomas's *Cambrian Register* of 1796 lists 30 monuments.
43 A full transcription of the excavation is in Smith (1987).
44 It should be noted that the Reverend Nicholas Owen's account should be treated as false. He is regarded as a notorious charlatan who appears to have plagiarised an original manuscript produced by the Reverend John Thomas in the early 1760s.
45 I should stress that this monument has been poorly recorded.
46 Skinner's *Ten day's Tours through the Isle of Anglesea* (1802).

47 This much-ruined monument consists of a capstone partially supported by two fallen uprights. There is no evidence of any cairn or mound.
48 Pertheduon is now collapsed, with its uprights either under or lying recumbent. Skinner's sketch (made in 1802) shows the monument to have three uprights; two lying away from the capstone.
49 Daniel (1950, 9) recognises eight classifications of burial monument. B-Dolmens are monuments that possess a polygonal chamber.
50 Lynch (1969a, 116) refers to the chamber as roughly polygonal.
51 A similar type pin has been found at Ty Isaf (BRE 5) in Breconshire (Grimes 1939, 131).
52 It presently stands within the formal gardens of Plas Newydd House.
53 Skinner appears to only mention the larger of the two chambers, and refers to the larger chamber as a separate cromlech.
54 Lynch (1969a, 121) suggests that the Glyn monument (ANG 12) is sub-megalithic in form. The monument consists of a single capstone that has been propped up against a natural limestone rock outcrop, forming a cavity. This monument was excavated but nothing was found.
55 See Lynch (1991).
56 SM No. A094.

CHAPTER SIX

57 The axe factory at Penmaenmawr, set within an extensive Bronze Age landscape, is formed from the augite granophyre scree that runs down the mountainside. Excavations here took place in 1920, where a series of rough-outs were found, which formed part of an extensive trading network over Britain. A Graig Lwyd mace head was found at Windmill Hill causewayed enclosure. Sadly, modern quarry waste dumping has destroyed much of the Neolithic activity around this part of the mountain.

58 Powell *et al* (1969, 307) classifies this site as a structure with a possible cist; or which has otherwise been wrongly classified as a chambered tomb.

59 Britnell (1991, 64) refers to Gop Cave as a rock shelter.

CHAPTER SEVEN

60 The RCHM (Merioneth) states that the site consists of a 'capstone of a demolished cromlech'. However, Daniel (1950, 197) doubts this site as being a Neolithic chambered tomb.

61 A similar relationship can be argued with that of the Bronze Age monuments located to the north of Gwern Einion (MER 1).

62 Originally noted in *Archaeologia Cambrensis* (1869, 134).

CHAPTER EIGHT

63 This site was described by Pennant 1783 as 'three chambers' (see Barnwell 1868, 481).

64 Simpson also provides an illustration of the monument with a representative account of the cupmark arrangement on the capstone (Simpson 1867, Plate IX).

65 Daniel (1950, 117) suggests there are 70 cupmarks.

CHAPTER NINE

66 Barker (1992) identifies 31 recognised monuments along with 16 sites that are listed as probable burial chambers.

67 A similar view is held by Tilley & Bennett (2001), with monuments on West Penrith, Cornwall.

68 This additional chamber is not present on two nineteenth-century illustrations made by Gardner Wilkinson (1871) and Barnwell (1884).

69 This site, known as Trefael (SN 1030 4030), comprises a single slab with at least 28 cupmarks; 17 of these are shallow depressions which, according to Barker (1992, 52), have been obscured by lichen. Lynch (1972, 79–80) suggests that this stone may well be a capstone from a now-destroyed monument.

70 See the artistic reconstruction drawing in Parker-Pearson (1993).

71 Fenton states four uprights supported the monument rather than three (1811, 31).

72 The field systems appear to be multi-phased, dating to the prehistoric, Roman and medieval periods (PRN 2631 and SM 14689 – Prehistoric, Roman and medieval field systems).

73 An account was written by an OS Field Officer in 1966.

74 Both monuments are listed in Barker (1992).

75 Noted by Lewis (1969, 137).

76 Personal communication between Barker and Lynch.

77 However, Grimes (1936c) and Daniel (1950) classify this monument as a burial chamber.

78 Not listed in Burl (1976).

79 Ward *et al* 1987, 9–13.

80 However, Barker (1992, 37) notes that certain stones incorporated into the bank, which were recorded by Frances Lynch in 1976, are no longer there.

81 First recorded by Grimes in 1936.

82 Ignore the recent Ordnance Survey 'Pathfinder' map for this area. The map clearly shows the tombs to be located about 100–200m west of their present position (inland, behind Ragwen Point).

83 I have previously suggested that this monument may house two chambers. In light of reinterpretation, I now consider the site to only have one chamber. Part of this reinterpretation is based on revisiting the site in December 2002.

CHAPTER TEN & APPENDICES

84 Both sites visited in August 1994.

85 Within the same paper, Barnwell has published three illustrations of the sites from various locations.

86 Of the other extant monuments that could have been included in Chapter 5, is the Cromlech Farm monument. This monument – described and illustrated by the Reverend Skinner in 1802 and excavated by George Smith of then Gwynedd Archaeological Trust in 2013 – was vandalised in April 2024. This sad event was reported by the author to the relevant authorities.

87 Grid referencing is taken from the regional Sites and Monuments Record (SMRs).
88 Distances are based on contemporary shorelines that are considered roughly similar to those during the Neolithic.
89 Sources: Cambria Archaeology, Clwyd-Powys Archaeological Trust, Glamorgan-Gwent Archaeological Trust and Gwynedd Archaeological Trust; and Whittle & Wysocki (1998).

BIBLIOGRAPHY

Anon., 1851. Account of the Fifth Annual Meeting of the Cambrian Archaeological Association, held at Tenby, *Archaeologia Cambrensis,* Series 2, 315.

Anon., 1864. Account of the Eighteenth Annual Meeting of the Cambrian Archaeological Association, held at Haverfordwest, *Archaeologia Cambrensis* (346–7).

Ashbee, P., 1978. *The Ancient British, Norwich,* Geo Abstracts.

Atkinson, R.J.C., 1961. 'Parc-le-Breos-Cwm', in *Archaeology in Wales* (1, 5).

—, 1968. 'Old Mortality: some aspects of Burial and Population in Neolithic England', in *Studies in Ancient Europe (Essays presented to Stuart Piggott),* Leicester University Press (83–93).

Aubrey, J., 1695. *Monumenta Britannica,* Parts 1 and 2 ed. Reprinted by Dorset Publishing Company, edited by J. Fowles.

Bagnall-Oakeley, M.E., 1889. *An account of some of the Rude Stone Monuments and Ancient Burial Mounds in Monmouthshire,* Monmouthshire & Caerleon Antiquarian Association.

Barber, C. & Williams, G.W., 1989. *The Ancient Stones of Wales,* Blorenge Books.

Baring Gould, S., 1902. 'The Exploration of Clegyr Voya', in *Archaeologia Cambrensis,* Series 6 (3, 1–11).

Barker, C.T. 1992. *The Chambered Tombs of South-West Wales: A re-assessment of the Neolithic burial monuments of Carmarthenshire and Pembrokeshire,* Oxbow Monograph 14.

Barnwell, E.L., 1868. 'Alignments in Wales', in *Archaeologia Cambrensis,* Series 3 (14, 169–79).

—, 1869. 'Cromlechs in North Wales', in *Archaeologia Cambrensis,* Series 3 (15, 118–47).

—, 1872. 'Notes on some South Wales Cromlechs', in *Archaeologia Cambrensis,* Series 4 (3, 81–143).

—, 1877. 'Early remains in Carmarthenshire', in *Archaeologia Cambrensis,* Series 5 (1).

—, 1884. 'On some South Wales Cromlechs', in *Archaeologia Cambrensis,* Series 5 (1, 129–44).

Baynes, E.N., 1908. 'The Excavations at Din Lligwy', in *Archaeologia Cambrensis,* Series 6 (8, 183–210).

—, 1909. 'The Excavation of Lligwy Cromlech in the County of Anglesey', in *Archaeologia Cambrensis,* Series 7 (9, 217–31).

—, 1910–11. 'The Megalithic remains of Anglesey', in *Trans. Hon. Soc. Cymmrod* (3–91).

Bender, B., 1978. 'Gatherer-hunter to farmer: a social perspective', in *World Archaeology* 10, No. 2 (204–22).

Bezant Lowe, S., 1912. *The Heart of Northern Wales* (Vol. 1).

Bowen, D. & Pritchard, O., 2023. *Hunting the Wild Megalith, Self publication.*

Bowen, E.G. & Gresham, C.A., 1967. *History of Merioneth.* vol. i, Dolgellau.

Boyd Dawkins, W., 1901. 'The Cairn and Sepulchral Cave at Gop, near Prestatyn', in *Archaeological Journal 58* (322–41).

Bradley, R., 1993. *Altering the earth*, Society of Antiquaries of Scotland, Monograph Series 8.

—, 1998. *The Significance of Monuments*, Routledge.

—, 2000. *The Archaeology of Natural Places*, Routledge.

—, 2002. *The Past in Prehistoric Societies*, Routledge.

Britnell, W., 1979. The Gwernvale Long Cairn, *Antiquity*, 53 (132–4).

—, 1984. 'The Gwernvale Long Cairn, Crickhowell, Brecknock', in W. Britnell & H. Savory, *Gwernvale and Penywyrlod: Two Neolithic Long Cairns in the Black Mountains of Breconshire*, Cambrian Archaeological Monographs No. 2 (43–93).

—, 1991. 'The Neolithic', in J. Manley, S. Ganter & F. Gale (eds.). *The Archaeology of Clwyd,* Clwyd Archaeology Service.

Britnell, W. & Savory, H., 1984. *Gwernvale and Penywyrlod: Two Neolithic Long Cairns in the Black Mountains of Breconshire*, Cambrian Archaeological Monographs No. 2.

Britnell, W. & Whittle, A., (eds.) 2022. *The First Stones: Penywyrlod, Gwernvale and the Black Mountains Neolithic Long Cairns of South-East Wales,* Oxbow Books.

Brown, A.E., 1963. 'Records of surface finds made in Herefordshire, 1951–60', in *Trans. Woolhope Natur. Field. Club,* XXXVII (76–91).

Burgess, C., 1980. *The Age of Stonehenge*, Dent.

Burl, A., 1976. *The Stone Circles of the British Isles,* Yale University Press.

—, 1985. *Prehistoric Stone Circles*, Shire Archaeology.

Burnham, H., 1995. *A guide to ancient and historic Wales: Clwyd and Powys*, CADW.

Carlisle, N., 1811. *A Topographic Dictionary of the Dominion of Wales.*

Case, H.J., 1969. 'Neolithic explanations', in *Antiquity* 43 (176–86).

Caseldine, A., 1990. *Environmental Archaeology in Wales,* Cadw Welsh Historical Monuments & Dept. of Archaeology, St David's University College.

Castleden, R., 1992. *Neolithic Britain: New Stone Age Sites of England, Scotland and Wales*, Routledge.

Chapman, R., Kinnes, I. & Randsborg, K., (eds.) 1981. *The Archaeology of Death,* Cambridge University Press.

Children, G. & Nash, G.H., 1994. *Monuments in the Landscape: The Prehistory of Herefordshire*, Vol. I, Logaston Press.

—, 1996. *Monuments in the Landscape: The Prehistory of Monmouthshire,* Vol. IV, Logaston Press.

—, 1997. *The Neolithic Sites of Cardiganshire, Carmarthenshire and Pembrokeshire,* Vol. V, Logaston Press. Reprinted and revised in 2002.

—, 2001. *Monuments in the Landscape: The Prehistory of Breconshire,* Vol. IX, Logaston Press, Hereford.

Clough, T.H. McK. & Cummins, W.A., 1988. *Stone Axe Trade: The petrology of prehistoric stone implements from the British Isles*, Vol. 2 CBA Research Report No. 67.

Cloutman, E., 1983. 'Studies of the vegetational history of the Black Mountain Range, South Wales', Unpublished Ph.D. thesis, University of Wales.

Cook, N., 2004. *Prehistoric Funerary and Ritual Sites Project – Pembrokeshire 2003-2004*, Cambrian Archaeology.

Cooney, G., 2000. *Landscapes of Neolithic Ireland*, Routledge.

Corcoran, J.X.W.P., 1969. 'The Cotswold-Severn Group', in T.G.E. Powell, J.X.W.P. Corcoran, F.M. Lynch and J.G. Scott (eds.), *Megalithic Enquiries in the West of Britain*, Liverpool University Press.

Crampton, C.B. & Webley, D.P., 1968. 'A section through Mynydd Troed long barrow, Brecknock', in *Bull. Board Celtic Studies* 22 (71–7).

Crawford, O.G.S. 1920., 'Account of the Excavations at Hengwm, Merionethshire, August and September 1919', in *Archaeologia Cambrensis* (1921; 99–133).

—, 1925. *The Long Barrows of the Cotswolds*, Gloucester.

Cummings, V., 2002. 'All cultural things: Actual and conceptual monuments in the Neolithic of western Britain', in C. Scarre (ed.), *Monuments and Landscape in Atlantic Europe*, Routledge (107–21).

—, 2009. *A View from the West: The Neolithic of the Irish Sea Zone*, Oxbow Books.

Cummings, V. & Richards, C., 2011. 'Building the Great Dolmens Excavations at Garn Turne, Pembrokeshire, Data Structure Report'. Site code: GT11 and GTQ11 (*Uclan Report*).

—, 2014. 'How to build a dolmen: exploring Neolithic construction at Garn Turne', in *Current Archaeology*, Vol. 286 (32–5).

—, 2021. 'A Monumental Catastrophe: Investigating the Collapsed Dolmens at Garn Turne, South-West Wales', in *Monuments in the Making: Raising the Great Dolmens in Early Neolithic Northern Europe*, Oxbow Books (179–220).

Cummings, V. & Whittle, A., 2004. *Places of Special Virtue: Megaliths in the Neolithic Landscapes of Wales,* Oxbow Books.

Daniel, G.E., 1937. 'The Chambered Barrow in Parc-le-Breos-Cwm, South Wales', in *Proceedings of the Prehistoric Society*. iii (1937; 71–86).

—, 1950. *The Prehistoric Chambered Tombs of England and Wales*, Cambridge University Press.

—, 1958. *The Megalithic builders of Western Europe*, Hutchenson.

Daniel, G., 1972. *Megaliths in History*, Thames & Hudson.

Darvill, T.C., 1982. *The Megalithic Chambered Tombs of the Cotswold-Severn Region*, Vorda Research Series No. 5.

—, 1989. 'The Circulation of Neolithic Stone and Flint Axes: a case study from Wales and the mid-west of England', in *Proceedings of the Prehistoric Society* 55 (27–43).

—, 2004. *Long Barrows of the Cotswolds and Surrounding Areas,* Tempus Publishing.

David, A., 1990. 'Some aspects of the human presence in west Wales during the Mesolithic', in C. Bonsall (ed.), *The Mesolithic in Europe*, John Donald (241–53).

David, A. & Williams, G., 1995. 'Stone axe-head manufacture in the Preseli Hills, Wales', in *Proceedings of the Prehistoric Society* 61 (433–60).

Davis, M., 1945. 'Types of Megalithic Monument of the Irish Sea and North Channel Coastlands: A Study of Distributions', in *Antiquity* 25 (125–44).

Devaraux, P., 2001. *Stone Age Soundtracks, The Acoustic Archaeology of Ancient Sites*, Vega.

Dimbleby, G., 1973. 'Report on two soil samples from Dyffyn Ardudwy', in *Archaeologia* 104 (4–5).

Done Bushell, W., 1911. 'Among the Prescelly circles', in *Archaeologia Cambrensis*, Series 6 (11, 287–333).

Driver, T., 1992. 'Shorter notes: St Lythans Chambered Tomb, South Glamorgan', in *Archaeologia Cambrensis* Vol. CXLI (181–2).

Dronfield, J., 1996. 'Entering alternative realities: Cognition, art and architecture in Irish passage-tombs', in *Cambridge Archaeological Journal* 6 (37–72).

Evans, J.G., 1975. *The Environment of Early Man in the British Isles*, Harper Collins.

Farrington, R., 1769. *Snowdonia Druidica*.

Fenn, P., Nash, G.H. & Waite, L., 2007. 'Cist Cerreg: A reassessment of a ritual landscape. Landscape Enquiries', in *Clifton Antiquarian Club*, Vol. 11 (135–38).

Fenton, J., 1848. *Cromlechs of Llanwnda, Pembrokeshire* (London).

Fenton, R., 1804–13. *Tour in Wales.* Published by the Cambrian Archaeological Association in 1917.

—, 1811. *An historical tour through Pembrokeshire*. London.

Figgis, N.P., 2001. *Prehistoric Preseli*, Atelier Productions.

Flemming, A., 1999. 'Phenomenology and the megaliths of Wales: a dreaming too far?' in *Oxford Journal of Archaeology* 18 (119–25).

Forde-Johnson, J.L., 1956. 'The Calderstone, Liverpool', in T.G. Powell, T. & G.E. Daniel, *Barclodiad y Gawres: The excavation of a Megalithic Chambered Tomb in Anglesey*, Liverpool University Press.

Fowler, P., 1983. *Prehistoric Farming*, CUP.

Gavin Robinson, R.S., 1934. 'Flint workers and flint users of the Golden Valley', in *Trans Woolhope Natur. Field Club* (54–63).

Gibson, A., 1990. 'A cropmark enclosure and a sherd of later Neolithic pottery from Bryn Derwen, Llandysul, Powys', in *Montgomeryshire Collections*, No. 78 (13).

—, 1999. *The Walton Basin Project: Excavation and survey in a prehistoric landscape 1993-7*, CBA research report 118, CBA, York.

—, 2002. *Prehistoric Pottery in Britain and Ireland*, Tempus Publishing.

Grønnow, B., 1987. 'Meiendorf and Stellmoor Revisited: An analysis of late Palaeolithic Reindeer exploration', in *Acta Archaeologica* (131–66).

Greenwell, W., 1877. *British Barrows*, Clarendon Press.

Griffiths, W.E., 1956. 'The Cors y Gedol Cromlech', in *Journal of the Merioneth Historical and Record Society*, ii (293–6).

Grimes, W.F., 1932. 'Prehistoric Archaeology in Wales since 1925: The Neolithic Period', in *Proceedings of the Prehistoric Society of East Anglia* 7 (85–92).

—, 1936a. 'The Megalithic Monuments of Wales', in *Proceedings of the Prehistoric Society* Vol. 2 (106–39).

—, 1936b. 'The Long Cairns of Breconshire Black Mountains', in *Archaeologia Cambrensis*, XCI (259–82).

—, 1936c. *Map of South Wales showing the distribution of Long Barrows and Megaliths,* Ordnance Survey.

—, 1938. 'Excavations at Meini Gwyr, Carmarthen', in *Proceedings of the Prehistoric Society* 4 (324–5).

—, 1939a. 'The excavation of Ty Isaf Long Cairn, Breconshire', in *Proceedings of the Prehistoric Society,* V (119–42).

—, 1939b. 'Bedd y Afanc', in *Proceedings of the Prehistoric Society* 5 (258).

—, 1945. 'Early Man and the Soils of Anglesey', in *Antiquity*, xix (169–74).

—, 1948. 'Pentre Ifan Burial Chamber, Pembrokeshire', in *Archaeologia Cambrensis,* 100 (3–23).

—, 1951. *The Prehistory of Wales*, The National Museum of Wales.

—, 1960. *Excavations of Defense Sites 1939–45, I: Mainly Neolithic and Bronze Age,* Ministry of Works Archaeological Reports No. 3.

Grinsell, L.V., 1981. 'The later History of Ty Illtud', in *Archaeologia Cambrensis* (131–9).

—, 1984. *Barrows in England and Wales,* Shire Publications.

Hawkes, J., 1937. *The Archaeology of the Channel Islands: Vol. 2, The Baliwick of Jersey.*

Healey, E. & Green, S., 1984. 'The Lithic Industries', in W. Britnell & H. Savory, *Gwernvale and Penywyrlod: Two Neolithic Long Cairns in the Black Mountains of Breconshire*, Cambrian Archaeological Monographs No. 2 (113–34).

Hemp, W.J., 1926. 'The Bachwen Cromlech', in *Archaeologia Cambrensis,* (429–31).

—, 1927. 'The Capel Garmon Chambered Long Cairn', in *Archaeologia Cambrensis,* 82 (1–43).

—, 1930. 'The Chambered Cairn of Bryn Celli Ddu', in *Archaeologia Cambrensis*, 1xxx (179–214).

—, 1935a. 'Arthur's Stone, Dorstone, Herefordshire', in *Archaeologia Cambrensis,* XC (288–92).

—, 1935b. 'A Possible Pedigree of Long Barrows and Chambered Cairns', in *Proceeding of the Prehistoric Society* 1 (108–14).

—, 1938. 'Cup Markings at Treflys', *Caernarvonshire*, XCIII (140–1).

Hodder, I., 1990. *The Domestication of Europe*, Blackwell.

Houlder, C.H., 1978. *Wales: An Archaeological Guide*, Faber & Faber.

—, 1988. 'The Petrological Identification of Stone Implements from Wales', in T.H. Clough and W.A. Cummins (eds.), *Stone Axe Studies*, Vol. 2 (133–36 & 246–60).

Hughes, G., 1996. *The excavation of a Late Prehistoric and Romano-British settlement at Thornwell Farm, Chepstow, Gwent, 1992*, BAR, British Series No. 224.

Hughes, W., 1999. *Monuments in the landscape: The Prehistoric Sites of the Gower & West Glamorgan*, Vol. VII, Logaston Press

Huntley, B., 1990. 'European vegetation history: Palaeovegetation maps from pollen data – 13,000 yrs. B.P. to present', in *Journal of Quaternary Science* Vol. 5, No. 2 (183–222).

HWCC., 1981. *Countryside Treasures of Herefordshire*, Hereford & Worcester County Council.

Jacobi, R., 1980. 'The Upper Palaeolithic in Britain, with special reference to Wales', in J.A. Taylor (ed.), *Culture, Environment in Prehistoric Wales*, BAR, British Series No. 76 (15–99).

Jarman, M.R., Bailey, G.N. & Jarman, H.N., 1982. *Early European agriculture*, Cambridge University Press.

Jelly, K. & Nash, G.H., 2016. 'New over old: an image-based reassessment of Le Déhus passage grave's Le Gardien du Tombeau, Guernsey', in *Time and Mind* 9(3) (245–65).

Jones, M.H., 1906. 'NW Carmarthenshire Antiquaries', in *Transactions of the Carmarthen Antiquarian Society*, 2 (141–2).

Jones, T., 1809. *History of the county of Brecknock,* Vol. 2.

Jones, W.B., 1863. 'Double Cromlech on Carn Llidi, in the Parish of St David's, Pembrokeshire', in *Archaeologia Cambrensis,* Series 3, 9 (73).

Jones, W.B., & Freeman, E.A., 1856. *The History and Antiquities of St David's* (London & Tenby).

Joussaume, R., 1985. *Dolmens for the Dead: Megalithic Building throughout the World*, Batsford.

Kinnes, I., 1992. 'Non-Megalithic Long Barrows and Allied Structures in the British Neolithic', in *British Museum Occasional Paper* No. 52.

Kytmannow, T., 2008. *Portal Tombs in the Landscape: The Chronology, Morphology and Landscape Setting of the Portal Tombs of Ireland, Wales and Cornwall.* BAR British Series 455.

Laws, E. & Owen, H., 1897–1906. *Pembrokeshire Arch Survey.*

Lhuyd, E., 1695. 'Additions to the entries for Carmarthenshire and Pembrokeshire', in Camden's *Britannia* (Gibson edition).

—, 1699. *Parochalia.*

Lillie, M., 2015. *Hunter, Fishers & Foragers in Wales: Towards a social narrative of Mesolithic lifeways*, Oxbow Books.

Longueville Jones, H., 1865. 'Pembrokeshire Antiquities', in *Archaeologia Cambrensis,* Series 3, 11 (281–5).

Lowe, W.B., 1912. *The Heart of Northern Wales.* i, Llanfairfechan.

Lubbock, J., 1872. *Pre-Historic Times,* Williams & Norgate.

Lukis, J.W., 1875. 'On the St Lythan's and St Nicholas' Cromlechs and Other Remains, near Cardiff', in *Archaeologia Cambrensis,* Series 4, 6 (171–85).

Lynch, F.M., 1967. 'Barclodiad y Gawres: Comparative Notes on the Decorated Stones', in *Archaeologia Cambrensis,* Vol. CXVI (1–22).

—, 1969a. 'The Megalithic Tombs of North Wales', in T.G.E. Powell, J.X.W.P. Corcoran, F.M. Lynch & J.G. Scott (eds.), *Megalithic Enquiries in the West of Britain*, Liverpool University Press (107–48).

—, 1969b. 'The Contents of Excavated Tombs in North Wales', in T.G.E. Powell, J.X.W.P. Corcoran, F.M. Lynch & J.G. Scott (eds.), *Megalithic Enquiries in the West of Britain*, Liverpool University Press (148–74).

—, 1970. *Prehistoric Anglesey,* Anglesey Antiquarian Society.

—, 1972. 'Portal Dolmens in the Nevern Valley, Pembrokeshire', in F.M. Lynch & C. Burgess (eds.), *Prehistoric Man in Wales & the West*, Adams & Dart (67–84).

—, 1976. 'Towards a chronology of megalithic tombs in Wales', in G.C. Boon & J.M. Lewis (eds.), *Welsh Antiquity (Essays mainly on Prehistoric Topics. Presented to H.N. Savory upon his retirement as Keeper of Archaeology,* National Museum of Wales (63–79).

—, 1991. *Prehistoric Anglesey: the archaeology of the island to the Roman conquest,* Anglesey Antiquarian Society.

—, 2000a. 'The Early Neolithic', in F.M. Lynch, S. Aldhouse-Green and J. Davis (eds.), *Prehistoric Wales*, Sutton (42–78).

—, 2000b. 'The Later Neolithic and earlier Bronze Age', in F.M. Lynch, S. Aldhouse-Green and J. Davis (eds.), *Prehistoric Wales*, Sutton (79–138).

Lynch, F.M., Aldhouse-Green, S. & Davies, J., 2000. *Prehistoric Wales.* Stroud: Sutton.

Lynch, F.M. & Burgess, C., (eds.) 1972. *Prehistoric Man in Wales and the West*, Adams and Dart.

Manby, G.W., 1801. *The History and Antiquities of the parish of St. Davids, South Wales.*

Masters, L., 1981. 'Chambered Tombs and Non-Megalithic Barrows in Britain', in C. Renfrew (ed.), *The Megalithic Monuments of Western Europe*, Thames & Hudson (97–112).

Mathiassen, T., 1943. *Stenalderbopladser i Aamosen,* Copenhagen.

Megaw, J.V.S., 1984. 'The Bone? Flute', in W. Britnell & H. Savory (eds.), *Gwernvale and Penywyrlod: Two Neolithic Long Cairns in the Black Mountains of Breconshire*, Cambrian Archaeological Monographs No. 2 (27–8).

Morgan, W.E.T. & Marshall, G., 1921. 'Excavation of a long barrow at Llanigon, Breconshire', in *Archaeologia Cambrensis* 79 (296–9).

Morris, R.W.B., 1989. 'The Prehistoric Rock Art of Great Britain: a survey of all sites bearing motifs more complex than simple cup-marks', in *Proceedings of the Prehistoric Society* 55 (48–88).

Murphy, K., 1985. 'Marros Mountain, Eglwys Cummin', in *Archaeology in Wales* 25 (36).

Nash, G.H., 1997. 'Monumentality and the Landscape: The Possible Symbolic and Political Distribution of Long Chambered Tombs around the Black Mountains, Central Wales', in G.H. Nash (ed.), *Semiotics of Landscape: Archaeology of Mind*, BAR International Series 661 (17–30).

—, 1998. *Exchange, Status and Mobility: Mesolithic Portable Art of Southern Scandinavia,* BAR International Series 640.

—, 2000. 'Re-evaluating monumentality: Arthur's Stone, Dorstone, Herefordshire', in *Trans Woolhope Natur. Field Club* Vol 56 (1–14).

—, 2006. 'Cup-and-ring petroglyph on the Neolithic chambered burial monument of Garn Turne, Pembrokeshire, SW Wales', in *Rock Art Research*, Vol. 23(2) (199–206).

—, 2008a. 'Encoding a Neolithic Landscape: The Linearity of Burial Monuments along Strumble Head, South-west Wales', in *Time & Mind*, Vol. I(3) (345–62). https://doi.org/10.2752/175169708X329381

—, 2008b. 'Long or round? Evaluation programme and results at the Neolithic chambered monument of Arthur's Stone, Herefordshire', in *Trans Woolhope Natur. Field Club* Vol. L Pt 1 (37–50).

—, 2020. 'Megalithic Art: A Visual Repertoire for the Dead', in Smith, C. (ed.) *Encyclopedia of Global Archaeology*, Springer, Cham. www.doi.org/10.1007/978-3-030-30018-0_1525

—, 2021. 'Contextualising megalithic rock art on Neolithic chambered tombs: a Welsh perspective', in C. Charette, A. Mazel and G.H. Nash (eds.) *Indigenous Heritage and Rock Art Worldwide Research: In Memory of Daniel Arsenault*, Archaeopress (14–31).

—, 2023. 'Discovery of a cupmarked stone on the boundary of Tai'r Waun Isaf and Tai'r Waun Uchaf, Llanfabon, Mid-Glamorgan (ST 10220 93489)', in *Archaeology in Wales*, Vol. 61 (3–6).

Nash, G.H., Brook, C., Wellicome, T. & Rees, C., 2020. 'Discovery of human remains at the Trefael Stone, North Pembrokeshire, South-west Wales, SN 10274 40227', in *Archaeology in Wales,* Vol. 57/58 (117–21).

Nash, G.H., Brook C. & Wellicome, T., 2020. 'Preliminary Field Investigations at Trellyffaint, Pembrokeshire, South-West Wales', in *Archaeology in Wales,* Vol. 57–8 (123–30).

Nash, G.H., Brook, C., Wellicome, T., Dunne, J. & Casanova, E., 2021. 'How excavating a Pembrokeshire Portal Dolmen illuminated Neolithic dairy farming in Wales', in *Current Archaeology*, Vol. 350 (20–5).

Nash, G.H., Elliot, R., George, A., Hopkins, C., McQueen, E., Strutt, A. & Waite, L., 2007. 'The Eastern Rhossili Down Project: Landscape Assessment and Reappraisal of the Sweynes Howe North Monument. First Interim Report', in *Clifton Antiquarian Club Journal,* Landscape Enquiries, Vol. 11 (87–106).

Nash, G.H., George, A. & Waite, L., 2007. 'Cupmarks discovered on the Cae-Dyni chambered monument, Criccieth, Caernarvonshire, North Wales', in *Clifton Antiquarian Club Journal,* Landscape Enquiries, Vol. 11 (33–40).

Nash, G.H., James, C. & Wellicome, T., 2015. 'The excavation of the Neolithic Portal Dolmen monument of Perthi Duon, Ynys Môn (Anglesey)', in *Archaeology in Wales*, 54 (25–34).

Nash, G.H. & Pope, R., 2023. 'New rock art discovery: Plas Maen Stone, Cymau, Flintshire', in *Archaeology in Wales*, Vol. 61 (41–4).

O'Connor, T.P., 1987. 'Report on the cremated bone from Din Dryfol, Anglesey, in C.A. Smith & F.M. Lynch', in *Trefignath and Din Dryfol: The Excavation of Two Megalithic Tombs in Anglesey*, Cambrian Archaeological Monographs, 3, (129–30).

Olding, F., 2000. *The Prehistoric Landscape of the Eastern Black Mountains,* BAR British Series 297.

Owen, G., 1603/1892. *The Description of Pembrokeshire*, Parts 1–4 (1603), (with notes and appendix by H. Owen).

Owen, N., 1775. *A History of the Island of Anglesey.*

Parker-Pearson, M., 1993. *Bronze Age Britain*, English Heritage.

Pennant, T., 1783. *Tours in Wales*, Reproduced by J. Rhys (ed.), Caernarvon, 1883.

Peterson, R., 2003. *Neolithic Pottery from Wales: Traditions and Constructions of Use*, BAR British Series 344.

Phillips, C.W., 1936. 'An Examination of the Ty Newydd Chambered Tomb, Llanfaelog, Anglesey', in *Archaeologia Cambrensis,* xci (93–9).

Piggott, S., 1954. *Neolithic Cultures of the British Isles,* Cambridge University Press.

—, 1962. *The West Kennet Long Barrow,* HMSO.

Pitts, M., 1980. *Later Stone Implements,* Shire Archaeology Series.

Powell, T.G.E., 1973. 'Excavation of the Megalithic Chambered Cairn of Dyffryn Ardudwy, Merioneth, Wales', in *Archaeologia Cambrensis,* 104 (1–49).

Powell, T.G.E. & Daniel, G.E., 1956. *Barclodiad y Gawres,* Liverpool University Press.

—, 1956. *Barclodiad y Gawres: The excavation of a Megalithic Chambered Tomb in Anglesey,* Liverpool University Press.

Powell, T.G.E., Corcoran, J.X.W.P., Lynch, F.M. & Scott, J.G., 1969. *Megalithic Enquiries in the West of Britain,* Liverpool University Press.

Pringle, J. & Neville George, T., 1970. *British Regional Geology: South Wales,* HMSO (2nd edition).

Pritchard, H., 1871. 'Mona Antiqua: Tyn Trefoel or Dindryfol', in *Archaeologia Cambrensis,* Series 3, 2 (300–12).

—, 1873. 'Cromlech at Ty Mawr', in *Archaeologia Cambrensis,* Series 5, 1 (22–30).

Ray, K. & Thomas, J., 2018. *Neolithic Britain: The Transformation of Social Worlds,* Oxford University Press.

—, 2020. 'Houses foundational: gathering histories at Dorstone Hill, Herefordshire', in A. Barclay, D. Field & J. Lear (eds.), *Houses of the Dead,* Oxbow (107–19).

RCAHMW, 1976. *An Inventory of the Ancient Monuments in Glamorgan,* Vol. 1, part 1, Stone & Bronze Age, HMSO.

RCAHM(W), 1986. *An Inventory of the Ancient Monuments in Breconshire (Brycheiniog): Later Prehistoric Monuments and Unenclosed Settlements to 1000 AD (Part I)*, HMSO.

RCAHM(W), 1997. *An Inventory of the Ancient Monuments in Breconshire (Brycheiniog): The Prehistoric and Roman Monuments (Part II)*, HMSO.

RCAM (Wales), 1937. *An Inventory of the Ancient Monuments in the County of Anglesey,* HMSO.

RCAM (Wales), 1956. *An Inventory of the Ancient Monuments in the County of Caernarvonshire, Part I,* HMSO.

RCAM (Wales), 1964. *An Inventory of the Ancient Monuments in the County of Caernarvonshire, Part III,* HMSO.

RCAM (Wales), 1917. *An Inventory of the Ancient Monuments in the County of Carmarthenshire,* HMSO.

RCAM (Wales), 1914. *An Inventory of the Ancient Monuments in the County of Denbigh,* HMSO.

RCAM (Wales), 1912. *An Inventory of the Ancient Monuments in the County of Flintshire,* HMSO.

RCAM (Wales), 1921. *An Inventory of the Ancient Monuments in the County of Merionethshire,* HMSO.

RCAM (Wales), 1925. *An Inventory of the Ancient Monuments in the County of Pembrokeshire,* HMSO.

Rees, C. & Jones, M., 2015. 'Neolithic houses from Llanfaethlu, Anglesey', in *PAST: Newsletter of the Prehistoric Society* 8 (1–3).

Rees, S., 1992. *A guide to ancient and historic Wales, Dyfed,* Cadw.

—, 2012. 'Excavations at Carreg Coetan Arthur chambered tomb, Pembrokeshire', in *Archaeologia Cambrensis,* 161, (51–163).

Rees, T., 1815. *A Topographical and Historical Description of South Wales,* Sherwood, Neely & Jones.

Renfrew, C., 1976. 'Megaliths, territories and populations', in S. de Laet (ed.), *Acculturation and continuity in Atlantic Europe,* de Tempel (98–220).

—, 1979. *Investigations in Orkney,* Society of Antiquaries.

Roberts, C. & Manchester, K., 1995. *The Archaeology of Disease,* Cornell University Press.

Rowley-Conwy, P., 1981. 'Mesolithic Danish Bacon: Permanent and temporary sites in the Danish Mesolithic', in A. Sheridan & G. Bailey (eds.), *Economic Archaeology: Towards an Integration of Ecological and Social Approaches,* BAR International Series 96 (51–65).

Rutter, J.G., 1949. *Prehistoric Gower: An early archaeology of West Glamorgan,* Welsh Guides.

Salmon, N., 1728–9. *A New Survey of England, wherein the defects of Camden are supplied and the errors of his followers remarked.*

Sant, J., 2000. *Stone Spotting in Herefordshire,* Moondial.

Savory, H.N., 1953. 'The Excavation of Twlc y Filiast Cromlech, Llangynog, Carm.', in *Bull. Board Celtic Studies,* xv (225–8).

—, 1956a. 'The Excavation of the Pipton Long Cairn, Brecknockshire', in *Archaeologia Cambrensis,* 105 (7–48).

—, 1956b. 'The excavation of 'Twlc-y-Filiast' cromlech, Llanynog, (Carm.)', in *Bull. of the Board of Celtic Studies* 16, (300–8).

—, 1973. 'Pen-y-wyrlod: a New Welsh Long Cairn', in *Antiquity,* 47 (187–92).

—, 1980. 'The Neolithic in Wales', in J.A. Taylor (ed.), *Culture and Environment in Prehistoric Wales,* BAR British Series 76 (207–32).

—, 1984. 'The Penywyrlod Long Cairn, Talgarth, Brecknock', in W. Britnell & H. Savory, *Gwernvale and Penywyrlod: Two Neolithic Long Cairns in the Black Mountains of Breconshire,* Cambrian Archaeological Monographs No. 2 (13–36).

Scott, W., 1933. 'The chambered tomb of Pant y Saer, Anglesey', in *Archaeologia Cambrensis,* 38 (185–228).

Sharkey, J., 2004. *The Meetings of the Tracks: Rock art in Ancient Wales,* Carreg Gwalch.

Shee-Twohig, E., 1981. *The Megalithic Art of North-Western Europe,* Oxford University Press.

Sherratt, A., 1981. 'Plough and pastoralism: Aspects of the Secondary Products Revolution', in I. Hodder, G. Issac & N. Hammond (eds.), *Pattern of the Past,* Cambridge University Press (261–305).

Silsoe, 1983. *Soil Survey of England & Wales.*

Skinner, Reverend J., 1802. *Ten Days Tour through the Island of Anglesey* (reprinted with introduction by T. Williams, 2004).

Smith, A.G. & Cloutman, E., 1988. 'Reconstruction of Holocene vegetation history in three dimensions at Waun-Fignen-Felen, an upland site in South Wales', in *Phil. Transactions of Royal Society,* B 322 (159–219).

Smith, C., 1992. *Late stone Age Hunters of the British Isles,* Routledge.

Smith, C.A., 1981. 'Trefignath Burial Chambers, Anglesey', in *Antiquity* 55 (134–6).

Smith, C.A. & Lynch, F.M., 1987. *Trefignath and Din Dryfol: The Excavation of Two Megalithic Tombs in Anglesey,* Cambrian Archaeological Monographs, No. 3.

Smith, I.F., 1974. 'The Neolithic', in C. Renfrew (ed.), *British Prehistory: A New Outline,* Duckworth (100–36).

Stanford, S.C., 1990. *The Archaeology of The Welsh Marches* (2nd ed.) (2–73).

Stanley, W.O., 1870. 'On the tumulus in Plas Newydd Park, Anglesey', in *Archaeologia Cambrensis,* Series 4, I (51–8).

Startin, B. & Bradley, R., 1981. 'Some notes on work organisation and society in prehistoric Wessex', in C.N.L. Ruggles & A.W.R. Whittle (eds.), *Astronomy and Society in Britain during the period 4000–1500 BC,* BAR British Series 88 (289–96).

Stewart, L., Nash, G.H. & Cowell, R., 2021. *The Calderstones: A Prehistoric Tomb in Liverpool,* National Museums Liverpool.

Stuiver, M., Reimer, P.J., Bard, E., Beck, J.W., Burr, G.S., Hughen, K.A., Kromer, B., McCormac, F.G., v.d. Plicht, J. and Spurk, M., 1998. *Marine delta 14C and radiocarbon ages, Radiocarbon,* University of Edinburgh Press.

Stukeley, W., 1778. *Itinerarium Curiosum,* Centuria II (London).

Taylor, J.A., (ed.) 1980. *The Culture and Environment in Prehistoric Wales,* BAR British Series 76.

Thomas, D., 1799. *Cambrian Register.*

Thomas, J.S., 1988. 'The Social Significance of Cotswold-Severn burial practices', in *Man,* 23 (540–59).

—, 1993. 'The politics of vision and the archaeologies of landscape', in B. Bender (ed.), *Landscape, Politics and Perspectives,* Berg.

—, 1988. *Rethinking the Neolithic,* Cambridge University Press.

—, 1999. *Understanding the Neolithic,* Routledge.

Tilley, C., 1993. 'Art, architecture and the landscape in Neolithic Sweden', in B. Bender (ed.), *Landscape, Politics and Perspectives,* Berg.

—, 1994. *A Phenomenology of Landscape: Places, Paths and Monuments,* Berg.

Tilley, C. & Bennett, W., 2001. 'An archaeology of supernatural places: the case of West Penrith', in *Journal of the Royal Anthropological Institute*, 7 (335–62).

Traherne, G.G.T., 1911. 'Brief note on my work in Laugharneshire', in *Transactions of the Carmarthenshire Antiquarian Society*, 6 (58–60).

Vulliamy, C.E., 1921. 'The Excavation of a Megalithic Tomb in Breconshire', in *Archaeologia Cambrensis,* Series 7, LXXVI (300–5).

—, 1923. 'Further excavations in the Long Barrows at Ffostyll', in *Archaeologia Cambrensis,* Series 7, 3 (320–4).

—, 1929. 'Excavation of an unrecorded Long Barrow in Wales', in *Man*, XXIX, No. 29 (34–6).

Wainwright, G.J., 1967. *Coygan Camp*: *A Prehistoric Romano-British and Dark Age Settlement in Carmarthenshire,* The Cambrian Archaeological Association.

Walker, K., 2018. *Axe-heads and Identity: An investigation into the roles of imported axe-heads in identity formation in Neolithic Britain*, Archaeopress.

Ward, J., 1915. 'The St Nicholas chambered tumulus, Glamorgan', in *Archaeologia Cambrensis,* Series 15 (253–320).

—, 1916. 'The St Nicholas Chambered Tumulus, Glamorgan', in *Archaeologia Cambrensis,* Series 16 (239–67).

—, 1918. 'Some prehistoric sepulchral remains near Pendine, Carmarthenshire', in *Archaeologia Cambrensis,* 18, Series 6 (35–79).

Warrilow, G., 1986. 'The Pollen', in W. Warrilow, G. Owen, & W.J. Britnell, 'Eight ring-ditches at Four Crosses, landysilio, Powys 1981–85', in *Proceedings of the Prehistoric Society* 52, (53–88).

Watkins, A., 1928. 'Arthur's Stone', in *Trans. Woolhope Natur. Field. Club*, XIV (149–51).

Webley, D., 1959. The Neolithic Colonization of the Breconshire Black Mountains, *Bull. Board Celtic Studies*, XVIII, 1958–60 (290–4).

—, 1961. 'Y Garn Llwyd, Newchurch West, Monmouthshire: A Reassessment', in *Bull. Board Celtic Studies*, XIX, 1960–2 (255–8).

Westerby, E., 1927. *Stenalderbopladser ved Klampenenborg*, Copenhagen.

Whittle, A., 1985. *Neolithic Europe: A Survey,* Cambridge University Press.

—, 1988. *Problems in Neolithic Archaeology,* Cambridge University Press.

—, 2003. *The archaeology of people: dimensions of Neolithic life,* Routledge.

Whittle, A. & Wysocki, M., 1998. 'Parc-le-Breos-Cwm transepted long cairn, Gower, west Glamorgan: date, contents and context', in *Proceedings of the Prehistoric Society,* 64 (139–82).

Wilkinson, J.G., 1870. 'Avenue and Cairns about Arthur's Stone in Gower', in *Archaeologia Cambrensis*, Series 4, 1, (23–45).

—, 1871. 'Cromlechs and other remains in Pembrokeshire', in *Collectanea Archaeologia,* Vol. 2, part 2 (219–40).

Williams, A., 1953. 'Clegyr Boia, St David's, Pembrokeshire: Excavations in 1943', in *Archaeologia Cambrensis,* 102 (20–47).

Williams, W.W., 1875. 'Excavations at Pant y Saer Cromlech, Anglesey', in *Archaeologia Cambrensis,* (341–8).

Wymer, J.J., 1977. *Gazetteer of Mesolithic sites in England and Wales*, CBA (Council for British Archaeology), Research Report No. 22.

Wyndham, H.P., 1775. *A Gentleman's Tour through Monmouthshire and Wales in the Months of June and July 1774.*

Yates, M.J. & Jones, M., 1991 'Excavation and Conservation at Capel Garmon Chambered Tomb, Betws-y-coed, Gwynedd, 1989', in *Archaeology in Wales,* 31 (1–5).

bold entries indicate main entry for the site; ***Bold italic*** signify illustrations outside the main entry.

INFORMATION IN BRACKETS: (site number, site group) if in the gazetteer; (county ref. no.) if mentioned in the text only.

SITE GROUP KEY: BMG: Black Mountains Group; GPG: Gower Peninsula Group; SEG: South-East Wales Group; YMG: Ynys Môn Group; NG: North Wales Group; HG: Harlech Group; LPG: Llŷn Peninsula Group; SWG: South-West Wales Group; IM: Isolated Monuments

SITE INDEX

Altar Stone, Nevern *see Llech-y-Tribedd*
Altar, The, Colston, Little Newcastle (85, SWG) 210, **213–4**, 218
Arthur's Stone, Dorstone (14, BMG) 13, 26, 28, ***30***, 31, 38–40, 47–8, 51, 64–5, **66–71**, 72–3, 111, 158
Arthur's Stone, Llanrhidian *see Maen Ceti*

Bachwen, Clynnog (57, LPG) 16, 28, ***29***, ***31***, 161–2, **163–5**, 171
Barclodiad Y Gawres, Llangwyfan (30, YMG) 2, 8, 17–9, 97–8, 104, **105–10**, 117–8, 165, 228
Bedd Taliesin, Llanfihangel (99, IM) 162, 233–4, **235–6**
Bedd-yr-Afanc, Meline (69, SWG) 177–9, **190–2**
Belas, Knap, Glos (GLOU 1) 76
Bodowyr, Llanidan (32, YMG) 97, **112–3**, 119, 124
Bron-y-Foel-Isaf-West, Llanenddwyn (51, HG) 147–8, **150–1**, 155, 168–9
Bryn Celli Ddu, Llanddaniel-Fab (33, YMG) ***3***, 6, ***7***, 8, 10, 13, 16–7, 19, 25, 30, 97–8, 107, 109, **113–9**, 122, 125, 141, 166, 247

Bryn yr Hen Bobl, Llanedwen (34, YMG) 20, 97, **119–22**, 126, 141
Bryn, Caernarfon (CRN 16) 98, 137

Cae-Dyni, Criccieth (CRN 14) 162, 169
Cae-yr-Arfau (GM 30) 85
Calderstones, Liverpool (LANCS 1) 8, 16, 18, ***18***, 98, 110, 118
Capel Garmon, Llanrwst Rural (46, NG) ***6***, 7, 102, 131–2, 139, **140–2**, 189, 236
Carn Besi, Llandyssilio East (88, SWG) 162, 210–11, **218–9**, 221
Carn Llidi, St David's (81, SWG) 26, 200, 203–4, 206, **207–8**, 218, 226, 231
Carn Wnda, Llanwnda (71, SWG) 191–2, **194–5**, 208, 226
Carneddau Hengwm North, Llanaber (54, HG) 147–8, 150, **155–6**
Carneddau Hengwm South, Llanaber (55, HG) 147–8, 150, **157–9**
Carreg Coetan, Newport (66, SWG) ***5***, ***11***, 138, 171, 175, 177–8, **183–4**, 187, 247
Carreg Samson, Llanwnda *see Carn Wnda*
Carreg Samson, Mathry (75, SWG) 26, 176, 191, **199–201**, 209, 226

Cashtal-yn-Ard, Isle of Man (MAN 1) 111
Cathole Cave, Gower 247
Cefn Isaf, Llanystumdwy (59, LPG) 161, 165, **166–8**, 169–70
Cerrig Llwydion, Cynwyl Elved (100, IM) 110, 233, **237–8**
Cerrig y Gof, Newport (67, SWG) 177–8, ***178***, 183, **185–7**, 206
Cist Cerrig, Treflys (60, LPG) 136, 161, **168–9**
Cleppa Park, Coedkernew (24, SEG) 85, **91**
Clyro Court Farm Long Barrow, Clyro (12, BMG) 42, **63–4**
Coed-y-Cwm (GM 116) 85
Coetan Arthur, Caernarfon (CRN 17) 98, 137
Coetan Arthur, Llanrhidian *see Maen Ceti*
Coetan Arthur, Llanystumdwy *see Ystum Cegid Isaf*
Coetan Arthur, Newport *see Carreg Coetan*
Coetan Arthur, Penllech *see Mynydd Cefn Amwlch*
Coetan Arthur, Penrhos-Lligwy *see Lligwy*

Coetan Arthur, St David's (78, SWG) 26, **32**, 78, **203–4**, 207, 226

Cors-y-Gedol, Llanddwye-is-y-craig (53, HG) 147–8, 150–1, **153–5**, 224

Croesllechau, Bronllys (6, BMG) 28, **52–4**

Cross Lodge Long Barrow, Dorstone (15, BMG) 13, 38–40, 64, 70, **71–2**, 73

Cuckoo Stones, The, Carew (89, SWG) 210, **219–20**

Devil's Quoit, Angle (92, SWG) **9**, 205, 221–2, **224–5**, 227

Din Dryfol, Aberffraw (31, YMG) viii, x, 20, 97–8, 105, **110–2**, 125

Dunseal Long Barrow, Dunseal (16, BMG) 38, 40, **72–3**

Dyffryn Ardudwy, Llanenddwyn (52, HG) 6, 10, **10**, 24, 98, 103, 125, 127, 147–8, 150, **151–3**, 155–6, 173, 189–90

Eithbed Cemetery Group (N, Central, S), Maenclochog (90, SWG) 155, 162, 210, 219, **220–1**

Ffostyll North, Llanelieu (2, BMG) 32, 38, 42, **45–6**, 47, 52, 54, 59, 155

Ffostyll South, Llanelieu (3, BMG) 32, 38, **42–5**, 47, 52, 54, 95, 155

Ffynnondruidion, St Nicholas (76, SWG) 20, 22, 191, 195–7, **201**

Ffyst Samson, St Nicholas (73, SWG) 191–2, 195–6, , **197–8**, 201

Four Crosses, Abererch (61, LPG) 161, 168, **169–70**

Four Crosses, Llandeilo (Powys) 4

Fourknocks, Ireland 110

Garn Gilfach, Llanwnda (72, SWG) 191–4, **195–6**, 198, 200, 227, 231

Garn Goch, Llangatwg (11, BMG) **62–3**, 73, 167, 212

Garn Turne, St Dogwells (86, SWG) **17**, 26, 176, 210, 213–4, **215–7**, 218, 247

Garn Wen (3), Llanwnda (70, SWG) 155, 191, **192–3**, 194, 202, 220–1

Gavrinis, Brittany 19

Glyn (ANG 12) 126, 128–9, 144

Gop Cairn, Trelawnyd (47, NG) 25, 131–2, **142–3**

Gop Cave, Trelawnyd (48, NG) 129, 131, **143–4**, 247

Gwal-y-Filiast, Llanboidy (83, SWG) 210, **211–2**, 234

Gwal-y-Filiast, St Lythans see Maes y Felin

Gwern Einion, Llanfair (50, HG) 138, 145, 147, **148–50**, 151, 168–70

Gwernvale, Crickhowell (10, BMG) viii, x, 6, 11, 24, 29, 31, 35–6, 38–9, 47, 55–6, **59–62**, 63, 68, 70, 184, 212, 247

Hanging Stone, The, Burton (91, SWG) 27, 103, 113, 124, 205–6, 208–9, 212, 218, 221, **222–4**, 233–4

Hendre Waelod, Llansantffraid-Glan-Conwy (44, NG) 131–2, 135, **137–8**, 141, 168–70

Hen-Drefor, Llansadwrn (37, YMG) 97, 112, **125**

Heston Brake, Portskewett (26, SEG) 10, 85–6, **93–5**

King Orry's Grave, Isle of Man (MAN 2) 140

King's Quoit, Manorbier (93, SWG) **9**, 205, 221–2, 225, **226–7**

Le Dehus, Guernsey 49

Little Lodge Barrow, Aberllynfi (13, BMG) 39, 42, 47, **64–5**

Llanfechell Burial Chamber, Ynys Môn 248

Llanymynech Hill, Montg. 28, 110

Llech-y-Drybedd, Nevern see Llech-y-Tribedd

Llech-y-Filiast, St Lythans see Maes y Felin

Llech-y-Tribedd, Nevern (64, SWG) 171, 176–8, **179–80**, 187, 198, 225

Llety'r Filiast, Llandudno (40, NG) 131, **132–3**

Lligwy, Penrhos-Lligwy (39, YMG) xiv–xv, 2, 11, 97–8, **128–9**, 144

Lower Luggy Long Barrow, Montg. (MNT 3) 248

Maen Ceti, Llanrhidian (18, GPG) 75, **78–80**

Maen y Bardd, Caerhun (41, NG) 131, **133–5**, 141

Maes y Felin, St Lythans (23, SEG) 75–7, 85–6, **89–90**, 91, 93,

Morfa Bychan A, Marros (94, SWG) 27, 32, 155, 220–2, 226, **227–9**, 233

Morfa Bychan B, Marros (95, SWG) 32, 155, 220–2, 226–7, **229–30**, 233

Morfa Bychan C, Marros (96, SWG) 32, 155, 220–2, 226–7, **230**, 233

Morfa Bychan D, Marros (97, SWG) 32, 155, 220–2, 226–7, **231–2**, 233

Mountain, Mynachlog Ddu (84, SWG) 210–1, **212–3**, 221

Mynydd Cefn Amwlch, Penllech (62, LPG) 161, **170–1**

Mynydd Troed, Talgarth (9, BMG) 24, 38, 50–1, 54, **58–9**, 64

Newgrange, Boyne Valley, Ireland 8, 19, 106

Notsgrove, Glos (GLOU 4) 76

Pant y Saer, Llanfair-Mathafarn-Eithaf (38, YMG) 97, **126–8**, 129, 190

Parc-le-Breos-Cwm, Penmaen (17, GPG) 7, 9, 26, 75, **76–8**, 82–3, 90, 228, 248

Parc-y-Cromlech, Goodwick (77, SWG) 191–2, **202**, 205

Parc-y-llyn, Ambleston (87, SWG) 210, 213–4, **217–8**

Parkwood Barrow/ Chambered Cairn (HRF 2) 38, 40

Pattern Stone, Bryn Celli Ddu 17–8, 109, 116–7, *118*

Pen-yr-Alltwen (GM 514) 85

Pen yr Wyrlod, Llanigon (1, BMG) **40–2**, 59, 64

Penarth, Clynnog (56, LPG) 161, **162–3**, 171

Penmaen Burrows, Tilston (21, GPG) 7, 75, **82–3**

Pentre Ifan, Nevern (68, SWG) *ii*, 11, 15, 26, 29, *31*, 123, 176–7, 185, **187–90**, 191, 199–200, 209, 215, 237

Penywyrlod, Talgarth (7, BMG) viii, 6–7, 31, 36–9, *37*, 47, **54–6**, 68, 140, 248

Perthi Duon (ANG 17) 98, 112–3

Pipton Long Cairn, Glasbury (4, BMG) 32, 36, 39, 42, **47–9**, 51, 54, 64–5, 68, 189

Plas Newydd, Llanedwen (35, YMG) 27, 97, 103, 113, 115, **122–4**

Porth Llwyd, Caerhun (42, NG) 131, **135–6**, 141, 145

Presaddfed, Bodedern (28, YMG) 15, 97, **102–4**, 123

Quanterness, Orkney 44

Rowen East (CRN 2) 135

St Elvies Farm, St Elvies (80, SWG) 133, 178, 203, **205–7**, 208, 224–5

Samson's Quoit, Nevern *see Llech-y-Tribedd*

Sling, Llandegai (43, NG) 97, 131, **136–7**

Sweyne's Howes North, Rhossili (19, GPG) 75–6, **80–1**, 83

Sweyne's Howes South, Rhossili (20, GPG) 75–6, **81–2**, 83

Tan-y-Muriau, Rhiw (63, LPG) 161, 171, **172–3**

Thornwell Farm (MON 4) 85–6

Tinkinswood, St Nicholas (22, SEG) 7, 25–6, 75–7, 85, **86–9**, 90–1, 93

Trefael Stone, Nevern *176*, 248

Treffynnon, Llandeloy (79, SWG) 199–200, 203, **205**, 209, 234

Trefignath, Holyhead Rural (27, YMG) viii, 97, **98–102**, 104, 111, 123, 125, 248

Tref-y-garnedd, Penllech *see Mynydd Cefn Amwlch*

Trellyffaint, Nevern (65, SWG) 4, 11, 164, 176–8, **180–3**, 218, 223, 248

Tresewig, Llanhowell *see White House*

Trewalter Llwyd, Mathry (74, SWG) 191, 197, **198–9**

Twlc y Filiast, Llangynog (98, IM) 133, 212, 224, **233–5**, 248

Ty Illtyd, Llanhamlach (8, BMG) 11, 30, 38, **57–8**, 59, 240

Ty Isaf, Talgarth (5, BMG) 6, 9–11, 20, 25–6, 32, 36–9, 47–9, **50–2**, 59, 68, 71, 76, 78, 105, 140–1, 172, 189, 212

Ty Mawr, Llanfair Pwllgwyngyll (36, YMG) 97, 113, **124**

Ty Newydd, Llanfaelog (29, YMG) 20, 97, **104–5**, 110

Tyddyn Bleiddyn, Cefn (45, NG) 131–2, **139–40**

Tyn-y-Coed, Llangar (49, NG) 131–2, **144–5**

Wayland's Smithy (BERKS 1) 62, 184

West Kennet Long Barrow (WILTS 4) 36, 127

White House, Llanhowell (82, SWG) 198–200, 203, 205, **209**

Y Gaer Llwyd, Shirenewton (25, SEG) **92–3**, 95

Ystum Cegid Isaf, Llanystumdwy (58, LPG) 161–2, **165–6**, 168

GENERAL INDEX

Abingdon ware *see pottery*
animals 2, 11, 15, 36, 43, 49, 56, 61, 83, 87, 94, 127, 129, 144, 177, 184, 231
   birds of prey 86
   cat 43
   cattle 2, 4, 13, 15, 27, 36, 40, 64, 87, 111, 214, 225, 240
   deer/elk 13–4, 24, 40, 61, 64–5, 139, 177
   dog 46, 139
   goats 43–4, 87, 111
   horses 46, 61, 87, 111, 143
   marine life/fish 2, 11, 15, 24, 109, 129, 177
   ox 43, 46, 94, 116–7, 143
   pigs/boar 4, 13–4, 43–4, 46, 87, 111, 139
   sheep 2, 27, 56, **56**, 64, 87, 111
arrowheads (*see also flint*) 4, 13, 15, 21, 39, 51, 70, 86, 89, 105, 116–7, 122, 127, 131, 142, 153
Atkinson, R.J.C. 5, 36, 77, **77**
axes 4, 13–6, **19–23**, 24–5, 39–40, 49, 51, 70, 85–6, 90, 105, 122, 134, 144, 175, 191, 201, 235
   axe groups 21
   Langdale axe factory, Cumbria **20**, 21
   flint 19–22, 39, 51, 64, 85, 105, 201

axes cont.
   Graig Lwyd (Penmaenmawr) factory 16, 21, 23, 64, 122, 134, 144
   Preseli factory, Pembs 21–2, 175, 191
   stone 4, 13, 15, 19–25, **20**, 39–40, 49, 51, 64, 70, 85–6, 90, 122, 144, 201, *201*

Bagnall-Oakeley, M. 91, 93–4
barrows 17, 78, 86, 190, 211, 221, 237–8
   Arthur's Stone, Dorstone *see site index*
   Bach Long Barrow *see site index*
   Clyro Court Farm Long Barrow *see site index*
   Cors-y-Gedol *see site index*
   Cross Lodge Long Barrow *see site index*
   Dunseal Long Barrow *see site index*
   Little Lodge Barrow *see site index*
   Llety'r Filiast *see site index*
   Lower Luggy Long Barrow *see site index*
   Parkwood Barrow/ Chambered Cairn *see site index*
   Pipton Long Barrow *see site index*
   Rowen East *see site index*
   Tan-y-Muriau *see site index*
   West Kennet Long Barrow *see site index*
Baynes, E.N. 11, 32–3, 100, 106, 111, 129

Beaker vessels *see pottery*
Black Mountains Group xvi, 6–10, 14, 16, 19, 24–5, 28, **34–73**, 95, 140, 172, 189, 212
Bronze Age 2, 4–5, 11, 13, 16, 22–3, 25, 28, 49, 52, 63, 64, 66, 70, 72–3, 75, 78, 82, 86, 89, 91–2, 105–6, 111, 113, 119–21, 125–9, 132, 134, 137, 141–2, 147–8, 150, 155, 162, 164, 176–8, 181, 186, 195, 198, 204, 219, 225, 235–7, 238
   Neolithic/Bronze Age transition 5, 27
burials *see human remains*

Case, H. 3, 5, 36, 240
Caseldine, A. 13, 24, 58
chert **16**, 44, 59, 101, 127
Clegyr Boia *see settlements*
Climatic Optimum 13, 24
Colt Hoare, R. 53, 60
copper 49, 94, 132
Cotswold-Severn monuments 6–8, **6**, 19, 22, 37, 39, 41, 47, 49, 51, 53–4, 56, 59, 62, 65, 68–9, 72, 75–6, 82, 86, 88–9, 91, 93, 95, 102, 125, 127, 132, 139–42, 144–5, 147–8, 156, 168, 172, 189, 228
Coygan Camp *see settlements*

Crawford, O.G.S. 28, 32, 37, 43, 54, 58, 61, 63, 66, 68, 91–4, **94**, 154, 156
crops *see farming*
cupmarks 8, 11, 16, 18, 29, 66, 98, 113, 118, **118**, 162, 164–5, 169, 176–9, **176**, 181–2, **182**, 186–7, **186**, 217
cursus monuments 7

Deveraux, P. 239
Doorstone 70, 71, 88, 138, 168, 189
Dorstone settlement *see settlements*
Dronfield, J. 239

Ebbsfleet ware *see pottery*
earth-fast monuments *see monuments*
Eisteddfod 31–2
enclosures viii, 4, 7, 13, 23, 50, 93, 148, 155, 168, 186, 204, 220, 230
Evans, J.G. 3, 12
Evans, T. 236
excarnation *see human remains*

farming 1–4, 14, 16, 25, 36, 40, 61, 73, 93, 175, 177
  crops 2, 4, 16, 93, 177
Fenton, R. 20, 53, 61, 185, 193–6, 199, 201, 215, 224–5
flint 4, 6, 11–16, **16**, 19–22, 24, 39–41, 44, 46, 49, 51, 56, 59–61, 64, 70, 72, 85, 89, 101, 105, 111, 116, 121, 127, 129, 131, 139, 141–4, 177, 183, 190–1, 196, 201, 230, 235
  arrowheads 13, 15, 89, 116, 127, 142
  axes 19–22, 39, 51, 64, 85, 105, 201
  blade/knife **16**, 39, 56, 129, 131, 142, 144
  tools 4, 12, 21, 101, 142, 183, 201, 235
Fintshire 131, 144, 164
Flemming, A. 239
flute, bone **37**, 56, **56**
Fussell's Lodge 62

gallery grave *see monuments*
gender encoding 21, 26, 240
glacial landforms 35, 79, 113, **169**, 195
Golden Valley, Herefs 13–4, 39–40, 66, 68–73
gongriffen *see monuments*
Gors Fawr stone circle 210, 219
Gower Peninsula, The 8–9, 23, 25, 70, 75–83, 221, 228
grave goods 11, 86, 240
Great Orme Head/ mines 21, 132–3, 137
Grimes Graves, Norfolk 23
Gwent Levels 25, 85, 93

Hay Bluff 47, 65–6
henges 7, 13, 25, 182, **182**
  Bryn Celli Ddu **3**, 10, 17–8, 98, 116–7, **118**
  Meini-Gwyr 210, 221
  Stonehenge 23, 28, 175, 191, 210
  Woodhenge 23
Holocene 13
Hughes, W. 80
human remains 9, 11, 26–7, 32, 39, 41, 44, 46, 49, 51–2, 54, 56, 61–2, 64–5, 77, 82–3, 86, 88, 94, 102, 109, 111, 116, 120, 126–9, 137, 139–40, 143–4, 173, 177, 186, 189, 195, 203, 229, 240
  articulated 11, 51–2, 240
  cremation burial 9, 27, 32, 44, 49, 52, 61, 109–10, 116, 177, 184, 186, 195, 229, 240
  disarticulated 9, 11, 26, 36, 44, 49, 56, 86, 88, 120, 186, 240
  excarnation of 9, 55, 61, 116, 184, 240
hunting/gathering/fishing 1–5, 12, 15, 24–5, 35–6, 61, 70, 145, 163, 177, 240
hut circles 186, 204

infant mortality 26
Irish Sea Province/ Zone **5**, 6, 8, 92, 98, 102, 112, 121, 125, 127, 151, 154, 175, 185, 240
Iron Age 13–4, 50, 89, 122, 155, 168, 177, 204

Jacobi, R. 13
Jones, Revd H. Longueville 30, 57–8, **57**, 110, 116, 204, 225–6
Jones, Theophilus 28, 52–3, **53**, 60
Jones, W.B. 207–8
Joussaume, R. 16, 98

Keith, Sir Arthur 41, 44, 88
Kongemose period 24

landnam 3
Langdale axe factory *see axes*
Lhwyd, E. 28
long mounds *see monuments*
Lubbock, J. 1, 26, 76
Lukis, J.W. 86–7, 89

McQueen, E. **31**
Megalithic art 8, 16–9, 98, 107, **108–9**, 110, 117–8
Megalithic tombs vii, 11, 16–9, 24–5, 29, 33, 63, 76, 78, 86, 98, 103, 107–10, **108–9**, 117–8, 128–9, 135, 139, 162, 169, 176, 182, 190, 199, 203, 205, 214, 216, 220, 230, 233–4, 236–8,
  number of vii, 24–5, 27
  sub-megalithic 98, 132, 137, 144, 193–5, 204, 227, 236
Meini-Gwyr, Preseli *see henges*
Mesolithic period (*c*.10,000–4,000 BCE) vii, 1–3, 5–6, 11–5, 23–5, 35–6, 39–40, 61, 64, 70, 72, 91, 131, 177, 204, 225, 236, 240

Mesolithic–Neolithic transition 2, 12–3
monuments, types of
  barrows *see* barrows
  Cotswold-Severn monuments *see* Cotswold-Severn
  earth-fast monuments 9, 9, 26–7, 81, 124, 137, 151, 154, 175–6, 191–2, 194, **194**, 201–6, 208, 216, 219, 222, 224, **225**, 227, 237, 239
  gallery grave **8**, 77, 86, 93, **93**, 95, 98, 100, 104, 111, 125, 178–9, 190–1, **190**, 238
  gongriffen (passage graves, Sweden) 27
  hybrid monuments 10, 47, 51, 59, 62, 68, 75–7, 189
  long mounds 2, 6, 68, 71, 73, 75–6, 90–1, 104, 112, 125, 147–8, 163, 166, 171–2, 213, 227–8, 237, 239
  multi-phased construction 13, 38, 45, 48, 50, 98, 112, 156
  passage graves 10, 16–9, 27–8, 49, 71, 82, 98, 101, 103, 105–6, 109–11, 113, **114**, 116–7, 119–24, 139, 142–3, 162, 165–6, 223, 228–9, 239
  Portal Dolmens 5–6, **5**, 28, **31**, 86, 92, 105, 113, 124, 131–5, **134**, 137, 147–8, 151, 153–4, 156–8, 161–3, 167, 169–72, 175, 177–80, 184, 203, 209–10, 213, 219, 235, 239
Mynydd Carningli 29, 177, 179, **181**, 187

Olding, F. xiii, 37, 66, 68, 155

Paget's disease 27
Palaeolithic, Late Upper 11–2, 61
Palaeolithic, Upper vii, 6, 24, 35, 60, 70, 131–2
passage graves *see* monuments
Pennant, T. 29–30, 125, 157–8, 164–5
Pen y Fan, Brecon. 38, 57

Peterborough ware *see* pottery
Piggott, S. 1, 37, 129
population dynamics 23–7
Portal Dolmen *see* monuments
Portal Dolmen classification ix, 7
pottery 1, 4, 11–3, 15, **15**, 21, 24, **37**, 39–41, 44, 46, 48–9, 52, 59, 61, 77–8, 83, 88–9, 94, 101–2, 105, 110–1, 116, 120–1, 127, 129, 133, 139, 141, 144, 152–3, **182**, 183–5, 190, 195–6, 235, 240
  Abingdon ware 4, 39, 56, 78
  Beaker vessels 41, 49, 86, 88, 105, 121, 126–7, 128–9, 141, 144, 152–3, 184
  Ebbsfleet ware 4, 39, 78, 141
  Grooved Ware 4, 129, **182**, 183–4
  Irish Sea carinated ware 102
  Medieval pottery 94, 102
  Peterborough ware 4, 39, 121, 144
  rude pottery 87, 185, 195–6
  Western style 39, 77, 95, 121, 127, 190
Preseli Mountains, Pembs 8, 22–3, 175, 177–9, 201, 210–3, 216, 218, **218**, 221

Ramsey Island 207
Ray, K. viii, 39–40, 69–70, 239
Rees, S. xiii, 16, 39, 178, 182, 184, 209, 213, 217, 236
Renfrew, C. 26, 45, 73
rock art 11, **109**, 110, 164–5,
  Welsh Rock Art Organisation 110
rock outcropping 68, 97, 113, **118**, 176, 191, 198, 201, 203–4, 208, 216–7, 225, 227–8, 233

St David's Head, Pembs **14**, 15, 25–6, 191, 196–7, 200, 203–6, 209–10, **210**, 225
settlements of Neolithic date
  Clegyr Boia settlement, St David's 2, 13–5, **14**, 26, 40, 176, 203,

settlements cont.
  Coygan Camp 2, 13, 15, 176
  Dorstone settlement 13–4, 40, 70, 72
  Silbury Hill, Wilts 142–3
Skinner, Revd J. 29–30, 97, 102, 104–6, 113–4, **113**, 116, 119, 123, 125, 128
Stone Age vii
stone circles 25, 31, 75, 92, 132, 147–8, 150, 210, 219–21
Strumble Head **186**, 191–3, 195–7, 199, 200, 203, 205, 221, 225
Stukely, W. 28
Swansea, Lord 76–7

Thomas, D. 29–30, 106,
Thomas, J. viii, 5, 39–40, 69–70, 117, 239
Tilley, C. viii, 22, 36, 66, 70–1, 147, 175, 177, 179, 212, 239
tools 4, 12, 21, 23–4, 39, 61, 83, 101, 115, 118, 122, 142, 183, 201, 235
  flint 4, 12, 21, 101, 142, 183, 201, 235

viewshed analysis 161
votive deposition 21
Vulliamy, C.E. 41, 43–4, 46, 64–5

Waite, L. 162, 169
Western Neolithic pottery *see* pottery
Whittle, A. viii, 5–6, 36, 56, 60, 77, 147, 161, 175, 239
Woolhope Naturalists' Field Club 32, 40, 68
Wye Valley 42, 46, 64–5, 69

Y Das, Brecon. 47